America After Tocqueville

America After Tocqueville complements Harvey Mitchell's earlier book, *Individual Choice and the Structures of History: Alexis de Tocqueville as Historian Reappraised* (1996). Mitchell's new study draws on *Democracy in America* to study the condition of democracy in the United States in our own time.

Many of the difficulties we have in grasping Tocqueville's fullest intentions in his seminal work lie in his marginalization of problems he raised in "The Present and Probable Future Condition of the Three Races that Inhabit the Territory of the United States," the last chapter that concludes the first volume of *Democracy in America*.

Three aspects of American democracy shape Mitchell's book. He shows that they cannot be considered apart from his predictions about the future relationship between the three original populations – the red, the white, and the black – who lived side by side yet remained apart in the United States, which he visited in the 1830s. The first centers on the tensions between ideas of equality and a political system that tries to keep it within bounds. The second is the relationship between this system and the dynamics of American capitalism. The last revolves around the criteria of inclusion and exclusion in American life.

Mitchell asks if Americans have surrendered to what Tocqueville called the materialization of life; if that compromise means they have abandoned their original spiritual quest; and if Americans are on the way to a radical alienation from politics.

Harvey Mitchell is Professor Emeritus of History at the University of British Columbia. His many works include *Individual Choice and the Structures of History: Alexis de Tocqueville as Historian Reappraised* (Cambridge University Press, 1996); *The Underground War against Revolutionary France: The Missions of William Wickham 1794–1800* (1965); and *Workers and Protest*, co-authored with Peter Stearns (1971).

America After Tocqueville

Democracy Against Difference

HARVEY MITCHELL
University of British Columbia

CAMBRIDGE
UNIVERSITY PRESS

PUBLISHED BY THE PRESS SYNDICATE OF THE UNIVERSITY OF CAMBRIDGE
The Pitt Building, Trumpington Street, Cambridge, United Kingdom

CAMBRIDGE UNIVERSITY PRESS
The Edinburgh Building, Cambridge CB2 2RU, UK
40 West 20th Street, New York, NY 10011-4211, USA
477 Williamstown Road, Port Melbourne, VIC 3207, Australia
Ruiz de Alarcón 13, 28014 Madrid, Spain
Dock House, The Waterfront, Cape Town 8001, South Africa

http://www.cambridge.org

First published 2002

Printed in the United Kingdom at the University Press, Cambridge

Typeface Sabon 10/13 pt.   *System* QuarkXPress [BTS]

A catalog record for this book is available from the British Library.

Library of Congress Cataloging in Publication Data available

ISBN   0 521 81246 1   hardback

For Ruth

Contents

References to Tocqueville's Democracy in America   *page* viii

Preface   ix

I   PATHS TO DEMOCRACY IN AMERICA

1   Introduction: Thinking about American Democracy   3

2   Democracy's Experiment: From Inequality to Equality   23

3   Achieving a Democratic Civil Society   49

II   BEGINNINGS AND DEMOCRACY

4   Beginnings and History: Red and White in Tocqueville's America   75

5   The New England Township Before the Revolution: Tocqueville's American Pastoral   114

6   A Second Beginning: Black and White in Tocqueville's America   132

III   AMERICAN DEMOCRACY ON TRIAL

7   Difference, Race, and Color in America   185

8   Maintaining American Democracy   213

9   The State, Authority, and the People   242

10   Conclusion   276

Works Cited   295

Index   311

References to Tocqueville's *Democracy in America*

Throughout the text, I refer to the Bradley edition of *Democracy in America* (see note 2, chapter 1).

Bradley's Volume I is divided into chapters. Volume II is divided into four books, each of which in turn is divided into chapters. Hence, "I" refers to Volume I, followed by chapter number and page number. "II" refers to Volume II, followed by book number, chapter number, and page number.

Preface

This book has its roots in my earlier book, *Individual Choice and the Structures of History: Alexis de Tocqueville as Historian Reappraised* (1996), which pursued Tocqueville's passionate belief that if people in the modern age wanted to enlarge the conditions of their liberty, they could not neglect the study of the past. His passion for "pondering the future" was just as intense. He conjured up the phrase for his readers with magisterial hyperbole, yet serious purpose – not common in a man only thirty – to articulate his reasons for thinking and writing about American democracy. America seized his imagination and would not let it go, from his very first visit to his declining years, during which he continued to correspond with Americans he had befriended. He summoned up his intellectual powers to tell his readers in Europe that they must recognize and acknowledge America as a wholly new and daringly innovative social and political experiment that would weigh heavily, not only on the future of Americans, but of Europeans as well. My earlier book dwelt on Tocqueville's conception of the fragile links between individual agency and large historical forces that live on opposite sides of an opaque curtain. It did not neglect the ways in which much of the power of *Democracy in America* rested on his sharp contrasts between aristocratic and democratic society. The most important revealed quite different notions of individual liberty, individual worth, and historical change.

Tocqueville's reflections on the conditions of the Indian and slave populations of the United States before the eruption of the Civil War I left for separate study. My decision proved to be the beginning of the present book. His analysis and predictions about the future of the native and black peoples in America, as I came to see them, add new meaning to his sense of the past, raising such questions as the origins of cultural difference that led to the devastating effects of Western civilization on the cultures of aboriginal North American and North African people, and, not least, on the people from large parts of equatorial Africa who suffered the deaths and indignities of forced passage to and settlement in the New World. The meshes and clashes of Western and non-Western cultures in North America forced Tocqueville to ponder the future of democracy and opened his mind to the comparative history of civilizations.

My understanding of how the three races in Tocqueville's America existed alongside one another, touched one another, yet remained isolated from one another, would have eluded me had I not sought answers to his belief that the black and aboriginal populations could not be fitted into his larger scheme of understanding the foundations of American democracy, at the center of which equality was the inextinguishable reality, not only in its crude and obvious form, but in its most subtle manifestations. His most profound and provocative ideas, his pessimism and his optimism, derive from a prolonged reflection on the meaning of that ethos. He sought to keep in their place what were for him the dangerous excesses of equality that in their striving for sameness threatened not only personal and political liberty but the quality of life itself. The emotional investment that values some aspects of equality as good and better than others, of devaluing others as unworthy, and of the disagreements caused by these conflicting beliefs is even more intense today. While many Americans believe that the American Constitution can offer solutions to some of these problems, and are certain about its soundness, the unease caused by the debate on how to grasp the dynamics of democratic authority and the deployment of its power to ensure a decent distribution of equality is imperfectly understood. For the time being, that question lies on the margins of theoretical consciousness. Finally, it is impossible to move into this territory without studying how and with what consequences Americans valorize the material satisfactions of a capitalist consumer society – the hunger for which Tocqueville believed would and could not be stilled, and which will surely continue unabated, not only in America, but in all parts of the world.

This book could not have reached its present form without the drafts of confidence that a growing familiarity with new subjects and disciplines inspired. In its earlier versions, it benefited from Ed Hundert's and David Bates' best criticism. Their encouragement helped me to complete it. My thanks are due as well to other friends with whom I discussed many of the ideas that took on solid shape in the book. They are Kim Adams, Ed Broadbent, Harvey Chisick, Lynn Cohen, Mark Glouberman, Howard Kushner, Paul Nelles, Eduardo Nolla, Luisa Pesante, Roger Seamon, Steve Straker, and Geoffrey Winthrop-Young. I wish to express my appreciation to Lewis Bateman, my editor at Cambridge University Press, for his enthusiasm, and to Ronald Cohen for his fine editorial hand.

PART I

PATHS TO DEMOCRACY IN AMERICA

I

Introduction: Thinking about American Democracy

The United States presents the most pressing example of how democracy and modernity were and continue to be, in their most vital aspects, identified with one another. It is not only as if the one depends on the other. From the moment they were coupled, each imposed some considerable force upon, or at least challenged, the other to discover how they combined to shape thinking about civil and political society. There may be a sting hidden in the apparently benign design that binds them together. While people in many places in the world claim that they are laying both the foundations of democratic rule and reaping the benefits of modern market forces and technology, the evidence seems to contradict the claim that the second rests on the first. Indeed, the recent history of non-Western parts of the world reveals that capitalism, on the one hand, and Enlightenment ideas and values, including democratic forms and practices, on the other, can move in opposite directions. The lesson we might draw is that the expansion of democratic values, outside selected Western oriented societies, is more apparent than real.[1] The real point in this book, however, is that they appear to exist as well in a beleaguered condition in the United States, which possesses the material resources and political traditions that at one time were believed to be immune from known, and as yet unknown, hostile forces. It may indeed be that the democratic ethos has been in a state of siege, almost from the beginning

---

[1] The widespread view that crisis plagues the major democracies is considered by several authors in *Disaffected Democracies. What's Troubling the Trilateral Countries?*, eds. Susan J. Pharr and Robert D. Putnam (Princeton: Princeton University Press, 2000).

of its American incarnation when the newly formed United States presented itself heroically to an astonished world after the American Revolution. Some sixty years later, Alexis de Tocqueville remarked in his incomparable book that while democracy was the wave of the future, in America it carried a large burden that might plague its health and raise doubts about its survival. And he said this at the very time that democratization was profoundly changing politics.

My book focuses on the nature and limits of diversity and equality, the several axes around which egalitarian principles and the American political system rotate, and the relationship between politics and economic life. In its darker mood, it asks if democracy, conceived as a deliberative process in the public life of citizens, may in fact be a utopian dream, irrelevant to their search to satisfy their immediate and special interests either as workers, consumers, home owners, or as members of minority groups and of religious denominations, and so on. It appears to be easier to remain locked into those roles and to attach oneself to single causes than to find good reasons to support a unified political cause that overrides them. If all the compulsions of modern economic life are decoupled from the idea that democracy entails deliberation and argument, the first may reign triumphant over and effectively negate the second.

Is democratic civil society defined by the market, or is civil society able to determine the limits that may be placed on it? The economics of capitalism may indeed exclude from the lives of citizens almost everything except the commands of private interest, and create a mental environment for an overpowering but mistaken identity between it and democracy. Neither a rigid notion of politics as total struggle and opposition, nor a benign one of politics as cooperation, which is more in keeping with supposed democratic values, but which is ultimately nonexplanatory, helps. If, instead, the goals of democracy are seen as taking place within a framework of conflict over power sharing, and not as a supposedly rational debate between competing interests seeking what is commonly praised as consensus, the altered focus might work to the benefit both of liberal political philosophy and a democratic culture in which serious thought is given how best to bring voice to ever increasing numbers of people. The contradiction between democracy's appearance and its reality, and the gap between its utopian dress and rude experience, might thus stand exposed. If so, then the process of democratization that Tocqueville witnessed, yet was fearful of, in the first half of the last century, may be given new life.

My book does not pay ritualistic homage to Tocqueville as an infallible guide to the American democracy of his own time or to modern capitalist democracy in ours. Rather it asks how we might understand how he illuminates, but also how he fails to discern, the disparities between professions of faith in democracy from which most questions of power have been excluded, and the existence of the hard facts of economic, cultural, and other differences. As a starting point, I take one of the more sobering conclusions in the first volume of *Democracy in America*, which comes in the form of a warning. Besides the difficulty of getting people to participate in government, he writes, there remains the problem of supplying them with the experience to govern themselves well. He was, of course, alluding to the experiences Americans would unquestionably face, and upon the foundation of which they would either succeed or fail to gain the capacity to live as free citizens. Then comes the muted bombshell in his last great chapter, "The Present and Probable Future Condition of the Three Races that Inhabit the Territory of the United States." The Indians and Negroes were absent from the Anglo-American polity – the "absolute and immense democracy" – that he considered to be unique in the world not only, because, as he put it, America was the first nation to embark on such a perilous journey, but for other reasons that are just as compelling. The chapter sharply grips all his themes in a tight fist and thrusts before us his concept of the connections and tensions between history and civilization.

Later, in the second volume, we find an observation that may be placed in startling juxtaposition with Tocqueville's pessimism, and one that – we must wonder if he intended it this way – seems to take the edge off his darkest foreboding about the capacity of white Americans to keep both their democracy alive and to resolve the problems of the existence of alien peoples in their midst. He believed that he had located the secret of America: The American citizen thrives on success supported by an abstract belief in human perfectibility that responds to constant change with irrepressible optimism. "Thus, forever seeking, forever falling to rise again, often disappointed, but not discouraged, he tends unceasingly towards that unmeasured greatness so indistinctly visible at the end of the long track which humanity has yet to tread."[2] What may lie ahead

---

[2] The references and quotations are from Alexis de Tocqueville, *Democracy in America*, trans. Henry Reeve, ed. Phillips Bradley, 2 vols. (New York: Vintage Books, 1945). Hereafter, references will be bracketed and incorporated in the text (I, chap. 17, 341; chap. 18, 343; II, Bk. 1, chap. 8, 34–35).

is, at the same time, measured by chance, a chance Americans are willing to take.

Not only do the rich eagerly embrace it, but also the poor. They harbor the hope that the rapidly changing society in which they live will not keep them in one place for long. In this respect, they tend to think of themselves as equal, not different. They find it easier to imagine a level playing field that seemingly preserves feelings of independence than an uneven one in which success is vouchsafed to the few and denied to the many. When they see fellow citizens rise from obscurity to wealth, they attribute the change to vice, Tocqueville observed, rather than admit their own lack of virtue or talent (I, chap. 13, 235). They are captured by the aura of the average; and while democratic institutions feed their hunger for equality without being able to satisfy it fully, their envy of the rich and the successful generates, contrary to expectations, no long-lasting resentments, but instead a climate of disappointment. Public opinion "draws them to a common level and creates a species of imaginary equality between them, in spite of the real inequality of their conditions. This all-powerful opinion penetrates at length even into the hearts of those whose interest might arm them to resist it; it affects their judgment while it subdues their will" (II, Bk. 3, chap. 5, 192). In America, in short, resemblance and difference are both invoked to support equality. So powerful is the tendency to recreate, so to speak, equality, that it works against independent thinking. The desire for the same, the simple, and the general demands laws and rules that will cover all and privilege no one. All are gambling on a benevolent future. The market, the place where competitiveness is worshipped, indeed creates social strata, but no one seems, Tocqueville implies, to believe that it creates a permanent hierarchy:

> Nothing tends to materialize man and to deprive his work of the faintest trace of mind more than the extreme division of labor. . . . The Americans . . . change their means of gaining a livelihood very readily. . . . Men are to be met with who have successively been lawyers, farmers, merchants, ministers of the Gospel, and physicians. . . . The whole life of an American is passed like a game of chance, a revolutionary crisis, or a battle (I, chap. 18, 443).

> Those who live in the midst of democratic fluctuations have always before their eyes the image of chance; and they end by liking all undertakings in which chance plays a part. They are therefore all led to engage in commerce, not only for the sake of the profit it holds out to them, but for the love of constant excitement occasioned by the pursuit (II, Bk. 2, chap. 19, 165).

Although these passages would seem to indicate that he was quite accurately describing what we might call equality of opportunity, which does not see inequality of income and inferior social rank as an insurmountable barrier to social and economic success, he chose to concentrate on what he preferred to call equality of condition comprising legal equality, social equality, and equality of respect. Clustered together, they significantly transformed the landscape of politics, for, thought of as inseparable and as one, equality of condition kept people peacefully engaged in the task of achieving success, while transferring the task of government to a few. Tocqueville was the first modern thinker to predict that Western society would be organized along democratic lines and that in America, more triumphantly than elsewhere, democracy would be identified with modern commerce. A parallel development was not, he implied, discernible in France. While, therefore, the popular will took root both in America and in France, there was another important aspect in which their particular histories ensured that its manifestations would differ, especially at the level of the state's action upon citizens, lighter in the first, heavier in the second. One might say that persons as citizens stood out more prominently than persons as subjects in America than in France, where the reverse was true. In short, the legacies of sovereignty, taken in their European context, did not press so insistently in America.

Beyond those specific national characteristics, which uniquely differentiated a new from an older, traditional one, modern democracy exerted an unusual power for good or ill. Equality that was, Tocqueville said, central to the democratic ethos – distinguishing it from all others – had two sides, one civil, the other political: "The principle of equality may be established in civil society without prevailing in the political world. There may be equal rights of indulging in the same pleasures, of entering the same professions, of frequenting the same places; in a word, of living in the same manner and seeking wealth by the same means, although all men do not take an equal share in the government"(II, Bk. 2, chap. 1, 100). From that insight, Tocqueville drew two conclusions. In the first place, since the demand for equality was so closely tied to the search for economic security, or more straightforwardly self-interest, it might lead to the strengthening of feelings of self-satisfaction and complacency within competing but not unpeaceful self-centered groups, and to the deadening of the sense of collective effort needed to maintain political institutions, and, as importantly, a vibrant civil society from which it draws its lifeblood. In the second place, the materialization of mind might lead to a profound despiritualization of society – "to hit upon what is expedient without heeding what is just, to acquire knowledge without faith, and prosperity apart from virtue" (I, Introduction, 13). In that case, standing in the wings was a "tutelary power" eager to assume the role of benevolent despot, sublimely detached from the citizenry but giving it the material satisfactions it wants. Such a description fits one side of Tocqueville's analysis of the relationship of the social and the political in an American population sharing an equality of condition.

The other, more hidden, because conceptually weaker, side of his analysis is that American democracy was fated to seal, not reduce, the distance between the social and the political. Tocqueville did not overcome the difficulties of conceiving how an informed political elite could prevail against the full weight of the people without whose support it could not move. The only way he found to extricate himself from the conceptual tangle was to place his hopes on voluntary associations – in his view, the crucible of democratic action, and the fount from which presumably politics came to life. Now, almost two centuries later, it is crucial to ask two questions. The first is whether democracy has the energy to defend itself from its impulse to resist the difficulties of making and enacting political decisions, and even more radically, whether depoliticization – perhaps the trivialization of politics is the apter description – is democracy's endgame, and if that was its destination all along. The second, related to the first, is whether the dynamic of the market is the source of the debasement of political culture, indeed, of culture *tout court*.

To deal with these questions, I have chosen to carve out one small portion of the past history of American democracy to consider how it has shaped the present, and to discuss what forces – mainly internal to democracy itself – are changing its image and its reality. My study also moves to the present, where Native and Afro-Americans have made the search for equality their own, hoping that because it has worked, albeit imperfectly, for white Americans, it should work for them, even while they express much uncertainty that it will. My book, however, is not limited by a consideration of those who live on the far side of difference. Equality and difference, I contend, are questions that must be placed in the deeper context of existing but malleable political practices. For example, in one of its aspects, American democracy favors, at least in the abstract, the value of universality, while, in another, it clings to the known, and frowns upon any suspicion of special treatment. The search for and stress on identity as the sole criterion for determining the substance of equality seems to me to be a form of narcissism, which spurs on the claims of those who deny the force of universalistic arguments by repudiating the project of the Enlightenment on the grounds that it is itself a form of cultural narcissism, springing arrogantly, they say, from an utter incomprehension of and disregard for other cultures.[3] The title of this book is meant to focus our minds on these two constructions of the relationship between democracy and difference.

From one point of view, we may gain some understanding of their relationship when we see how people deal with the issue inside a culture that mobilizes political forces that subtly contradict the democratic forms and goals of voluntary associations in a thousand different ways. The contradictions may be found in other areas in American politics, and call into question the viability, liveliness, and purposes of American political life. It may well be, as I have been alluding, that politics, which calls on the active participation of a significant segment of the citizenry, may no longer be the ultimate arena in which these questions are decided; and it is not certain that voting in elections, which has long been thought to be democracy's ultimate test, but which more and more, because they ask citizens to confirm their immediate rather than their common interests, should be the identifying mark of democracy.[4] Such as it is, voting is for many Americans the full extent of their political literacy, and it is not to be dismissed on the argument that elections are crude indicators of voters' wishes, or that the political class and citizens collude, the first to stay in power, the second to gain as much as possible from the electoral bouts of periodic bribery. Even so the importance of voting seems to diminish as more than half of the American electorate chooses to stay away. Included in that figure are those sections of the population that feel themselves to be the most marginal and the most vulnerable – including Afro- and Native Americans, who have been part of America

---

[3] Jürgen Habermas, *The Inclusion of the Other. Studies in Political Theory*, trans. Ciaran Cronin (Cambridge, Mass.: MIT Press, 1998) similarly argues that while persons as such are equal to all other persons, they are also absolutely different from all others: "The equal respect for everyone else demanded by a moral universalism sensitive to difference thus takes the form of a *nonleveling* and *nonappropriating* inclusion of the other *in his otherness*." His emphasis, p. 40.

[4] Bruce Ackerman views these low turnouts at elections with equanimity, on the one hand, seeing in them the reality of what he calls normal politics, and, on the other, arguing that, even when only 51 percent of voters – those deeply involved in seeking support for their movement constituting 20 percent, and 31 percent making up the rest – come out, they are a significant portion of the people who will go on to the final stage of transforming normal politics by altering the Constitution in a fundamental and revolutionary way. See his *We the People. Foundations* (Cambridge, Mass. and London: The Belknap Press of Harvard University Press, 1991), pp. 269–80.

from its inception – and who have turned away from politics and politicians whom they believe don't address their needs.

It is more true than ever that the better educated and the economically favored sections of society who bother to vote today constitute the largest part of the electorate, and do so because their stakes are higher. Yet, across the class and color spectrum, the majority of Americans have all but handed over politics to professional politicians and experts, who fulfill their own desire for money, success, and power, which they purchase by seeming to meet, although on a less reduced scale, the needs of the better-off, and on a significantly reduced scale, the same desires in the less-advantaged population. When Tocqueville noted the decline in the quality of American political life, and warned against the demagogues who were seeking office, he was sounding an alarm bell that has been rung often in the last century and a half.

These were telling symptoms for Tocqueville, but the causes were not immediately visible. The deepest urges of equality might lead radically away from politics. In their search for security, the illusions of wealth, and power, Americans may indeed gain the equality they desire – the equality that Tocqueville admired and feared at the same time. He stressed that the energetic pursuit of wealth in America has benign effects on its civic life and ultimately on its political life, bringing to them some of that energy, but he also feared that too close an identity between them, or confusion about the boundaries separating them, would prove injurious to the distinctively different requirements of civic and political concerns. He recalls for us that Americans in his lifetime did learn, albeit imperfectly, how laws may be fashioned to restrain the power of human passions – preeminently the passion for money and success – on the smaller scale of public life in the New England township that he admired. The route that Americans today are traveling to achieve equality shows strong signs of leading them to a place where the impersonal rules that operate in the market operate as well in the public forum, both of which are bounded by the world of postmodern global capitalism.

Both as an abstract notion and in its practical manifestations, democracy is varied in its meanings and a contentious area of concern among its various exponents. It is salutary to be reminded that democracy and slavery existed side by side in Athens, and were certainly not felt to be irreconcilable in the Southern United States. Athenian democracy did not rest unequivocally on abstract universalistic ideals. In America, these had their origins in a belief in Christian, not a universal brotherhood, and which, moveover, was to be realized fully in the next world. The

Christian ideal was then used as a foundation for a secular and humanist universality that supposed a principle of equality of all persons. Americans were forced to deal with the gap between official professions of faith in something that may not be capable of being actualized and is distant from their actual experience; and for most of their history, they have found the means to step away from the discrepancy by eschewing utopian longings, while paying homage to the principle of equality. No easy comparisons can be made between American and Athenian democracy. A sense of the past is crucial first to see how, in the case of democracy, one cannot escape from its two faces, one abstract, the other historical. Athenian democratic political life nourished itself on a belief in the unrivaled goodness of the public realm. This was its untested abstract side. According to Pericles, known to us in Thuycidides' ironic account of his Funeral Speech, even the citizens who were most occupied with their private affairs supposedly took an interest and participated in the debates affecting affairs of state. The democracy that they defended and he extolled was one in which:

> we are governed for the many and not for the few . . . As far as private interests are concerned, everyone has equal access to the law; but you are distinguished in society and chosen for public service not so much by lot as because of your individual merit. Furthermore, your poverty will not keep you in obscurity if you can do something worthwhile for the city. We are generous towards one another in our public affairs, and though we keep a watchful eye on each other as we go about our daily business, we don't get angry at our neighbor if he does as he pleases, and we don't give him dirty looks, which are painful though they do not kill. Painless as our private lives may be, we are terrified of breaking the laws. We obey them as they are administered by whoever is in power, especially the laws meant to relieve victims of oppression, whether they have been enacted by statute or whether they are the unwritten laws that carry the undisputed penalty of shame.

Pericles is in full, eloquent flight, praising both political egalitarianism and, if not the sturdy individualism that Americans like to think as rooted in free choice, at least an enduring respect for a person's right to lead his life substantially free of obstruction from the state. But a fuller freedom was not extended to all persons, to those human beings deemed incapable of exercising it in the public realm and therefore not considered the equals of those who could. The collective life of Athens acknowledged the private social realm of slaves, foreigners, women, and manual workers, but did not regard them as fully autonomous and hence capable of participation in the deliberative process from which they were

excluded, or simply counted out.[5] In contrasting Athens' virtues with
Sparta's defects, Pericles surely indulged in the rhetoric of universality
when he spoke of the government "for the many and not for the few,"
and when he spoke about "everyone" having "equal access to the
law." We may read this as a declaration affirming the rights of all the
Athenians. But these rights would be in the safekeeping of the Athenian
citizenry, a select and exclusive group. The whole people, we hear him
say, was constituted by men who could be of service to the state; their
service rested on their individual capacities. Moreover, their poverty
would not be an impediment to the service of the city. They were ready,
he adds, to obey the laws, especially those to relieve the oppressed. But
though we know that women were among his listeners, and, as well, that
slaves and the propertyless were likely present, they were not considered
the politically significant part of his audience, because they were deemed
sufficiently different (either because of their gender, or had been deprived
of their free status, or were lacking in material resources). They were not
thought to have the actual ability to perform political service. But what
could Pericles have had in mind when he spoke about ensuring protection for the oppressed? Simply that, for he acknowledges that citizens,
because they represent themselves, can protect themselves, while others,
who are not in that fortunate condition, would depend on and gain the
protective support of a generous citizenry. What prospect was there that
the protected would ever win the right to work their way past their tute-
lage to present themselves? There is evidence that more and more poorer
Athenians no longer needed that protection. According to a recent study,
democratic reforms "shifted the domestic balance of power toward the
poor and the navy. . . . [for at] the height of democratic government,
trireme rowers were full citizens," and were "generally from the lower
classes."[6] Women, however, remained outside the inner circles of citizenship. At the end of the Oration, Pericles praised the women of Athens
in the audience for not being "worse than your nature's inferior, and in
having the least possible reputation among males for good or ill," but
we may infer that he also meant that their differences were such as to
make them unsuited for political life.[7]

[5] J. Ober, *Mass and Elite in Democratic Athens* (Princeton: Princeton University Press,
   1989), pp. 6–7.
[6] Bruce Russett with William Antholis, "The Imperfect Democratic Peace of Ancient
   Greece," in Bruce Russett, ed., *Grasping the Democratic Peace. Principles for a Post-
   Cold War World* (Princeton: Princeton University Press, 1993), 59.
[7] Thucydides, *The Peloponnesian War*, trans. Walter Blanco (New York: W.W. Norton,
   1998). Citations and references from pp. 73–76.

Much later, when we turn to the early modern period of Europe's past, we find that John Locke, addressing the question of authority and liberty, believed that the generous protective hand extended to the unself-represented was not enough: "But whatever have been the occasion [of our misfortunes] . . . we have need of more generous remedies. . . . It is neither declarations of indulgence, nor acts of comprehension, such as have yet been practiced or projected among us. . . . Absolute liberty, just and true liberty, equal and impartial liberty is the thing that we stand in need of."[8] Others who were as much concerned with equality perceived some of the problems that lay in store for a democratic society that would take up the question about the nature of reasoned debate, including a debate over who should be included in the art and practice of deliberating, and about those who were deemed to be political equals sharing in public life. The Rousseauian civic ideal, for example, predicated a shared collective life of a small homogeneous population with differences reduced to a minimum. Thus, when Rousseau thought of the people whose voices demanded to be heard, and when heard, thereby entered politics, he had in mind an integrated community, sharing acceptable beliefs and agreeing on actions, in which intrusive differences were barely, if at all, to be tolerated. Superiority and inferiority were banished in the name of a disciplined equality, stabilized but frozen in time, and in that way, not only keeping foreigners out, but in keeping a tight circle around the conduct of politics.

Little of this same urge persists in modern democratic pluralistic societies, where liberal ideology softens, and indeed alters, the parameters of difference. The balance between superiority and inferiority in fact passes from a negative to a positive register as conditions of acceptability change over time. In the broad and middle stretches of the population in modern America are people who qualify for degrees of equal consideration, because they are thought to be fairly equal in their capacity to achieve a sense of self, if not completely, yet substantially, within a society sharing a common set of goals. The thought and expectation are both given legitimacy, because the Fourteenth Amendment to the U.S. Constitution contains the words "equal protection" and "due process" in the same sentence, thereby establishing a foundation for the application of the law without regard to a person's ethnicity, gender, and religion.

Though these constitutional safeguards exist, the impediments to the full protection of the law and due process have by no means all

---

[8] John Locke, *A Letter Concerning Toleration* (Buffalo, NY: Prometheus Books, 1990), pp. 11–12.

been reduced, if only because not all Americans feel that they are self-represented adequately either in their private lives or in their lives as citizens. A crucial reason for this is that democracy, whether of the Rousseauian or the pluralistic variety, can deal more easily with sameness and the general, but is uncomfortable with the phenomenon of difference – in short, with the particular, with the part that is not part of the whole, and finds reasons for seeing it as dissonant, and hence worthy of exclusion. When that excluded part questions the hierarchical social order, it seeks to intrude and to destabilize it, and does so by hoping to unmask those in power on the grounds that their exclusionary basis of power rests on specious and illegitimate grounds. On the individual psychological level, a person may find it unsettling when measuring his sameness with, and his difference from, others. Thus, if it is sameness that is sought, difference is minimized. It is as if the energy propelling this human tendency to look for resemblance works to make invisible the difference in others. True, excellences are applauded in every field of human striving, and the more diverse the fields of endeavor, the more equally is achievement distributed. Democracy acknowledges distinction and distinctions, even celebrates them, but it also has a tendency to flatten them, as if, in responding to a deep reductive urge, it seeks almost instantaneously to restate a principle of general achievement, available to all. Any achievement, in other words, that does not threaten to have a label of permanent superiority attached to it is found to be acceptable. In this way, the craving for a sense of equality is constantly, if perhaps often only seemingly, reestablished and reasserted. The impulse to affirm equality may also be seen as an affirmation of a belief in its universality.

The equality ideal purports to see persons as individuals, rather than as persons belonging to distinct groups, yet by uttering and acting on the first principle, while not entirely repudiating the second, a tension of ambiguity is created. The argument that each person is capable of making his own way in the social world, bringing to it nothing but his self, is indeed central to the American liberal individualistic creed, strengthened by a fierce and often brutal competitiveness. The ambiguity also may be seen to work from the opposite direction when group loyalties, and the search for identity within the boundaries set up by those loyalties, are given primary importance, as they are, for example, in social relationships that meet what might be called opportunities for, and expectations of, meeting psychological and material interests. For all the criticism this tension has received from those who have appealed to a gentler America, it is seen by some as positive on the grounds that its reregistration of identity is not only an inescapable but a desirable aspect of the democratic dynamic. The replenished identity loops back and keeps the dynamic alive, but not by sealing off the possibility of breaching the boundaries. Indeed, movement across the boundaries does occur when it is seen as advantageous. But when the person comes clothed in an alien skin, or in other respects is seen to be part of an alien group, the welcome he receives is at best mixed; and the equal treatment that he and the group of which he is part desire is not easily given. Charges of special treatment are hurled about when he is singled out for special recognition and treatment, together with the blanket criticism that equality is threatened; the impulse is to do away with, not to acknowledge, difference. Those advocating departures from the norm say that these are justified because they incorporate respect for differences and collective forms of distinction. Both the critics, who argue against measures to right historical wrongs, and the defenders of Afro- or Native Americans – to name the two most disaffected constituencies – who keep a balance sheet in which they subtract past resentments from equal rights policies, do little to convince us that they have moved beyond simple notions of equality. If this is so, the harmful effects pile up from the present inability – perhaps refusal – to rethink the ways in which democracy draws the lines to and away from difference, and, when doing so, how it affects equality and liberty. It may be that the democratic default system acts so powerfully that it conceals its flaws. Or that it averts its eyes from the sheer force of the play of power in the politics of inclusion and of resentment in democratic society.

There can, nevertheless, be no doubt that although beset with enormous problems, democracy remains after almost two centuries of political debate a spoken but confused ideal that most Americans support, however imprecisely, sentimentally, and incoherently they speak about it. Across a wide spectrum of democratic opinion, the conviction that people are basically equal in value and have equal moral worth, even if ability is not equally available to all, remains ostensibly strong, but often it is submerged by feelings of despondency on the part of those who live on unequal shares, and by feelings of angry impatience or cultivated indifference by others who are better placed. In developing his "difference principle," John Rawls argues that anyone favored by the accidents of nature should not assume a right to, nor should society introduce public policies that would sanction, superior moral claims and greater material rewards. "The naturally advantaged are not to gain merely

because they are more gifted but only to cover the costs of training and
education and for using their endowments in ways that can help the less
fortunate as well. No one deserves his greater natural capacity nor merits
a more favorable starting place in society."[9]

Rawls' original position is based on questioning those inequalities
considered to be arbitrary on moral grounds, because the inequalities are
assumed to derive from natural gifts. Yet, even as he established the principle of enhancing the possibilities of equality, he seemed to question it
by subordinating it to liberty.[10] His scheme was also ideally founded on
an expectation that impartial judgment will in practice produce justice,
as if everyone can or will agree intuitively on how to distinguish its features. He also placed confidence in the beneficial effects of consensus-
making that would ensure a fair chance of satisfying diverse and
conflicting goals and political aims.[11] Can, however, a sharper focus on
these questions be achieved, one that will clarify the facts yielded by
detailed study that will in turn be tested against and alter the mental and
emotional landscape that make up the American ideal, refining some of
its strokes, erasing others, and introducing new ones? One way to
achieve this focus is to reexamine the urge to see all members of a group
in the same light, and, in the instance of Native and Afro-Americans, to
see them – as so many of them refuse to see themselves – not as units of
an undifferentiated mass airing the same grievances, but as persons with
a sense of how they differ among themselves, and from others who are
not Native or Afro-American, as well as how they resemble them. Here
we encounter the difficult problem of how and to what ends the individual achieves his sense of being part of a distinctively separate community or collectivity, or contrariwise seeks to find it outside its bounds.

In an unexpected way, France, along with the major nations that
espouse Western values, is at the present time wrestling with the problems of immigration – integrating peoples from distant and alien cultures, the legacy of an imperialist past. No modern nation, however,
matches the unique conditions and peculiar circumstances of America.
It was in the United States, a self-professed egalitarian society, that the
dilemma of creating a democratic society in which Anglo-Americans,
aboriginal, and newly freed slave populations might share a body of

[9] John Rawls, *A Theory of Justice* (Oxford: Oxford University Press, 1971), pp. 101–02.
[10] Ibid., p. 250.
[11] John Rawls, "The Domain of the Political and Overlapping Consensus," *New York
University Law Review,* 64 (1989), 234.

values, was first contemplated, if only by a few, and was most tragically experienced. Nowhere in the rest of the Americas did such a juxtaposition exist. It became the more pressing as the slave proportion of the American mainland population rose in the eighteenth and nineteenth centuries. This stubborn phenomenon was without precedent in other parts of the hemisphere. Other colonial peoples, such as the Spanish, Portuguese, and French in the New World, where there were larger black populations and where emancipation came earlier, nonetheless lived in a political culture that conspicuously lacked parliamentary and common law traditions, and failed, even if the color bar were not so virulent, to elevate ideals of civic and political engagement in quite the same way. Though these traditions had some force in the British Caribbean island colonies, their cramped dependence on the mother country, their achievement of independence so-long delayed, created a different mix of receptivity to equality and liberty. If we look farther afield, to Czarist Russia's expansion eastward in Asia, we find that it also registered a very different political culture, in which political inclusion was not seriously considered until the last century, leaving a very different imprint on vastly diverse populations experiencing economic backwardness and little exposure to democratic forms.

The very different trajectory traced by the contact of Europeans and non-Europeans in the United States also distinguishes it from the European encounters with peoples from other cultures almost two hundred years later. Only now do they in France (and in other parts of Europe) constitute a large enough migrant mass to request full inclusion in the host society. But a subtle change has occurred. They were formerly called migrant workers. Today they are simply designated as immigrants, and the idea that they are also workers who might be assimilable has been, if not entirely dropped, given only heavily qualified support. I am also thinking of the mixed responses in France, for example, to demands made on its democratic traditions by the presence of a Muslim population for whom the idea of a distinction between the temporal and the spiritual, and hence the political and religious, is thought to be barely conceivable by the host country. As well, the absorption of Africans from the defunct French empire remains troubling. These are pressing problems awaiting creative political answers. In France, the issue of *laicisme,* or what has been called the substitution of a secular catechism for a Catholic one, has resurfaced acutely in recent years in the realm of public education, where Muslims challenge the state's efforts to keep out culturally distinguishing features, such as dress, from the classroom.

(Professing Christians and Jews long ago made their peace with the laicised school regime.) Relations between Church and State in France are conceived inside a context that encompasses a tradition of universal rights that constitute an ethos deemed superior to any notions of inviolable religious rights. Many French citizens find it difficult to accept the particular and the plural on the grounds that universal application of principles legitimately subsumes them. The more brutal reality, however, is that the immigrants whose visibility at times evokes indifference, but at other times, foments hatred, creates a perfervid climate in which their absolute otherness seems unbreachable. In America, Church-State relations are less rigid, and therefore more open to controversy and wavering decision, often finding apparently final resolution in findings of the U.S. Supreme Court, only to be challenged in successive rounds of litigation. Debate over religious issues, rarely if ever distinguished from social questions, remains sharply divisive.

Newcomers to America did not encounter an empty continent – even if they quickly created a myth that it was to all intents and purposes uninhabited – and in a short time they also brought to it an enslaved population. Both the Amerindian and slave populations were kept at a distance by draconian measures. Also, unlike the other countries in the Western Hemisphere that were still in a semi-colonial state (including Canada which was, moreover, still not as democratic in its political institutions as the United States was by the mid-nineteenth century), the United States proudly professed its republicanism and its democratic aspirations and claimed to live by their dictates, though the clashes between the holdovers from eighteenth-century republican ideas of virtue and the popular and often-aggressive democratic will were on the minds of Americans before, during, and after Tocqueville's visit. Nowhere else, apart from France perhaps, did these ideals so critically raise questions of the meanings of equality. Moreover, the fact that Tocqueville distinguished the revolutionary (French) and the non-revolutionary (American) content of the two species of equality helps explain why we continue to think of the two democracies as fraternal rather than identical twins.

And so I take up Alexis de Tocqueville's announcement in the 1830s that he was describing a new civil society in America. In isolating the features of the specific ethos that differentiated one society from another, he sought out those ideas and values that formed them. In turn, he aspired to gain historical perspective, knowing that historical periods are not easily, totally, and finally demarcated from one another. Although hardly startling, this theory of the past is of high importance. In Tocqueville's case, we find that his determination to address the problems of a future democratic civil society and government nearly always – as if working against his will to draw the social contrasts as sharply as he could – brought to his mind the ironic persistence of older values and how some might be, not so much salvaged, as given some new and firm basis for survival. The most pressing need, as he saw it, and as we may perhaps also be enabled to see by his exploration of just such a challenge, was how to envisage a democratic society that would keep alive yet actively transform the varieties of human experience. Already he saw that this new civil society that replaced the lost world of a society bound by tradition, caste, rank, and privilege might, unless it looked closely to its foundations, itself in turn become a lost world.

Tocqueville's claim on us rests not only on his beguiling oracular utterances. It is founded more permanently, it seems to me, on his capacity to touch deeply points of high intensity in American society. In the years since, they have in some instances proven to be even more critical. In a very powerful way, a good many of his perceptions continue to govern American views of those older, as well as the newer, sources of tension. This book embraces those insights to heighten awareness of what has befallen the American dream, but it does not accept them uncritically. Americans have traveled far since those distant times, when a covenant brought to the shores of America English dissenters, who prided themselves on listening to and acting on their conscience. From the depths of that conscience, they took steps toward the creation of a social solidarity based on their conception of, and belief in, a unique correspondence of authority and liberty. Today, the older notion of authority embedded in those politics has long since vanished. It lies dispersed among several points of power. Originally this dispersal was designed to prevent the abuses of uncontrolled power exercised from one center. However, one may ask what consequences follow from the more extreme examples of fragmented authority that are visible today, and whether they may be inherent in democracy itself. Democracy, needing no authority other than itself, can, it seems, shape political culture in any way it wishes, creating new forms for itself in a time of rapid change and advanced technology. It follows that democracy is likely to move beyond politics as we have known it. It is thus an open question whether, living in a nation-state, which has lost many of its conventional signposts, and, even more critically, in a changing globalized capitalist economy, which overrides old boundaries, Americans are intent on trying to preserve and

extend to different groups whatever remains of that politics of affection
and loyalty that presumably gave life to the small local communities so
admired by Tocqueville. It is even more open to question that they are
prepared to endure the risks, and welcome the opportunities, of crossing borders. One may ask whether they can make the communications
technologies that monitor and manipulate mass democratic desires,
needs, and opinion work for them.

This book takes up some of the problems of the history of the
American democratic experience. The focus in Part I, Chapter 2 is on
Tocqueville's high regard for the Federalists, who, in their determination
to create a democratic state, firm enough to neutralize the centrifugal
actions of states' rights, would, at the same time, be capable of preserving liberty in a sea of expanding equality. Interwoven in my discussion
are the processes by which inequality in the privileged setting of an aristocratic regime were questioned, and succumbed to affirmations of
equality. The Federalists are important because their pronouncements
continue – if not to determine, but still called on – to confirm or inval-
idate different views of the intent of the American founders. European
thinkers also remain important because they were much present in the
minds of the Americans who shaped the Constitution and strove to give
body to their concept of politics and the principles of a good society.
I also call on some of their nineteenth- and twentieth-century European
and American successors who have added to the discussion on the future
of democracy. We will do well, as we traverse this territory in this and
other chapters, to be mindful of Tocqueville's view that political theory
by itself has no lasting value unless it addresses actual political practices.
Unlike the Founding Fathers who, he believed, bent their minds to the
practical exigencies of governing, those who lost themselves in the thick-
ets of abstraction prove to be poor guides in dealing with a culture
that calls itself democratic, and is somewhat uncomfortable with grand
theory that advocates sudden change in the conditions of property and
people, and from which it recoils instinctively (II, Bk. 3, chap. 21, 270,
274). Political theorists were, to be sure, helpful, but they were not to
be granted a special role as explorers of the American democratic
essence. As a political theorist and a social critic, Tocqueville was intent
on finding concrete ways to achieve a reasonable balance between the
oft-opposing commands of equality and liberty.

Chapter 3 is devoted to a discussion of how, both in Tocqueville's view
and in the opinion of one of his valued correspondents, John Stuart Mill,
and of twentieth-century political theorists, a democratic civil society

might retain its capacity to enlarge its range and continue to engage the population as citizens helping to make collective decisions benefiting all of them. The chapter introduces questions, first, about Tocqueville's belief in the vibrancy of voluntary associations that he attributed to the vast energies released by commerce, and which he argued were the source of political engagement and the positive enemy both of the materialization of private life and withdrawal from public life. It also asks, second, what we are to make of the Tocquevillian paradox that a market society appears to act as a sorcerer, creating prosperity, but at the same time throwing people into the turmoil of facing their duties as citizens.

Part II occupies the middle portion of the book. Chapters 4 to 6 rest on a notion of successive beginnings. The thread that unites them centers on Tocqueville's understanding of how America's treatment of the Native and slave populations might determine its future, as well as whether there was a future for them. Chapter 4 describes how the European mind came to imagine a new beginning after the Atlantic discoveries. It was a mind that saw the world as its own to explore and inhabit. The chapter evaluates Tocqueville's response to Native American culture the displacement of which he accepted as the inevitable outcome of the clash between Western and non-Western cultures, but which also strained his dedication to universal humanistic values. Chapter 5 offers an analysis of his reading of democracy in the New England township as a close fit between authority and liberty. I use the words "A Second Beginning" in my title for Chapter 6 to designate how, in thinking about the aftermath of the creation of the Federal Union, Tocqueville could not make the imaginative leap to include an active role in it for either the aboriginal or the black population. The chapter tries to understand the meaning of his near elision of groups of people from the new democracy by considering the context of his culture and time and the options that were then available.

Part III's Chapter 7 looks at a few works of the American imagination, its fiction, and its poetry to see how they approach the question of race and color, and it reviews, in contrapuntal fashion, the ideas of political theorists and polemicists on how American democracy deals with or confronts conflicts arising from the recognition of difference while trying to measure and ensure equality. I do not make a full turn in Chapter 8 to a historical discussion of voluntary associations, nor do I undertake a comprehensive critique of the empirical works of the phenomena. I have chosen instead to engage with contemporary social and political theorists who have focused on it as the spur to modern democratic action. The chapter deals with two issues of critical importance. The first issue evaluates Tocqueville's stress on the power of voluntary associations to keep the spirit of civic action and political concern alive by looking at how their modern advocates and critics regard them under the canopy of organizations that dwarf them in size. It does so within a context of how the prevailing ideas and practices of democratic consensus, which rely heavily on their putative virtues of dispersing power, but which may be more importantly understood as a branch of administrative control, have concealed the ways in which power is exercised. The second issue evaluates the impact of the enormous changes modern corporate and global capitalism have created, and attempts to assess whether it is the source of an irrevocable debasement of democratic politics. More radically, it asks whether politics as Americans knew it and now practice it will have an opportunity in a swiftly changing economy to make it work for them, or whether they will have only its forms, and not its substance, facing them. Chapter 9 takes up a problem that eludes final resolution even when it is given serious consideration. I have chosen, as in Chapter 8, to treat the sources of democratic authority in the context of political philosophy, with some references to American constitutional practices. The attempt to locate a stable source of democratic authority may, even if it proves to be a cul de sac, nevertheless not be an entirely futile exercise. How does one conceptualize it beyond moving full circle back to its source – the people? And how is the people's will to be read? The Federalists believed that they could best put minds to rest by distinguishing between a republic and a democracy, vesting final power in those who acted as the people's representatives. However, because in the very act of separating power between the three branches of government, they avoided a consideration of what might occur in times of crisis and who would be best able to deal with it, they left behind as a legacy periodic reexaminations of the original purposes of constituting power, bringing to the fore different claimants calling themselves the undisputed heirs of the popular will.

2

Democracy's Experiment:
From Inequality to Equality

The disputes over race and color in the United States were not absent from the debates over the provisions of the U.S. Constitution. However, the question of what structures of government would best express the goals of the American Republic, particularly the fears expressed over the unmediated force of the popular will, was their major focus. This aversion to full popular sovereignty cannot be fully understood without a clearer idea of why, even as many participants in the debate rejected the aristocratic ethos, and questioned the notion that the British Parliament faithfully and legally represented all British subjects, they worked to consolidate a bourgeois concept of personal worth, and forcefully used it as an argument to keep alive social distinctions and political inequality. It was within that concept that Anglo-Americans sought to locate non-whites, but the place they chose for them was not an unambiguous one, if only because bourgeois liberalism could not satisfactorily reconcile its confidence that rational thought was, in theory at least, vouchsafed to all, with their earliest doubts that all human beings were capable of it, even whites. The result was to present future generations of Americans with a chronically uncertain notion of where they were all supposed to fit – at the center, or on the edge, of equality, somewhere in between, or more disputably, as it were, nowhere.

Tocqueville and the Federalists

Whatever the observations made about Tocqueville's motives for traveling to, and his permanent interest in, the United States, one of the most important surely must be his vision of the New World as a point of

beginning, a point from which humanity by a free choice embarked on
a new stage in its social and political evolution. Present in *Democracy
in America*'s structure is a narrative of crossing-over, of a passage
toward, a new mental, as well as a geographical, space. The older space
from which it departed contained in itself a testamentary prophecy that
enjoined the bearers of the message to fulfill it by comprehending, experiencing, and carrying out a providential will. Inherent in the prophetic
narratives that, in the instance of the founding of the first Anglo-
American colonies, carried notions of the chosen people entering the
promised land, is error as well as promise, tragic despair as well as hope.
Anglo-American democracy became for Tocqueville a testing-ground for
the faltering aspirations and failures of modern civilization. He looked
at Anglo-American democracy in two broad ways. First, as a unique crucible for testing democratic political theory and practice, and, as well, as
a system of governance, radically different from the aristocratic forms
that, whatever changes the French Revolution had introduced, continued to hold sway in most of Europe. Second, he saw democracy as a
cultural and psychological product of distinctive habits and customs,
encapsulated in the French word *moeurs*. Hard to translate, its meaning
may best be understood as a cluster of moral and affective responses to
the material and the non-material boundaries of life. Underlying both
perspectives was a keen sense of the historical changes that created this
novel democratic experience, or, as he often stated and implied, this
experiment in civil and political society, not excluding, in a wider sense,
its affective experiences.

Tocqueville's stress on experiment was not misplaced. The sense of the
new was pervasive in the United States. He found it everywhere he went
and, not least of all, in his perusal and deep study of the collection
of *The Federalist* papers, the work of James Madison, Alexander
Hamilton, and John Jay, who invoked the authority of classical and
eighteenth-century political philosophers to support their vision of a sound
national polity. Their work, and those others who were active in forging
a new sovereign state, appealed to Tocqueville, as much by their firm
familiarity with the practical problems and legitimate endeavors of government as by their readings on politics on which they sharpened their
minds. Not only was the United States embarking on a new political
path. The experiment in self-government in a popular republic could be
undone, as Hamilton and Madison stated in their objections to Jefferson,
by too frequent appeals to the popular will. Indeed, Tocqueville enlisted
Jefferson, "the greatest democrat whom the democracy of America has

yet produced," to support his doubts about popular democracy. He did so by reproducing Jefferson's letter to Madison in 1787 some two months after the papers of *The Federalist* were being sent to the press:

> The instability of our laws is a very serious inconvenience. I think that we ought to have obviated it by deciding that a whole year should always be allowed to elapse between the bringing in of a bill and the final passing of it. It should afterwards be discussed and put to the vote without the possibility of making any alteration in it; and if the circumstances of the case required a more speedy decision, the question should not be decided by a simple majority, but by a majority of at least two-thirds of each house (I, chap. 13, 214, Jefferson to Madison, December 20, 1787, translation of M. Conseil).

Hamilton and Madison were unquestionably more confident about the superior nature of a representative form of self-government they saw embodied in the American republic – distinguishing it from the aristocratic and stadtholder republics in Europe, the Venetian, and the Dutch – than they were about a democratic republic, with its potential for civil disturbance. For them, a republic is "a government which derives all its powers directly or indirectly from the great body of the people, and is administered by persons holding their offices during pleasure, for a limited period, or during good behavior. It is *essential* to such a government that it be derived from the great body of the society, not from an inconsiderable proportion or a favored class of it."[1]

In the tenth *Federalist Paper*, Madison stated that "[t]he two great points of difference between a democracy and a republic are: first, the delegation of the government, in the latter, to a small number of citizens elected by the rest; secondly, the greater number of citizens, and greater sphere of country, over which the latter may be extended." He was a frank advocate of mediation, stating that public views demanded refinement and enlargement "by passing them through the medium of a chosen body of citizens, whose wisdom may best discern the true interest of their country ... Under such a regulation, it may well happen that the public voice ... will be more consonant to the public good than if pronounced by the people themselves, convened for the purpose."[2] In the untried world of democratic politics, citizens had to be trained to apprehend public interest. And, ever on the outlook for the urge to put local self-interest first, he deliberately subordinated it to "the permanent and

---

[1] *Federalist* No. 39 in *The Federalist*. From the original text of Alexander Hamilton, John Jay, and James Madison (New York: The Modern Library, n.d.), pp. 243–44.
[2] *Federalist* No. 10, p. 59.

aggregate interests of the community."³ Most of all, neither faction nor its cause can be removed; "relief is only to be sought in the means of controlling its effects."⁴ Yet this could not and would not be achieved unless it was candidly recognized that the spirit of party and faction is itself necessarily involved in the making of the laws that regulate the "various and interfering interests."⁵ The perils of faction could not be contained if the majority became part of the faction, in short, when passion overwhelmed the public good and the rights of minorities. The task of government was to find the means to prevent the majority oppression of private rights and public good. Morality and religion would not have the strength to deal with a situation in which "the impulse [to oppress] and the opportunity [were] suffered to coincide."⁶ His view that theoretical defenses of pure democracy stood in the way of an understanding of political reality, and his critique of what he labeled perfect equality, are worth citing *in extenso*:

> [I]t may be concluded that a pure democracy, by which I mean a society consisting of a small number of citizens, who assemble and administer the government in person, can admit of no cure for the mischiefs of faction. A common passion or interest will, in almost every case, be felt by a majority of the whole; a communication and concert result from the form of government itself; and there is nothing to check the inducements to *sacrifice the weaker party or an obnoxious individual.* Hence it is that such democracies have ever been spectacles of turbulence and contention; have ever been found incompatible with personal security or the rights of property; and have in general been as short in their lives as they have been violent in heir deaths. Theoretic politicians, who have patronized this species of government, have erroneously supposed that by reducing mankind to a perfect equality in their political rights, they would, at the same time, be perfectly equalized and assimilated in their possessions, their opinions, and their passions.⁷

An enlarged nation, a national body that cared for "the great and particular interests" of the people, diminished the threat of an officious and dominant majority exerting its will. While factions were dangerous in small democracies, they were less so – in fact, they were salutary – in large republics. As he put it, the variety of sects dispersed over "the entire face of it (the Confederacy) must secure the national councils against any danger from that source." "Wicked project[s]" (such as equal division of property, abolition of debts, and religious sectarianism) would encounter resistance from the whole body of citizens, who would not be

---

³ Ibid., p. 54.   ⁴ Ibid., p. 57.   ⁵ Ibid., p. 56.   ⁶ Ibid., p. 58.
⁷ Ibid., pp. 58–59. My italics.

taken in by such schemes because they would reject interests so narrowly conceived. Thus, Madison counted on the people to deflate and scatter the power of a factious majority intent on "schemes of oppression." The sheer number of sects would achieve two unintended consequences. First, they would serve to fragment the power of illegitimately conceived majorities and hence protect the minority of the educated and the propertied and safeguard the republic. Second, because of their large number, they would also keep the people dispersed in pursuit of different goals, and, as often as not, neutralize one another's efforts:

> Ambition must be made to counteract ambition. The interest of the man must be connected with the constitutional rights of the place. It may be a reflection on human nature, that such devices should be necessary to control the abuses of government. But what is government itself, but the greatest of all reflections on human nature? If men were angels, no government would be necessary. If angels were to govern men, neither external nor internal controls on government would be necessary. In framing a government which is to be administered by men over men, the great difficulty lies in this: you must first decide to control the governed; and in the next place oblige it to control itself.[8]

It is plain that Madison captured democracy's propensity to swallow up differences. In its pure form, democracy erased all distinctions, the good as well as the bad. To preserve the first, one had to learn to tolerate the second. Those who advocated pure democracy were lending themselves and everyone else to an injurious attack on good sense and good order. It was, furthermore, based on a false premise that a simple equality benefited everyone, instead of bringing advantage to no one, unless they were willing to take on the role of oppressors of the weak and of the dissenting individual. Pericles, we recall, was anxious to ensure that no one in Athens would suffer oppression. Tocqueville, as we will later see, was concerned to protect the voice of the "stranger."

But there was more to be considered. The eighteenth-century debate on America's future political character drew a deliberate distinction between republican and democratic forms of government. As we may see from Madison's warnings, it was the problem of ensuring the stability of the polity by a filtering process capable of resisting the gyrations of a democratic majority fluctuating in the winds of public opinion that was most exercising. Calling on the people "would carry an implication of

---

[8] *Federalist* No. 51, p. 337. For the eighteenth-century debate on the countervailing passions, see Albert O. Hirschman, *The Passions and the Interests. Political Arguments for Capitalism Before Its Triumph* (Princeton: Princeton University Press, 1977).

some defect in the government, [and] frequent appeals would, in a great measure, deprive the government of that veneration, which time bestows on everything, and without which perhaps the wisest and freest governments would not possess the requisite stability."[9] There were, moreover, no philosopher-kings, such as Plato wished for. Modern societies could no longer even call on them in their imagination, but they could call on their own "prejudices" – that is, their reverence, hallowed by time – for the Constitution of which they were the authors. Yet, because the people might not only be forgetful but swayed by the passions of their representatives and sway them in turn by their own, there had to be some means of controlling them. "[I]t is the reason, alone, of the public, that ought to control and regulate the government. The passions ought to be controlled and regulated by the government."[10] And the superiority of the American governments "lies *in the total exclusion of the people, in their collective capacity*, from any share in the *latter*, and not in the *total exclusion of the representatives of the people* from the administration of the *former*."[11]

Hannah Arendt captures well the distinction between majority decision and majority will that the Federalists were trying to make – a distinction that our contemporaries find hard to sustain. She saw the problem as arising "where the majority, after the decision has been taken, proceeds to liquidate politically, and in extreme cases physically, the opposing minority . . ." It is then that the "technical device of majority decision [will] degenerat[e] into the 'elective despotism' of majority rule." Lest there be any misunderstanding, Arendt also reminds us that the Anglo-American debate was conducted within a framework of constitutionalism, in which the solidity of written documents marking the American beginnings of civil and political society expressly eschewed majority despotic rule.[12] The beginnings were, however, central to what was key to the American Revolution. "Crucial to any understanding of revolutions in the modern age," she insists, "is that the idea of freedom and the experience of a new beginning should coincide."[13] What made the American Revolution unique, distinguishing it from the French rupture, Arendt says, is that Americans grasped the difference between the "passion for public or political freedom" and "the more vehement,

---

[9] *Federalist* No. 49, pp. 328–29.   [10] Ibid., p. 331.   [11] *Federalist* No. 63, p. 413.
[12] Hannah Arendt, *On Revolution* (New York: The Viking Press, 1963), pp. 163–64, 227.
[13] Ibid., pp. 21–22.

but politically essentially sterile, passionate hatred of masters, the longing of the oppressed for liberation."[14] Liberating the political from the social spared Americans the tumult and violence of the people. Yet, while revolution might make this manifest, Arendt tells us that freedom is itself a beginning; "it carries its own principle within itself, or, to be more precise, . . . beginning and principle, *principium* and principle, are not only related to each other, but are coeval,"[15] and that the experience of being free came after liberation when Americans proceeded with the task of creating an "independent government and found[ing] . . . a new body politic."[16] It was to be a body politic that lodged and defined freedom within the boundaries and limits posed by the Constitution. It was the repository, moreover, of the authority needed to maintain the republic's integrity.[17] Where, before, freedom and power coincided, now freedom and authority did.

Arendt's distinction between majority decision and majority will helps to clarify why Tocqueville unequivocally admired and took the side of the Federalists after 1789, who, he said, by resisting the democratic tendencies of America, at least gave the new nation time to settle down and inscribe their wise apprehensions on the minds of the more fervently democratic Jeffersonians (I, chap. 10, 184). It was the overwhelming power of the majority that Tocqueville feared. By citing at length passages from *Federalist* paper No. 51, he made it clear that he agreed with Madison that one of a republic's main responsibilities was to prevent a situation in which one part of society can with impunity oppress another. He endorsed Madison's formulation that the people had to be protected against themselves to avoid harming the entire protective armature of the republic's political structure and the civil society upon which it rested. Not only was the despotism of rulers to be abhorred and kept at bay, but the unjust despotism of the majority could well rouse the minority to defend itself, producing anarchy, and bringing an end to civil society (I, chap. 15, 279). The goal of government had to be justice, even to the point of losing liberty if it was required:

> It [justice] is the end of civil society. It ever has been, and ever, will be pursued, until it is obtained, or until liberty be lost in the pursuit. In a society, under the forms of which the stronger faction can readily unite and oppress the weaker, anarchy may as truly be said to reign as in a state of nature, where the weaker

[14] Ibid., p. 121. [15] Ibid., p. 214. [16] Ibid., p. 26. [17] Ibid., 152–53.

individual is not secured against the stronger: and as, in the latter state, even the stronger individuals are prompted by the uncertainty of their condition to submit to a government which may protect the weak as well as themselves, so, in the former state, will the more powerful factions be gradually induced by a like motive to wish for a government which will protect all parties, the weaker as well as the more powerful (ibid., 280).

Tocqueville discussed the future of the American experiment with former president John Quincy Adams in Boston in 1831, three years after his defeat by Andrew Jackson, Jefferson's ideological heir, who had earlier defeated Adams' father, John Adams, in the 1800 presidential elections. He listened to Adams' disapproval of the practice of calling conventions to discuss political questions, which had the effect of bypassing and usurping the legitimately juridical powers of constituted political bodies.[18] As William Appleman Williams also tells us, Adams "challenged America to become truly unique by mastering its fears. It was Jefferson and his followers who did not face up to the tension that freedom involved by denying that it was possible to be free and disciplined. Adams insisted that was the only meaningful definition of freedom. . . . 'The great object of civil government,' Adams declared in his first annual message to Congress, 'is the improvement of the condition of those who are parties to the social compact.' "[19] By questioning the identification of electoral politics with democracy and sound government, as if the one explained or expressed the other, and just as significantly by affirming his belief in the conjunction between freedom and discipline, Tocqueville went further. He suggested that the right of franchise should not be the only criterion of either freedom or the purposes of a civil society. Bluntly he rejected the belief that universal suffrage guaranteed the *wisdom or excellence* of the popular choice (I, chap. 13, 209. My emphasis). Direct election, he insisted, as for the House of Representatives, brought the worst place-seekers to power. He gave thanks to the provisions for indirect elections to the Senate by members of the elected state legislatures, who change the popular authority by "refining its discretion and improving its choice . . . [T]hey represent only the elevated thoughts that are current in the community and the generous

[18] Alexis de Tocqueville, *Oeuvres*, ed. André Jardin, with the collaboration of Françoise Mélonio and Lise Queffélec, 2 vols. (Paris: Gallimard, 1991), I, 74. Hereafter cited in this and succeeding chapters as *Oeuvres*.
[19] Cited in Gore Vidal, "Reel History. Why John Quincy Adams Was the Hero of the Amistad Affair," *New Yorker*, November 10, 1997, p. 120.

propensities that prompt its nobler actions rather than the petty passions that disturb or the vices that degrade it" (I, chap. 13, p. 212).[20]

But, even while he thought such restrictions desirable, he was not confident that the "rare and brief exercise of [the people's] free choice, however important it may be, will not prevent them from gradually losing the faculties of thinking, feeling and acting for themselves, and thus gradually falling below the level of humanity" (II, Bk. 4, chap. 6, 339). They were healthy safeguards, but Tocqueville strongly declined to support those who put their entire faith in the political devices and mechanisms of electoral management as the single and simple guarantor of free choice. They would fail to notice, he predicted, that over time the ability to discern the boundaries between choice and electoral manipulation would fade. At the same time as John Quincy Adams spoke in deploring tones to Tocqueville about the growing practice of excessive appeals to the democratic will, it was just as imperative, Adams told Tocqueville, to acknowledge the existence and problem of two Americas – the America of New England and the America of Southern slavery.

Thus, when Tocqueville asked his readers to keep in mind that "The aspect of civic society has been as much altered as the face of the political world" since 1789, [and] amounted to an irresistible force (II, Preface, v–vi), the wonder of the social and political experiment – its origins, strengths, weaknesses, and likely outcome – stayed with him as the chief feature of a political culture that demanded explanation. The very notion of experimentation was long-lived, moving through several lives and several societies, preceding and continuing, but encompassing Tocqueville's own. It had earlier invited scathing scorn from Edmund Burke, who warned against facile analogies between chemical experimentation and experimenting with human lives.

Standing in a space separating himself from the Anglo-Irish conservative critic, Tocqueville offered his own substantive reading of the experimental. It rested on his personal observations in America, the lessons of the French Revolution – which elicited an ambivalent response to Enlightenment rationality – and his careful reading of many of the same writings that inspired the educated classes on both sides of the Atlantic before after 1776 and after 1789. That the clock could not be turned

---

[20] For a study of Madison's complex view that a natural aristocracy was needed for wise government, see Alan Gibson, "Impartial Representation and the Extended Republic. Towards a Comprehensive and Balanced Reading of the Tenth Federalist Paper," *History of Political Thought*, 12 (1991), 263–304.

back was a belief shared by many, such as François Guizot, who in 1837, two years after the publication of Tocqueville's first volume, wrote that "Democracy is a war cry; it is the banner of the many situated below against the few placed on high. A banner raised sometimes in the name of the healthiest rights, sometimes in the name of the crudest and outraged passions, sometimes against the most iniquitous usurpations, sometimes against the most legitimate superiority."[21]

In 1859, the year of Tocqueville's death, his friend, John Stuart Mill, declared that "There is confessedly a strong tendency in the modern world towards a democratic constitution of society, accompanied or not by popular political institutions." He singled out the United States as the "society and the government [which] are most democratic." It could indeed be a fatally oppressive society by virtue of invoking the sanctity of majority choice as against the choices made by individuals.[22] In classical times, philosophers, Mill said, countenanced practices that regulated "every part of private conduct by public authority, on the ground that the State has a deep interest *in the whole bodily and mental discipline of every one of its citizens.*"[23] In conditions of chronic warfare, the regulations that were needed by states in ancient times when facing attack from their neighbors ruled out the luxury of choosing self-discipline. Strangely, Mill seemed to remember Sparta and to forget the Athenian school of freedom bequeathed by Thuycidides' Pericles. In modern times, Mill goes on to say, military discipline was no longer required, mainly because spiritual and temporal authority had been separated, leaving private lives freer from legal interference, but not from the dead weight of majority religious convention, nor from "the disposition of mankind, whether as rulers or as fellow citizens to impose their own opinions."[24] Unchecked by moral conviction, that power would increase. He opposed to it a robust individualism, which "recognizes no authority whatever in Society over the individual, except to enforce equal freedom of development for all individualities." He equated this with his notion of a democrat who imposed "the tyranny of society over the individual." The just society he hoped would take shape in the future would rest on humanity's capacity to find the means to "unite the greatest individual liberty of action, with a common ownership in the raw material

---

[21] Cited in Pierre Rosanvallon, *Le moment Guizot* (Paris: Gallimard, 1985), pp. 83–84.
[22] John Stuart Mill, *On Liberty* (Indianapolis and New York: Bobbs-Merrill, 1956), 6–07.
p. 17. My emphasis.   [24] Ibid., p.18.

of the globe, and an equal participation of all in the benefits of combined labor."[25]

Mill approached the question of power and discipline across time in a way that relates freedom over one's own body and mind to the meanings of self-discipline and its ties with the order and disciplinary acts available to society and the state, as well as those of its disciplinary institutions that act in the name of the tacit wishes of society and in the name of state authority. Like Tocqueville, Mill dwelt on the increasing power of centralized administration, pointing to what he said was the demonstrable fact that "where everything is done through the bureaucracy, nothing to which the bureaucracy is really adverse can be done at all." It drew to itself the best minds of the community, and thus created the conditions for the "more complete . . . bondage of all, the members of the bureaucracy included."[26] If Tocqueville did not doubt that democracy would in time overtake and displace older ideas of authority in the private and public realms of existence, he was even less certain than Mill that democracy would be a creative or a negative force in human society. Related closely to his expressions of doubt was the prior question: Would citizens be able to use democratic forms to achieve their goals as free individuals? What could modern active citizenship mean? Were the organs of representative government, from the township to the state legislatures and to the national Congress, activated by a vigilant press and voluntary private societies, capable of exercising the power to strengthen a democratic civil society?

To retain the sense of closeness to be found within the township, Tocqueville placed immense value on these continuing efforts of citizens to immerse themselves in their organizational life to offset the tendency to live wholly within their families, businesses, trades, and their small communities. But it was not only civil engagement upon which a liberal democratic society must rely. One was the weight of the Constitution, the other the power of the federal government. Tocqueville's analysis of the Constitution provides some further evidence of his conception of civil society. American courts looked to the Constitution as the fount of all authority and thus for answers to deal with opposing views of how a republic might resolve differences among its citizens. It, and not the laws, was said to represent the will of the whole people, binding legislators as

[25] John Stuart Mill, *Autobiography* (New York: Columbia University Press, 1960), pp. 179, 162.
[26] John Stuart Mill, *On Liberty*, p. 137.

well as citizens. It was not only an instrument to be used against the tyranny of political assemblies, but the means of sorting out conflicts arising from differing visions of American society, most of all the ways in which liberty and public order were to be measured (I, chap. 6, 102–07). At the same time that the clash of interests was regulated through judicial compromise and acceptance of inevitable differences in civil and political society, the federal government also possessed some power to create a sense of unity standing, above separate interests and the jealously guarded independence of units smaller than the nation, particularly the states, which, Madison believed, were not receptive to the increasing pace of economic life. The failure to concentrate efforts to achieve such a sense was due to the failure of the people to retain the consciousness to "rise above itself" as it did when it sought to create itself as "single and undivided" (I, chap. 18, 423). Thus a lively sense of the creative force of law, a government answering to the needs and desires of citizens (unlike the governments of European nations), and a capacity to move beyond the compulsions of local loyalties constituted the features of a sound democratic civil society.

There is a tendency to idealize democracy as a goal to strive for, but one never to be reached in its entirety, leaving in its wake crushed, but never totally inextinguishable, hopes. There is also pressure to dwell on its imperfections and corruptions. The first is to be found among disenchanted revolutionaries who transfer their spent energies to more pacific and less destabilizing meliorative paths to reach their objectives. The second issues from a deep aversion for democracy, in its liberal readings more than in its populist ones. The jeremiads that often follow the pessimistic appraisals of the flaws in democracy are aimed at playing to the voice of the people, the so-called neglected heartland of America. But there is also a naive notion that Western political societies, founded on constitutions embodying unequal measures of principle and practical wisdom, are broadly democratic because they consult their citizens through the machinery of electoral processes by means of which they are said to express their will and expect that it will be carried out in one form or another. Much of this is disingenuous. No thoughtful person – and Tocqueville, as we saw a moment ago, was such a one – really believes that such procedures constitute democracy. Despite Rousseau's very different concept of politics, especially his suspicion of the alleged benefits of continuous and active citizen participation, the appeal to a semi-divine and wise Legislator as a point of reference, indeed, as a founder, is not unsimilar to the sacred qualities that were attached to the U.S. Constitution and the Founding Fathers who fashioned it. For

Tocqueville, who shared much of that respect, the Constitution was seen, as, indeed, it was seen by its framers, as a guide against the inevitably errant wishes of the populace. Errancy was expected and accepted as a human failing by the Founding Fathers. It was not used to justify a cynical withdrawal from or exploitation of the public realm.

We have seen through Mill's eyes how the ancient Greeks were supposed to have looked at democracy. The Greek word *demos* conjures up unruly crowds and demagogues, as well as a polity of citizens gathering in the *agora*, the public space in the small Greek city, where citizens made decisions affecting all of them. Tocqueville, like many of his contemporaries, but particularly Benjamin Constant, was mixed in his admiration for the robust, and, as he put it, virile and virtuous nature of Athenian democracy. But he knew that neither it, nor what he believed were the near pathological and destructive democratic theater and rhetoric of the elected French revolutionary neighborhood bodies, could serve as a desirable or defensible model for modern democracy. Besides, what Tocqueville saw lurking there was the dead zone of democratic despotism in his own country, which assumed alarming powers under Louis Bonaparte after the 1848 Revolution, and might, in a different and distinctive form, Tocqueville thought, manifest itself in America, where arbitrary government could work against individual freedom by a seemingly plausible defense of equal rights. It was easier to exercise executive power by persuading citizens that such power represented their real interests, especially when they tended to support measures that put greater store on treating all alike.

The only sure thing was that democracy was an almost totally novel phenomenon, one that was strictly speaking a product of the modern age, one that was being identified, not with a small city-state, but with a large national territory, and one that got its bearings from what he called, as we have noted, an equality of condition – that principle of equality that powerfully shaped an existing body of anterior and independent modes of thought and feeling. The dissection of the psychic roots of the desire for equality could not be separated from previously existing intellectual and affective modes. That was certain. But nearly equally, the equality principle would shape them. In this rough formulation of their mutual interaction there was, if not fully concealed, at least obscured the potential clash between, and the possibilities for conflict generated by, the tenacity of *moeurs* and the movement toward equality. By the equality principle or equality of condition, Tocqueville did not mean equality in fact, nor did he mean that men were born free, as the 1776 American Declaration of Independence and the 1789 French

Declaration of Rights stated. Nor, again, did he mean economic equality. Distinctions of wealth, of course, existed in America as in Europe. The rich and the affluent, however, behaved defensively, even to the point of withdrawing from political life into their private worlds, waiting out the triumph of the democratic party (he wrote soon after the Jacksonians swept the polls). They demonstrated a false acquiescence, even an obsequiousness, in public, but privately expressed their scorn for and fear of the poor. There was no question that they hated democratic institutions, but they went through the motions of acceptance in a society pledged to equal access to the polls (I, chap. 10, 186–87), except for blacks and Native Americans. Economic dependence and economic inequality, both created by specific contractual obligations, were not inimical, he thought, to equality of citizenship in a civil society. Besides, he was fairly certain that the ever-expanding economic opportunities and the rapid rise and fall of fortunes would both act against huge concentrations of wealth. By equality, he meant the cultivation of a credo of equal human dignity and equal esteem powerful enough to neutralize economic inequality. In the domain of politics, there was no need for a political contract enshrining the reciprocal obligations of rulers and ruled, but only the belief in a transcendent vision of equality. This was sufficient to make it work in the daily practices of life. It marked the end of privilege of ascribed status that provided the dynamics of a traditional hierarchical society of classes and castes.

From Quality to Equality

The *moeurs* of a caste society made it possible for its members to know who was entitled to earn their sympathy and support. When social change came, neither education nor civilization explained the softening, gentleness, mildness, compassion, and pity of a society in which equality of conditions prevailed, as much as equality itself. Castes looked inward; they looked after their own and were insensible to the sufferings of others; a society without castes extended its gaze outward and took in more of humanity. Castes, I would add, were made up of people who thought of themselves as possessing qualities not universally shared, and who believed that a breach of justice would occur were anyone to suggest otherwise. Castes subsisted on the notion of quality. In the case of the European aristocracy, these qualities were carried by blood. Those outside it were, as Tocqueville said in his brief reference to Roman attitudes, treated barbarically as strangers. Similarly, American slaveholders were not moved by the suffering of their slaves, yet not as unmoved as their harsher counterparts in European colonies (II, Bk. 3, chap. 2, 172–77).

An ideal aristocratic society was one of equals for those deemed to have passed the tests of birth and hence of *qualité*. People of quality, *gens de qualité, gens du monde*, created an exclusive identity of quality, possessed by themselves alone and denied to others. Pascal, to whom Tocqueville turned, understood the practices of caste well. "It is a great advantage," he said "to be a man of quality, since it brings one man as forward at eighteen as another man would be at fifty, which is a clear gain of thirty years" (II, Bk. 3, chap. 19, 258–59). Pascal went on to make clear that he had no illusions about idealized claims of a naturally endowed quality, and entertains us with his maxims on its accouterments, the external apparel that clothed highly birthed individuals, braced for the exercise of authority and against those who would challenge it. Tocqueville had no illusions either. For the privileged, quality was inseparable from merit and denoted superior well-being. In his 1836 *Etat social et politique de la France* Tocqueville provided a fuller picture of caste. For the privileged members of a caste society, one might say that "democratic" forms of liberty existed but at the expense of all outside the charmed circle. But as Tocqueville presciently observed, it was from these forms that democratic equality sprouted when fissures began to erode the strict caste differentiations, as blood lines were diluted by noble landholders in search of wealth through commerce and the venal purchase of state offices. Divisiveness and hierarchy seriously compromised the tenuous links of the *esprit de corps* of the caste itself, with the result that assigned and self-attributed qualities were driven further apart. The idealized equality promised by a cohesive caste ran up against changing attributions and perceptions of quality, all originating in motives of self-regard. The illusion of quality lasted as long as a condition of social stasis remained undisturbed, or at least could be assumed to exist. Once the illusion was shattered by increasing hostilities and rivalries internal to the caste, the entire social edifice in which equality based on the aristocratic notion of quality was replaced with the notion of equality extended to all.[27]

---

[27] See "Etat social et politique de la France avant et depuis 1789," in *Oeuvres complètes d'Alexis de Tocqueville*, 18 vols. (Paris: Gallimard, 1950–98), (*L'Ancien Régime et la Révolution*) 2, part 1, 33–66. Materials from the *Oeuvres complètes* will hereafter be cited as OC. To date, only volume 6, part 3, and volume 17 remain to be published.

The illusion of aristocratic equality came to an end through jurisprudential changes after 1789. Sieyès, whom Tocqueville was later to see as the quintessential voice of a radical and full-scale offensive against the Old Régime, questioned the very foundation of caste differentiation, and challenged it to oppose the singular and undifferentiated national will, a powerful rallying point for those who debated and defended a startlingly novel theory of constitution making.[28] Nevertheless, the will of the nation was best entrusted, not to all, but to a qualified section of the people. The interests and capacities Sieyès singled out as features of a just civil and political society sharply divided the population according to property, education, and general fitness for political life. This had the effect of disqualifying the greatest portion of the population. In any rational civil society, all nevertheless had the right to the protection of their persons, property, and liberty, though not all had the right to take part in political life. Civil rights were natural, but political rights had to be earned. Since there were natural human differences, inequalities naturally existed in the capacity for work, productivity, and happiness. While Sieyès said that "nature does not pass out mental gifts exclusively to a single race of men," he also said "those whom nature or circumstances have marked with the seal of nullity" [should be allowed] "to fall."[29] Equality was, as far as he was concerned, clearly a naive idea, and the call for it in a large modern nation was he believed misconceived. "If in a small space you wish to retain equality, you condemn the nation to a simplicity of industry and of happiness which could be sustained only with the degradation of the faculties of imagination and will. We would have to roll back the human species."[30] Sieyès was no partisan of the Rousseauian quest for a return to simplicity. He embraced instead the very developments that the Genevan hated – the division of labor,

---

[28] For a discussion on this point, see Harvey Mitchell, *Individual Choice and the Structures of History. Alexis de Tocqueville as Historian Reappraised* (Cambridge: Cambridge University Press, 1996), pp. 243–44.

[29] Cited by William H. Sewell, Jr., *A Rhetoric of Bourgeois Revolution. The Abbé Sieyès and "What is the Third Estate"?* (Durham and London: Duke University Press, 1994), p. 163. Stressing Sieyès' "amnesia" on the question of privilege, Sewell sees a deep contradiction in his political thought. While Sewell correctly points to Sieyès' conceptual struggle with legitimate and illegitimate privileges or *availabilities*, as Sieyès called them, it may be argued that for him, differentiation was an inescapable aspect of human society. Like Plato before him, he drew a straight line between those enabled for rule and those disabled for it, or in their lexicon, those possessing, and those not possessing the requisite qualities.

[30] Cited in ibid., p. 161.

the unequal distribution of wealth, and the growth of inequalities at all levels of life, private and public.

But no one in civil society would be denied the legal protection of their rights. Sieyès seems to have taken it as granted that men who were not gifted by nature would, for that very reason, be kept from the acquisition of interests and capacities that qualified for full participation in political life. The corollary of interests and capacities was autonomy; the combination of these produced an autonomous will, a will dependent solely on oneself.[31] "The difference between *natural and civil rights* and the *political* rights of citizens," he said:

> consists in the fact that natural and civil rights are those rights *for* whose preservation and development society is formed; and political rights are those rights *by* which society is formed. For the sake of clarity, it would be best to call the first ones passive rights, and the second ones active rights. . . . All inhabitants of a country must enjoy the rights of passive citizens . . . all are not active citizens. Women, at least in the present state, children, foreigners, and also those who would not at all contribute to the public establishment must have no active influence on public matters.[32]

Sieyès did much to set down the foundations of the moderate 1791 Constitution that ended a privileged caste society. While it widened the limits of civil society, the Constitution kept a lid on full expressions of a democratic polity. We should not overlook Sieyès' egregious glances into a future society organized along strict rules of division of labor, with Negroes, "auxiliary instruments of labor," acting in an intermediary role between whites and "new races of anthropomorphic monkeys" destined to be slaves.[33]

By Tocqueville's time, as he saw in America, the illusions of a self-contained caste structure had been exposed, but he thought that the illusory aspects of democratic societies had a long history stretching out before them. Still, whether or not a society was built upon castes, there were hard social and psychological realities to be found everywhere:

> Among men, there exists, irrespective of the societies in which they live, and independently of the laws that they have developed, a certain quantity of actual

---

[31] Emmanuel-Joseph Sièyes, *Qu'est-ce que le tiers état*, ed. Roberto Zapperi (Geneva: Librairie Droz, 1970), p. 139. See also Sièyes' *Préliminaire de la constitution: Reconnaissance et exposition raisonnée des Droits de l'Homme et du Citoyen* (Versailles, 1789) in *Ecrits politiques*, ed. Roberto Zapperi (Paris: Editions des Archives Contemporaines, 1985), pp. 20–21.

[32] Sièyes, *Préliminaire*, pp. 36–37. Italics in original.

[33] Sièyes, *Ecrits politiques*, p. 75.

or conventional goods, which naturally can be the property of only a small number of people. At their summit, I place birth, wealth and knowledge. Any social conditions in which all citizens were noble, enlightened and rich would be inconceivable. The goods of which I am speaking differ among themselves, but they possess a common feature, and that is, that only a small number of people can share them, and for this very reason, these attributes can be acknowledged only for those who possess exceptional judgments and selective ideas. Thus these goods form so many aristocratic elements which, set apart and entrusted in the same hands, are to be found among all peoples and in every historical epoch. When all those who are endowed with these exceptional advantages work together with government, a powerful and durable aristocracy exists.[34]

In this rather astonishing passage, Tocqueville departs from historical specificity and identifies goods with qualities of excellence, or of excellences pertaining to birth, wealth, and knowledge. Found in all societies, such goods are rare and not evenly divided. Though quality is instantiated in practical and tangible forms, he also seems to speak of it in an abstract sense, and seems about to raise the question of how societies recognize it and the degree to which they reward it. If he seems more at ease with the practical manifestations of quality, for our purposes it is important to note his indecision on the question of the existence of a natural aristocracy. But he seems inclined to strike a blow in favor of the notion. However hard he might find it to render a coherent account, he again relies on an analysis of how individuals behave – in this instance, when aristocratic societies are destroyed. They instinctively fear everything above them, and must make an enormous effort to admit that the science or the impartiality of justice and respect for the law possesses solidity. People exhibit jealousy of neighbors, who, once having been their superiors, are now their equals, and to complete the circuit come to doubt themselves.[35] In these conditions, excellences or quality are, Tocqueville implies, grudgingly recognized but never totally sustained. It is in the transition from aristocratic to democratic society that the notion of quality or excellence is forfeited. What operates to keep the notion alive, even if only as an ideal in an aristocracy, seems to come to an end.

The possession of quality bestows power. It also demands the assumption and execution of roles – the acting out of power. People in a state of inequality react. Their actions take place on a subordinate plane. With

---

[34] "Etat social et politique de la France avant et depuis 1789," in OC 2 (*L'Ancien Régime et la Révolution*) part 1, 46.
[35] Ibid., 57.

the widening of notions of quality – that is, with the movement toward equality – power becomes less concentrated. It becomes diffused throughout the population. The older attitudes separating individuals and groups from one another suffer challenge, and are to be displaced by other, more subtle forms of differentiation. As Tocqueville recognized, no one, even in a society with equality of conditions, is wholly disinterested. So, while for the ethos of quality there is substituted one of equality, the operations of power remain. As well, new social conditions multiply qualities and roles. In the new democratic society, everyone can now play a role; but, while power is indeed more diffused, it is not unconcentrated or fragmented. In other words, democratic society does not equalize power. It shifts it around. Power no longer subsists on what are now regarded as obsolete and unfair notions of quality. It feeds on a fair, though not total, accretion of feelings of social certainty, a far cry from the certainty of social degradation and the uncertainty of future security. Nominally all have qualities in democratic societies, but at the same time some are given different and greater or lesser valorization. Consequently, for the broadest sections of democratic society, equality subsumes qualities and presumes shared qualities or a minimum number of them that are identified with a notion of common humanity, but this need not obliterate a hierarchy of qualities, as Tocqueville feared it might through the sheer weight of leveling. He thought of the declining opportunities for individuals who sought to express the lofty ambitions associated with aristocratic societies. Democratic people were more absorbed by the commands of the present. To counteract this democratic failing, which fosters obedience, on the one hand, and domination over others, on the other, they ought to be subjected to difficult and dangerous challenges to raise them above, and to give them an enlarged notion of, themselves. Up to a point, he included in his vision people who deliberately stood aside from the mass, their only ambition being to be outside it in order to criticize it (II, Bk. 3, chap. 19). Their refusal and their taste or talents for objectification might also be seen as an enactment of a role, but this has at best a negative power, not the unblinkingly positive power of natural qualities that remain unaltered in a society transformed by equality.

Nowhere does Tocqueville say this more bitingly than at the end of his chapter entitled "What Are the Real Advantages Which American Society Derives from a Democratic Government?" Defiantly challenging those who hated or praised democracy without, as he said, having an adequate knowledge of the subject, he asked the question that is

foundational for anyone inquiring into the nature of civil society and
authority, one that cannot be ignored if we are to deal with the question
of how far he was prepared to delve into the implications of his own
prognosis:

> We must first understand what is wanted of society and its government. Do
> you wish to give it a certain elevation of the human mind and teach it to regard
> the things of this world with generous feelings, to inspire men with a scorn of
> temporal advantages, to form and nourish strong convictions and keep alive the
> spirit of honorable devotedness? Is it your object to refine the habits, embellish
> the manners, and cultivate the arts, to promote the love of poetry, beauty, and
> glory? Would you constitute a people to act powerfully upon all other nations,
> and prepared for those high enterprises which, whatever be their results, will
> leave a name forever famous in history? If you believe such to be the principal
> object of society, avoid the government of the democracy, for it would not lead
> you with certainty to the goal.
>   But if you hold it expedient to divert the moral and intellectual activity of
> man to the production of comfort and the promotion of general well-being; if a
> clear understanding be more profitable to man than genius; if your object is not
> to stimulate the virtues of heroism, but the habits of peace; if you had rather
> witness vices than crimes, and are content to meet with fewer noble deeds, pro-
> vided offenses be diminished in the same proportion; if, instead of living in the
> midst of a brilliant society, you are contented to have prosperity around you; if,
> in short, you are of the opinion that the principal object of a government is not
> to confer the greatest possible power and glory upon the body of the nation, but
> to ensure the greatest enjoyment and to avoid the most misery to each of the
> individuals who compose it – if such be your desire, then equalize the conditions
> of men and establish democratic institutions (I, chap. 14, 262).

What is Tocqueville telling us? Is he saying that he has a taste for
many, if not all, of the qualities of a non-democratic society, but that he
is also trying to balance his preferences by acknowledging the advantages of a democratic one? Reading him this way is justifiable only if we
fail to take into account that he meant or at least implied that the contrasts were between two kinds of excellence; and that they were incom-
mensurable, that, indeed, given the *moeurs* of each society, neither the
qualities of the first nor of the second could cross over to the other. The
clear utilitarian values of democratic society would be inimical to a
society that valorized the aesthetic and the non-functional. Not that he
denied that poetry and science could not flourish in a democratic society,
where they would assume different forms and express different goals.
The more practical aspects of science, he said, already commanded more
admiration than the theoretical in a democratic society. Philosophically,
its forbears were Bacon and Descartes who, in questioning all authority

except that of individual judgment, laid the groundwork for the demo-
cratic questioning of political authority as well, an aspect of life to which
Descartes did not seek to apply his method. This trend was negative.
"[I]t would seem as if human opinions were reduced to a sort of intellectual dust, scattered on every side, unable to collect, unable to cohere"
(II, Bk. 1, chap. 1, 3–7). He felt differently about the future of literature.
Poets were likely to turn their attention from the particular to the universal, Tocqueville said. He regarded the American passion for equal
treatment so overwhelming in its power as to efface and drive out the
benefits of various forms of differentiation, but not so inevitably powerful as to rob human beings of their capacity to repress the evil tendencies in either of the two societies. Yet he was more concerned with
the problematic success of such efforts in an egalitarian society (I, chap.
14, 262–63).

Equality and Liberty

Where might such exertions be concentrated? Tocqueville was drawn to
show that liberty was essential to individual growth and fulfillment – in
other words, as the glue that would keep quality alive. But before looking
at this question further, we should recall that he did not adhere rigidly
to the either/or choice between equality and liberty that he appeared to
be presenting. He made it clear that he spoke neither of absolute equality nor of absolute liberty. Only in the imagination was it possible to
posit an extreme point where liberty and equality would blend and meet.
"Let us suppose," he wrote, "that all the people take a part in the government, and that each one of them has an equal right to take part in it.
As no one is different from his fellows, none can exercise a tyrannical
power; men will be perfectly free because they are all entirely equal; and
they will all be perfectly equal because they are entirely free" (II, Bk. 2,
chap. 1, 99–103). Once having posited this imaginary state, he set it aside
but did not abandon it as an ideal, and proceeded to deal with imperfect forms of both equality and liberty. Civil equality can exist in the
absence of political equality. Liberty, similarly, may be found in various
forms, not least in aristocratic societies, and need not be exclusively associated with democracy. In excess, liberty can be oblivious of others,
upsetting order and social life. Because it is a more obvious source of
discord, it is not easily overlooked, and so it is kept in bounds. Not so
with equality. Its excesses are not so easily acknowledged, because
not so easily perceived, so that over time they can become a source of

violence. It is not that democratic societies do not want or cherish liberty, but its virtues pale in comparison with those attributed to equality. That is why Tocqueville saw liberty as endangered by equality.

Why was it so powerful? Tocqueville made much of the interchangeability of roles: People could change them with relative ease. The rifts dividing them were not permanently settled. No one regarded him- or herself as condemned to a class of menials or to perpetual servitude. Once the change from an aristocratic to a democratic age was successfully negotiated, once "the public mind, which is never affected by exceptions, assigns general limits to the value of man, above or below which no man can long remain placed," once human beings occupied a common level, "a species of imaginary equality between them, in spite of the real inequality of their conditions" would be created (II, Bk. 3, chap. 5, 192). The notion – here unambiguously stated – that democratic peoples live by the illusion, rather than by the reality, of equality, raises important questions about the power of belief to determine societal and personal values. If it serves to stabilize society, it may be argued that it serves citizens against disorder. If, however, it serves to keep people in a state of inequality, even while they believe they are not living in such a condition, then the fiction, it might be argued, becomes an evil, since it not only deceives, but is a source of self-deception. The issue remains vital, because not only did it create disputes about the boundaries to be imposed on equality in Tocqueville's time, but continues in today's social environment in a mixture of cynicism and hope.

The weight of social change to be borne by the self was always a question that spoke powerfully to him. We remember how much importance he attributed to the responses of the heart to the vagaries of life, especially in times of great change. Once the notion of equality was let loose in the world, and once it appeared to be reaching a state of complete fulfillment, the greater was the compulsion to demand it in excess. The desire becomes insatiable:

> Among democratic nations, men easily attain a certain equality of condition, but they can never attain as much as they desire. It perpetually retires before them, yet without hiding itself from their sight, and in retiring draws them on. At every moment they think they are about to grasp it; it escapes at every moment from their hold. They are near enough to see its charms, but too far off to enjoy them; and before they have fully tasted its delights, they die (II, Bk. 2, chap. 13, 147).

Thus the quest for equality presents itself as a great siren, but, like the siren, the quest continues, and never surrenders its charms, if, indeed, they can be proven to be such. It will always elude human beings, because it cannot, by its nature, and, also because of theirs, be fully grasped. Those who live in democratic societies, however, have no choice; they are driven to satisfy the pleasure principle embodied in a belief in full equality, but they cannot do so without first adhering to the dictates of the work principle, with all its exactions and anxieties. Consequently, in democratic times, individuals are caught in a vise. They must be bent to work, not by external force as in pre-democratic times, but by an inner compulsion. It was not the ascetic compulsion of early New England Puritanism that saw work and its rewards as proof of a fulfillment of, and in harmony with, God's will. Asceticism was left behind by the pure drive, not to embrace materialist philosophy, but toward material gain, so totally unmodulated as to create a society in which intense pleasure seeking was followed by the spectacle of blasted hopes and desires, of "soul[s] . . . more stricken and perturbed, and care itself more keen" (ibid.).

Tocqueville, it may also be said, foresaw a possible prospect of human alienation, hollowness, and shallowness. But he did not express total disillusion. A belief in equality was the major practical achievement of a democratic society, however imperfect it was in reality. He believed in equality as an ideal, and refused to think of it as an empty illusion. He saw it as unattainable in its perfected form – whatever in reality that might look like – and was very much concerned to avoid egalitarian leveling. He saw equality's more positive side. The yearning for it created a spirit of independence, especially the political independence that militated against the servitude of political dependence (II, Bk. 4, chap. 1, 305) that created conditions in which equals could be manipulated to desire the same objects by a government democratic in name, but despotic in practice. There was more to Tocqueville's praise of equality. A state of equality is just, and its justness constituted "its greatness and its beauty" (II, Bk. 4, chap. 8, 351). The power of the appeal of equality has not diminished. Even if it is trumpeted aloud naively as a real and total presence in American social and political life, it remains personally or socially beneficial for large sections in society, however those benefits are calculated, and even for all who lived separate lives in America and protested that their imposed separateness caused them to suffer unequal treatment.

On balance, Tocqueville worried more about the future of a society that tended to sacrifice all to equality and often, in its fervid support of it, did not perceive how, when unrestrained or taken to extremes, it could in fact produce the unintended result of placing everyone on a single footing, obliterating all differences, including positive ones, and pressing everyone into the same mold. For Tocqueville, this blindness was an invitation to governments to oppress all equally in the name of a chimerical equality. Governments fulfilled their own dynamic. They were driven to aggrandize power, and, in the case of democratic states, did so with the instruments they had at hand: the desire for equality impelled governments to achieve it, but at a price that they alone reckoned. Mobilization of the equality principle was only one, but nevertheless, a significant, source of real and potential government tyranny. Such an equality would be the opposite of greatness and justice. It thrived in a democratic culture that ascribed no bounds to the human intellect, yet at the same time, identified it with the beliefs and wishes of the majority, rather than, as in a non-democratic society, with a particular individual or class. In a culture ruled by an egalitarian ethos, individuals place greater faith in the mass of humanity who, so to speak, are thought to incorporate its values into the very marrow of their beings. Hence they are able to express their weaknesses and strengths more openly than people in non-democratic societies. This democratic shift in manners and morals tends to erase differences and makes them all alike. Thus, although democratic peoples are inclined to push the boundaries of thought to its limits, they are held in check by their fellows, for whom any ultimate or permanent right to stand above the crowd reeked of privilege (II, Bk. 1, chap. 2). Such an equality would, as Tocqueville saw it, be an equality of vulnerabilities, rather than strengths. He could of course not know the full extent of the first. But he certainly knew that the equality principle was, while tending to flatten out life, not yet creating a community of equals. He saw that equality was not fully accepted by all those who paid homage to it, neither by plantation owners, who thought they were preserving the ideals of the Greek democratic polis by living up to a conception of the attributes of citizenship that excluded slaves, nor by northerners, who thought of society as divided between the elect and the non-elect. Both in the North and South, citizens would come to feel themselves beleaguered by the hand of the law to give up what they believed they already had in the way of equality, and also forced to find means of sharing it with others outside their immediate communities.

What we must now do is see to what point Tocqueville's stress on liberty as the source of new qualities – excellences – is at least in part reconcilable with the trend towards greater and greater equality. Did he think that quality, which is intrinsically differentiating, could survive in a democratic society, and that it need not have the negative values associated with the privileges of aristocratic society? Or was the struggle lost? Would a shift toward liberty be seen by those who lived by the credo of equality as a smoke screen for the creation of a new caste system based on a presumed superiority, in the American case, the assumed, but not proven, superiority of wealth? For the most part, Tocqueville placed his hopes on those few spirits in America who possessed the intellectual courage – who showed independence of thought, and were not taken in by slogans – (I, chap. 15, 277) and who could use what powers they had to cultivate the constitutional safeguards of a liberal democracy to put a brake on the excesses of equality. This in itself presumed the existence in America of individuals who prized excellence and were prepared to defend the differences based on them instead of succumbing to the insistent cries of fervent egalitarians. He stationed himself against moralists who inveighed against pride. Without it, human beings condemned themselves to ordinariness. They needed "a more enlarged idea of themselves," which pride alone, not humility, could provide (II, Bk. 3, chap. 19, 262–63). Thus, while equality carried with it the risks of a uniformity of responses from a compliant social body; while its tendency toward undifferentiation was to be deplored; and while diversity, indeed, pride, could be seen as a positive force in strengthening the self and freedom, how such a set of beliefs could be translated into the practical realm was a tougher problem. How indeed could democratic peoples break out of the common mold, assert their singularity, their individuality, and their distinctiveness? (II, Bk. 3, chap. 26, 298f).

But there was another side to Tocqueville's reading of individuality. Love of money was, in its single-mindedness, if anxious-making, also highly disciplining (just as in its earlier phases the small democratic community founded on individual conscience created the self-discipline of a tightly knit civil society). Anglo-Americans were a driven people and they were all traveling down the same path toward democratic conformity, uniformity, and mediocrity. They had become a people living fragmented and restless lives, endlessly seeking diversion and never achieving satisfaction. Tocqueville asks us to consider whether what he is describing is an exclusively Anglo-American social and psychological reality:

The remark I here apply to America may indeed be addressed to almost all our contemporaries. Variety is disappearing from the human race; the same ways of acting, thinking and feeling are to be met with all over the world. This is not only because nations work more upon each other and copy each other more faithfully, but as the men of each country relinquish more and more the

peculiar opinions and feelings of a caste, a profession, or a family, they simultaneously arrive at something nearer to the constitution of man, which is everywhere the same. Thus they become more alike, even without having imitated
each other. . . . All the nations which take, not any particular man, but Man
himself as the object of their researches and their imitations are tending in the
end to a similar state of society . . . (II, Bk. 3, chap. 17, 240–41).

Tocqueville reaches beyond the future of America to the future of
Western society, indeed to the future of the "entire human race." While,
to be sure, people were becoming more and more alike, they were also
gaining more and more knowledge about people in different parts of
the world. Democracy is indeed universal in its thrust. No one is left
untouched. Behold, he says, "one vast democracy, each citizen of which
is a nation. This displays the aspect of mankind for the first time in the
broadest light." Peoples will become more transparent to one another.
The individual will, by shedding his particularity, begin to glimpse universal Man, and in the process find traces of God's universal and eternal
plan. This is democracy's greatness. By making human beings accessible
to one another, it promises them the gift to gain a greater, if veiled, understanding of themselves, though leaving much in "thick darkness." Some
opacities might yield to probing, but the mysteries would remain mysteries. No human inquiry could reach beyond a certain point. What
Goethe, Chateaubriand, and Byron were already doing to open up "the
obscurer recesses of the human heart" would be enlarged by the poets
of the democratic age who might explore the "vicissitudes and . . . future
of the human race" taken as a whole (II, Bk. 2, chap. 17, 75–81).

Thus, while Tocqueville contemplated the distant vistas of American
democracy and modernity, choosing to sound danger signals but not sur-
rendering to the darkest vision he saw, the particular, the concrete, and
the individual remained the empirical foundation for the patterns he
drew – yet another instance of his paradoxical style. The copious notes
he made while in America were recorded, not to prove preconceptions,
but to recreate the real world as far as he could discern it. He worked
his observations into his analysis without smothering them in excessive
generalizations. *Democracy in America* amazes us by an attention to
detail that catches a truth. Taken in the aggregate, these details always
bring us back to the purpose in mind – Tocqueville's assessment of the
threads that American society needed tightening, and those that needed
to be loosened.

3

Achieving a Democratic Civil Society

The tensions between equality and liberty, as well as those between liberty and authority, counted as the markers of a democratic civil society, but the science of politics lay in isolating those institutions that gave it practical life. This was the project to which Tocqueville devoted his observing eye and intellectual energies. What made Americans behave as a people sharing common interests paradoxically had almost everything to do with their sense of themselves as sovereign individuals. Thus, one of the features of American civil society that Tocqueville explored was its deep roots in the tradition of communal and mutual helpfulness, and the sharing in tasks through the voluntary associations that he said were stronger in America than even in England. How this was achieved was one of the mysteries that Tocqueville tried to penetrate. There were the political associations, also founded in English political traditions, that sought to enlist partisan support for political programs. The relationship between politics and the power of public opinion was an integral part of American democracy as well. Finally, the role that religion played in securing the fabric of civil society had properly to be defined. Taken together, these elements revealed much, he claimed, about the American experiment. We will look at each of them.

Some Contrasting Conceptions of Civil Society

We might begin first with another, a rather distant, vision of a civil society, a pre-modern democratic one, for it sharpens the outlines of Tocqueville's modern one. Tocqueville, we are told, had read *The Republic*, from which he supposedly would have gleaned the ideal principles that power is constituted for the good of all and not in the interest of those who govern; that it belonged naturally to the most enlightened and virtuous members of society; that citizens existed in a state of fraternity; and that their education in virtue, respect for the laws, and fear of the gods was best entrusted to the wisest.[1] Such a curiously banal construction would have baffled Tocqueville. He would have more likely found in *The Republic* Plato's pronounced condemnation of liberty and the blossoming of human diversity he prized, and he would have also encountered an even more critical account of equality. The democratic constitution Plato described in *The Republic* fostered an undesirable "variegated pattern of all sorts of characters." At the same time, democracy encouraged "an equality of a peculiar kind for equals and unequals alike." This indiscriminate equality, so condemned by Plato, dulled judgment, put everything on an equal footing, encouraged activity for the sake of activity, and countenanced disorderliness and unrestrained behavior in politics as well as in private life. As for liberty, it too suffered no constraint in a democracy: It was tantamount to license, and was a sure road to despotism. In an eventual struggle between the plundered rich who would defend themselves in the most reactionary ways against the irresponsible spendthrifts and layabouts who would take over the assemblies, the great mass of the people would finally turn to a man who championed them, but already was in fact the despot waiting to take over, bringing the democratic edifice tumbling down to destruction. Democracy's contempt for, and refusal to submit to, authority and its disregard for the exceptional and the good, reached its nadir by bestowing honor to "anyone who merely calls himself the people's friend."[2] Was it perhaps this prediction that Tocqueville had in mind in his protests against modern democratic despotism?

It seems so, at least in certain respects. Democratic people were pulled in opposite directions, one to new ideas, the other to an abdication of thought. Indeed, given that certain kinds of laws were inimical to the

---

[1] Discours de M. Lacordaire, January 24, 1861, *Oeuvres complètes d'Alexis de Tocqueville*, 18 vols. (Paris: Gallimard, 1950–98), 16 (*Mélanges*) 312–31, citation at 327. Hereafter cited as *OC*. Tocqueville had read *The Laws* (ibid., 555–57), from which he concluded that Plato had no problem in justifying aristocratic regimentation of the people, especially if it manifested itself as "a small, vicious, thoughtless, and turbulent democracy." He criticized Plato for not being able to imagine the good that was to be found in individual liberty and the variousness of human behavior.

[2] *The Republic*, trans. Francis M. Cornford (London: Oxford University Press, 1941). See chap. 31, viii, 557–65, from which I paraphrase and quote.

first, the mind would soon surrender its will to the general will, the absolute power of the majority. For Tocqueville, the place of authority in a democratic and equal society could not be shrugged off easily. It was, to be sure, to be found in the democratic majority will, which carries greater weight than individual judgments, but in order for it to be legitimate, it was to be distinguished from its power to coerce, and the best guardian against it was a free and inquiring mind (II, Bk. 1, chap. 2, 13). The danger was that people painted collective judgment under a kind of religious light. They did so, of course, to defend a common set of beliefs and values that gave them a sense of themselves. Tocqueville claimed that the true sources of democratic tyranny were to be located, not in an excessive liberty but a shackled liberty, not in undisciplined variety as much as in conformity: These were the snags in the democratic fabric. Variety, in the classical version, encouraged mindless activity, and could not be a well-founded structure for human striving. For Tocqueville, as well, such mindlessness is the opposite of the varieties of human experience. However, much less catastrophically than the Greek philosopher, he did not think that equality produced a runaway taste for variety for its own sake. Instead, it fostered a dull uniformity of response. The steps leading to a despotic regime are thus unsurprisingly only partially the same for Plato and Tocqueville. The French aristocrat placed his hopes on liberty as a force restraining the enthusiasm for conformity that could lead in the direction of a popularly supported despotism. It is on this point that the differences between them are greatest.

An important question is struck by Plato's determination to draw boundaries across which there could not or should not be movement, and Tocqueville's argument that there might indeed be some benefits from such mobility, missing in classical Greece, but now a permanent feature of Western society. Rapid change and the flight from the traditional were not only inimical to the classical sense of order, but as well to the pre-revolutionary condition of European society, with which he contrasted America, where he observed opportunities for the cultivation of a new civil society. He was historically attuned to the coming of an egalitarian one whose rough edges he hoped might be refined. While not losing sight of these refinements in his approach to democratic equality, he was the first significant commentator to see that democracies placed equality and difference at the center of political debate. This cannot be stressed too strenuously.

Two undated fragments, probably written after the publication of *Democracy in America*, offer us a glimpse of Tocqueville's ideal notion of democracy, but as well the principles of a democratic civil society. In the first of these, he asked, "What is democracy?":

It consists in the greatest possible share of liberty, enlightenment, and powers, given to each individual.

What is a democratic government? It is a government which, instead of suppressing human liberty, finds a thousand ways to come to its aid instead of confining it within barriers from every angle. It opens up all kinds of new perspectives [from which to view it]. Instead of imposing on liberty new hindrances, it succeeds in destroying all those that stand in the way of its progress. It does not channel liberty, but places at its disposal enlightened [views], [and] the resources which may permit it to . . .

This is a government that places each citizen, even the most humble, in a condition of [enabling him to act] with as much independence, and of making of his independence as much use as is available to the most exalted citizen . . .

[It is a government] which does not oblige any one to [accept] an equality of poverty, but one that places everyone in a condition of becoming prosperous with honesty, work and merit . . .[3]

In the second fragment, he defined democracy as fostering equality by founding it on political rights:

The tendency of legislation [is] to render conditions *equal.* Absolute equality before the law.

The effort of society to make available to all the poor such institutions that would allow them to place themselves in a condition of raising themselves by their own efforts.

Primary education [is] of capital importance.

No obstacles to improvement. Every facility to do so. The greatest possible independence left to the individual.

Full liberty, full responsibility, [all possible] facilities [to do so] . . . To make available to all citizens every facility to improve his destiny through his own efforts, not to impose on society [the task] of improving him directly and primarily for the sake of society.

Democracy is liberty combined with equality, *socialism* is equality without liberty.

Society assuming direct responsibility and with its own resources to meet the needs of citizens only when it is proved beyond doubt that they cannot succeed in doing so on their own . . .

Democracy takes up its position on the foundations of society; the edifice is new, the foundations are ancient. Socialism [is driven] to change them (at least in so far as it is a question of property) . . .

[3] OC 3 (*Ecrits et discours politiques*) part 3, 196. Because prominence was given to the concept of the "social republic" only in the 1840s, and especially in the period leading up to and after the 1848 Revolution, it is likely that these notes were jotted down at about that time.

The *democratic* and *social* republic are two terms that are not only different, but in a certain sense opposed [to one another].[4]

Thus, Tocqueville introduced his concept of the foundations of a democratic civil society. It should blunt the judgment that he failed "precisely to define démocratie."[5] It ought also to demonstrate that his understanding of democracy was richer than, for example, some of the minimal criteria that have been adduced to justify its use as a term designating forms of government.[6] In societies calling themselves democratic, individuals, for him, as the last extract shows, were ideally autonomous persons armed with the resources and power to take part as equal citizens effectively making decisions affecting their lives, and through the processes of democratic government, as he wrote, "open[ing] up all kinds of new perspectives." There was thus inscribed in his notion of democracy a recognition that individuals, who, although not equally endowed by nature nor favored by income, nor compensated through public policy to overcome social and economic disadvantages, could equally take part in public life. Such a government would create the conditions to enable citizens to act, and to act as citizens. Within these terms, democracy was defined as "liberty combined with equality," and "absolute equality before the law" was to be respected.[7] Again, within

---

[4] Ibid., 197. The ellipses and the emphasis are in the original passage.
[5] James T. Schleifer, *The Making of Tocqueville's Democracy in America* (Chapel Hill: University of North Carolina Press, 1980), pp. 273–74. Nevertheless, Schleifer comments: "His extraordinary ability to imagine and to consider so many different uses [of democracy], to resolve the idea so continuously in his mind, led to the richness and profundity of his insights."
[6] For example, Jon Elster, who writes, "I understand the term [democracy] in a minimal sense, as any kind of effective and formalized control by citizens over leaders or policies: 'effective' to exclude ritual forms of participation, and 'formalized' to exclude rebellion as a means of control. The *existence* of democracy does not depend on whether the control is ex ante or ex post, direct or representative, one-step or two-step, divided or undivided, or based on a narrow or broad electorate. See his "Deliberation and Constitution Making," in *Deliberative Democracy*, ed. Elster, (Cambridge: Cambridge University Press, 1998), 98.
[7] Tocqueville, it is not surprising to learn, was not prepared to go as far, for example, as Isaiah Berlin, who believed that "equality may demand the restraint of liberty of those who wish to dominate; liberty – without some modicum of which there is no choice and therefore no possibility of remaining human as we understand the word – may have to be curtailed in order to make room for social welfare, to feed the hungry, to allow justice or fairness to be exercised." Isaiah Berlin, "Pursuit of the Ideal," *The Proper Study of Mankind*, eds. Henry Hardy and Roger Hausheer (London: Chatto and Windus, 1997), pp. 10–11. Tocqueville was, however, prepared to consider that in the interest of preserving order and peace, governments might have to restrict the absolute freedom of political parties. Another point of comparison may be made between Tocqueville and

these terms, there is no extended treatment, to be sure, of how, except in a marginal way, economic inequality might be lessened. That question aside, citizens were not to be singled out and penalized for their differences, whatever they were and however they might be recognized through institutions and endeavors outside the public realm of politics.[8] Tocqueville's focus is on what makes such democratic societies work. American society was suffused by a desire and need for the new, but there was no need to fear that in the search to satisfy them, they would ever be thought immoral, or that those engaged in these daily pursuits would misuse their liberties. In America, democratic energies appeared to be released by "commercial passions":

> The passions that agitate the Americans most deeply are not their political, but their commercial passions; or, rather, they introduce the habits of business into their political life. They love order . . . and they set an especial value upon regular conduct, which is the foundation of solid business. They prefer the good sense which amasses large fortunes . . . ; general ideas alarm their minds, which are accustomed to positive calculations; and they hold practice in more honor than theory (I, chap. 17, 308).

Again, as in the useful contrast we drew between a classical democratic polity and Tocqueville's modern one, another may be drawn between Rousseau's and Tocqueville's polity, particularly because Rousseau often had Athens and Sparta in mind. Nothing could be more opposed to Tocqueville's admiration for the advances in economic life than Rousseau's praise for an imagined Geneva as a model civil society in which supposedly conscientious citizens followed the precepts of a responsible civic and political life without being unduly distracted by their needs as traders and craftspeople. To be sure, the charms of Tocqueville's New England township reflect, intentionally or not, some

---

Etienne Balibar, "Ambiguous Universality," *differences: A Journal of Feminist Cultural Studies*, 7.1 (1995), 65–66. Balibar says that what he calls "equaliberty," which draws on an old Roman formula (*aequa libertas*), "has never ceased haunting modern political philosophy in modern times, from Tocqueville to Rawls."

[8] The democratic citizen as described here may be compared with the rational individual – that is, one governed by rationality, as Richard Rorty understands it: "Rationality is roughly synonymous with tolerance – with the ability not to be overly disconcerted by differences from oneself, not to respond aggressively to such differences. . . . It [this ability] is a virtue that enables individuals and communities to coexist peacefully with other individuals and communities, living and letting live, and to put together new, syncretic, compromise ways of life. So rationality in this sense is sometimes thought of, as by Hegel, as quasi-synonymous with freedom." *Truth and Progress. Philosophical Papers* (Cambridge: Cambridge University Press, 1998), vol. 3, pp. 186–87.

of Rousseau's beliefs about an uncorrupted democratic polity, but Tocqueville had no illusions about its ability to escape unscathed in the modern world. Even in Rousseau's Geneva, however, differences of achievement were rewarded. One of Rousseau's starting points was the modern magnification of personal differences from which all other inequalities emerged and came to be enforced through universal competition, including most of all the perils of luxury. Both the best and worst, the virtues and vices, of human beings thus became a permanent feature of civil society.[9] Civil society could not thereby ignore questions of distributive justice, but these were best determined by each individual's services to the state as far as their abilities could be assessed. Only a well-constituted state could make such demands without being thought coercive.

Like Tocqueville, Rousseau turned to classical examples. The orator Isocrates praised the primitive Athenians for distinguishing between two kinds of equality. The first was an equality distributed indifferently among all. It was actually inequality masquerading as equality. The second differentiated persons by rewarding the meritorious. But the distinction Isocrates drew could not be the whole story, Rousseau said. Surely there was no society so corrupt as to fail to differentiate between the moral and immoral, virtues and vices. Magistrates were wisely led to judge actions rather than the persons who committed them on the grounds that to attempt to do the second would lead to a quagmire of doubt and confusion, and deflect the purposes of sound judgment. Magistrates thus confined themselves to the application of the strict laws, leaving the public to decide moral questions – who was good, who was bad. To be sure, the public as judge might be imposed upon, but it could never be corrupted. As judge it could better appreciate the real services of citizens, and these were judged presumably by how well these advanced the polity. In the end, therefore, Rousseau is telling us that civic merit is what counts, not any presumed and ultimately incalculable personal merit. The reward for merit, and hence the foundations of real equality in civil society, could not be achieved without differentiation. The inner motives of human beings were, if not inconsequential, unfathomable. It was what they did that led to good or bad consequences.[10]

---

[9] *Discourse on the Origin and the Foundations of Inequality Among Men*, ed. and trans. Victor Gourevitch (New York: Harper and Row, 1986), pp. 194–95.

[10] Ibid., p. 230.

Thus, after all, an imperfect equality was possible. The stress on Rousseau as the thinker who signified inequality as the marker of civil society obscures his concern with the problem of how real societies might evaluate and value equality. We should remember, yet again, that when Rousseau thought he had found the foundations of a civil society which ensured equal liberties to all, his vision was that of a small undifferentiated community, not only with shared traditions and values, but an acute sense of the need to subject particular interests to the common interest. In the absence of such self-discipline, the coercive power of government should be required. Indeed, the future conditional is expressly stated: "Now, the smaller the ratio of individual wills to the general will, that is to say morals to the laws" he stated, "the more does the repressive power have to increase. Hence in order to be good, the government, then, has to have relatively more force in proportion as the people is more numerous."[11]

Rousseau's notion of a civil society stopped short of the modern, but it also left the question of how equality and differentiation would be tackled in a populous state covering a wide territory unexamined. Tocqueville was painfully aware of the perils lying before the advance of the state's power to coerce a large population. He did not ignore Rousseau's warnings, but he was not beguiled by the virtues of a small republic, however much the New England township appealed to him, where, if there were concern for the community, there was also a propensity to mediocrity, as well as the possibility that in times of strife, no one escaped the tyranny of a small state, with its invasion of private rights. He conceded that in the absence of great resources and great wealth, the stakes were not high enough for citizens to succumb permanently to the whims of a tyrant. He did not underestimate the problems of a large state, where political passions fatal to republican government came in abundance, "not only because they aim at gigantic objects, but because they are felt and shared by millions of men at the same time," while virtues do not increase in the same proportion (I, chap. 8, 165–67). Montesquieu's words must also have rung loudly for him:

It is in the nature of a republic to have only a small territory; otherwise, it can scarcely continue to exist. In a large republic, there are large fortunes, and consequently little moderation in spirits: the depositories are too large to put in the hands of a citizen; interests become particularized; at first a man feels he can

---

[11] *The Social Contract*, ed. and trans. Victor Gourevitch (Cambridge: Cambridge University Press, 1997), Bk. 3, chap. 1, p. 84.

be happy, great, and glorious without his homeland; and soon, that he can be great only on the ruins of his homeland.

In a large republic, the common good is sacrificed to a thousand considerations; it is subordinated to exceptions; it depends upon accidents. In a small one, the public good is better felt, better known, lies nearer to each citizen; abuses are less extensive there and consequently less protected.[12]

Tocqueville was agitated by the question of how a nation could be forged from the experiences of the small community of the New England township, where he located the origins of American democracy. For him, as for Rousseau, authority possessed a sacred character. For Rousseau, equality indifferently shared, demanded, in the event of a threat to the general will, coercion, and much more often in states with large populations. Without falling back on a notion of the general will, but sensitive to the political passions of the majority in a large state, Tocqueville had to find reasons for stepping beyond Rousseau's and Montesquieu's self-limiting prohibitions against large states. He found it paradoxically in the multiplication of passions. In a large state, knowledge and civilization are more advanced, especially in great cities, "which are the intellectual centers where all the rays of human genius are reflected and combined." In a great nation, unlike in a small one, "government has more enlarged ideas, and is more completely disengaged from the routine of precedent and the selfishness of local feeling; its designs are conceived with more talent and with more boldness" (I, chap. 8, 167–68). He clearly left behind the attachments to the small republic, whether in its classical mode or in the model of the Swiss canton. With the example of the American creation of the Federal Union before him, he believed a first positive step had been taken towards nation-founding. We may see that for Rousseau, political sovereignty was a burning issue. He located it in the unerring general will, which reaffirmed his position in the *Second Discourse* that the public is rightfully the sovereign arbiter of good and evil. For Tocqueville, democratic sovereignty was an American fact. It was no longer, as in pre-democratic polities, concealed or sterile. It was out in the open. In America, society governed itself for itself. Declaring that the democratic franchise was an irrepressible force, Tocqueville could say that "The people reign in the American political world as the Deity does in the universe. They are the cause and the aim of all things; everything comes from them, and everyone is absorbed in them" (I, chap. 4, 60).

---

[12] Montesquieu, *The Spirit of the Laws*, trans. Ann Cohler, Basia Miller, and Harold Stone (Cambridge: Cambridge University Press, 1989), Bk. 8, chap. 16, p. 124.

Tocqueville posited that the daily give-and-take of commercial transactions – the turbulence and calculations of the market – spilled over,
with beneficial effects, into civil and political transactions. Later he came
to believe that commerce was not necessarily a highway to a healthy
democracy, but instead might become a detour. Retreating from his early
optimism, he would reserve judgment on its long-term effects upon a
democratic society when its citizens might become so totally absorbed
and overwhelmed by the amassing of wealth that they would come to
neglect the properly separate and autonomous sphere of private associations and institutions where apprenticeship in the habits of citizenship
took place. His view of a potentially negative relationship between commerce and politics recalls one of Montesquieu's warnings, even if the
eighteenth-century philosopher believed in the overall civilizing effects of
commerce:

> [Intrigue] is not dangerous in the people, whose nature is to act from passion
> ... The misfortune of a republic is to be without intrigues, and this happens
> when the people have been corrupted by silver; they become cool, they grow
> fond of silver, and they are no longer fond of public affairs; without concern
> for the government or for what is proposed there, they quietly await their
> payments.[13]

Tocqueville's travels along the curves of political theory took him a
long way from Montesquieu, if only because the French traveler in
America witnessed the operations of a living democratic republic where
commerce shaped so much of the American political fabric. The multiplication of needs as commerce quickened is more insistently built into
Hegel's theory of civil society than are Montesquieu's more leisurely comments on the economy: "[I]n the actual attainment of selfish ends ...
there is formed," Hegel wrote, "a system of complete interdependence,
wherein the livelihood, happiness and legal status of one man is interwoven with the livelihood, happiness and rights of all. On this system,
individual happiness &c, depend, and only in this connected system are
they actualized and secured."[14] In "a state of unimpeded activity," civil
society expands its population and its industry. When the "amassing of
wealth is intensified," generalizing the links between people by their
needs and the means devised to distribute them, profits are created. At
the same time, there comes into existence a class of workers who cannot

[13] Ibid., Bk. 2, chap. 3, p. 14.
[14] From *The Philosophy of Right*, trans. T.M. Knox (Oxford: Oxford University Press,
1942), paragraph 123, p. 123.

"enjoy the broader freedoms and especially the intellectual benefits of civil society."[15] The conflicts ensuing from the competition to ensure them, at first locally, and then on a much grander scale, became, in Hegel's view, a question of urgency for the public authority. It must then preserve the security of particular ends and interests en masse, inasmuch as these interests meet his abstract "universal," actualized in the historical particularity of a commercialized society.[16]

The restless agitation and collisions of Hegel's civil society demanded political order. It was to be supplied, not by all, but by a small aristocratic landowning class with the leisure, talent, and inclination to determine public policy. This notion of the political sets aside the idea of universal participation. The belief that all should take part in political deliberation would lead away from diversity and a plurality of interests in a society that, he maintained, recognized but did not exploit differences, to a society that obliterated useful distinctions. But the more important point, Hegel maintained, was that the state, as representative of the universal interest, subordinated all singular interests. Here we may see how Tocqueville's view differed from Hegel's: For Tocqueville, commerce actually fructifies politics, and does so democratically, because commerce itself resembles a democracy of buyers and sellers, who exchange roles in the market. The conflicts and competing interests the market engenders are transferred to the political realm, where they are debated and resolved on a continuing basis. Hegel did not seriously consider disinterest in the political on the part of the greatest part of the population, while Tocqueville, like Montesquieu, regarded indifference to politics as the very negation of the political. Tocqueville's vision was also opposed to Marx's and Engels'.[17] Their notion of the political clearly points to the intensification of class conflict as being the decisive moment of change from one form and control of distribution to another. In such a theory, the essence of the political was to be found in the ultimate revolutionary transfer of control of the state from one class to another. Marxist theories of the state had to account for the notion of its autonomy, and, at the same time, to identify it with the voice of the liberated masses, and ultimately as the voice of a totally liberated society. This

---

[15] Ibid., paragraph 243, pp. 149–50.   [16] Ibid., paragraph 249, pp. 151–52.

[17] According to Jürgen Habermas, *Between Facts and Norms. Contributions to a Discourse Theory of Law and Democracy*, trans. William Rehg (Cambridge, Mass.: MIT Press, 1996), p. 478, they criticized "the bourgeois order as the juridical expression of unjust relations of production, [and thus] enlarge[d] the concept of the political itself."

they signally failed to do. Tocqueville, of course, could not offer a com-
mentary on Marxist and post-Marxist theory, but he distrusted any
theory of the state that vested so much power in it and its institutions
as a threat to the health of civil society. Moreover, he was sure that
revolution signaled an end to the possibility of bringing order to civil
society through the political process, and would thus mark the end of
the political.

For Marx, the political was embedded in and came to life in the revolutionary challenge to existing structures. The political came into being
precisely because of those relations of production. Tocqueville accepted
them as a disruptive force, but as a civilizing influence as well. He found
in the free exchanges of goods in the market a model for the free
exchanges of opinions in the forum. It was upon such a process that
he expected, not without severe doubts, however, that politics, as a
necessary and valuable part of human activity, would flourish. It might
thus be on-going, and not, as Marx theorized, the end of a stage in
civilization.

What Makes American Civil Society Tick?

On the political and civic stage, Tocqueville was impressed by the ways
in which Americans exchanged opinions on every issue, whether trivial
or large, as if such expression were an extension of their enthusiasm for
the capitalist market place. Just as commerce sharpened mental energies,
so was civil society enriched when mental horizons were broadened
through the exercise of the individual's participation in the public forum.
American political associations, based on traditions originating in
England, whereby citizens met in public to express their political differences and took part in the electoral process, were the best if imperfect
guarantee against the tyranny of the majority. In America, where slight
differences of opinion divided the minority from the majority, political
associations concentrated on reforming rather than overturning the laws.
So intent was Tocqueville on comparing the peaceful nature of political
associations in America with their more troubled origins and propensity
for violence in France, that he seemed willing, at one point in his analysis, to exaggerate the reason and free will of Americans, praising their
independence of thought and willingness to seek compromise in a quest
for a common understanding (I, chap. 12). Americans acquire their
knowledge of the laws by the practical science of participation, he said
in a burst of hyperbole, partly discounting his later critique of the

mediocre level of politics. He did not, it is true, step aside to avoid looking at political corruption. How could democratic politicians be more virtuous than the citizens who voted for them? "They [the citizens] are . . . led, and often rightly, to impute his [the politician or man of wealth] success mainly to some of his vices; and an odious connection is thus formed between the ideas of turpitude and power, unworthiness and success, utility and dishonor" (I, chap. 13, 235). Nonetheless, without intending it, democratic institutions provided a kind of prophylaxis against the rankest kind of corruption; "[public men] bring about good results of which they have never thought" (I, chap. 14, 250). His evidence that independent judgment was a fragile thing in America took him in another direction. He turned to the lawyers and the judicial process to dampen the unfettered, nonreflective, democratic will:

> When the American people are intoxicated by passion or carried away by the impetuosity of their ideas, they are checked and stopped by the almost invisible influence of their legal counselors. These secretly oppose their aristocratic propensities to the nation's democratic instincts, their superstitious attachment to what is old to its love of novelty, their narrow views to its immense designs, and their habitual procrastination to its ardent impatience (I, chap. 16, 289).

Thus, although their enthusiasms needed to be restrained, Americans are distinguished from Europeans by taking part in making the laws and acquiring the knowledge of the forms of government from the art of governing. The procedures of juries and the forms of parliamentary life were in turn carried over into the daily lives of people (I, chap. 17, 330). As Tocqueville also put it, Americans "transport the habits of public life into their manners in private." Thus, by a series of cascading effects are created the democratic *"habits of the heart"* and "character of mind" (I, chap. 17, 310, his italics). These habits of the heart and character of mind produce liberty and, along with it, a powerful energy, for Tocqueville, the two most important advantages of democracy (I, chap. 14, 261–62).

Both were vouchsafed by political rights. Just as the spread of wealth nurtures desire and respect for property, so the exercise of political rights produces in a democracy, whatever difficulties may be faced by a citizenry still learning its advantages, a valuable substitute for the fading traditions of moral right, faith, and sentiment. Political rights in the American democracy are the instruments to which an intelligent and rational citizenry turns to overcome their passions; without them society would succumb to fear and the rule of force. "[R]ight is simply . . . virtue introduced into the political world." Once imported into politics, right perceives the difference between anarchy and tyranny. Once, moreover, society takes measures to connect right, political rights, and "private interest . . . the only immutable point in the human heart," the disagreements citizens have are freely and openly expressed and cement social bonds (I, chap. 14, 254–56). In this passage, Tocqueville unreservedly commits himself to a republican notion of democratic politics, putting conscious political engagement first. A democratic society will work to recognize the diverse and often incompatible ways in which citizens working through political associations view the world. Democracy, in short, demands political argument.

Democracy also rested significantly on the strength of America's religious traditions. Tocqueville's own religious sensibilities, seemingly of an aristocratic age, have a distinctly modern edge. His sense of contingency and uncertainty is consistent with modernity's skepticism, though he found the roots of the skeptical tradition in the early modern age and its offshoots in post-Revolutionary Europe distasteful and even dangerous. Historically, the linkage he posited between the inseparability of religion and liberty in America, fitted both his own and early America's convictions that liberty "considers religion as the safeguard of morality, and morality as the best security of law and the surest pledge of the duration of freedom" (I, chap. 2, 46). The early Anglo-American democratic community was hardened by the Puritan assurance of individual conscience. By the nineteenth century, it had been transformed into a singular type of American individualism, the source of the materialism of mind whose power, he believed, might endanger the health of civil society. Tocqueville was critical of its most egregious expressions, not only as a diversion from what had made Anglo-Americans strong in the earliest years of their democratic experiment, but also as an impediment to the creation of a more extended national polity. The way to finesse or mitigate excessive materialism was to urge democratic governments to make room for it, not by forbidding what could not be eradicated, but by inculcating a respect for religious belief (II, Bk. 2, chap. 15, 152–56). But this was a strategy that might not always work in an age when neither religion nor "the state of society" (a clear notion of society's goals) was of commanding power. Still, because human beings searched for answers to their future, making it impossible to "confine their minds within the precise limits of life, and . . . [who] are [thus] ready to break the boundaries and cast their looks beyond," religious faith could be used to direct those feelings into religious channels (II, Bk. 2, chap. 17, 160). But it would be an error of some magnitude to conclude that Tocqueville favored the introduction of religious preferences into the political arena, for there they would become a plaything and trivialized. What would happen to religion in a country whose people changed their governments frequently? "[I]f Americans, who have given up the political world to the attempts of innovators, had not placed their religion beyond reach, where could it take firm hold in the ebb and flow of human opinions? . . . The American clergy were the first to perceive this truth . . . and saw that they must renounce their religious influence if they were to strive for political power" (I, chap. 17, 323). Tocqueville, relying mainly on his Unitarian friends for their views, was, even if he averted his eyes from the actual play between religion and politics, more intent on fortifying the principle that the independence of religious principles would be compromised if they were harnessed to political power.[18] More, their benign effect on American mores would be lost in a blatantly open alliance of religious denominationalism and politics. Consequently, he took heart from the more salubrious alliance between rightly understood self-interest and religion, commending those American preachers who spoke to their congregations of earthly comforts and prosperity and showed them how religion favored freedom and public peace (II, Bk. 2, chap. 9, 135).

Most of all, Tocqueville gave a central role to voluntary associations, other than commercial ones, in the formation of a modern democratic civil society. Americans came together in:

> associations of a thousand other kinds, religious, moral, serious, futile, general, or restricted, enormous or diminutive. The Americans make associations to give entertainments, to found seminaries, to build inns, to construct churches, to diffuse books, to send missionaries to the antipodes; in this manner they found hospitals, prisons, and schools (II, Bk. 2, chap. 5, 114).

Tocqueville rested his case for voluntary associations on a counterintuitive argument. Equality weakened rather than strengthened individuals. For while they prided themselves on their independence, as lonely individuals, they were prompted to seek the help of others to compensate for their weakness. The great and positive side of such associations was their capacity to interpose themselves as a counterweight against the government, which, in an economy of greater specialization and

---

[18] Robert W. Fogel writes in *Without Consent or Contract. The Rise and Fall of American Slavery* (New York and London: W.W. Norton, 1989), p. 462 note 83 that Tocqueville overlooked the antagonism between Protestant denominations and the factious fights within them.

technological change, would step in and do things for people, rather than let them do things for themselves. It could more readily move against the isolated person than against an association alive to and able to protect its sense of solidarity. It was the intellectual and moral associations that Americans needed most to nurture, for a democratic civil society could not do without them. "In democratic countries the science of association is the mother of science; the progress of all the rest depends upon the progress it has made" (ibid., 118). He also declared it to be an art, "the mother of action, studied and applied by all" who participate in public associations "the universal or, in a manner the sole, means that men can employ to accomplish the different purposes they may have in view" (II, Bk. 2, chap. 7, 125).

Whether science or art, the technique of association helped to ensure the tranquillity of society, but only under certain conditions. Political and civil associations were reciprocally linked; each strengthened the other, but the first were essential to the second in an active democracy. Every society could, to be sure, count on having civil associations simply because people must come together to get things done in common, but, in the absence of political organizations, it was certain that the first would be ineffectual and weak, and just as certain that civil society itself would experience a diminution of its energy. Should political associations ever become subject to harassment, even while civil associations were left undisturbed in the belief that people left to their everyday needs would be safely diverted from political activity, the chances of social and civil instability would multiply. Fortunately, in America, there was no real danger that the state would move to curb their activities. It was a mistake to believe that the fierce competition for political power was a prologue to an abuse of liberty. Indeed, because Americans who gathered in these political bodies were just as, if not more, concerned to keep their commercial undertakings intact, they made sure to stay within the borders of order. By enjoying "a dangerous freedom" – the freedom to gather peacefully for political purposes – they acquired the art of avoiding the extremes of freedom. Just in case liberty for political purposes was taken too far, or was seen and acted upon as an absolute value, limits on it were justified, but if they were imposed in the name of peace, Tocqueville suggested, without extending his comment, society would lose its élan (ibid., passim). Thus he did not elide the question of unbridled freedom, and seemed to be ready to consider that it could be injurious to society.

Democracy was inconceivable without public opinion, which was to be distinguished from "public spirit – the instinctive, disinterested, and undefinable feeling which connects the affections of man with his birthplace" (I, chap. 14, 250–51). Because it was inescapably and intricately woven into the processes of political action, it shaped political parties and it was to its effects that Tocqueville was responding when he spoke of the unparalleled influence in a democratic society by organs of opinion – the newspaper most of all – on the minds of the public (ibid., Bk. 2, chap. 6). On balance, he believed that the press civilized democracy. "[N]ewspapers frequently lead the citizens to launch together into very ill-digested schemes, but if there were no newspapers there would be no common activity. The evil which they produce is therefore much less than that which they cure." Why? Only the press can speak above the crowd and address itself to its interest, to bring them "some intelligence of the state of their public weal" (II, Bk. 2, chap. 6, 120). At the same time, "[a] newspaper can survive only on the condition of publishing sentiments or principles common to a large number of men" (ibid., 122). Thus the most advanced organ of information in his day exerted enormous power and was bound, he predicted, to exert more as the conditions of equality increased.

At the time of the American Revolution, under the guidance of truly significant thinkers and politicians, public spirit was a positive force (I, chap. 15, 276). But it took a dark turn soon after. Tocqueville looked at its sources and manifestations in non-democratic and democratic societies. In the first, public spirit acts importantly as a permanent, even secret, force within and against despotic regimes. In the second, public opinion begins by circulating openly, picking up support and opposition along the way before it becomes hardened as orthodoxy – orthodoxy because the *doxa* [the opinion] of the majority makes it straight, correct, and right. Its power is consequently much greater than the power of a monarch, because democratic peoples have both the right of making and executing the laws – a right denied the monarch who, no matter how absolute, can never succeed in stifling all opposition. Resistance will make itself felt no matter how many cards are stacked against it. Democratic opinion, by contrast, is more like the holy of holies; there is nothing beyond it to which one can appeal. It dictates the contexts and the confines within which the opinions of individuals may be safely expressed. Woe to them if they cannot resist a blockade of unanimous public opinion. The result is a democratic tyranny where the broadsides of the dissenter fall on deaf ears. His civil rights are not extinguished, but he is shunted to one side. He has been deprived of an audience in a society that regards him as eccentric, a troublemaker, and therefore properly treated as an outcast. "You will remain among men," Tocqueville says of the "*stranger*," "but you will be deprived of the rights of mankind" (I, chap. 15, 274). The prophecy gives a semi-Hobbesian reading of democracy that is composed of human beings who find it difficult to acknowledge superior arguments. No one in a Hobbesian state, morever, is required to be a willing participant in his own death, and to that extent the individual's rights remain undisturbed in such a state.

Tocqueville describes a democratic society in which a person can live, but not as part of a community that shuns him because the only thing it wishes to hear is how praiseworthy it is, how what it represents and strives for cannot be submitted to question. The authorities may not hunt the "*stranger*" down for his denial, but there is no need, since he has nothing anyone desires – his exclusion is total. He is left alone in the isolation of his self to comfort him. Tocqueville asked the peoples of democracies to do two things – to take their responsibilities as citizens seriously, and to listen to those among their fellows who had *strange* ideas. These individuals could be intellectuals, but they were not to be given any special status or privileges. They could also be politicians, but of high purpose and caliber, or they could be others with unusual resources of mind and energy – the innovators he speaks about. Their fate – and the fate of democratic peoples – rested ultimately on their capacity for "a strong and sudden effort to a higher purpose" (II, Bk. 3, chap. 21, 277). By this he meant the continuing struggle to achieve a heightened sense of civilization, which he was not afraid to identify with democracy despite its blemishes and risks.

His other point is more valid. Without a critical oasis outside itself, American democracy cannot grasp the full consequences of the insidiousness of mass opinion – of the democratic will gliding along the circumference of a circle pushing everyone and being pushed by everyone. There is no break in the circle. Especially because the private and the public are not sharply delimited, they tend to absorb one another. All is open to scrutiny. Authority may then be frivolously, not seriously, tested, and character is diminished. Thus reduced, one acceptable mold shapes the American mind. If dissent is expressed it is done privately – that is, to strangers from other cultures, and not to one's closest neighbors. In public everyone, except the American "*stranger*" – the innovator – speaks the same language. In this way, democracies insulate themselves, both from within and from outside (I, chap. 15, 273–78). But such a solipsism does not, in Tocqueville's view, destroy the legitimacy of democratic authority, which depends wholly on majority will – a question to be explored more fully in Chapter 9.

In his critique of American imperviousness to new opinions and intellectual life, Tocqueville overshot and missed his target. Forgetting his enthusiasm over the double advance of civilization and intellectual life in a commercialized world, he failed to address the juxtaposition of American conformity and creativity in philosophy, the arts and sciences, and technology. Thus he painted a bleak picture. What was evident to him was the high psychic cost of a conformist America. For the intensity of feeling roused by the fear of being left behind – shaped by a powerful need to emulate one's neighbors – is never dulled. It is itself a function of opinion, of the esteem sought from others, which, if not granted, is a chronic source of depression and insanity (II, Bk. 2, chap. 13, 146–47).

Americans are also, he added, more comfortable with received opinions. It is not that their minds are at rest; they are in constant agitation, but not because they seek the truly new. Rather the fascination with superficial novelties is a function of commitment to known principles, while new principles are avoided. The truly radical view is suspected. It must stand the test of everyone's opinion, who regards his opinion as good or as bad as his neighbor's; and everyone's intellect is thought to be no better than anyone else's. Hence Americans want the wings of their innovators clipped. The great mass of people is ignorant of and is indifferent toward them and their new ideas. The consequence is that public opinion in America weighs down with equal force on the vast majority, but since the vast majority creates it, the circle of conformity and acquiescence is complete. Moreover, because Americans are continually "in action," which absorbs them totally, there is time only for such new ideas as have an immediate relevance for their practical concerns. Tocqueville made a slight concession in concluding his dim picture of opinion. Time, events, and the isolated workings of each person's thought might in fact change opinion. But, if so, the change is likely to be inwardly absorbed, not externally admitted or signified, leaving what he called "the empty phantom of public opinion . . . strong enough to chill innovators and to keep them silent and at a respectable distance." How this surreptitious invasion of received opinions is negotiated nevertheless remains mysterious (II, Bk. 3, chap. 21). Thus, Tocqueville acknowledges that opinion can change, but only because opinion engineers change on its own terms. Democratic individuals need the illusion that nothing really changes without mass consent, and that change occurs because they will it to happen in ways not upsetting to the majority.

From a present-day vantage point, we are told that members of associations that are close to the pulse of their everyday concerns – their "lifeworld" – make up a civil society, a public that seeks "acceptable interpretations for their social interests and experiences and who want to have an influence on institutionalized opinion-and will-information."[19] We also find an elaboration of the Tocquevillian concept of civil society in the following definition:

> Civil society embraces a multiplicity of ostensibly "private" yet potentially autonomous public arenas distinct from the state. The activities of such actors are regulated by various associations existing within them, preventing the society from degenerating into a shapeless mass. In a civil society, these sectors are not embedded in closed, ascriptive or corporate settings; they are open-ended and overlapping. Each has autonomous access to the central political arena, and a certain degree of commitment to that setting.[20]

There is, of course, a serious problem raised by the notion of "autonomous access" as well as with the suggestion that they are "open-ended." As we shall see in Chapter 8, the vaunted value of associations sometimes founders when they turn out to be single- rather than open-minded – that is, when, rather than contributing to the health of civil society, they monopolize public life as organized interest groups. Such groups can escape the charge of parasitism only by convincing the general public that their demands on it and the political institutions they wish to influence will not be achieved without at least some of the benefits of wider deliberation in the public realm. Perhaps the crux of the problem lies precisely in the divergence between the theoretical striving for, and the degradation of, the democratic ideal when the public mis-

---

[19] Jürgen Habermas, *Between Facts and Norms*, p. 367.

[20] *Democracy and Modernity*, ed. S.N. Eisenstadt (Leiden, 1992), cited in ibid. Valuable discussions of the concept of civil society may be found in Norberto Bobbio, "Gramsci and the Conception of Civil Society," in *Which Socialism?* trans. Roger Griffin, ed. Richard Bellamy (Minneapolis: University of Minnesota Press, 1987); Jean Cohen and Andrew Arato, "Politics and the Reconstruction of Civil Society," in *Cultural-Political Interventions in the Unfinished Project of the Enlightenment*, eds. Axel Honneth et al. (Cambridge, Mass. and London, MIT Press, 1992), 121–44; Antonio Negri, *The Savage Anomaly. The Power of Spinoza's Metaphysics and Politics* (Minneapolis and Oxford: University of Minnesota Press, 1991), pp. 136–43.

takenly support associations that claim to represent the general interest, but in fact represent only themselves.

We must finally deal with a question that will be the subject of extended discussion in Part II. Tocqueville attempted to introduce difference as a positive force in democratic society without importing with it the undesirable features of an aristocracy, and without approving in their stead unqualified egalitarian principles and policies. There was not the slimmest opportunity for a practical democratic solution for the Native and Afro-Americans, whose differences he saw in a negative light. Though most Americans have rejected an undifferentiated egalitarianism, their convictions continue to waver: They say, on the one hand, that greater measures of equality remain a practical goal. On the other hand, they do not abandon their belief that the exploitation of some differences will not likely be overcome. At the same time, many of the responses to these questions are riddled with ambiguities. And it is hard to keep them in mind when hard questions demand unambiguous answers to real events. For instance, positive valence is bestowed both upon pride of identity and the image of universalism. Neither has established an unchallenged place in the democratic ethos, even as democratization, viewed as the expansion of citizenship, has enlarged the processes of inclusion. Never before have differences based on race and identity been so vaunted and so disputed. Partisans of each claim that they are serving the cause of equality best. This tangled web catches contradictory impulses. One nourishes feelings of superiority, the other feelings of kinship, with selected groups of people. Both add to the difficulty of clarifying solutions to the sources of democratic malaise.

All this suggests that it would not be a simple matter for democratic civil society to pursue the option of opening the possibility of recognizing different excellences centering on race. It was in this direction that just over twenty years ago, Charles Taylor said democracies might wisely move, with each of the partial communities becoming focal points of activity that need not prevent them from finding connections to the whole.[21] If so, what does the relativization of excellences, or to adopt the more benign notion of an incommensurability of values, do to the premises of Enlightenment rationality? All three – relativism, pluralism, and rationality – divide liberals, who have had to deal with them in the light of the critique of the Enlightenment and are tending to erase sharp

---

[21] Charles Taylor, *Hegel and Modern Society* (Cambridge: Cambridge University Press, 1979), pp. 114–18, 131–33, 136.

distinctions between themselves and conservatives. One might say, ever since Herder spoke about feeling as a substrate of thought and knowledge, that it is impossible to ignore his notion of *Einfühling* – empathy – and the *Volk* – folk culture and organicism – both of which he saw as the basis of community to which people always return as the solid meaning of their existence. Denial of its power simply disrupts. But it need not be parochial. "There is," he wrote, "a symbolism common to all people – a great treasure vault in which is preserved the knowledge belonging to the whole human race."[22] With this statement, Herder declared himself as one who hoped to expand the meaning of the Enlightenment by making room for the particular. The sentiment is echoed by Martha Nussbaum, who uses almost identical words when she says that the self-critical citizen – the citizen who submits tradition to the rational requirements of consistency and justification – is one who has the imagination to ask what it would be like to be as a person different from himself.[23] Noble sounding, certainly Herderian, resembling also Hans-Georg Gadamer's idea that a "fusion of horizons" will effectively break barriers between peoples. He asserts:

> [W]e must always already have a horizon in order to be able to place ourselves within a situation. For what do we mean by 'placing ourselves' in a situation? Certainly not just disregarding ourselves. . . . [I]nto this other situation we must also bring ourselves. . . . If we place ourselves in the situation of someone else, for example, then we shall understand him, i.e. become aware of the otherness, the indissoluble individuality of the other person, by placing ourselves in his position. This placing of ourselves is not the empathy of one individual for another, nor is it the application to another person of our own criteria, but it always involves the arraignment of a higher universality that overcomes not only our particularity, but also that of the other.[24]

Clearly Gadamer is on the side of the angels, in hoping that the process of fusion will permit different people to say something of meaning to

---

[22] Cited in Ian Watt, *Myths of Modern Individualism* (Cambridge: Cambridge University Press, 1996), p. 189.

[23] Martha Nussbaum, *Cultivating Humanity. A Classical Definition of Reform in Liberal Education* (Cambridge, Mass.; Harvard University Press, 1997). Her book is a stimulating guide through the different and diverse worlds in which, she argues, that Americans must try to steer paths, away from a closed parochialism, toward a commonly shared acknowledgment of the value of differences. She believes that the innovative programs on some university campuses open students and their parents to critical thought, and that though it is often alien to those who fail to question tradition, it remains fundamental to democracy.

[24] Hans-Georg Gadamer, *Truth and Method*, trans. of the 2nd edition edited by Garrett Barden and John Cumming (New York: The Seabury Press, 1975), p. 272.

one another, and that it will produce a difference in the way they see the world. This hope is similar to Etienne Balibar's contention that the struggle against inequality will "ever suppress the problem of cultural diversity," or difference,[25] as if he were echoing Tocqueville's concern for preserving within a democratic society the sense that human achievement rests on a need to recognize it. The cultivation of difference was an aristocratic goal, and it became the more deeply entrenched as it came under siege from outside its ranks. Paradoxically, it became for Tocqueville, even as he registered the final doom of such a society, the source for his insistence that difference and equality might survive together in a democratic society.

Tocqueville's confidence in the action of associations and civil society upon one another might be illusionary if an important question is ignored, and we owe it to Tocqueville's own doubts that we can ask it. They arise from his ideas on how a balance might be created to prevent the market from displacing the forum and diverting people from their responsibilities as citizens. The question for him was whether civic and political responsibility was durable enough to survive the drive to give priority to the accumulation of wealth. The question for Americans now is whether they will regard the compulsion to regard all the products of a mass society, be they political or non-political, as having equal and interchangeable value. What happens to civic mindedness if the only meaningful equality is an equality of consumers, if equality of consumption is the only equality that possesses real value? Marx dealt with this one way. He saw in the commodification of life a necessary prelude to the revelation of its folly. The conflict between desires and needs would fall away. Tocqueville does not paint his critique in colors of the apocalypse. While he was disappointed by the conformity that bourgeois individualism reinforced, the ways in which he saw how Americans sought to identify themselves in groups, associations, and communities remained for him a source of the mental energy they required to transfer their concerns to, and mobilize their power for, political action, however uncertain he was about the political and larger goods that their exchanges would achieve.

He had preferences for what he believed were the individual and social differences that made civil society tolerable. The democratic ethos was originally strained in the disputes between partisans of greater democratization and the Federalists, who took steps to ensure their control over

[25] Etienne Balibar, "Ambiguous Universality," 70.

the masses. The Americans who gained by the expansion of political democracy felt no urgent need, however, to expand it for the benefit of those outside the circles of social acceptance. Feelings and habits of superiority persisted. Racial differences were seen negatively, and, if proofs of achievement were nevertheless available, they were rationalized as freakish and hence not entirely as an instance of natural merit. So, on the one hand, in pre-Civil War America, the principle of equality was preached against a background of a suspicion of difference, whether it arose within the relatively closed community of whites, or in the cast-off communities where presumed differences from the existing norms of race and concepts of civilization legitimately consigned the greatest majority of them.

PART II

BEGINNINGS AND DEMOCRACY

4

Beginnings and History:
Red and White in Tocqueville's America

In looking at the past, Tocqueville always coupled and contrasted beginnings with endings. The demise of the *ancien régime*, the attempts to restructure society and politics after 1789, but especially the Jacobinization of, or overwhelming concentration on, politics, loomed over his analysis of what was coming to an end and what was awaiting birth. These metaphors of closures and beginnings are to be found in *Democracy in America*; in his 1836 sketch for, and his uncompleted study of, *L'Ancien Régime et la Révolution*; and in his references to and recollections of a society of ranks, castes, elitism, and a bureaucracy, which were only weakly, if at all, checked by the quasi-juridical, quasi-legislative *parlements*. They carry with them the odors of tradition and the perfumes of a future. When Tocqueville was still an aspiring young magistrate in 1829, he looked back to the vertiginous past of the Revolution. Defending his client, he questioned the argument that the time had come to call for a moratorium on the Revolution – on the quest for liberty itself – on the grounds that the state, as the embodiment of stability, had interests more sacred than those belonging to the individual citizen. He wanted, to be sure, to see the Revolution brought to an end, not only as a concept but as a tradition that legitimated periodic challenges to authority that detracted from the need to concentrate on practical policy decisions. Only a well-conceived constitution, which had so far eluded Frenchmen, could create a legitimate authority and protect individual liberty.[1] In his

---

[1] *Oeuvres complètes d'Alexis de Tocqueville*, 18 vols. (Paris: Gallimard), 1950–98), 16 (*Mélanges*), 68. Hereafter cited as OC. The argument is taken up in François Furet's call for an end to the idea of the Revolution as an unchanging, yet renewable, starting point

mature years, after his American experience and after the promise and
disillusionments of 1848, he recalled in the opening sections of *L'Ancien
Régime* how the early makers of the Revolution, with equality and liberty
as their goals:

> wanted not only to create democratic institutions but free ones as well, not
> only to destroy privileges, but to recognize and to consecrate rights. It was a time
> of youth, enthusiasm, pride, of generous and sincere feelings, which, despite the
> errors that were committed, will forever be kept alive in the memory of human-
> ity, and which will, for a long time to come, disturb the sleep of all those who
> seek to corrupt or reduce the people to a condition of servility.[2]

Still the old clung to the new. Indeed it was one of Tocqueville's
premises that much of the framework of state power developed in the
ancien régime survived and became more entrenched by the actions of
the revolutionaries. Instead of keeping to their original goals of ensuring liberty, they tended to conflate and treat civil and political society
as one by giving a false reality to the sacred but unexamined principle
of the "sovereignty of the people." Consequently, all foundered on a
thoughtless understanding of how it could be realized in an age demanding an informed electorate and properly constituted methods of knowing
its will. The fall-out thickly blanketed the thoughts and the lives of the
generations following 1789 who scrambled to establish forms of constitutional liberalism, but became entangled in the effort. So heavily did
the past burden the post-Revolutionary scene that intellectual-politicians
such as Benjamin Constant and Royer-Collard failed to make a lasting
impression on the Restoration governments that were set in place after
1814–15. The destruction of Restoration France, however, did not mark
a true ending, as Tocqueville impatiently wished – only a change in the
seemingly never-ending and irresolvable cycle of debate on the nature of
the polity best suited to meet the needs of the nation.

in modern history. See Furet's *Interpreting the French Revolution*, trans. Elborg Forster
(Cambridge and Paris: Cambridge University Press and Editions de la Maison des
Sciences de l'Homme, 1981). Jürgen Habermas considers what he calls the "*cultural
dynamic released by the French Revolution*" as carrying forward its energies into the
future and suggests that it must be a starting point for considering how a "radical
democratic republic might even be *conceived* today." See his *Between Facts and Norms.
Contributions to a Discourse Theory of Law and Democracy*, trans. William Rehg
(Cambridge, Mass. and London: MIT Press, 1996), pp. 470–71. It is fair to say that
Tocqueville's position may be located on a spectrum halfway between Furet and
Habermas, but this does not mean that Habermas ought to be located at the extreme
end of it and therefore in total opposition to Furet. Like Furet after him, Tocqueville
recoiled from radical solutions.

[2] OC 2 (*L'Ancien Régime et la Révolution*) part 1, 72.

In little more than a year after the July Revolution of 1830, Tocqueville journeyed, without losing sight of the politics of France, as far as the forests of Michigan. The political failure of the Bourbon Restoration instantiated for Tocqueville yet one more historical turn of the French Revolution's transformation of the abstract ideas of the Enlightenment. Many of them, it is well known, elicited his scorn. He looked forward to the time when they might more properly be seen from their post-Revolutionary perspective and at last treated within the restraints of a set of well-defined and practical constitutional institutions. The debacle of 1830 threw him off balance and challenged his assumptions about European culture. He welcomed America with relief. There his new experiences invited further musings on beginnings and ends. Instead of the problems of an older society, he saw a new one with a political culture, barely fifty years old, taking pride in its new beginnings and turning a blind eye to the devastations of the Native American cultures that were approaching their end. The juxtaposition of these changes – one in Europe, the other in North America – became a basis for Tocqueville's ideas on civilization and cultural difference. For all its youth and exuberance, he found in America a legacy of deeply entrenched attitudes about both. Already the debates over the killing of Native American tribes and the future of the remaining ones had fallen into familiar grooves. Resettling the latter in the western reaches of the continent sanctioned a politics of forgetfulness. There were few regrets, only the triumphalism of superior civilization. A similar set of beliefs, enshrined almost as a dogma, separated the black and white cultures, with the difference that the economic well-being of the latter rested on the labor of the former. Tocqueville shared some of, but turned a critical gaze upon, these assumptions.

In America, he found himself in a world turned upside down. Civilized man and the barbarian Native American had changed places.[3] The barbarian was invested with a negative savagery or positive primitivism, depending on degrees of European self-consciousness. Tocqueville, as we shall later see, made these distinctions, but they tended to merge even in his own mind. In the wilderness, the European disappeared, if only

---

[3] References to "barbarous," "barbarians," "savages," "primitive," and "civilization" capture contemporary usages. The terms, "primitive" and "civilization" cannot be dispensed with in any discussions in which comparisons are made. They need not be associated with an inferior state of being, on the one hand, nor with a "superior" one, on the other. Finally, I use such terms as "Indians," "Indian," "Native American" and "native" interchangeably.

briefly, from the publicly sanctioned sphere of European conventions. Words appeared to have lost their familiar meaning, and time took on a new one. Signs replaced words in the changed ecology. They were more transparent: "Civilized man walked as a blind man, incapable not only of making his way in the labyrinth through which he was traveling, but even of finding the means to sustain life. It is in the midst of these very difficulties that the savage triumphed; for him the forest had no veils."[4]

There are etymological links between savagery and forest. The word savage comes from the Latin *silva*, "wood." The savage is the man who lives in forests; he is *homo sylvestris*. So much is the wilderness part of him that he is by definition constitutionally unable to be civilized.[5] Paradoxically, but inevitably, in this setting, the Native American was superior to the civilized Frenchman, and alone capable of delivering him from disorder and disorientation and depositing him at the site of a new truth. Civilized man, newly aware of his blindness in the forest darkness, now gained an unexpected insight: Without aboriginal man he was impotent in the wilderness. Several steps were needed to bring the double meaning of this discovery home to Tocqueville. He quickly threw aside preconceptions of Native Americans that he had gathered from Chateaubriand and James Fenimore Cooper. Expecting traces in them of the "lofty virtues that had given birth to the spirit of liberty," and of their reputed physical robustness, he saw very different human beings. They were of small stature, their legs were thin and twitching, and their skin color was not copper red,[6] but a dark bronze. Altogether they exuded an impression of:

---

[4] "Quinze jours dans le désert," in Alexis de Tocqueville, *Oeuvres*, ed. André Jardin with the collaboration of Françoise Mélonio and Lise Queffélec, 2 vols. (Paris: Gallimard, 1991), I, 390. Hereafter cited as *Oeuvres*. On Tocqueville's and Gustave de Beaumont's visit to Michigan, see George W. Pierson, *Tocqueville and Beaumont in America* (New York: Oxford University Press, 1938), p. 229; James T. Schleifer, *The Making of Tocqueville's Democracy in America* (Chapel Hill: University of North Carolina Press, 1980), pp. 62–63; André Jardin, *Alexis de Tocqueville, 1805–1859* (Paris: Hachette, 1984).

[5] Very useful are the discussions by Jan Nederveen Pietersen, *White on Black: Images of Blacks and Americans in Western Popular Culture* (1990; reprint, New Haven: Yale University Press, 1992), pp. 30–31, and Ronald Sanders, *Lost Tribes and Promised Lands: The Origins of American Racism* (Boston: Little Brown, 1978), p. 202.

[6] "Quinze jours dans le désert," *Oeuvres*, I, 361. On the evolving designations of "red" to identify Native Americans (both by themselves as well as by Europeans), and, how, when both participated in observing themselves in order to make sense of each other's differences, they also come to the realization that physical differences did exist, and that it would be an error to ascribe overmuch to a cultural construction of racial categories, see Nancy Shoemaker, "How Indians Got to Be Red," *American Historical Review*, 102

wretchedness and misery. Their physiognomy signified that profound deprivation that a prolonged abuse of the benefits of civilization can alone bestow.
One would have said: [nothing less than] the [physiognomy] of men belonging
to the lowest depths of the populations living in our great European cities. And
yet they were still savages. To the vices that they took from us was mixed something barbaric and uncivilized which rendered them a hundred times more repulsive. . . . Standing before us – and it is a pitiful thing to say so – were the final
remnants of that famous Iroquois Confederation whose 'virile' wisdom was no
less celebrated than their courage that for so long a time held the balance of
power between the two greatest European nations.[7]

Tocqueville gave up his expectation that the explanation for the
ascending stages of civilization would be determined, in America, as in
Europe, by territorial extent and degrees of wealth, and that, once the
latter were properly taken into account, it would be possible to discern
how the development of civilization might be understood and measured
by human time. More so in the New World than in the Old, he had
thought, because it would be in the first that multiple, coexisting, images
of different social states would be revealed. America, he had anticipated,
would be "the only place where all the transformations in the social condition to which man had submitted could be plotted, and where it would
have always been possible to perceive [those changes comprised in] a vast
chain descending from ring to ring, ranging [in condition] from that of
the opulent urban patrician to the savage of the wilderness. There, in a
word . . . I expected to find the structure of the entire history of humanity."[8] This was not to be. Shifting his categories, he postulated America
as a single society. Whether in its populated or empty spaces, it was
shaped by ideas of equality and republicanism, penetrating the very
marrow of life. The exception was the savage life. Civilization, when
transported to America, gave to the savage state only what the natural
order of things was prepared to absorb from it.[9] Why? The presumption
was that the savage's perceptions of his needs was narrow, for he had no
way of knowing what was valuable in civilization, except the material
goods it could produce. Turning to the distinctions between Europeans
and non-Europeans, Tocqueville wrote:

(1997), 625–44. Alden T. Vaughan, "From White Man to Redskin: Changing Anglo-
American Perceptions of the American Indian," *American Historical Review*, 87 (1982),
917–53 points out that the designation "redskin" was not in normal use until the
nineteenth century.
[7] "Quinze jours dans le désert," *Oeuvres*, I, 361–62.
[8] Ibid., 365.   [9] Ibid., 366.

Philosophers have believed that human nature was the same everywhere and varied only as institutions and laws created different societies. Every page in the history of the world gives the lie to this view. Nations like individuals possess their own particular physiognomies and show them throughout history. The characteristic traits of their countenance is reproduced through all the transformations they experience. Laws, *moeurs*, religions change; power and wealth change places; the external aspects of things vary; dress differs, some prejudices are obliterated or take the place of others. In the midst of these diverse changes you always recognize the same people. Something inflexible appears at the center of human flexibility.[10]

At its most fundamental level, despite whatever differences he noted between Anglo-, French-, or Spanish-Americans, the gulf between two parallel cultures, one civilized, the other savage, was too great to be overcome. No matter what particular Europeans brought to America, the triumph of the white race, now seen as synonymous with civilization, was assured. Indeed, Tocqueville's allusions to the barriers between civilized and uncivilized are couched in terms of skin color and blood,[11] whiteness and redness, or if not redness, of a darkish color, visibly, and therefore, it would seem, intrinsically different and separate. The outcome could not be halted. Civilization was both a destructive and a creative force. It marked ends as well as beginnings. It registered as well moments of sublimity – the emotions of "religious terror" called up by the immensity of the apparent chaos of the wilderness, pulsating with vegetative life, seemingly eternal, hence superior to the changing fortunes of human beings spread over an old continent, but at the same time made new by the end of one culture and the start of another. Human power over nature was the enactment of God's will. Nature did not have a chance, and the savages who roamed freely throughout its vast reaches would also succumb. The prospects of change raised conflicting feelings of pride and regret that remained for the most part at this inchoate level.[12]

The one occasion of mutual recognition may have occurred during Tocqueville's and Beaumont's journey to Saginaw. In the landscape of the unknown, the barriers of language, prejudice, and fear encircled civilized and savage man alike. For brief instances, the circle was broken spontaneously, as if the tensions of non-comprehension were too menacing

[10] Ibid., 401–02.
[11] The references to white race and white blood are to be found in ibid., 382, 406, 409.
[12] Tocqueville raises these images in "Voyage au Lac Oneida," in ibid., 353–54, and in "Quinze jours dans le désert," ibid., 391–92, 409.

for both the white men and the red. It was then that the two parties, eyeing one another, together created some meaning from the encounter. Tocqueville and Beaumont for a moment relaxed their guard against an Indian who was following them, when they unexpectedly were halted in their tracks by a figure whom they mistook for an Indian, but were startled to discover was an American dressed in Indian garb. He had chosen to live among the Indians, whom he valued more, he said, than the life of white society. Then he began an exchange in Chippewayan with the Indian who had been following them, sharing as equals, it seemed to Tocqueville, ideas on the merits of their respective rifles. Only then were their fears stilled. "It was quite remarkable," Tocqueville wrote, "to see the pleasure with which these two men, by birth and manners so different from each other, shared their ideas." Fear, a universal emotion, had kept the two travelers and the Chippeway apart and hostile. Tocqueville described the release of tension as a moment of human connection, but not one – retracting somewhat his earlier remarks – that placed either them and the American on an equal footing with the Indians: "[Europeans] blended the love of savage life with the arrogance of civilization and preferred the Indians to their compatriots without, however, recognizing them as their equals."[13]

We are left to guess at what a fuller narrative might tell us. For one thing, what is available to us are only his interpretative skills, and, moreover, even though unpublished in his lifetime, they would not have been destined for anyone but European readers,[14] and not the Indian's, though white-red contacts over time offer evidence of how the aboriginals chose various strategies to interpret themselves to Europeans, including how they believed Europeans wanted to see them. And, for another, even if we had the Indian's version, we would still be left with a problem of puzzling through at least two, if not more, interpretative muddles.

Tocqueville also discovered that as Europeans moved into the interior of the continent, not only did they not succumb to their impotence, they were forging a totally new society, one that differed not only from the aboriginal's, but distinct as well from the one they had left behind. What was new for these transplanted "nomads," as they extracted from civilization and enlightenment only what was pleasing to their sense of

---

[13] Ibid., 383.
[14] Together with "Voyage au Lac Oneida," "Quinze jours dans le désert" was published after his death by Gustave de Beaumont, in *Oeuvres complètes de Tocqueville*, 9 vols. (Paris: Michel-Lévy frères, 1864–66), 5, 173–258.

well-being, were its material products, as they advanced with their axes and newspapers through the American stillness and solitude.[15] In the widest, yet ironic sense, they were still nomads, but, in Tocqueville's conceptual scheme, civilized ones, carrying history on their shoulders. They were creating a singular civilization,[16] a new beginning – one that, while existing in proximity with America's indigenous peoples, would finally negate and destroy their way of life, and take their lives as well. Such was Tocqueville's prediction. True, everything about the pioneers on the frontier appeared primitive, but fifty centuries in the Old World had formed them, during which time they had pierced the secrets of nature, leaving behind earlier forms of barbarism, ignorance, and isolation (I, chap. 17, 302). Their knowledge of the past, curiosity about the future, and readiness to argue about the present found new historical meaning in America. Tocqueville found there the beginnings of a new civilization, but it proved to have a negative side. In viewing Anglo-Americans as pragmatic historians with a belief in a limitless and benign future, the question he took on was how history would present them with challenges from peoples who were grappling with their own notions of beginning and of Americanness.

Jack Greene captures well the place America held in the European intellect and imagination:

[T]hey [people in the seventeenth century] thought in terms not of *finding* an existing utopia but of *founding* one in the relatively 'empty' and inviting spaces of North America. . . .

North America presented itself as an immense, sparsely populated, and bounteous territory that was 'open for experimentation.' Apparently with 'neither a history nor any political forms at all,' it invited people to consider how, in as yet unarticulated space, Old World institutions and socioeconomic, religious, and political arrangements might be modified to produce the best possible commonwealths.

[V]irtually every one of the New England colonies . . . represented an effort to create in some part of the infinitely pliable world of America – a world that would perforce yield to English mastery – some specific Old World vision for the recovery of an ideal past in a new and carefully constructed society.[17]

Tocqueville, of course, distinguished the signs marking the arrival of Europeans in, and the beginnings of their colonization of, America, and

---

[15] *Oeuvres*, I, 373. Tocqueville uses the term "nomads" to describe the pioneers.

[16] Ibid., 365.

[17] Jack P. Greene, *The Intellectual Construction of America. Exceptionalism and Identity from 1492 to 1800* (Chapel Hill and London: University of North Carolina Press, 1993), pp. 51, 52, 54–55. Italics in the original.

the signs of its original inhabitants. He was on the track of aboriginals in his adventurous trek through Michigan. He could assign a beginning to the early European settlement of the "new" continent. It was harder, if not impossible, to seek out the beginnings of the human occupation of America. Nevertheless, the two, when considered as parts of the entire history of humanity, it seemed to him, could be measured on one scale. There was then for him a single and universal human nature joined in a chain from the past to the present. As I noted earlier, Tocqueville spoke of human nature as inflexible, though it came dressed in various garbs, mores, and manners as material circumstances changed. Apparently the incoherence did not strike him. In one breath, he could contrast primitive, savage and barbaric, and civilized human states, and, in the next, he could speak of a single human nature.

In Claude Lévi-Strauss's description of the longings for and hopes vested in the lost Atlantis, we catch a glimpse of early modern Europe's image of an unspoiled fixed point, which carries some of the echoes of European and non-European contacts:

a continent barely touched by man whose greed could no longer be satisfied by their own continent. Everything would be called into question by this second sin: God, morality and law. In simultaneous yet contradictory fashion, everything would be verified in practice and revoked in principle: the Garden of Eden, the Golden Age of antiquity, the Fountain of youth, Atlantis, the Hesperides, the Islands of the Blessed, would be found to be true; but revelation, salvation, custom and laws would be challenged by the spectacle of a purer, happier race of men (who, of course, were not really purer or happier, although a deep-seated remorse made them appear so.[18]

The twentieth-century post-colonial search for origins is, however, slanted away from an age-old, but, in the nineteenth century, increasingly romanticized, obsession with the distant, presumably heroic, though savage, dawn of human society, to ethnographic explorations, designed to destroy myths and release information about the different, but most of all, the historical contexts of human nature. Theoretically more advanced than Tocqueville's understanding of European and non-European cultures, Lévi-Strauss's journey from the universality of the human race to the particular, from singularity to differences, and back again, left him with the hypothesis that all non-Western peoples would come to see themselves as "temporarily backward rather than

[18] Claude Lévi-Strauss, *Tristes Tropiques*, trans. John and Doreen Weightman (New York: Athenaeum, 1973), p. 74.

permanently different."[19] A further step toward the erasure of backwardness, but not of cultural difference, is taken by Castoriadis who
writes that "we [Europeans] at the same time claim that we are one
culture among others *and* that this culture is unique, since it recognizes
the alterity of the others (which wasn't the case before, and what other
cultures do not acknowledge to us)." Castoriadis rightly declares that
the historical determinants of human rights do not exhaust their meaning
nor the permanence of their value, so that, for example, the value of
equality, though a historical creation of Western culture, "tends to transform history, including also the history of *other* peoples."[20]

There is a point of convergence in the ideas of both the twentieth-
century's theoreticians and those of their earlier proto-ethnographer
companion. The lost Atlantis that Lévi-Strauss depicted as an imaginary
second Eden – a place to which human beings were said to wish to make
the journey back in time to a fixed point from which they might start
afresh – is somewhat analogous to Tocqueville's soliloquy in the forest,
where he summoned up Milton's *Paradise Lost* to express his admiration for its solitude and his disenchantment with civilized life.[21] But this
was a mental state more tinged with Romantic feelings than with anthro-
pological conjecture about, or evidence of, early human societies.[22]

Traces were much on his mind as Tocqueville speculated on the
earliest peoples who inhabited the New World. He thought about the
traces left behind by early cultures and compared them with what was
to become the culture of Anglo-Americans, once its English origins were
transported from the Old to, and transformed in, the New World. But

[19] Claude Lévi-Strauss, *Structural Anthropology*. Vol. 2, trans. Monique Layton (New
York: Basic Books, 1976), p. 53.
[20] Cornelius Castoriadis, *Philosophy, Politics, Autonomy: Essays in Political Philosophy*
(Oxford: Oxford University Press, 1991), pp. 37–38, 135. As a real example, he writes
about the clash of African Muslim and Western attitudes toward female circumcision,
and the dilemma facing two friends from each of these cultures. They wish to preserve
their friendship, yet each feels he must argue for his value system. The first argues for
the practice, the second argues against it, as the denial of a universal human right.
Castoriadis argues that the Western value is universally valid.
[21] "Quinze jours dans le désert," in *Oeuvres*, I, 381–82.
[22] In his Introduction to *Liberty, Equality, Democracy* (New York and London: New York
University Press, 1992), pp. xv–xxiii, Eduardo Nolla notes that Tocqueville must be
taken seriously not only as a political prophet, but as a philosopher, though one with a
powerful commitment to the problems of political life. Nolla's important critical edition
of *De la Démocratie en Amérique*, 2 vols., including Tocqueville's notes, was published
by Librairie Vrin (Paris, 1990). His Introduction makes a valued contribution to
Tocquevillian scholarship. See also his essay "Autour de l'autre démocratie," published
by Instituto Suor Orsola Benincasa (Naples, 1994).

much of this was somewhat like the conjectural history of previous centuries. He preferred the evidence of historical and political sociology, as he conceived it in his day: How one could expand the practical knowledge of the world's peoples by studying their social lives and their political organizations. He looked to the ways that history structured their density and their impactedness, while disentangling their various parts. In that domain, Tocqueville found the meaning in and mystery of much of the past. He visualized beginnings as a threshold over which human beings must pass before they consciously enter history. Its meaning was not complete without introducing as an essential part of human history the idea of willed and intentional action striving to impress itself upon and against the vast aggregates of the past. When individuals simultaneously intend an action *and* act, they do so as intending and free, though not totally self-defining, agents. Intentionality was the very marrow of beginnings in history. Before thinking could become historical, a cognitive separation had to occur, in other words, between origins *toute longue* and active human consciousness. History for Tocqueville was meaningless without initiation; it was nothing without will.[23] With just a touch of self-conscious rhetoric, he wrote at the conclusion of *Democracy in America* – rounding off his original idea that it was will that gave the Pilgrims the strength to suffer the unknown terrors of the Atlantic and begin anew (I, chap. 2, 35) – that the new democratic nation some two centuries later needed but the will to ward off the "mighty evils" to be "virtuous and prosperous" (II, Bk. 4, chap. 7, 352). Clearly such an affirmation of the will's free action was meant by Tocqueville to signify not only a beginning registered, but one not available for non-Western people who were stuck at a point of material stasis from which they could not advance.

The greatest evil for Tocqueville lay in the internal contradictions of a democracy that could not consistently adjust itself to the conflicts that he saw arising from the desire for material satisfaction and a political culture requiring some sacrifice of private life if it were to survive. Another evil was slavery and racial discrimination (I, chap. 18, 371). The third evil was the treatment of the aboriginal peoples (ibid., 354). How might we make sense of Tocqueville's stress on beginnings and freedom, his condemnation of slavery and the displacement of the Native

---

[23] See Harvey Mitchell, *Individual Choice and the Structures of History. Alexis de Tocqueville as Historian Reappraised* (Cambridge: Cambridge University Press, 1996), pp. 61–62, 160, 260, 262, 264, 266.

Americans, which he based on both observation and deduction, and the reasons he adduced, if not categorically to deny, but certainly to question, the possibility that the aboriginal and black American populations would become integrated into Anglo-American democracy? What was at stake was not only the survival and expansion of the democratic ethos with its roots in European institutions as they were metamorphosed in America. A strong part of him identified the meaning of civilization and history with a universal quest for liberty. In the modern world, that search superseded the ancient liberty of hunting and gathering peoples, whom he likened to the European nobles at the height of the Middle Ages (I, chap. 18, 357), and, not least, the black population before it was enslaved. Not only did American democracy encounter a clash of three cultures in Tocqueville's time. He is rightly seen as among those who were most acutely aware of the crisis to which Americans were moving – including the threat of civil war. In the end, he believed not only that human will decided between good and evil, but that there was no reason to believe that intelligence and virtue were necessarily and simply related, or that they were history's favorites.

François Furet takes up aspects of this question in his argument that Tocqueville abandoned his conceptual democratic scheme as all-inclusive, not so much because he did not recognize Native and Afro-Americans as racially different, but because their social organizations were incompatible with American democracy.[24] In a variation of this theme, Françoise Mélonio maintains that the internal strains of American democracy led a disillusioned Tocqueville to abandon the preeminence he had bestowed on it in favor of a two-model theory of the future, one American, the other English, thereby strengthening his notion of liberalism as a precarious conquest over the forces of irrationality.[25]

Though Furet's and Mélonio's views carry weight, they elide some key issues. Tocqueville's concept of American democracy is less complete than they make out, for while it dealt brilliantly with its strengths and weaknesses, it did not account for all of the latter. And the reason for this failure is that he obscured the meaning or took for granted the two strains of thought that served as the foundations for his theory. One was the dual legacy of the Enlightenment. Critical though he was of many of

---

[24] François Furet, "The Conceptual System of 'Democracy in America'," in *The Workshop of History*, trans. Jonathan Mandelbaum (Chicago and London: University of Chicago Press, 1984), pp. 182–84.

[25] Françoise Mélonio, "Tocqueville et les malheurs de la démocratie américaine (1831–1859)," *Commentaire*, 10 (1987), 381–89.

its claims, he inherited its notion of civilization and history. At the very best, the exoticism of non-European cultures assured the recognition of difference. At the very worst, cultural stagnation awaited them. In either case, they seemed to be approaching ends, rather than beginnings. The other stream of thought that Tocqueville inherited, and which informed his defense of a future democracy, was the idea that liberty and equality were universally rooted needs. But there was an even older and perhaps even more important stream of Judeo-Christian thought, he maintained, that fed on memory, led to reflection on the nature of beginnings, and was carried into European historical consciousness. Later it inspired the American democratic ethos. In lauding these and many of its other features, he was somewhat inclined to over-stress its benign side, thinking of it as a tolerant and positive vision of a democratic citizenry dedicated to equality and liberty.[26] Though not unaware of the underside of Christianity, especially in the southern United States, he tended to minimize the burden of intolerance carried with it by thinking of it as more vestigial than it proved to be. If an interracial society was, as he believed, not in the offing, what implications does this conviction have for his theory that joined beginnings and freedom and found its best expression in a democratic America?

As he reached the end of *Democracy in America*, he tenaciously insisted that the modern world had not yet taken its final historical shape, and that there was no doubt in his mind that "I go back from age to age up to the remotest antiquity, but I find no parallel to what is occurring before my eyes" (II, Bk. 4, chap. 8, 349). When reaching out for an explanation for the beginnings and direction of American democracy, Tocqueville posited a break with the past, an articulation of a free choice that marked a break in time, a moment of speculation, an instant when a wager was made on an experiment with the future. Beginnings and freedom are linked in Tocqueville's idea of historical time, with the second being inseparable from the first and the source from which it had the potentiality to become an active force. Beginnings he saw as a mental construct, allowing the historian and historical actors alike to act in the world by freeing their minds and inclinations away from the past and directing them toward the future. This I see as a key to what Tocqueville

[26] In 1843, he wrote six anonymous articles for his shortlived newspaper, *Le Siècle*, on the abolition of slavery. In the second and fourth of these, he attributed to Christianity the source of the principles of equality and liberty, both of which were given dignity by the French Revolution and through it were carried to the world. See "L'Emancipation des esclaves," OC 3, (*Ecrits et discours politiques*) part 3, 88–89, 124–25.

tried to accomplish as a historian. Though not directly related to the argument developed in these pages about the importance he gave to historical beginnings and ends, it is Frank Ankersmit's contention that Tocqueville did not bind himself to the tasks of conventional narrative representation. He argues that *Democracy in America* itself has no real beginnings and no end. Tocqueville turned instead to metaphor, and above all, to paradox, thence to arrive at a point where he turns away from finding the center or theory of democracy, and that it exists rather in a state of sublimity.[27] The putative absence of beginnings in the sense Ankersmit gives it, and the dominating presence of irony and paradox, which are, to be sure, inescapable features of Tocqueville's philosophy of history, does not alter, as I have shown, my reading of Tocqueville's intent in the *Democracy* and his larger purpose as a historian.

If freedom is to be considered neither a product of human vanity nor wishful thinking, empirical foundations are required to lend support to it as a human possibility. We might do well to turn to Montesquieu, the likeliest source of the two kinds of liberty that Tocqueville probably recalled. One, Montesquieu described as philosophical, "an exercise of one's will, or . . . in the opinion that one exerts one's will"; the other, he described as political liberty, which "consist[s] only in having the power to do what one should want to do and in no way being constrained to do what one should not want to do" in a state ruled by laws.[28] For Tocqueville, the first form of liberty was the work of the spirit and the imagination, yet was also inescapably rooted in history. If one asks, as he did, how the exercise of the will is translated into political action, or how the human psyche impresses itself on society, we may gain a firmer understanding of how he moved from the first to the second form of freedom while maintaining the distinction between them. Freedom conceived as an exercise of the will served as a groundwork for Tocqueville's consideration of what purposes are served by what may be called willing – in brief, how willing is transformed into political freedom. Historical inquiry revealed to him the enormously difficult problem of creating a coherent account of the manner in which freedom seems to force its way into the world and dissolves at the same moment. He called on histori-

---

[27] See Frank R. Ankersmit's original treatment, "Tocqueville and the Sublimity of Democracy, Part I: Content," *La Revue Tocqueville/The Tocqueville Review*, 14 (1993), 173–200; Part II: "Form," ibid., 15 (1994), 193–217. esp. in the latter, 195–201.

[28] Charles-Louis de Secondat de Montesquieu, *The Spirit of the Laws*, ed. and trans. Anne Kohler et al. (Cambridge: Cambridge University Press, 1989), Bk. 12, chap. 2, p. 188; Bk. 11, chap. 3, p. 155.

cal memory to think back to even more distant beginnings and to their outcomes as distinctive historical events, subject to, but not invariably driven by, narrative rules. To his recollection of the non-European past in America, we must now turn.

"Prehistorical" America

America was a beckoning sentinel, the site of a new civilization.[29] It had been for centuries. As Tzvetan Todorov remarks, "Even if every date that permits us to separate any two periods is arbitrary, none is more suitable, in order to mark the beginning of the modern era, than the year is 1492.... We are all the direct descendants of Columbus."[30] Tocqueville carried with him the European need to ethnologize the aboriginals of America. In the incremental ethnologies of previous Europeans was embedded the entire edifice of European science, which informed his understanding of civilized and savage states – of the European and non-European minds. The American aboriginals, he noted on the basis of a still-primitive ethnography, were related to Asian nomadic peoples, living like them in wild freedom, and in a land they had penetrated without, he mistakenly believed, leaving anything of permanence behind (I, chap. 1, 23–24). Tocqueville had read a slightly plagiarized version of a German novel published in 1798 (*Erscheinungen am See Oneida*),[31] which fictionalized the story of a French emigre fleeing the Revolution and finding refuge and a new beginning in the wilderness near Lake Oneida. Tocqueville's attempt to look for signs of his existence almost forty years later, which he recounts in *Voyage to Lake Oneida*, is a Romantic evocation of a "new Eden" that surrendered to the overpowering force of nature, leaving almost no traces of an attempt to found a civilization. After clearing a portion of the forest and establishing more than the rudiments of a civilized life, the emigre suffered the death of his wife and found himself alone. He was, as Tocqueville imagined, a being who was no longer able to live with men, nor live without them, a being neither savage nor civilized, a being who was nothing so much as a form of human debris, "similar to those trees in the forests of America that

---

[29] For an imposing examination of some of the unexpected features of the concept of civilization, see Jean Starobinski, *Blessings in Disguise; Or, the Morality of Evil*, trans. Arthur Goldhammer (Cambridge, Mass.: Harvard University Press, 1993), pp. 17–34.

[30] Tzvetan Todorov, *The Conquest of America: The Question of the Other* (New York: Harper and Row, 1984), p. 5.

[31] See André Jardin, *Alexis de Tocqueville, 1805–1859*, pp. 119–20.

the wind had the power to uproot but not to kill, standing but dead."[32] The primeval forest spread its towering branches over, and obliterated virtually all signs of human impressions, covering them with darkness.

But Tocqueville did not remain in this mood for long. From this poetic, semi-religious journey of his imagination, he went on a month later to write *Quinze jours dans le désert*, a record of his travels to "the limits of European civilization," a geography that revealed the concrete signs of indigenous life. As he recorded in one of his exchanges with the white settlers he met, the traces of that life melted away as the Native Americans retreated further and further into the unreachable parts of the continent. They are "a race," one of his interpreters told him, "not made for civilization. It kills them."[33] That they were not fitted for it had become part of the prevailing Anglo-American credo some time before Tocqueville's discovery of its prevalence among the whites he met. Before the end of the previous century, George Washington, in a message to Congress, stated, "We are more enlightened and more powerful than the Indian nations; we are therefore bound in honor to treat them with kindness, and even with generosity" (cited in I, chap. 18, 364). Thomas Jefferson spoke of the "genius and mental powers" of Native Americans, but added that "great allowance [must] be made for those circumstances of their situation which call for a display of particular talents only."[34] It seems clear that in speaking about talents this way, he was referring to inherited capacities – that is to say, to Native American capacities, and thought of Afro-American talents in the same way. Looking at the Native Americans alone, Jedidiah Morse agreed with Jefferson,

---

[32] *Oeuvres*, I, 359. For his notes on his journey, see also, 148–49. References to it are also to be found in *Democracy in America*, I, chap. 17, 306. An interesting reading of the journey is offered by Irena Grudzinska Gross, *The Scar of Revolution. Custine, Tocqueville and the Romantic Imagination* (Berkeley, Los Angeles, Oxford: University of California Press, 1991). A larger treatment of the French Romantic view of civilization is to be found in Pierre Michel, *Un mythe romantique. Les barbares 1789–1848* (Lyon: Presses Universitaires de Lyon, 1981). For the view that Tocqueville did not overly romanticize the Native Americans, and in fact contributed to a modern social scientific understanding of primitive peoples, see Harry Liebersohn, "Discovering Indigenous Nobility: Tocqueville, Chamisso, and Romantic Travel Writing," *American Historical Review*, 99 (1994), 746–66. His article is also valuable for its bibliographical citations on travel writing and the ethnographical studies of the period.

[33] *Oeuvres*, I, 360. Cf. Senator Thomas Hart Benton's words: "Civilization or extinction has been the fate of all people who have found themselves in the track of advancing whites." See Michael Rogin, *Fathers and Children: Andrew Jackson and the Subjugation of the American Indian* (New York: Alfred Knopf, 1975), p. 210.

[34] Thomas Jefferson, *Notes on the State of Virginia*, ed. W. Peden (Chapel Hill: University of North Carolina Press, 1955), p. 62.

concluding that "the character of the Indians is altogether founded upon their circumstances and way of life. A people who are constantly employed in procuring the means of a precarious subsistence, who live by hunting the wild animals, and who are generally engaged in war with their neighbors, cannot be supposed to enjoy much gaiety of temper, or a high flow of spirits."[35] "A relatively unpopulated country . . . far from the great seats of civilization," Tocqueville reflected, "is one generally inhabited by a population that is often virtuous but almost always poor and ignorant."[36] Here was a people that *refused* to take that vital step away from their nomadism and, by refusing, accepted their own destruction. This fact of recognition cannot be reconciled with the categorical view that it was inconceivable for Europeans of the eighteenth and nineteenth centuries "to have regarded Indians as persons with a psychology of their own."[37] In the past, as in the present, Tocqueville opined that there are:

> nations whose first education has been so vicious and whose character presents so strange a mixture of passion, ignorance, and erroneous notions upon all subjects that they are unable to discern the causes of their own wretchedness, and they fall a sacrifice to ills of which they are ignorant.
>
> I have crossed vast tracts of country formerly inhabited by powerful Indian nations who are now extinct; I have passed some time among remnants of tribes, which witness the daily decline of their numbers and of the glory of their independence; and I have heard these Indians themselves anticipate the impending doom of their race. Every European can perceive means that would rescue these unfortunate beings from the destruction otherwise inevitable. They alone are insensible to the remedy; they feel the woes which year after year heaps upon their heads, but they will perish to a man without accepting their cure. Force would have to be employed to compel them to live (I, chap. 13, 239–40).

Tocqueville also relied on the written accounts of Frenchmen and of Americans. Not only had he consulted and challenged, as we saw, Chateaubriand and Cooper. He showed greater confidence in accounts by some of his countrymen – including Charlevoix,[38] Volney,[39] La

---

[35] Jedediah O. Morse, *The History of America*, 2nd ed. (Philadelphia, 1795), p. 31.

[36] *Oeuvres*, I, 1362, note b.

[37] Richard Drinnon, *Facing West: The Metaphysics of Indian-Hating and Empire-Building* (New York: Meridian, 1980), p. 332.

[38] François Xavier de Charlevoix (1682–1761), the Jesuit scholar and author of *Histoire et description de la Nouvelle France avec le Journal historique d'un voyage fait par ordre du Roi dans l'Amérique septentrionale*, 6 vols. (Paris, 1744).

[39] Constantin François de Chasseboeuf, comte de Volney, *Observations générales sur les Indiens ou Sauvages de l'Amérique du Nord*, published as an appendix to his *Tableau du climat et du sol des Etats-Unis*, 2 vols. (Paris: Courcier, 1803).

Rochefoucauld-Liancourt,[40] and Ernest de Blosseville[41] – but he also read
the reports published in the Congressional Record on these questions
by the Unitarian minister, Edward Everett, member of Congress for ten
years from 1825, and then four terms as governor of Massachusetts; by
William Clark, of Lewis and Clark fame, who served as Superintendent
of Indian Affairs at St. Louis; by Lewis Cass, Secretary of War in the
Jackson Cabinet; and by John Bell, reporter for The Committee on
Indian Affairs in Congress. Through them, Tocqueville tried to find the
voices of the aboriginals. He did not thereby ask himself how written
and oral histories cross, contradict, or confirm one another. Still it is not
impossible to construct, as he did, a coherent and plausible record of
what was happening to them. Michael Geyer, writing on the extinction
of memory in the twentieth century – a much briefer time span – suggests that "The effectiveness of the vestiges of memory is dependent upon
historical imagination and historical consciousness – not a procession of
images and facts from the past, but the readiness to assure oneself of the
past beyond the existence of witnesses."[42] How that transfer from
memory to history is to be accomplished Geyer does not say, except to
suggest that historical consciousness is a stage in cognition in which we
can know about and judge the past.

The important point is that contact between Europeans and aboriginals uncovered some of the complex, and highly ambivalent, ways that
permitted indirect access to the thoughts each formed about the other.
It is still possible to be naive, of course, and to ascribe, for example, in
acts of contrition, a different, even superior, order of spirituality to aboriginals, and, at the same time, recognize their capacity to adapt to and
survive in hostile environments, until European contact upset their
ecology. Europeans and aboriginals alike imputed, sometimes generously,
at other times, cynically, beliefs to one another, and did so, in some cases,
by expediently assuming that they used concepts that were cognitively
alike. Based on what he observed and was told, Tocqueville records that
some aboriginals spoke about the Great Spirit that governed their lives,

[40] La Rochefoucauld-Liancourt, *Voyage dans les Etats-Unis d'Amérique, fait en 1795, 1796 et 1797*, 8 vols. (Paris: Du Pont, an VII).
[41] Viscount Ernest de Blosseville, translator of John Tanner, *A Narrative of the Captivity and Adventures of John Tanner, during the Thirty Years Residence among the Indians in the Interior of North America* (New York: G. & C. & H. Carvill, 1830). The title of the translation is *Mémoires de John Tanner; ou, Trente Années dans les déserts de l'Amérique du Nord* (Paris: A. Bertrand, 1831).
[42] Michael Geyer, "The Place of the Second World War in German Memory and History," *New German Critique*, no. 71 (Spring-Summer 1997), 7.

and used the same term to describe the Christian God. Individual victims' memories were not that scarce, and were readily available. Red-Jacket, an Iroquois chief who resisted missionary zeal, observed how the existence of multiple Christian sects undermined the power of the Christian God, who should have had, he thought, a single voice. "These matters are difficult for red men to understand," Red-Jacket was purported to have said. "But let my father (the missionary) repeat them to our kin who are the closest neighbors of the white men. And if what he says will prevent the white men from stealing our territories and our herds as they do day by day, my father will be able to return to the red men and find them more open [to the Christian message]."[43]

Thus, if there were some degree of incommensurability between these language-users, the demographic facts were candidly spoken of, and we may see that the story of how the retreat to the western parts of the continent created hardships is not distorted. Observers before, during, and after Tocqueville's travels were more impressed by the vast, general changes in the human landscape than by those that bore upon individual lives. Tocqueville made the most of reports that revealed how Americans, though feeling superior to the aboriginals, did not wholly ridicule them. That "the Indians are attached to their country by the same feelings which bind us to ours," they did not deny. It was as if reds and whites recognized in the other common feelings, so that at least at one level, they could indeed identify with one another. But this recognition of a common humanity was partly negated by the negotiators' allusions to "superstitious notions connected with the alienation of what the Great Spirit gave to their ancestors," and finally, while recognizing their resistance to the sale of land "which contains the bones of our fathers," white negotiators noted the gradual weakening of Indian resistance to their blandishments (I, chap. 18, 351, note 5). The great divide between the two sides to the negotiations was widened, first, by differing conceptions of property – the land held communally by the aboriginals, not by any "one in particular" – in short, private property, the foundation of contract law as Europeans had come to understand it. As important was the consequence of the scattering of the aboriginals. Driven further from their homes, their communal organization was shattered, and with it, the memories of their origins (ibid., 352).

---

[43] *Oeuvres*, I, 215–17. See also, 1327, note 3. Red-Jacket (1758–1830) fought to preserve tribal independence, struggled against the missionaries, and in 1821 was able to have a law passed to protect the reserves.

Unfortunate, but perfectly legal, Tocqueville noted ironically. All exchanges were concluded, first with due regard to the formalities of the law, and, second, following from this, transfers of land were concluded, it was reported – doubtless with due self-regard – with "humanity and expediency," and justified "by the natural superiority allowed to the claims of civilized communities over those of savage tribes" (ibid., 353–54). The superiority was based in large part on the high regard accorded the formation of an English body of law based on precedent over centuries. The English and the Americans not only retained the law of precedents, building up their legal opinions and court decisions on those of their predecessors. On the basis of precedent law, public order was maintained. Hence legality was identified with authority untainted by arbitrary uses of power. So successfully internalized in the population was this reverence for past decisions that nothing was initiated without appeals to the law. Since nearly every political question was resolved into its judicial elements, the language of dispute and conflict was framed accordingly, so much so that it became the lingua franca of American life. Whether themselves men of the law or not, the Americans who dealt with the Indians on land transfers incorporated this ethos and bore down on them without compunction. This species of legality, based on a single and hegemonic explanation of the origins of property, sanctioned the erasure of other notions of property (I, chap. 16, 285).

The brutal penetration of the continent by land-hungry Anglo-Americans drove away the game the Indians needed for life, dissolved their social ties, left few traces of their language, and obliterated their origins; in fact, ended the life of their "nation," leaving memories that exist only "in the recollection of the antiquaries of America and a few of the learned in Europe" (I, chap. 18, 352). As Tocqueville originally put it in one of his letters to his mother in 1831, which contains a description of the forced migration of the Choctaws, often in the same words as those used in the *Democracy*, the dispersal of this people was executed legally, but was still more destructive than any violent engagement. American democracy was showing its true colors as the "nomad families of pioneers" moved west. Oblivious of personal attachments, revealing the "distinctive attributes" of democracy – its "thoughtlessness, violent passions, instability, and anxiety – . . . . [t]he pioneers march in advance of the white race through the American wilderness, like a kind of advance guard assigned the task of driving the Indians ahead of it by destroying the wild life . . . and finally opening the way of civilization following it." He continued, "It is impossible to doubt that not only will a single nation not be left in North America in a hundred years, but not even a single man belonging to the most remarkable of the Indian races."[44] The "sufferings" of the Choctaws, he did not have "the power to portray" (I, chap. 18, 352). More negotiation was needed to dispose of the Cherokees. In 1791, the federal government promised support for the Cherokee occupation of their own lands, even to the point of declaring that the Cherokee people had the right of punishment over any non-native transgression of their territory. From this pledge, the Union moved in 1829 to announce that the Cherokees could expect support only if they took up their lives and moved beyond the Mississippi, "as if," Tocqueville wrote bitingly, "the power which could not grant them protection then would be able to afford it to them hereafter!" (ibid., 366–67, and 366–67, note 24 and note 25).

Tocqueville could not resist citing *in extenso* the protestations of the Cherokees, which reveal their self-understanding as a people possessing a memory of the past, a social organization, including conceptions of property, now under severe threat of destruction. After ascribing to God's will the power reversals that saw a previously strong "red man" fall under the domination of the "white man," we may see in the Cherokee petition to the Congress in November 1829 a verbal strategy that conceded to the Americans what they wanted to hear – namely, that the "red man" was "ignorant and savage," and that the reversal of fortunes that placed him at a disadvantage in his negotiations with the government's commissioners was providential:

> *By the will of our Father in heaven, the Governor of the whole world, . . .* the red man of America has become small, and the white man great and renowned. When the ancestors of the people of the United States first came to the shores of America, they found the red man strong; though he was *ignorant and savage,* yet he received them kindly. . . . At that time the Indian was the lord, and the white man the suppliant. But now the scene has changed. The strength of the red man has become weakness. . . . Thus it has happened to the red man in America. Shall we, who are remnants, share the same fate?
>
> The land on which we stand we have received as an inheritance from our fathers, who possessed it from time immemorial, as a gift from our common Father in heaven. They bequeathed it to us as their children, and we have sacredly kept it, as containing the remains of our beloved men. The right of inheritance we have never ceded nor ever forfeited. . . . We know it is said of late by the state of Georgia and by the Executive of the United States that we have forfeited this right, but we think this is said gratuitously. At what time have we made the

---

[44] Tocqueville to his mother, December 25, 1831, OC 14 (*Correspondance familiale*), 153, 160.

forfeit?. . . . Was it when we were hostile to the United States and took part with
the King of Great Britain during the struggle for independence? If so, why was
not this forfeiture declared in the first treaty of peace between the United States
and our beloved men? Why was not such an article as the following inserted in
the treaty: 'The United States give peace to the Cherokees, but, for the part they
took in the late war, declare them to be but tenants at will, to be removed when
the convenience of the states within those chartered limits they live shall require
it.'? That was the proper time to assume such a possession. But it was not thought
of; nor would our forefathers have agreed to any treaty whose tendency was to
deprive them of their rights and their country (ibid., 367–68, italics added).

But the rights were wiped out along with notions, raised in the petition, of time – the time when the Cherokees were, as they said, the
masters, and the time they lost their power, the time of ancient rights
and the time of treaties, the time of contracts and promises. Formalities
of the law were observed. Treaties were concluded. And the Indians were
taken "by the hand and transport[ed] to a grave far from the land of
their fathers." What was not left open for real debate were the premises
and procedures that deprived the Indians of any claim that they had to
possess their land. Spanish methods, Tocqueville said, were characterized by physical atrocities, yet they did not rob the Indians of all their
rights. As well, in the earliest period of the Spanish contact with the
Indians, their clergy preached conversion, not destruction, on the
grounds that, like all people, the Aztecs had souls and could come to
accept Christianity. Las Casas and Bernadino de Sahagun were led,
through their intense examination of Aztec culture, to question the superiority of their own without finding a way to give it up entirely lest they
risk losing their own identity. Nevertheless the legitimation of the conquest of a people thought to be beyond redemption prevailed. Besides
precedent law, Tocqueville pointed out in his mixed feelings about the
Spanish conquest, that the laws of humanity, invoked by the Americans,
proved to be as effective in the destruction of the Indians as the san-
guinary methods of the Spaniards, who did not totally destroy them
because their labor was useful. "The more I contemplate," Tocqueville
wrote, "the difference between civilized and uncivilized man with regard
to the principles of justice, the more I observe that the former contests
the foundation of those rights, which the latter simply violates" (ibid.,
368 and notes 28–29). The comment is such as to warrant the strongest
suspicion that Tocqueville reversed the conventional meanings of civilized and uncivilized. The supreme law-making bodies in each state now
could exercise their sovereignty, satisfying themselves that their total
power over the Indians was incontestable (ibid., 426). In a last effort,

the Cherokees appealed, first to the Supreme Court, and then to President Andrew Jackson, to end the treaty-breaking "Indian Removal" policy. On March 5, 1831, Chief Justice John Marshall wrote that "A people once numerous, powerful and truly independent . . . have yielded their lands by successive treaties, each of which contains a solemn guarantee of the residue, until they retain no more of their formerly extensive territory than is deemed necessary for their comfortable subsistence." According to the Constitution, the courts were given power to arbitrate disputes between a state and its citizens, and, as well, foreign states, citizens or subjects. The Cherokees were, however, neither a state nor a foreign nation, because as a nation it was not foreign to the United States. Thus, though the Cherokees had rights, the court was not the place to assert them, and a supposed place of redress was never suggested.[45]

Late in December 1831, Tocqueville did some investigating of his own. He met and spoke with Sam Houston, one-time governor of Tennessee, who had gone to live among the Crees in the Arkansas district, where he married the daughter of a Cree chief, and lived, according to Tocqueville, a half-European, half-savage life. Unlike Houston, Tocqueville was unconvinced that the federal government would carry out a generous policy of recognition permitting the Indian nations to live in the upper portion of Arkansas, where their lands would be protected from sale and white settlement of any kind. There, Houston predicted, they would gradually leave their savage state and become "civilized." And, among them, the Cherokees, who cultivated the land and who, he said, alone among the Native Americans, had a written language, were the most advanced. The same was not true of the northern and western tribes, who would simply be driven further and further west as the white population migrated.[46]

Focus on the Cherokees continued. On March 3, 1832, in *Worcester v. Georgia*, Marshall found that the state of Georgia had illegally arrested two Congregationalist missionaries within an Indian nation protected under the treaty clause of the Constitution: "The Cherokee Nation . . . is a distinct community, occupying its own territory . . . in which the law

---

[45] Marshall's decision in *Cherokee Nation v. State of Georgia*, 30 U.S. (1831). Cited in Samuel Carter III, *Cherokee Sunset* (New York: Doubleday & Company, 1976), p.113. See also Theodore W. Allen, *The Invention of the White Race.* Vol. 1: *Racial Oppression and Social Control* (London and New York: Verso Press, 1994), pp. 33 and 243, note 45.

[46] *Oeuvres*, I, 258–63.

of Georgia can have no right to enter but with the assent of the Cherokees."[47] Associate Justice Joseph Story, whose *Commentaries on the Constitution of the United States* Tocqueville read in preparing for his interviews, also cast a futile vote in favor of the Cherokees. Story concluded that they had no future now that removal was a certain prospect, and was even more scathing in his denunciation of American expropriation:

> an absolute dominion over the whole territories afterwards occupied by them, not in virtue of any conquest of, or cessation by, the Indian natives, but as a right acquired by discovery. . . . The title of the Indians was not treated as a right of property and dominion, but as a mere right of occupancy. As infidels, heathens and savages, they were not allowed to possess the prerogatives belonging to absolute, sovereign, and independent nations. The territory over which they wandered, and which they used for their temporary and fugitive purposes, was in respect to Christians, deemed as if it were inhabited only by brute animals.[48]

Thus, within a year, two decisions. The first denied the existence of a Cherokee nation vis-à-vis the United States, thus granting to the latter the right to treat it not as an equal. The second, however, denied Georgia the rights given the United States. The opportunity for enforcement or non-enforcement was open. In the event, President Jackson did not put an end to removal.

As Tocqueville generally saw the workings of the law, both the judiciary and the citizenry agreed that unresolved political questions could be transformed into judicial ones (I, chap. 16, 290). Yet, in the process, force was the final arbiter. The aboriginals were both the source of their own eventual disappearance and the victims of an alien culture (I, chap. 17, 302). History recorded both human pity and pitilessness, but partook of neither. It revealed ambiguities only for those who wanted to see them. Tocqueville compared two kinds of barbaric societies. The Native Americans, a conquered people, lacked what other barbaric societies – for instance, conquering societies, like those invading Rome – had pos-

---

[47] Cited in William G. McLoughlin, *Cherokee Renascence in the New Republic* (Princeton: Princeton University Press, 1986), p. 444.

[48] Cited in Robert A. Williams Jr., "The Algebra of Federal Indian Law: The Hard Trail of Decolonizing and Americanizing the White Man's Indian Jurisprudence," *Wisconsin Law Review*, no. 2 (1986), 256. Story apparently believed that Tocqueville did not acknowledge his indebtedness to his own work. See *OC* 7 (*Correspondance étrangère d'Alexis de Tocqueville*), 80–81, note 2. But Tocqueville held Story in high esteem, not only saying how much he had benefited from his work, but apparently also doing his best to have him named a correspondent of the Institut français. Tocqueville to Sumner, October 28, 1839, ibid., 80–81.

sessed, the will to raise "themselves to civilization by degrees and by their own efforts":

> Whenever they derived knowledge from a foreign people, they stood towards them in the relation of conquerors, and not of a conquered nation. When the conquered nation is enlightened and the conquerors are half-savage, as in the invasion of the Roman Empire by the northern nations, or that of China by the Mongols, the power that victory bestows upon the barbarian is sufficient to keep up his importance among civilized men and permit him to rank as their equal until he becomes their rival. . . .
>
> [W]hen the side on which the physical force lies also possesses an intellectual superiority, the conquered party seldom becomes civilized. . . . [I]t is the misfortune of Indians to be brought into contact with a civilized people, who are also (it must be owed) the most grasping nation on the globe, while they are still semi-barbarian; to find their masters in their instructors, and to receive knowledge and oppression at the same time (I, chap. 17, 359–69).

Though he was hardly without sympathy for the Cherokees, Tocqueville saw them as a wounded people, but he was obviously not fully aware of the extent to which they had in fact by efforts of their own tried to assert their rights in the American Union. The possible exceptions to the general fate awaiting the Native Americans were the *métis*, who lived uncomfortably *between* two worlds, and, in addition, were divided by competing Christian sects.[49]

Tocqueville had more to say. His conjectural historical description of the territories and aboriginal inhabitants of North America stands in sharp contrast with what he took to be the almost paradisiacal quality of the West Indies and South America upon which he threw a momentary and perfunctory glance. Concealed below the paradise of Tocqueville's imagination, that "enchanting region," which "seemed prepared to satisfy the wants or contribute to the pleasures of man" (I, chap. 1, 21), he speculated, were the traces of even older human groups, now barely remembered. That was not a problem he set himself. Paradise, he thought, was a timeless present. It could not bear the weight of reflection. Similarly or identically, primitive societies existed in a time frame of repetition. Thus far, Tocqueville's tone is distancing. The more frustratingly, irrecoverable, past of the earliest peoples of the northern half of the North American continent induced in Tocqueville a more intense reaction: Their complete disappearance, and the total effacement of memory itself, attested to the fact that "the most durable monument

---

[49] *Oeuvres*, I, 404–06.

of human labor is that which recalls the wretchedness and nothingness
of man" (I, chap. 1, 26).

The origin of the judgment is clearly biblical (see Genesis 3: 17–19).
Here, unlike the situation in the southern portions of the continent
in the pre-Columbian period, which Tocqueville vaguely saw as one
unmarked by a laboring people, labor did make a difference to memory,
because the endurance of labor marked the duration of time. But there
was so little left of Native-American labor to mark their past – a few
utensils and strange instruments all molded by laboring hands. Whatever glory these people had once possessed was not memorialized in a
written language, scarcely an echo remained.[50] They had forgotten their
past, because of their dispersal and the resulting obscuring of their traditions (I, chap. 18, 345–46). But more decisive, in Tocqueville's theory,
was that without the "constant and regular labor that tillage requires,"
a slippage of memory somehow occurs (I, chap. 18, 356).[51] Was the fate
of these past peoples to be repeated and the human condition condemned
to negativity? Yes, for them, but not for those, at least not in those stark
terms, whose labor permanently left more visible traces. The former were
the victims of an almost total collective amnesia (I, chap. 18, 346).
Memory seemed, however, not to have fallen into total oblivion, at least
for the Cherokees who, as we saw, appealed in 1829 to a "time immemorial" when they peaceably had a right of inheritance to their lands (I,
chap. 18, 368). Moreover, it was also a fact that they were not averse
to cultivating the soil, driven to it by destitution, yet driven from it by
oppression (I, chap. 18, 364). One must wonder then whether their
memory had not been revived by the very contacts with the Europeans
who were depriving them of the right to exist; if so, it would be more
difficult to brush them aside as a people without a past. Tocqueville, in
fact, drew back slightly. For lurking beneath his rather easy dismissal of
an aboriginal loss of memory were his many references to their suffering. One can only observe that he sensed that there was no quick answer
as to how persons and collectivities deal with the memory of pain. Do
they keep it alive or do they forget?

---

[50] Tocqueville recognized that the Native Americans had a complex spoken language, but
he makes no unambiguous mention of a written one. See Appendix C in *Democracy in
America*, II, 354–55 in which he refers to the literature on the subject he consulted, he
admits, superficially. His other references appear in vol. I, 23 note 16, where he notes
that no existing studies had established firm evidence of the origins of the North
American aboriginal languages.

[51] Cf. Tocqueville's conversation with Sam Houston, who believed that the Mississippi
Valley had been the home of a culture more civilized than that of the Native Americans
of his own day. *Oeuvres*, I, 261.

To rescue himself from the ambiguous effects of memory, and to legitimate the displacement of the Native Americans, he used the standard Lockean view that by their very nature they had "occupied" the land "without possessing it." He did so uneasily, but at the same time it was clear to him that the contact between the aboriginal peoples and the Anglo-Americans exposed the primitive technology of the first, driving them to concede and to submit, at supreme cost to their way of life. Well that he did. At least he admitted lack of substantive knowledge. It is only now that historians can speak with some authority about the nature of Native American economic life, which did not exclude their concern for subsistence, the importance of agriculture for groups far enough south to cultivate and harvest more than 100 frost-free days, the practice of exchange, the gendered division of labor, along with the lack of private land ownership.[52] One may point to the sixteenth- and seventeenth-century exclusion by Anglo-Americans of non-Europeans from the land on the ground that property rightly belonged only to those who cultivated it as a deep-seated source of psychological resistance to differing, but just as likely misunderstood, notions of possession.[53] This stance was shared by most Europeans, including Tocqueville, who said that "the territory of a hunting nation is ill defined; it is the common property of the tribe and belongs to no one in particular, so that individual interests are not concerned in protecting any part of it" (I, chap. 18, 351).[54]

---

[52] See the opening essay by Neal Salisbury in *The Cambridge Economic History of the United States*, eds. Stanley L. Engerman and Robert E. Gallman, 3 vols. (Cambridge: Cambridge University Press, 1997). Vol. I: The Colonial Era.

[53] On this question, see Patricia Seed, *Ceremonies of Possession in Europe's Conquest of the New World, 1492–1640* (Cambridge: Cambridge University Press, 1995).

[54] A recent [December 11, 1997] Canadian Supreme Court decision on Native Canadian land rights in northern British Columbia, *Delgamuukw v. British Columbia*, 1010. strongly suggests the need for a reconceptualization of ownership and possession. In the Supreme Court judgment is found the notion of a spectrum respecting the "degree of connection with the land," ranging from aboriginal rights amounting to "practices, customs and traditions integral to the aboriginal culture of the group" that claims "the right but where the use and occupation of the land is insufficient to support a claim to title"; to middle-type activities, taking place on land, and even to a particular piece of land ("a site-specific right to engage in a particular activity"); to aboriginal title itself conferring "more than the right to engage in site-specific activities and which are aspects of the practices, customs and traditions of distinctive aboriginal cultures." Important in the decision is the argument that aboriginal title rested, from a theoretical standpoint, on "a prior occupation of the land by aboriginal peoples and out of the relationship between the common law and pre-existing systems of aboriginal law. Aboriginal title crystallized at the time sovereignty [the assertion by the Crown of its sovereignty] was asserted." The conventional notion of possession goes back to Locke's notion of property as coming into being when the first man who labored to cut the first sod of land made it his own.

The incredibly complex bundle of concepts, theories, half-theories, and rationalizations surrounding the nature of possession and property was a topic that had been – and continues to this day – tossed about ever since the explorers-cum-conquerors from the maritime powers of Europe crossed oceans, east and west, there to meet peoples whom they regarded as related to but different from themselves. Anthony Pagden reminds us that over a period of some 300 years, the Europeans built the New World by commanding accepted ways to think of the nature and moral status of Native Americans and of the African slaves imported for their labor. They did so by distinguishing between different kinds of human beings, with one moral code governing themselves and another for governing non-Europeans. What they could not easily do, Pagden maintains, was to take in fully the difficult notion that while they had their own history, peoples alien to it also had their own.[55]

But what could this mean? We might seek clarification in yet another way. First, the modern notions of history we incontrovertibly believe and argue and take credit for are rooted in the way Western civilization developed, and the ways we began to evolve historical theories to plot the past and at the same time to assume that we had discovered the only way to see it. How these theories could be accommodated to, or rather make room for, other countings of historical time, was baffling, because they were simply not understood, or were, on the slightest consideration, set aside as mistaken. Tocqueville was only one of many, including Marx, who thought non-European societies to be ahistorical. The other face of this conceptualization of the past, of course, was to impose European notions of history on these non-historical peoples, either to begin the process of explaining why they stood outside history before their lives crossed those of Europeans, or refusing them a place in a future history unless they conformed to European historical time.[56] When Tocqueville

---

[55] See Anthony Pagden, *Lords of all the World: Ideologies of Empire in Spain, Britain and France c.1500–c.1800* (New Haven: Yale University Press, 1995). On the same subject, but attacked from another angle, see V. J. Kiernan, *The Lords of Human Kind: Black Man, Yellow Man, and White Man in an Age of Empire* (1969; reprint New York: Columbia University Press, 1986). As Kiernan sees it, the European or White fear of the Yellow Peril and the Black Peril, obscured the fact that the non-European continents were suffering from the White Peril – in other words, the imperializing and colonizing domination of Europe.

[56] Cf. Pierre Clastres, *Chronicle of the Guayaki Indians*, trans. Paul Auster (Cambridge, Mass.: Zone Books, 1998). Clastres's book, which first appeared some twenty-five years ago, offers a discussion of how the Guayaki in Paraguay, in his view, were forced into history and in the process were destroyed.

spoke about and denied the existence of aboriginal memory, he confirmed to himself, as a historically conscious person, that forgetfulness was not in the cards for moderns. Thoroughly historicized, he did not find unimaginable the idea that there might be alternative histories. What was inconceivable was that there could be an alternative historicity itself. Non-linearity was for post-Enlightenment Europeans hard to grasp, and those who, like the aboriginals, failed to grasp linear temporality, were destined to be left behind to perish. Almost 200 or so years later, as time in its Western measuring mode appears to make concessions to other time countings, the question is whether historicized minds can encompass Ashis Nandy's rather mystifying declaration "that history can be dealt with from outside history,"[57] and whether, as the future is contemplated – and Tocqueville, like his contemporaries, linked past and future as unidirectional and inexorable – one can do so without asking if the ideas of progress of civilization are chimerical, and, indeed, whether Western notions of history are themselves conceptually restrictive. The answer must be no. Although the notion of time in aboriginal America, like time in South Asia, as Ashis Nandy tells us, may not have been calculated as past, present, and future in any firm way, history is in those cultures inseparable from myths and legends and enjoys no autonomous status. This does not mean that their notions of time's arrow reduces their symbolic power in a world that has become sensitive to the conquest of non-Western cultures.[58]

By the seventeenth century, the intricate turns and twists in the debate among Spanish theologians were, as Pagden tells us, theologically spent.[59] By the eighteenth century, several of the compelling questions

---

[57] Ashis Nandy, "History's Forgotten Doubles," *History and Theory. Studies in the Philosophy of History.* Theme Issue 34, no. 2 (1995), 44–66. Citation from 50.

[58] In an earlier study, *Traditions, Tyranny and Utopias* (Delhi: Oxford University Press, 1987), Ashis Nandy, drawing examples mainly from Asian, and specifically Asian-Indian examples, and relying on much psychoanalytic theory, writes in a typical passage, "The rejection of history to protect self-esteem and ensure survival is often a response to the structure of cognition. . . . For the moderns, history has always been the unfolding of a theory of progress, a serialized expression of a telos which, by definition, cannot be shared by communities on the lower rungs of the ladder of history" (p. 48). In his foreword to Nandy's book, Roger Garaudy, by characterizing Western countries as sick, presents as stereotyped a view of Western cultures as the cliched depiction of non-Western cultures as childish.

[59] For the disputes on the question in Spanish theology, see Anthony Pagden, "Dispossessing the Barbarians: The Language of Spanish Thomism and the Debate over the Property Rights of the American Indians," in *The Languages of Political Theory in Early-Modern Europe*, ed. Anthony Pagden (Cambridge: Cambridge University Press,

that had agitated sixteenth-century Spaniards, such as *dominium*, which
consisted of the various ways in which persons could be said to own
property and which problematized outright dispossession, were plucked
from their theological contexts. In this instance, Istvan Hont is our
guide.[60] The key figure in the European, and soon in American, thought
on property relations is, of course, Locke. Samuel Pufendorf's notion of
negative community, in which there were no property rights, echoed
Locke's rejection of the notion that the beginnings of private property
and human history were temporally simultaneous. While there were no
formal grounds for dominion in the negative community, it was nevertheless allowed as having potential force. For Jean Barbeyrac, the
justification for land occupied was the capacity (physical or otherwise,
Barbeyrac does not say) to cultivate it. But for us the important point is
that Pufendorf claimed, as others did, that the communal forms of ownership came to an end once the cultivators of the land achieved two
things: agreement to establish full private property and agreement
on the notion that communal property conduced more to conflict
than did private property, the virtue of which ensured a more just correspondence between individual capacity and reward. A couple of hard
residues survived: One, the premise that civil societies by definition were
the only societies that were based upon property; two, that *dominium*
was not the same as possession, since the first, not the second, implied
that the person having it could dispose of it through various forms of
exchange.

Tocqueville did read some of this literature, but selectively. Pufendorf
he saw (along with Grotius) as dealing with the development of international law, but as well with the fact that in civilized nations guaran-
teeing citizenship, some vestiges of barbarism remained.[61] The abbé
Raynal, who called for a slave revolution, and Diderot, who wrote some
of the more provocative accounts and theories of the savage state,
escaped his attention. Neither did he follow up Rousseau's thoughts on
property, which were Lockean, and where he would have found an

1987), 79–98. The central thinker in the debate was the Spanish Dominican, Francisco
Vitoria, professor of Theology at the University of Salamanca. In *The Devastation of
the Indies: A Brief Account*, trans. Herman Briffault (New York: Seabury Press, 1974),
Bartolomé de Las Casas revealed the nature of the systematic destruction.

[60] Istvan Hont, "The Language of Sociability and Commerce: Samuel Pufendorf and
the Theoretical Foundations of the 'Four-Stages Theory,'" in Anthony Pagden, ed., *The
Languages of Political Theory in Early Modern Europe*, 253–76.

[61] OC 16 (*Mélanges*), 232.

endorsement of cultivation of the land as the conventionally given pre-requisite for private ownership. Rousseau also famously deplored the practice of "usurping" territories held in common. "When Núñez de Balboa on the seashore," he asked, "took possession of the Pacific Ocean and of the whole of South America in the name of the crown of Castille, was this sufficient to dispossess all the inhabitants, and exclude from it all the princes of the world."[62] Wattell's classic text, published early in the nineteenth century, was also quite probably not known to Tocqueville, but he would not have quite agreed with its dictum that human beings had an obligation to cultivate the land given to them by God, and that if they did not, others, more industrious than themselves – the reference to Locke's industrious and rational man is transparent – could justifiably take it from them.[63] Rather, Tocqueville saw the problem not as one to be determined by appeals to God, but rather to history. Montesquieu, whom Tocqueville read carefully, took a more generous view in his brief notes on Native Americans, their nomadism, their disputes over uncultivated land. Most important was, first, that the division of land was the foundation of civil laws, and, second, that where there was no such division, social institutions were governed by "*mores* rather than *laws*. In such nations the old men, who remember things past, have great authority; one cannot be distinguished by one's goods there, but by arms and by counsel."[64]

Guizot's studies of the rise of civilization in France and Europe raised some further questions for Tocqueville on the nature of property in a non-European setting and, most of all, how the rules of property were laid down in parts of Europe, particularly France in the feudal period. The gist of the latter was that vassalage was the institutionalized means for the transfer of property from one generation to another, and that it presupposed notions of private ownership, though it was subject to the fulfillment of obligations, in the form of services, including warrierdom, from one vassal to another. Even more fundamental, Guizot declared, accepting a now generally accepted theory, was that the earth had to be worked, that its value rested on cultivation. An act of injustice would be committed should the possessor be denied the right to transfer land to

---

[62] Jean-Jacques Rousseau, *The Social Contract*, ed. and trans. Victor Gourevitch (Cambridge: Cambridge University Press, 1997), Bk. 1, chap. 9.

[63] M. de Wattell, *Le Droit de gens ou principe de la loi naturelle* (Paris, 1820), I, p. 113. Cited in Pagden, "Dispossessing the Barbarian," 92.

[64] Montesquieu, *Spirit of the Laws*, Part 3, Bk. 18, chaps. 9–17. Quotation from p. 291. Italics in the original.

his heirs. Indeed, such a right was a common practice in all times and in all places, and was one of the sources of stability and order. The right of inheritance, Guizot added significantly, was not confined to land. Hunting rights were equally passed in perpetuity from one generation to another. But he did not pursue the point. His major aim was to show that feudalism and Christianity between them advanced civilization up to a certain point, after which they stifled innovation, until the logjam was finally overcome by the irresistible force of the Third Estate that broke through the crumbling crust of the *ancien régime*.[65] Tocqueville most probably found in Guizot's lectures a basis for a general theory of civilization that, while it ineluctably marginalized primitive cultures, did not obviate responsibility on the part of those who called themselves civilized to have an open and, if possible, sympathetic understanding of earlier forms of social organization.

While Tocqueville liked to speak of the *moeurs* of a people, meaning the opinions, notions, and ideas that shaped their mental and moral habits, in order to understand how they formed political institutions (I, chap. 17, 310), he did not extend the term to aboriginal peoples. The testimony he gathered, however, was far less clear-cut. In fact, he asked about the forms of Indian government, and was told that it was patriarchical, although there were tribes that had begun, after contact with Europeans, to elect their chiefs and had also begun to use corporal punishment for theft, while murder remained a matter of tribal vengeance to the death. For Tocqueville, these features of aboriginal justice properly placed Native Americans outside the boundaries of a civil society, and the attributes of any kind of political association seemed to him to be non-existent.[66] As he moved away from the differences between hunting and gathering and agricultural societies to consider the unique features of the Native Americans, he found in them most of all a natural aristocratic bearing and a "freedom" from civilized but "incoherent"

---

[65] "Rédaction d'une grande partie des leçons de M. Guizot... depuis 11 Avril 1829 jusqu'au 29 Mai 1830," in OC 16 (*Mélanges*), especially 479, 482, 484, 486, 491, 493, 516–17.

[66] *Oeuvres*, I, 260, conversation with Houston. For a modern treatment of Cherokee political and economic life at the beginning of the nineteenth century, see William G. McLoughlin, *Cherokee Renaissance in the New Republic*, especially pp. 284–98. Between 1820 and 1823, what McLoughlin called a political revolution, allowed the Cherokees to create a bicameral legislature, a court system, and an electoral system, which replaced the decentralized town government under locally chosen headmen. Their laws were versions of white political structures. And in McLoughlin's words, they had "moved from *gemeinschaft* to *gesellschaft*, and from an oral to a written system of order." The Cherokee dilemma was that "in order to survive as red men, they were told they must become more and more like white men."

notions of evil and good. These he extolled, comparing them in Rousseauian manner with the barbarism of advanced cultures, where servility and poverty in the inferior classes created a psychology of humiliation (I, chap. 1, 24–26. Cf. I, chap. 17, 301–02).[67]

Tocqueville accepted as inevitable the physical and mental extinction of the Indians once they encountered civilized societies. He was unable to offer any idea of how Native Americans could present any lasting resistance to the power of the immigrants to exercise "tyranny," which reduced them to even greater disorder and made them "less civilized" and "more barbarous" than before (I, chap. 18, 346). Their only alternative was "war or civilization; in other words, they must either destroy the Europeans or become their equals" (I, chap. 18, 355). They could do neither, and those of mixed race were doomed to live on the margins of white society "in oppression and destitution" (I, chap. 18, 368). That their equality is still resisted well into this century is to be seen in the fact that for the most part their politics, both internal and in their relationship with the federal government, were set down and dictated by the Department of the Interior in the 1930s. "These Indian Reorganization Act constitutions," Jon Elster comments, "vary little across tribes, typically providing for a chief executive (tribal chairman), a small unicameral legislature (tribal council), and a non-independent judiciary (some judicial powers were vested in the tribal council). The U.S. government retained the right to approve any changes in the constitutional form. Later developments indicate that these constitutions 'work,' in terms of promoting economic development, only when they coincide with the pre-existing unwritten constitutions of the tribes."[68] If any change had been

---

[67] François-René de Chateaubriand came to this conclusion earlier. See, for example, his *Atala, René* (Paris: Garnier-Flammarion, 1964). American writers of the period, including James Fenimore Cooper, made the same point. Chateaubriand was more forthright in acknowledging that "it is clear that the *savages* were far advanced in that civilization which involved the combination of ideas." See *Chateaubriand's Travels in America* (1827), trans. Richard Switzer (Lexington: University of Kentucky Press, 1969), p. 120. On Indian land uses, see Richard White and William Cronon, "Ecological Change and Indian-White Relations," in *Handbook of North American Indians*, 4, 417–29. On the differences between Tocqueville and Chateaubriand, see Eva Doran, "Two Men and a Forest: Chateaubriand, Tocqueville and the American Wilderness," *Essays in French Literature*, no. 13 (1976), 44–61. In addition, see Martin Thom, *Republics, Nations and Tribes* (London and New York: Verso, 1995), pp. 119–49 for the American travels of Chateaubriand, as well of those who preceded and followed him.

[68] Jon Elster, "Ways of Constitution-Making," in *Democracy's Victory and Crisis*, ed. Axel Hadenius (Cambridge: Cambridge University Press, 1997), pp. 127–28. Elster's source is S. Cornell and J. P. Kalt, "Where Does Economic Development Really Come From? Constitutional Rule among the Modern Sioux and Apaché." Harvard Working Project on American Indian Economic Development (1993).

effected, it was in the fact that the U.S. government recognized that the tribes did in fact have unwritten constitutions and that they could not be ignored when imposing one from outside. But, as we have seen, despite the brutal treatment, United States law did not totally shut out the stubborn fact of a culture that had a right to exist and that they had integral communities before Europeans "discovered" them.

European civilization alone could escape the near total oblivion that was the fate of primitive societies. There was scarcely any ambiguity in Tocqueville's judgment:

> Civilization is the result of a long social process, which takes place in the same spot and is handed down from one generation to another, each one profiting by the experience of the last. Of all nations, those submit to civilization with the most difficulty who habitually live by the chase. Pastoral tribes, indeed, often change their place of abode; but they follow a regular order in their migrations and often return to their old stations, while the dwelling of the hunter varies with that of the animals he pursues (I, chap. 18, 357).

The time for theology had passed, but, as we noted earlier, it was not far from the minds of a number of people, including Tocqueville. If he makes no allusion to the Cain and Abel story, where we find the Lord God taking the side of pastoral, not agricultural labor, it is nevertheless useful to bring it to mind now, as we continue to explore how Europeans generally, and Tocqueville particularly, saw beginnings and ends, barbarism and civilization. It is striking that while Genesis speaks of nomadic and semi-nomadic tribes, it makes no mention of hunters, who were assumed by Tocqueville and others in the previous century, most notably Adam Smith, to stand, if not at the very beginning of organized human life, still not that distant from its origins. Though claiming to explain the origins of human knowledge, the Hebrew Bible leaves in semi-darkness the state before knowledge. It also speaks of the presence in Eden of the tiller of the soil and the gatherer, but not of the hunter (Genesis 2: 15–16): "The Lord God took the man and put him in the Garden of Eden to till it and keep it. And the Lord God commanded the man, 'You may freely eat of every tree of the garden.'" The tillage, it may be surmised, was meant to be of a most elementary kind, since in Eden the trees could not have demanded much tending, nor is there any hint that the animals and birds created by the Lord God were either tended or eaten. In his post-lapsarian state, man is condemned to work the earth. It is a degraded state to which man is henceforth subjected. And when the agriculturist, Cain, brings his offerings to God, they are rejected in favor of the gifts from Abel, the shepherd. The Lord God obviously prefers the simpler life of the shepherd to that of the farmer, who, confronted by the stubbornness of the soil, must now use his mind to make it yield its fruits. If it was the Lord God's preference to keep as much knowledge to himself as possible, it did not accord with the conjectural history that placed workers of the soil at the top of an ascending scale of civilization.[69]

Proto-anthropological and historical conjecture took over from biblical conjecture. With or without the Biblical markers of time, conjecture was the name of the game, as, for example, when Rousseau insisted when he laid down the gains and losses of civilization's advance over primitivism. Jean Starobinski long ago compared the loss of Eden with Rousseau's account of the origins of inequality,[70] but he does not mention the Cain and Abel story, which figures prominently in Rousseau's essay, *On the Origin of Language*.[71] There, Rousseau twice calls Cain a farmer and once refers to Abel as a herdsman. Moses, in Rousseau's reading, frowned on agriculture, "ascribing its invention to a reprobate, and having God reject its fruits."[72] God was right in seeing in Cain "the bad effects of his art. The author of Genesis saw further than Herodotus."[73] Savage and barbarian were not the same. The first is a hunter, the second, a herdsman. Only the tiller of the soil creates society and becomes a civil man, and as soon as he enters that state he is loaded down with labor and misery and proceeds to transform the world into a desert, the end point and endgame of social union. In Rousseau's account, some point is hypothetically reached when the loss of innocence and indolence – the natural state of humankind – is registered – that is, when pre-humans, hence, pre-cognitive creatures, become human. The point of contact making possible the transition from pre-human to human, from pre-knowledge to knowledge, was metaphorically the result of "the touch of a finger [that] shifted the globe's axis into line with the universe."[74] The hypothesis was that these creatures came together instead of continuing to live exposed to the elements. This was a stage in human life that registered the desire to satisfy needs beyond biological survival, needs so pressing that humans were forced to speak. The mystery of pre-civil life

---

[69] I owe much of this interpretation to Mark Glouberman, but the final version is mine.

[70] Jean Starobinski, *Jean-Jacques Rousseau. Transparency and Obstruction*, trans. Arthur Goldhammer (Chicago: University of Chicago Press, 1988), pp. 290, 295, 297.

[71] Jean-Jacques Rousseau, *On the Origin of Language*, trans. John H. Moran and Alexander Gode (Chicago and London: University of Chicago Press, 1986), p. 34 and note 38.

[72] Ibid., p. 37.   [73] Ibid., p. 38.   [74] Ibid., pp. 38–39.

would, however, largely remain a mystery. Still, he conjectured that togetherness and growing awareness of others created in successive stages a more mature civil society – mature, being in these terms, a more conflict-ridden, because, competitive society – a society in which comparisons, while bringing technological innovations, also brought into being the unsocial sociability behavior of a civil society. In Rousseau's world, to enlarge the community's capacity for communication by calling on it to extend loyalties and to appreciate competing sets of self-interest was not only too much to ask, but was surely destructive, since its very life was constituted by the corruption of morals and opinions that could not be overcome, and, moreover, narrowed its focus even more.

Against the popular opinion of his day, Rousseau suggested that surplus populations from barren lands peopled fertile territories, rather than the reverse, observing at the same time that, if true, it was strange that barren lands could produce a surplus population. He could not get beyond these puzzles. On the one hand, there is his contempt for the "civilized" climate produced by "the workshop of the world." On the other, there is his disparagement of the undeveloped Lapps and Eskimos who, he says, were so brutalized by their hostile climate that they could not form any real social union. By raising the question of the migrations to the fertile areas of the Middle East, he put on notice, so to speak, how to explain the migrations of peoples from the civilized parts of Europe to the lands of the rest of the globe. Once they had become sedentary, some civilized peoples left their settled conditions to occupy lands whose people were assumed, because of their aboriginal condition, to be, according to Rousseau, without speech. But, of course, he was mistaken.

What needs to be remembered, despite Rousseau's indebtedness to Genesis, is not only that we are presented with Cain as the ancestor of sedentary – that is, settled, culture – but that Lamech, the great-grandson of Cain, had sons who, as shepherds, musicians, and smiths, were linked to the city. Of these, musicians, carrying the stories of a people, do indeed figure in the stored memories of American aboriginals, who in fact did not live in cities, just as they did not in the biblical and Homeric myths. Thus, their memories could not be dismissed as the basis, in the instance, as we have seen, of the Cherokees, for their claims to land and justice. In any event, speech was not absent from Indian culture when the Europeans descended on the Americas as they soon found out. Rousseau's speechless universe existed in "the night of time" that could not be pierced. America's aboriginals, as seen by Europeans, were far from the first "self-born" people about whom little was known, but who were in Rousseau's anthropology without speech.[75]

Tocqueville set himself a slightly more tractable problem. The turning point from pre-human to human culture he saw as occurring when two cultures clashed, not as, in Rousseau's conjectures, when the sources of social conflict arose from within one culture. Tocqueville focused on the contact point that brought two cultures face to face. Primitivism was not to be despised, but it survived, in Tocqueville's mind, at best at the edges of history. He tended to stress its anomalous and ambiguous nature, robust and fragile at the same time, but as an essentially vanishing stage in human time. Yet as long as the aboriginals survived, their claims to their memories through oral tales, while not on a par with written records – much the preferred, because presumably more reliable, survivals of the past – had to be conceded some degree of plausibility. The sticking point, then, as now, is whether, even if first occupancy could be determined by invoking the phrase, "from time immemorial," it by itself overrode the human urge to perfecting knowledge, along the spectrum of which a sedentary social organization was deemed to be superior to a non-sedentary one. However, Tocqueville did not fully accept as a model for America Guizot's contrast between the conquering but superior and civilizing Romans who subdued the inferior and barbaric Gauls. In Guizot's lecture on the conquest, which Tocqueville preserved in his notes, we find references to the growth of Roman Marseilles likened to that of Boston, Baltimore, and New York: "In the first, as in the latter, may be seen a superior and victorious race developing in the midst of an inferior and vanquished people."[76] He did not take exception to Guizot's general argument, but he abhorred large cities as festering pools of riots, rabble, and revolution (I, chap. 17, 299–300, note 1). He had already described Manchester as "a foul drain," from which "the greatest stream of human industry flows out to fertilize the world. From this vile sewer, pure gold flows. Here humanity attains its most complete development and its most brutish; here civilization works its miracles, and civilized man is turned back almost into a savage."[77]

After the experience of 1789, reinforced by his more immediate memories of 1830, he could not regard the modern city as a wholly benign

---

[75] Ibid., pp. 33–42.   [76] "Séance du 22 mai 1830," in *OC* 16 (*Mélanges*), 525.
[77] *Oeuvres*, I, 504.

template of civilization, even if it were a historical necessity. Both as a post-revolutionary and as a Romantic, he could not unreservedly accept classical republicanism, as had the revolutionaries who had imposed a regime of terror in the name of virtue. He endorsed Rousseau's ideal of citizenship, which came to life for him in the small township and in the civic will of country people whose public actions formed the basis for a sound republicanism.[78] He summed this up best when he compared the lack of participation in the government of Florence and the cities of ancient Greece, which ruled over subjects in its extended territory, with the tumult and passions of a great manufacturing and commercial city and the representative democracy of an entire area in which the sense of order and morality of rural life served as a counterweight against the violence of urban populations, while their representatives in turn enlightened their fellow deputies from the countryside.[79] The upshot is that his first favorable contrast between barbarism and civilization, in which his admiration for the city at its center was unqualified, collapsed somewhat under the weight of the burdens that civilization brought with it.

Tocqueville's concept of civilization explicitly incorporated memory as one of its key elements. Though social theories had their roots in the Old – the first immigrants "could not found a state of things originating solely in themselves" (I, chap. 2, 46) – these theories took flight only when transplanted to the New, where liberated from the Old, they could be identified with a new beginning and shifted the balance from the past. The present intruded itself, as if surrounded by the aura of a "spectacle" – as an intentional moment of decision. Thus a new beginning pronounced itself as an act of will, of a freedom that rose above the past that had not prepared it (I, chap. 2, 26). The present moment and the momentous had truly become one in the New World. And the phenomenon continued to repeat itself, as wave after wave of new immi-

[78] After the Revolution of 1848, he stood again for a country seat in Normandy. Chapter 4 of his *Souvenirs* rides on waves of sentiment for his ancient ancestors, the rural population as "one vast family," the feelings of "affection" shown him by his supporters, and revulsion for the "demagogues of Paris." See OC 12 (*Souvenirs*), 106–14. However much he feared the city as a crucible of disorder, he could not ignore, indeed, he focused on the modern commercial and industrial city, especially the port cities of America, as the points around which the economic and political future of the American Union depended. See especially I, chap. 18, 405–09. He found no contradiction, arguing that the salubrious effects of township and state governments worked their way into and helped negate the chaotic tendencies of urbanized life.

[79] "Remarques générales sur la république florentine et principalement sur ce qui distingue ce qu'on nomme la démocratie de Florence des démocraties de nos jours," OC 16 (*Mélanges*), 548.

grants, "like a deluge of men arising unabatedly, and daily driven onwards by the hand of God," (I, chap. 18, 414) crossed the ocean and moved into the vast interior of the continent, virginal, waiting to be taken, "as if it had just risen from beneath the waters of the Deluge" (I, chap. 17, 302).

Tocqueville took their side. His history and theory of the coming of civilization, and particularly the emergence of democracy as the instrument of greater justice for humanity, does not ignore the sufferings of Native Americans who, in colossal numbers, were fated to slip away from the imperatives of European culture. Yet lodged within his narrative of the pain of their survivors was the discovery that they had other notions of time and memory, and that they indeed fastened upon European notions to prepare their claims for redress – an ironic development when we remember how firmly Tocqueville described the unbridgeable chasm between European and non-European cultures. This legacy has been transmitted to their children, but also significantly to white Americans. From their earliest contacts with Indians, the Anglo-Americans wanted to, but could not entirely, free themselves from the traces of their own raging history.

There were two beginnings for Tocqueville. One, the Native American, proved to be a false start, though indeed it was not one, but a series of starts, he believed, traceable to a distant prehistoric past. They became fragile on contact with the powerfully technologized Europeans. The other beginning was created by Anglo-Americans. The New England township tried to exist, so to speak, by itself, making itself immune from contact with, and indifferent to, the Native Americans. If Tocqueville had not gone on to write about them, readers would have closed his book without even the scantest knowledge that they had in fact been present from the beginning in that part of America that was to become the United States.

5

The New England Township Before the Revolution: Tocqueville's American Pastoral

History, American history, the stuff you read about in books and study in school, had made its way out to tranquil, untrafficked Old Rimrock, New Jersey, to countryside where it had not put in an appearance that was notable since Washington's army twice wintered in the highlands adjacent to Morristown. History, which had made no drastic impingement on the daily life of the local populace since the Revolutionary Wars wended its way back out to these cloistered hills.

Philip Roth, *American Pastoral*, p. 87

One had the impression of a process of ceaseless gradation. . . . The last word never seemed to be able to be uttered, for every end was a beginning, every last result the first of a new opening.

Robert Musil, *The Man Without Qualities*

The New England township was, from its inception, imbued with a sacred quality. In its founding lay the promise of a new society. Unfettered by the religious or political tyranny of the Old World, it would nurture a spirit of intense community loyalties through active neighborly participation, and hold at bay the disorderliness characteristic of imperfect societies. The limitations of the past would not cast a shadow on hopes for an abundant spiritual and material future. Nothing from the outside world would be permitted to destroy its tranquillity. Neither an oppressive religion, nor the king's arbitrary powers, nor the hostile savages in the countryside surrounding it would deter it from its course. The American pastoral was seen, whether realistically or mystically, as a union of families, living peacefully as they went about their daily tasks,

114

helping and caring for one another, taking pride in their individual achievements as well as the community's joint efforts, coming together to pray, and in public meetings to debate town policy. American civil society was founded on these beliefs. Tocqueville devoted an extended treatment of it in the opening chapters of the *Democracy*.

In Philadelphia and in Cincinnati as the winter of 1831 approached, Tocqueville's journal carries a record of his qualms about the unintended consequences of the uncertain link between the future of civilization and the spread of knowledge. The problem, as he saw it, begged for answers. We may reasonably expect that he intended to bring out the contradictory message in the relationship. Why, he asked, when knowledge becomes available to every one, does the general level of intelligence decline? Why, at the same time, when class divisions diminish, do the superior classes find their power in decline? Why, when the masses reach the point of acquiring the science or intelligence required to govern themselves, are there no great minds at hand to lend direction to society? On top of these questions, lay the belief that neither civilization nor reason assured perfection. Both were in history's path, but Tocqueville had no illusions, after the experiences of the recent past, that cumulative degrees of perfectibility lay along or at the end of it. If ever, he speculated, the world became entirely civilized – that is, rational – the human race might perhaps become a single people, for reason, like virtue, was not geographically determined. Its rules are inflexible; it follows the same route to the same goals. If people decide to use reason as a guide to action, their thoughts, beliefs, and feelings will be the same in all circumstances. The opposite is true if people stay wedded to their traditions and customs, remaining, as he put it, completely themselves, and becoming more and more separated from their neighbors. Such optimism may sound strange to those who think of Tocqueville as an opponent of the Enlightenment. As he explained almost a quarter of a century after he set down these reflections on America, he was partial to "the ideas of the eighteenth century, . . . or, at least the just, reasonable, applicable portion of those ideas, which, are after all, my own."[1] He was critical only of those who had no notion of how their ideas could be put to practical use.

These private thoughts were not devoid of a quiet display of rhetoric, but it is clear that a high measure of disquiet was buried in them. The

---

[1] Tocqueville to Beaumont, April 24, 1856, *Oeuvres complètes d'Alexis de Tocqueville*, 18 vols. (Paris: Gallimard, 1950–98), 8 (*Correspondance d'Alexis de Tocqueville et de Gustave de Beaumont)* part 3, 395. Cited henceforth as *OC*.

question was whether the change that robs people of their originality and character doesn't also rob them of their specific powers. Earlier that same year, in mid-summer, the processes of civilization elicited not his thoughts on reason, but on the power of aggression enshrined in the *laws* of war. Formulated by Europe in what he said was its most enlightened phase, they were being invoked to legitimate the dispossession of the Indians who, Tocqueville, in a totally ironic mood, declared, could rely on the protection of European civilization as the snow did on the heat of the sun. There was no doubt that it was in America that these questions were most acutely posed. Unlike the Spaniards, who came alone and easily cohabited with Native Americans, Englishmen came with their wives and children and immediately established a complete society.[2]

America was for that reason exciting. It was a cradle of a new civilization, while another was coming to an end. Beginnings could now, moreover, be spoken of as real, not in the phantom language that dimly evoked the past obscured by time and encircled by myth. Tocqueville had in mind a beginning point, and, while the future was obscure, there was also some clarity:

America is the only country in which it has been possible to witness the natural and tranquil growth of society, and where the influence exercised on the future condition of states by their origin is clearly distinguishable (I, chap. 2, 28).

The well-ordered polity, much in the minds of seventeenth-century Englishmen, as Jack Greene writes, would be one "presided over by saints, governed by a body of laws that conformed to those of God, and organized into a series of well-ordered covenanted communities knit together by Christian love and composed only of like-minded people with a common religious ideology and a strong sense of communal responsibility." The cost or the benefits of such a polity was a tightly controlled community in which church, town, and family maintained the "traditional social values of order, hierarchy, and subordination."[3]

In the minds of those who fashioned New England theology from its beginning, much of its authority rested on the notion that its stories of settlement were first prefigured in the Hebrew Bible and then refigured as a more authentic truth in the New Testament. Plymouth Rock was

---

[2] Alexis de Tocqueville, *Oeuvres*, ed. André Jardin with the collaboration of Françoise Mélonio and Lise Queffélec, 2 vols. (Paris: Gallimard, 1991), I, 141, 177, 179, 181. Cited hereafter as *Oeuvres*.

[3] Jack P. Greene, *The Intellectual Construction of America. Exceptionalism and Identity from 1492 to 1800* (Chapel Hill: University of North Carolina Press, 1993), p. 55.

thus foreshadowed in the Puritan mind by the Jewish covenant with God. The beginning was sought in the return to an idyllic past that had constantly to be tested from within the individual conscience as it related to others, and against the intrusions of the outside world. In the reenactment of the covenant was created, as Robert Bellah calls it, a "community of memory."[4] At the same time, Plymouth Rock was a point of departure, the landing after a journey. With its rich symbolic meanings of risk, uncertainty, fear of death, and fear of incompleteness, it recreated the Jewish covenant. There, in New England, Puritanism became almost as much a political theory as a religious doctrine (I, chap. 2, 36). Puritan religious doctrine, embedded in the sacred texts, not only inspired but legitimated the Pilgrims' democracy (ibid., 37). The ideas were old but their renewal and their realization constituted a fresh beginning. As Tocqueville put it quizzically, while also noting that the Connecticut legislators in 1650 enacted their penal laws by borrowing from the books of Exodus, Leviticus, and Deuteronomy, "The legislation of a rude and half-civilized people were thus applied to an enlightened and moral community" (ibid., 39). The adoption of customs that governed a primitive society – a nomadic society – formed the bedrock of Puritan beliefs, and the tests God imposed on Israel charted in the book of Exodus were the proving ground for the migrating waves of Israelites into the Promised Land, where they were vouched a progeny as numerous as the stars in heaven. The ancient covenant binding God and his chosen people became the prototype of an authentic community. The Puritan absorption of the Pentateuch story of tribulation, revelation, wandering, and deliverance, and the consequent cultivation of a self-image of sacrifice and salvation in a new land of spiritual and material plenty, was contrasted with a land preferably left behind, a Europe which was in the throes of a despotic consolidation of ranks and classes characteristic of a degraded, yet once vital, feudal society (ibid., 37). The "novel spectacle of a community homogeneous in all its parts" was moreover more perfect than that of antique democracy. It was in this sense that New England became "a region given up to the dreams of fancy and the unrestrained experiment of innovators" (ibid.). Benedict Anderson's concept of the social sharing of an imagined social space finds almost perfect expression in Tocqueville's New England.[5]

[4] Robert Bellah et al, *Habits of the Heart. Individualism and Commitment in American Life* (Berkeley, Los Angeles, and London: University of California Press, 1985), p. 212.
[5] Benedict Anderson, *Imagined Communities: Reflections on the Origin and Spread of Nationalism*, 2nd edition (London and New York: Verso, 1991).

This concept of a communitarian New England township should not be construed as a denial of Tocqueville's voluntarism, or as a contradiction of my argument that he advanced what may be called a theory of beginnings, freedom, and choice. The New England township, as he described it, putting stress on memory, a distinct geographical space, kinship, religion, and language, was an act of conscious contract – that is, an act of the collective will. He presented what he saw as an ideal type of community.[6] George Armstrong Kelly rightly points out that Tocqueville argued that such a community had to take special care to enhance "the rational exercise of freedom" so as to neutralize the expression of unlicensed or evangelical forms of religious observance. According to Kelly, Tocqueville's theory of freedom and control in a democratic society rested on a conviction that "religious belief was inseparable from free government and free public life because it was the channel of a self-imposed moral restraint that shaped and, in so doing, liberated the individual for participation in the republic."[7] By religious belief, Tocqueville meant, again Kelly tells us, Calvinism which "[t]heologically . . . gave men a discipline and a conditioning for freedom by binding them to each other in a purposeful, yet not extravagant, enterprise."[8] The dyad, authority and liberty, in the New England township was the point around which polity was made possible, and its fullest importance was related to another one, that of religion and liberty, thus investing authority with a sacred principle. As we shall see, the tension between authority and liberty could not be comfortably maintained within such a framework, since individual choice might not only erupt as license; it might more creatively break away and manifest itself as yet another return to a beginning for those averse to authority perceived as illegitimate (as it did for early dissidents such as Roger Williams).

---

[6] Brian C. J. Singer writes that the notions of cultural and contractual collectivities are complicitly linked, not oppositionally divided. See his article, "Cultural Versus Contractual Nations: Rethinking Their Opposition," *History and Theory*, 35 (1996), 309–37. Alain Touraine, in *What is Democracy*, trans. David Macey (Boulder and Oxford: Westview Press, 1997), p. 8, ignores the possibility of the compatibility between the two notions, when he calls to his aid Norberto Bobbio's contention that democracy comes into being with the denial of a communitarian conception of society by individualistic action. See Norberto Bobbio, *The Future of Democracy: A Defence of the Rules of the Game*, trans. Roger Griffith (Minneapolis: University of Minnesota Press, 1988).

[7] George Armstrong Kelly, *Politics and Religious Consciousness in America* (New Brunswick and London: Transaction Books, 1984), pp. 47, 55.

[8] Ibid., p. 76.

Barry Shain's use of the term "communalism" describes the same general features of a community bound by religious covenant. Indeed, the social contract that created, as Tocqueville wrote, the states of Rhode Island and Connecticut (ibid., 36), was nothing if not permeated by religious conscience. For Shain, however, the democracy of New England was not a crucible of individualism and of the autonomous self, but its very opposite.[9] The vision of the good in the townships was, he writes, "reformed Protestant and communal, rather than secular and individualistic."[10] A good inseparable from communal control was needed to restrain human beings from indulging their passion for unlicensed behavior. Religious communalism Shain claims to be at the heart of early American democracy. It has, he argues, been overlooked by more than one generation of American scholars, starting with Louis Hartz,[11] who have sought to make an iron-clad argument, in the words of Mark Roelofs, for individualism, "as the rock upon which all else in American politics was built."[12] For Shain this distorts the true nature of American political experience, at least until the final years of the eighteenth century. Even then, however much the ideas of the secular Enlightenment influenced the thought of the intellectual elites in the early United States, Americans did not embrace them universally. Instead, if Shain's view is accurate, they continued to be divided between a religiously oriented notion of politics and civil association, freedom, and authority, on the one hand, and, on the other, a vision that gives primacy to non-religious humanist views of individual liberty, civil association, and political action. He writes: "[T]he supporters of early 19th-century majoritarian democracy already had difficulty articulating and defending a politics of communally shaped morals. As the articulate elite embraced individualism in a complex and uneven fashion (particularly in the South), the needed conceptual vocabulary was increasingly lacking. In America, it became the unsought responsibility of the inarticulate residents of small towns and urban ethnic neighborhoods to sustain communally based

---

[9] Barry A. Shain, *The Myth of American Individualism. The Protestant Origins of American Political Thought* (Princeton: Princeton University Press, 1994), p. 3.

[10] Ibid., p. 4.

[11] Louis Hartz, *The Liberal Tradition in America: An Interpretation of American Political Thought since the Revolution* (New York: Harcourt, Brace and World, 1955).

[12] Mark Roelofs, "The American Political System: A Systematic Ambiguity," *Review of Politics*, 48 (1986), 326. Cited in Barry A. Shain, *The Myth of American Individualism*, p. 11.

ethics and political thought."[13] He thereby endorses James Hunter's interpretation of the continuation of this fundamental split between these two notions of American democracy.[14] Shain's reinterpretation of America's political founding does not so much mark an advance on Tocqueville's observations as it confirms them. It is an error to think of Tocqueville as an unabashed exponent of Lockean liberalism. He had already discerned the tensions between communalism and individualism in the New England township. Whatever its legacies remained to remind Americans of their local loyalties, they had already begun to embrace the creed of individualism, as he conceived it. It was admirable, but it could also be a source of fallible judgment, and, unless held in check, could draw persons into selfish disregard for others, resulting in a fatal disinterest in public life:

> Individualism is a mature and calm feeling, which disposes each member of the community to sever himself from the mass of his fellows and to draw apart with his family and his friends, so that after he has thus formed a little circle of his own, he willingly leaves society at large to itself . . . [I]ndividualism proceeds from erroneous judgment more than from depraved feelings; it originates as much in deficiencies of mind as in perversity of heart. [I]ndividualism, at first, only saps the virtues of political life; but in the long run it attacks and destroys all others and is at length absorbed in downright selfishness . . . [I]ndividualism is of democratic origin, and it threatens to spread in the same ratio as the equality of condition (II, Bk. 2, chap. 2, 104).

To underscore the way in which Tocqueville saw the New England polity, we must take note of his unique way of understanding it. Earlier we saw how recourse to the Genesis story threw needed light on the power of conjectural history. Rousseau's isolate, his half-human figure, moves to shed his innocence and join the first collective society in a non-theological recapitulation of how the not fully human becomes knowledgeable and therefore becomes more fully human. It is likely that Tocqueville had more than a perfunctory knowledge of the books of the Pentateuch, but it is also implausible that he, like Rousseau and others in Rousseau's century and in his own, would have made them the center of disputation. They stood as analogous, but nevertheless mythical, treatments of the development of civilization consciously inspired by philosophical history that incorporated the burgeoning literature on the existence of non-European peoples. On the other hand, the Pentateuch's

---

[13] Ibid., *The Myth of American Individualism*, pp. 149–50.
[14] James Davison Hunter, *Culture Wars: The Struggle to Define America* (New York: Basic Books, 1991), p. 132.

clear ring may be heard in his reading of the Connecticut Code and the Massachusetts 1648 penal code, which comprised a selection of sections from three of its five books. He more than likely absorbed the gravity of the covenant relationship with God's chosen people, the mixture of fear and love of God that pervades it, the enormous stress on the religious rituals and customs surrounding the actions of daily life, yet sacralized because of God's involvement in every one of them, and finally God's promise to enforce justice.[15]

The New England township was the site of the newly chosen people's quotidian interactions that were inseparable and undifferentiated from the active presence of God, and it was most importantly the site of bold thrusts into the future. This was the innovating spirit Tocqueville tried to capture. A democratic and republican political life was nurtured in the townships. As at Athens, (ibid., 42) the entire assembly of citizens took part in creating institutions embodying, in the words of Governor John Winthrop, the principles of moral and civil liberty that negated the evil propensities inherent in an unrestrained natural liberty,[16] subversive of the only acceptable authority – an authority in which free citizens voluntarily subjected themselves to God. Liberty, the liberty Winthrop called, "civil or federal . . . is the proper end and object of authority, and cannot subsist without it. . . . Whatsoever crosseth this, is not authority, but a distemper of it. This liberty is maintained and exercised in a way of subjection to authority; it is of the same kind of liberty wherewith Christ hath made us free" (ibid., 44–45). Athenian democracy, though in more perfect form; the severity and grudging benevolence of the Covenant; the Christian message of love: These were the features that distinguished private and public life in the townships. According to Tocqueville's reconstruction, the moral world governing private life is stable, predictable, and orderly. He asks us to believe that people passively, yet willingly, choose obedience to the moral law, without telling

---

[15] My understanding of the Pentateuch owes much to Jack Miles, *God. A Biography* (New York: Vintage Books, 1996).

[16] Here, Hannah Arendt's comments are of interest, since she, though somewhat polemically, also insists, in her gloss of the Mayflower Compact, on the Pilgrims' fear of the "so-called state of nature . . . as well as the unlimited initiative of men bound by no law. . . . The really astonishing fact . . . is that their obvious fear of one another was accompanied by the no less obvious confidence that they had in their own power . . . to combine themselves together into a 'civil Body Politik'." This mutual trust and confidence she finds quite remarkable, contrasting its open [American], with its conspiratorial character in other parts of the world. See *On Revolution* (New York: The Viking Press, 1963), pp. 166, 182.

us how he justifies speaking about the coupling of passive acceptance and active choice as a normal mental act. The paradox is simply allowed to stand as it is and to coexist alongside his characterization of the political world as a field of autonomous decisions that questions authority at every turn. The moral world, suffused with religious sentiment, is seen as the passage to the political, and because religion is the bedrock of civil liberty, it secures not only the law but political liberty itself (ibid., 46). Tocqueville could not be more admiring of a society animated by this urge to cross boundaries and to breach limits, but, through fear of the political unknown, drew back from fully testing the limits of the political world, as if to go beyond them was to enter a totally uncharted domain, loosened from its moorings in experience, leading to the subversion both of liberty and authority, and perhaps also heading toward the supersession of society by politics (ibid., 45–46).

Tocqueville elaborated upon the relationship between civil and political society. If care is not taken, his understanding might be misread on the semi-plausible grounds that he moved almost without pause to a consideration of the origins of Anglo-American democratic politics without first asking what constituted the foundations of sociability. Tocqueville tells us that Anglo-American society was from the beginning a democracy of *moeurs*, which for him derived from an equality of condition. That equality was in direct conflict with aristocratic social forms that valued, among other things, property relationships privileging caste, class, and deference, which were transformed from a bundle of feudal and semi-feudal customs into sanctioned laws. There seemed to be, he believed, a more natural fit between democratic civil and political society – as if the two were coterminous – than any fit between feudal *moeurs* and the legal and political forms that sanctioned them. Even in America, however, the situation was not without ambiguities. The fit he so hypothesized was confined to the regions east of the Hudson, and was not extended to those to its southwest as far as the Floridas, where aristocratic principles and the English law of inheritance were established, and which were modified only by the fact that while the existence of slavery gave plantation owners great power, it did not give them the power of patronage over tenants as in European aristocratic society. Moreover, such aristocratic *moeurs* as were to be found in America did not preclude the cultivation of ideas of freedom and independence. Indeed, southerners "furnished the best leaders of the American Revolution" (I, chap. 3, 48–49). They took, he said, a leading part in elevating the debate that led to the break with England from local- and religiously based notions of conscience to republican and secular values derived from civic humanism and transformed by the Enlightenment.

This additional paradox does not, however, obliterate his major point that "It is impossible to believe that equality will not eventually find its way into the political world, as it does everywhere else. . . . I know of only two methods of establishing equality in the political world: rights must be given to every citizen, or none at all to anyone" (ibid., 55). We thus return to equality as the distinguishing feature of democratic politics, and not to liberty, which is what democratic societies have to find the will and energy to defend, expand, and preserve.

Thus, when he said that "the various notions and opinions current among men and . . . the mass of those ideas which constitute their character of mind," he meant "the whole moral and intellectual condition of a people."[17] Liberty and authority, properly understood, were best seen not as a system of polarities. Again it was in the unique structure and dynamics of the township that the two fundamental aspects of public life could be perceived for the truly extraordinary experience it was. As if it came "directly from the hand of God" (I, chap. 5, 62), the village or township was the first manifestation of a natural, indeed, coarse and "semi-barbarous" sociability – yet vulnerable to a more advanced political intelligence. By this, Tocqueville meant politics practiced at the national level, self-consciously aware and intolerant of what it regarded as the restricted vision of a citizenry chiefly concerned with parochial interests. But it was the township's concrete and immediate concerns that kept political life vibrant. Should it vanish or be overtaken by great political assemblies or a strong and enterprising government, the liberty of deliberation based on the realities of experience of each citizen's character would itself disappear. Municipal liberty is "not the fruit of human efforts; it is rarely created by others, but is, as it were, secretly self-produced in the midst of a semi-barbarous state of society" (ibid., 63). These sacred points of initiation could in fact not be comprehended; just as the human spirit wisely shrank "from lifting the veil of the sanctuary" (I, chap. 2, 45), so a measure of wise self-defense shielded the human eye from the blinding light of truth, as it did the beginnings of local liberties best protected from profane probing. An indefinable but benign conversion occurred in town gatherings where citizens learned

---

[17] Cited in Harvey Mitchell, *Individual Choice and the Structures of History. Alexis de Tocqueville as Historian Reappraised* (Cambridge: Cambridge University Press, 1996), pp. 36–37.

not only to use but to enjoy liberty. In the absence of this life-giving force, the external, superficial, and shallow signs of liberty might be on display, but its inner essence would shrivel and hollow itself out. Its power lay in this indefinable essence, and only secondarily in its visible political forms, and because it did, liberty permeated everything.

The township was thus the public forum best suited to achieve harmony between freedom and authority. It respected the right of citizens to assert their own private interests without denying the authority of the common weal to exercise control over them with their consent. Indeed, power, flowing with the knowledge and approval of the citizenry from below to the top, rested on the confidence possessed by human beings in knowing that their exercise of independence and authority, the two most exciting things they most craved and needed, remained an active force (I, chap. 5, 67). These needs reflected the realities of everyday life, "the ordinary relations of life," Tocqueville called them. The passions that created social conflict were contained by the processes of active citizenship, which alerted them to the benefits of both public and private life. Their interpenetrability was the source of their strength, and the fulfillment of duty was indistinguishable from the exercise of a right. Independence and authority had so positive a meaning in the American psyche, because there was no opposition between them (ibid., 69–70). It derived, it would seem, from the double force of the Americans' willing obedience to God, and finding that they did so by facing practical problems. Every effort to do so confirmed order and liberty, and was in turn reaffirmed by the rituals of public life.

By their very nature, beginnings have ends and, through the sheer process of time, come to an end as well. Tocqueville's notions of beginnings, as we may now see more fully, combined the sacred or the near-mystical and the practical. God came to the side of the Pilgrims in a mysterious yet fecund way. Liberty for them did not simply issue from a collective covenant with God. It was for them, first, a matter of individual conscience, of individual, autonomous, and free dialogue with God, permitting them to understand, second, the covenant as a form of mutual vesting, of reciprocity, by means of which God agreed to a compact with the Elect – the new Saints whom God chose, yet who deliberately chose themselves to live up to divine demands. Tocqueville's famous linkage of religion and liberty did not, however, critically rely on a theodicy that ruled the lives of the Pilgrims, fearful that original sin would threaten the covenant by putting it under chronic, perhaps perpetual, siege. The individual struggle to lead exemplary lives and attract the good grace of God reinforced a belief that liberty was a question of choosing "to [do] evil as well as to [do] good" (I, chap. 2, 44). It was both the idea of communion and of free choice that constituted the foundation of political liberty that Tocqueville maintained inspired the parties to the covenant as it was reinterpreted in the Old World, and even more vehemently sworn to in the New. But liberty's future would rest on the processes of history, not on the withdrawal of God in response to the turning away by the Pilgrims from his commandments. If even ultimately the consequences of a broken covenant might be crucial to the working out of liberty, Tocqueville, neo-Pascalian as he was when it came to the ultimate meaning of evil and good, was no unswerving partisan of a rigorous and stern Christianity. He distanced himself from literal Christian meanings of a broken covenant. It was not important for his purposes to consider the mental stress of living in a society of saints. The significance of the covenant was that it set in motion the psychological preparation for the tasks Americans faced in dealing with the evils of this world. He was, however, not a mere observer. Posing the question as he did clearly implicated the ways in which he saw those evils.

How the democratic experiment would end was shrouded in obscurity. The notion of an end is tied to the question of process, to the practices that give voice to, and express the realities of, the goals expressive of democratic equality and liberty. The confluence, though perhaps not the harmonization of these goals, can only be gauged by asking whether and how the historical development of actual practices would guide them in a positive or a negative direction. Certainty of judgment about the future there could not be. What was sure was that passivity, but not only passivity – wrong choices as well – would both shape it negatively. It is not hard to see why Tocqueville's vision of, or preference for, a modern democratic culture that would not sacrifice liberty to equality rested on the efforts of the citizenry to keep intact their original pledge to vest one another with responsibility for keeping alive the ethos and practices of a closely knit community.

Tocqueville's idealized evocation of this political culture in New England tends toward the idyllic.[18] But is its true nature wholly and accurately described, as one of his critics contends, by recalling Arthur Miller's *Crucible*, where an ever-vigilant community worked to enforce

---

[18] On Tocqueville's definition of social states resembling Max Weber's "ideal types," see Robert Nisbet, "Tocqueville's Ideal Types," in *Reconsidering Tocqueville's "Democracy in America"*, ed. Abraham S. Eisenstadt (New Brunswick, N.J.: Rutgers University Press, 1988), 171–91.

self-discipline to conform to its moral and political structure?[19] Tocqueville's understanding and intention were more complex. At this point, the degree of political participation in the New England township is a question that must be raised. Turnout for elections in the New England town halls during the eighteenth century ranged from ten to twenty-five percent of eligible voters, but more significantly, open discussion in town meetings was discouraged. Order rather than representation was the goal. "Real freedom," it was generally held, "was possible only within a community of like-minded men."[20] This reinforces Tocqueville's major contention. The government of the town meeting could in fact err, not because participation was low, but in the very act of deliberation. Because the authority of government emanated from the governed, however small and unrepresentative that body was, likeminded citizens might correct the government's errors by taking on the parental role in a reversal of the traditional direction in which authority is expressed. Psychologically such a configuration induced in Tocqueville's view a health-giving and inextinguishable affection binding the citizen in a kind of adoration or "taste for order" in a society that "comprehends the balance of power, and [that] collects clear practical notions on the nature of his duties and the extent of his rights" (I, chap. 5, 70–71). In these early pages of *Democracy in America*, he did not admit or allow his vision to be darkened by the difficulties of dissent or of disaffection. Over the community there reigned a spirit of near-perfect conformity. Indeed the style of American politics created an exceptional kind of authority. The closest analogy that came to his mind were the specific forms of grammar that a language imposes on its users. And in the democratic township, the language of politics gathered up, so to speak, the conscious knowledge and the "invisible" sources of authority

---

[19] Stephen F. Schneck, "Habits of the Head. Tocqueville's America and Jazz," *Political Theory*, 17 (1989), 638–62, 650. Schneck relies on Michel Foucault's concept of power/knowledge to support his deconstruction of Tocqueville's notion of power in the American township.

[20] Michael Schudson, *The Good Citizen: A History of American Civic Life* (New York: The Free Press, 1998), pp. 17–18. The citation is from Bruce C. Daniels, *The Connecticut Town* (Middletown, CT: Wesleyan University Press, 1979), p. 75. Schudson concludes his discussion of American political practice during the colonial period in this way: "On the eve of the new nation, politics remained in the hands of gentlemen. The gentry ruled, notwithstanding representative institutions and a relatively broad electorate. . . . Looking back from beyond the democratic transition, colonial political practice still appears an extension of the social life and comfortable consensus of a gentlemanly elite" (p. 47).

and united them to stave off anarchy. Anarchy in fact could find no place in such a polity, since if every citizen possessed a share of power, authority could not be seen as exercising illegitimate power. From these impeccable foundations, the leap into the American Revolution was a leap into an even more profound legitimacy, into what Tocqueville characterized as a "mature and reflecting preference for freedom, and not," he deliberately said, "of a vague or ill-defined craving for independence." In this deliberate pronouncement, his aversion for a utopian future, the untried, and hence the dangerous, is quite pronounced (ibid., 72–73).

Tocqueville found it hard to sustain this unalloyed version of early American democracy. He half-heartedly endorsed what he took to be the realistic American premise that intelligence, based on self-interest, rather than honesty, was the best way to achieve obedience to the law. Individuals, American legislators found, were not quick to put themselves out for the community, if they did not deem such action personally worthwhile. What the community lost in honesty, and that was purchased at the price of "moral degradation," was balanced by the gains derived from political union. By such expedients were the laws executed. It would seem as if Tocqueville is saying that the political realm was, by its nature and in the interests of self-preservation, not primarily a moral entity (ibid., 81–82). But such a conclusion would be at least partly mistaken. For Tocqueville did not propose a notion of politics that totally or even partially identified political morality with a rigid adherence to a determined set of religious beliefs. America made room for a wide variety of sects, all of which acknowledged and struggled with the problems of human fallibility. Dishonesty was a human frailty, and hardly the most serious in the Christian tradition's compendium of vices. Giving it some space in society and in politics lay within the grand, almost unspoken, assumptions of political theory. He held the same view of what he called "honest materialism," which he said he envisaged from a practical perspective and was the best that could be expected from human beings.[21]

Not that he was insensitive to the professed moral ambitions of democracies, or unaware, as we have seen, of Montesquieu's identification of virtue as their leading principle. But it was not a republic of virtue in the Rousseauian sense, or one according to the Jacobin model that claimed his approval. Acting in the name of an abstract notion of good

---

[21] Tocqueville to Kergorlay, August 5, 1836, OC 13 (*Correspondance d'Alexis de Tocqueville et de Louis de Kergorlay*) part 1, 389.

was tragically misguided in its rapid and retrogressive sacrifice of present goods.[22] Indeed, Tocqueville presents us with a political theory whose focal point is a shared interest by governors and governed alike in retaining their unity as a coherent community. We may have in this instance an illustration of the keen scrutiny by means of which they measured each other's interests, so much so that each became accustomed to make concessions to the other. His conception of New England society thus made room not only for harmony, but for discord, not only for generosity, but for its absence. Not "regimes of truth," as Michel Foucault envisages the exercise of hegemonic power, but the calculation of interest, both individual and collective, is what Tocqueville was interested in, and comes closer to the realities of the township.[23] It is not implausible to draw from this eye-matching exercise an alternative construction of his use of the term "affection" to describe the unique nature of American politics (ibid., 69).[24] "Affection" comprehends, as he knew, the full range of emotions. Affection may be seen as a Tocquevillian trope to empower his depiction of American exceptionalism with its roots in the free religious conscience taking flight as political liberty. He knew perfectly well that the original religious foundations of the political experiment in the wilderness had in the course of successive historical stages been transmuted by the exigencies of practical experience. These did not, he thought, constitute a betrayal of the beginnings as much as a delicate balancing act to keep at least some of the powers of beginnings alive.

Even centralization had a different hue in America, where it crucially did not impinge on nor damage the initiating powers of locally elected officials. Hard as it was to persuade individuals to take an interest in the business of the public realm, and however less complex it might be to let a centralized government appropriate the deliberative and consultative powers of the citizenry, the key to a healthy political culture was not in prevention – not in laying down ground rules that prevented citizens

---

[22] For an interesting study dealing with the absence in Tocqueville of a concrete doctrine of public virtue, see Dalmacio Negro, "Virtue and Politics in Tocqueville," in *Liberty, Equality, Democracy*, ed. Eduardo Nolla (New York: New York University Press, 1992), 55–74.

[23] Cf. Stephen F. Schneck, "Habits of the Head," 639–40.

[24] Bruce James Smith uses the term, "politics of affection," in *Politics and Remembrance. Republican Themes in Machiavelli, Burke, and Tocqueville* (Princeton: Princeton University Press, 1985) in his chapter on Tocqueville to contrast the early democratic state of mind with modernity's assault on the spirit and the emotions that are now considered necessary for a sound politics.

from injuring each other, which amounted at best to maximizing a negative notion of liberty – but in free action. A politics in which "the alliance of the human will is to be obtained . . . must be free in its gait and responsible for its acts" was much more preferable – in fact, superior – to one in which the citizen had to choose between being "a passive spectator [and] a dependent actor in schemes with which he is unacquainted" (ibid., 94). Underpinning this theory of the political act is Tocqueville's "constitution of man" who cannot tolerate any prolonged infringement upon his liberty. In an imperfect world, he was ready to gamble on a society whose politics accommodated inefficiency and a momentary, perhaps even a chronic, state of disorder, rather than one with a "uniformity or permanence of design [and] the minute arrangement of details" (ibid., 95). Clearly with France in mind, he inveighed against the practices of a centralized administration. "I am suspicious," he stated categorically, "of a good that is united with so many evils, and I am not averse to an evil that is compensated by so many benefits" (ibid., 95, note 50). A state dedicated to and organized according to the first of these two conceptions of authority spelled the end of choice and decision, and marked the beginning of servitude – a condition into which human beings could, as the past had shown, be easily seduced either by their own lassitude or by a flawed conception of their own interests. It is not too much to say that Tocqueville saw a propensity to evil in the state as it assumed its modern features of coercion in the name of protecting material well being; even more damning was the action of depriving the citizen of the opportunity of facing life's risks and thereby "sacrifices his own free will" (ibid., 96).

To give additional weight to his theory of freedom and beginnings, he not only reiterated his conviction that "a durable and rational sentiment" of patriotism could only be founded on the citizen's appreciation of how thought, passions, and daily experience are rekindled by and in turn rekindle the laws of a country. Beginnings were thus renewed. With "every fresh generation [there] is a new people ready for the care of the legislator" (ibid., 97). In other words, the past cannot be escaped, but new generations of citizens arise to deal with its traces and face its legacy of unexpected crises. In France, a fatal error resulted from a total repudiation by the Revolution of past institutions that had acted as a counterweight to the "evils of the state" (ibid., 100). In America, it was not "too late to make the experiment" that would avoid these evils and serve as a healthy contrast to older political societies in which such choices were vanishing or had already vanished. To continue the experiment, the instinctive affinities or "transient exertions" – all the habits of heart that revered the past and its traditions, the "natural fondness" for country akin to the "love" bestowed on the "mansions of their fathers" – had to surrender to "rational" patriotism, a more durable attachment to country (I, chap. 14, 251). Americans needed, Tocqueville insisted forcefully, to give up childlike forms of citizenship for adult forms.[25] As we shall see, he found it hard enough to incorporate into his vision the fuller movement into maturity that others were later to see as the core of American promise, unfortunately blighted.

And so Tocqueville concentrated on what he believed to be the distinctive features of New England that were at least susceptible to rational political discussion in an America divided by race and by local community conflicts. "It is in part his own work," he said, when describing the citizen's mature exercise of civil rights. It led to the knowledge that civil rights and personal interests are intimately linked, since each reinforced the other and, by strengthening the nation, contributed to the goods of every citizen (ibid.). And the practical consequences of such action were clearly part, he declared, of a shift in historical time when a people is caught between the weight of the past and a vague comprehension of the future:

> The country then assumes a dim and dubious shape in the eyes of the citizens; they no longer behold it in the soil which they inhabit, for that soil is to them an inanimate clod; nor in the usages of their forefathers, which they have learned to regard as a debasing yoke; nor in religion, for of that they doubt; nor in the laws, which do not *originate in their own authority*; (my italics) nor in the legislator, whom they fear and despise (I, chap 14, 252).

The point of beginning meant nothing outside the creation of a new concept of authority, which in a democratic republic comprehends political rights. In this situation, caught between unreflexive, instinctual responses to monarchical forms of government and the as yet-to-be tested democratic forms that call on their reflexive powers, the imperfectly formed democratic citizenry are "stopped between the two in the midst of confusion and distress." They cannot go back. They must choose to go forward (ibid.). But the need in addition to retrieve the past

[25] For Ralph Ellison, too, America at that very precise time was going through a crisis of adolescence when "both individuals and nations flounder between accepting and rejecting the responsibilities of adulthood." Ralph Ellison, "Twentieth-Century Fiction and the Black Mask of Humanity," in *Shadow and Act* (New York: A Signet Book, 1966), p. 50. His gaze was directed specifically at the dilemma posed by the position of Afro-Americans in the fragile future of democracy.

demanded a knowledge of what use it would be put to, of saying no to what Tocqueville believed would be an illegitimate use of it. Reiterated here – as if to remind himself of his own starting point – is Tocqueville's conviction that beginnings do occur and that they are fraught with risk – risk that will not be free of error, but equally, risk that held out the possibility of human advancement. To the next series of beginnings we will now turn in the next chapter.

6

A Second Beginning: Black and White in Tocqueville's America

Americans, some hundred and fifty years after their Puritan beginnings, looked beyond their settled loyalties to time and place and set in motion a second beginning, which marked them as a mature nation. Freely and deliberately they "approached that lofty pinnacle of glory" by stepping into the space left empty by the dispersal of authority through the Articles of Confederation. The Madisonian view of the Constitution, as we have seen repeatedly, clearly influenced Tocqueville.[1] Madison was confident that the "good sense of the people of America" would not succumb to the "passions of the unthinking," and would prefer, "where power is to be conferred" to choose between the "GREATER, not the PERFECT,

---

[1] On May 30, 1787, during debates in the Federal Convention, Madison reported that Gouverneur Morris distinguished between a federal and a national supreme government, the former constituting a mere compact, while the latter amounted to a coercive operation. See James Madison, *Debates on the Adoption of the Federal Constitution in the Convention Held at Philadelphia in 1787; with a Diary of the Debates of the Congress of the Confederation*, ed. Jonathan Elliot (Washington, D.C.: Elliot, 1845), pp. 132–33. Cited in Liah Greenfeld, *Nationalism. Five Roads to Modernity* (Cambridge, Mass. and London: Harvard University Press, 1992), p. 427. Cf. *Federalist* No. 39, *The Federalist. From the Original Text of Alexander Hamilton, John Jay, and James Madison* (New York: The Modern Library, n.d.), pp. 249–50. For Madison, a national Constitution would vest ultimate authority in the majority of the people, who could change or abolish their established government. A federal Constitution would demand the concurrence of every state to alterations. The Constitution in its foundation was federal, not national, and "in the sources from which the ordinary powers of the government are drawn, it is partly federal and partly national; in the operation of these powers, it is national, not federal; in the extent of them, again, it is federal, not national; and, finally, in the authoritative mode of introducing amendments, it is neither wholly federal nor wholly national."

good."[2] He argued against a constitutional instrument in which "the authority of the whole society everywhere [would be] subordinate to the authority of the parts . . . a monster in which the head was under the direction of the members."[3] He declared against the partisans of state powers that

[U]ltimate authority, wherever the derivative may be found, resides in the people alone, and that it will not depend merely on the comparative ambition or address of the different governments, whether either, or which of them, will be able to enlarge its sphere of jurisdiction at the expense of the other. Truth, no less than decency, requires that the event in every case should be supposed to depend on the sentiments and sanction of their common constituents.[4]

Madison unequivocally located ultimate authority in the people, not in any fragment of it. In his own words, Tocqueville saw this as a unique historical moment. It was even more so than he knew, for not only did the Federalists decisively move to endow the central administration with greater powers, they did so without pausing to regret what Bruce Ackerman calls their illegal and truly revolutionary actions, which were needed to create a fresh foundational moment.[5] "It is new in the history of society to see a great people turn a calm and scrutinizing eye upon itself when apprised by the legislature that the wheels of government are stopped, to see it carefully examine the extent of the evil, and patiently wait two whole years until a remedy is discovered" (I, chap. 8, 117–18). "A wholly novel theory, which may be considered as a great discovery in modern political science," was how Tocqueville described the American Constitution. There was much about the Union it had founded that would certainly create problems, especially the question of determining the structures of democratic initiatives and review. What was uppermost in his mind, however, in giving his unqualified approval of the Founding, was the struggle between the decentralizers and centralizers. It was to the federal government that he referred when he said:

A government retains its sway over a great number of citizens far less by the voluntary and rational consent of the multitude than by that instinctive, and to a certain extent involuntary, agreement which results from similarity of feelings and resemblances of opinion. I will never admit that men constitute a social body

[2] *Federalist* No. 41, ibid., p. 260.   [3] *Federalist* No. 45, ibid., p. 296.
[4] *Federalist* No. 46, ibid., p. 305.
[5] See Bruce Ackerman, *We the People. Transformations* (Cambridge, Mass. and London, Belknap Press of the Harvard University Press, 1998), chaps. 2–3, for an excellent account of the decisive steps the Founding Fathers took in the forging of a nation.

simply because they obey the same head and the same laws. Society can exist only when a great number of men consider a great number of things under the same aspect, when they hold the same opinions upon many subjects, and when the same occurrences suggest the same thoughts and impressions to their minds (I, chap. 18, 408–09).

For Tocqueville, this constituted the vital principle of American political life. He joined this argument with what he understood republican government in the United States to mean – "the slow and quiet action of society upon itself . . . founded upon the enlightened will of the people. It is a conciliatory government, under which resolutions are allowed time to ripen, and in which they are deliberately discussed, and are executed only when mature. . . . What is called the republic in the United States is the tranquil rule of the majority . . . the common source of all the powers of the state." Still the will of the majority is not unlimited. "Above it in the moral world are humanity, justice and reason; and in the political world, vested rights" (I, chap. 18, 433–34). Thus citizens responded to their inner ear, pursuing a slow deliberate process in their public lives to do the right thing.

If we heed his argument that the politics of affection and the sense of community might be preserved within larger units of government, his admiration for America's second beginning is *not* remarkable for his failure to discuss the provision in the Constitution that counted only three-fifths of the slaves in apportioning representation in Congress.[6] But since he could not ignore his own respect for humanity, justice, and reason, it is also true that Tocqueville wanted to see where the strengths, weaknesses, fault points, and danger signals of American democracy might lead. They might either move toward the creation of innovative ideas to keep the American experiment alive and provide opportunities for further developing the means to deal with the dynamics of modern forms of authority and freedom, or they might lurch towards a corrupt form of democracy in which the authority/freedom nexus assumed sinister and nihilistic forms. Civil discord was a natural part of that nexus, but one in which, Tocqueville said, liberty was perfected, though it was

---

[6] The three-fifths compromise in the American Constitution followed the provision in the Articles of Confederation whereby the tax to be borne by the states would be based on 100 percent of the free population and three-fifths of the slaves. Originally the slave states wanted the slaves to be counted as zero percent for taxation purposes, and later they wanted them to be counted as 100 per cent of the population for purposes of political representation.

not until a polity was old that one would be able to appreciate its benefits (I, chap. 14, 256).

The problem is not usually stated in this way. Modernity's structures and discontents tend to be seen within a one-sided deterministic loop, and have been seen as a product of necessity. Despite the acknowledgment that historical actors do indeed deliberate and choose one action over another, and do so according to what they perceive to be their rational self-interest, the results of their actions are then explained and described in terms of a dynamic of inner necessity. This is how, for example, a particular case is constructed for the discriminatory implications of the Declaration of Independence, which, by accusing the crown of fomenting slave insurrections, implied that slave property was legitimate, or at least, not open to future challenge. Michael Rogin's argument is that the Declaration has carried its flawed beginnings into the present. It came into the world from the conflicting needs, demands, and wishes of a number of actors, who compromised their minor differences (Southern delegates wanted a more forthright approval of slave property), and accepted eighteenth-century ideas of the state of nature from which equal and inalienable rights were said to be derived, but at the same time argued for the "natural" inferiority of Native and Afro-Americans. That the debates circled around economic needs, wishes, and ideology is undeniable.[7]

But a presumably predetermined triptych is created by the conjoining, as a condition of American liberty, slavery, the theft of Indian lands, and, for good measure, the exclusion of Chinese and Mexican American labor. Modern America, in this deterministic version, had nowhere to go than along this journey. Tocqueville had something rather different in

[7] See Michael Rogin, "The Two Declarations of Independence," *Representations*, no. 55 (1996), 13–30. Jefferson was a key player. For his views on slavery, see *Notes on the State of Virginia*, in *The Complete Thomas Jefferson*, ed. Saul K. Padover (New York: Duell, Sloan & Pearce, 1943), pp. 605 and 644. Tocqueville had access to L. P. Conseil, *Mélanges politiques et philosophiques extraits des mémoires et de la correspondance de Thomas Jefferson*, 2 vols. (Paris: Paulin, 1833). Conor Cruise O'Brien is even more convinced that Jefferson, as a slaveholder, should be read out of the ethos of American civil religion. See *The Long Affair: Thomas Jefferson and the French Revolution, 1785–1800* (London: Sinclair-Stevenson, 1996). Like Rogin, O'Brien is too ready to impute racism. In the *Notes on the State of Virginia*, Jefferson expressed "a suspicion only, that the blacks, whether originally a distinct race, or made distinct by time and circumstance, are inferior to the whites." It was not "against experience to suppose that different species of the same genus, or varieties of the same species, may possess different qualifications." Still, one should not forget that Jefferson wanted to send free blacks to Africa, for only then would the origins of Anglo-American values be maintained.

mind. Of course, freedom and necessity meet. It is in an imagined space that an act is performed, and may thus be said to have a strong claim to determine the next act in a causal chain. His task was not only to chart how historical actors make choices. They did, it seemed to him, either with an arrogant belief in their own virtues and prescience, or in a less self-deceived way that took into account these dangers and tried to avoid them as much as possible. While ends could be predicted, there was something unexpected about how they actually turned out. Thus the element of uncertainty was always present. But this underlined rather than undermined the importance of taking freedom seriously. Thus, beginnings and ends are united, but the more crucial point he wanted to make is that the first determines the second by the contingent free act. If freedom, in all its modes, is to be endowed with power, then the notion of the free act had to be maintained. Without giving it weight, the historian would have nothing left to do but to chronicle the necessities of the past, and, more importantly, by fully accepting a necessitarian mode of historical explanation, he would eliminate or give up any plausible or realistic claim to assess "the historical work" of historical protagonists – that is, of actors contingently creating history. The jagged and distorted edges of historical work, forced into a box of historical necessity, would indeed shatter it and reveal it as a conceit.

We can now move toward the question of how he envisaged the processes by means of which beginnings meet their ends. First, Tocqueville turned away from the original thirteen states in which he said it was easier for freedom to flourish (I, chap. 8, 165–66) to consider how it might survive in a large modern one that was the crucible for the advancement of civilization and knowledge. Here, new ideas, genius, and a bold focus on larger issues, centered in populous cities, were generated, but only alongside the existence of significant disparities in wealth, conflict of interests, and suspect morality. But these were unavoidable trends. The modern nation could not be set back. What was avoidable in the modern nation, however, was the weakening of liberty. The American federal system not only had the potential to prevent it by ensuring the distribution of powers (I, chap. 8, 165–70), thus preventing the exercise of authority from one center, but also by calling on a citizenry that had accumulated a long experience in self-government. It had prepared them to understand that in fact legal fictions had founded the Federal Union, "an ideal nation, which exists, so to speak, only in the mind" (I, chap. 8, 172). As a true point of beginning, the American form of the modern nation was a work of the imagination, an artificial structure, one that demanded practical nurture capable of overcoming the centrifugal forces that might ensue from excessive focus on local issues. The larger concerns and vision of the modern nation were in fact not necessarily impeded by the private and civic concerns in the smallest municipality or at the level of the individual states. Indeed, as we saw, he rhapsodized civic life at the township and provincial levels – the solicitude of Americans for their schools, parsonages, churches, and roads, for order and policing (94–96), that distinguished them from other people, declaring them to be "enlightened and awake," unlike older societies that accepted uniformity and regularity. (See the important section "Political Effects of Decentralized Administration in the United States" in I, chap. 5, 89–101, quotation from 93.) This admiration for American vigilance against an authority wrongfully constituted by a combination of centralized government and centralized administration was not intended to weaken his case for a purposeful and effective federal government. The politics of intimacy was crucial to the viability of national politics: "Local freedom . . . which leads a great number of citizens to value the affection of their neighbors and of their kindred, perpetually brings men together and forces them to help one another in spite of the propensities that sever them" (II, chap. 4, 111). The politics of local affection so praised by Tocqueville, however, could have, and, as America moved from one crisis to another over slavery, did have consequences he may have overlooked. By placing so much weight on and praising the local springs of positive civic and political action, he could hardly question their right to say to their critics to desist from their challenges. There is a double edge to his belief in the passage cited near the beginning of this chapter that society exists only when people see things in the same light and when they share the same opinions about many things. Self-evident as this may seem, we are led to wonder whether Tocqueville had made his mind up on whether to accord precedence to local sensitivities or to the sensibilities of society as a whole. The defense of local and provincial interests were in fact invoked against interventions judged to be unjust, as they were by nullifiers and secessionists. As we shall see later in this chapter, he feared for the future of the Union, believing it to be weakened by such pressures, just as, for the same reasons, he expressed concern over the anti-slavery forces.

We may also turn to his praise of the free circulation of news and ideas. Localism was prevented from becoming a process of turning inward by the rapid consumption of communication – that is, by the great expansion of the newspaper press. In Tocqueville's opinion, the press was absolutely independent and served to combine "the utmost national freedom . . . with local freedom of every kind" (II, chap. 6, 121). Yet, though he believed the confluence of interests to be certain, another certainty negated it. The press and community reinforced their mutual needs by becoming such effective images of one another that, especially in democracies, the power of the crowd was such as to obliterate autonomous opinion (ibid., 122), paradoxically reversing the original desire of isolated individuals to escape their feeling of anonymity – of being lost in the crowd (II, chap. 6, 119).

Despite the attention Tocqueville gave to freedom of the press and association, inherent limitations in average intelligence remained an obstacle to political wisdom (I, chaps. 11–13). So was sheer ignorance (I, chap. 15, 277). For him, democratic government was the last, and presumably a superior, stage in human history, but, for that reason, one that presupposed a high degree of enlightenment and culture. Were democratic peoples, and Americans in particular, capable of reaching awareness of where their interests lay? He was not sure. If they were not as enlightened as other peoples, they nevertheless were in a better position to "repair the faults they [might] commit" (I, chap. 13, 239), because of their earliest experience in self-government. A self-correcting process might actually be operative in America (I, chap. 14, 248). In addition, there was, as he put it, "a secret tendency in democratic institutions" that worked to ensure the community's prosperity despite its vices and errors (I, chap. 14, 250). This tendency to create prosperity and a democratic equality of condition had become irresistible, cutting off any choice to recapture a society that retained traces of such older values as heroism, reverence for the arts, and honor. The only choice left was to calculate how best to discern what was to be nurtured and what was to be repressed in democracy (I, chap. 14, 262–63). Ignorance and shallowness were powerful forces in a society whose politicians tended to accede to the will of the majority, and actively and almost automatically seeking its approval, molding themselves to its wishes (I, chap. 15, 276–80). Yet these same legislators exerted a countervailing force that to some extent opposed the "idea of right to the feelings of envy; the permanence of religious morality to the continual shifting of politics; the experience of the people to their theoretical ignorance; and their practical knowledge of business to the impatience of their desires" (I, chap. 17, 337). The quotidian, in a word, rooted as it was in a respect for morality, kept idle speculation and uncontrolled passion in check.

The American nation's "love of novelty," "its immense design," and "its ardent impatience" perhaps posed the greatest danger (I, chap. 16, 289). The American character equated novelty with improvement; progress was an unassailable creed. A hunger for "perpetual change" kept Americans in a "perpetual feverish agitation," so that they spent their lives in a kind of lottery, "a revolutionary crisis, or a battle" (I, chap. 18, 443). A new species of humanity had been created (I, chap. 18, 410). We might dub him *homo americanus*. Restraints existed to offset the risks of extremism of any kind, but especially those that brought out the worst aspects of private and public life. Tocqueville catalogued the instruments that acted in America against grand but futile movements of change, and argued that the conservatism of the legal profession and the jury system that encouraged citizens to think of a world beyond their immediate interests were the most significant (I, chap. 16). Even more important was the congruence in America of religion and liberty (I, chap. 17). Innovation was, it was clear, not a good in itself. It could be destructive. What better way to achieve the first without sliding into the second than the civil associations, embodying intellectual and moral goals. They were necessary civilizing agents, precisely because they were the voluntary expression of citizens seeking to help one another, without any political purposes in mind (II, Bk. 2, chap. 5, 114–18).

Political society and civil society, nevertheless, did not exist across a great divide. "It is difficult to say," Tocqueville reflected, "what place is taken up in the life of an inhabitant of the United States by his concern for politics. To take a hand in the regulation of society and to discuss it is his biggest concern and, so to speak, the only pleasure an American knows." And he went on to say:

> I am persuaded that if ever a despotism should be established in America, it would be more difficult to overcome the habits that freedom has formed than to conquer the love of freedom itself. That ceaseless agitation which democratic government has introduced into the political world influences all social intercourse. I am not sure that, on the whole, this is not the greatest advantage of democracy; and I am less inclined to applaud it for what it does than for what it causes to be done.... Democracy ... produces ... an all-pervading and restless activity, a superabundant force and an energy which is inseparable from it and which may, however unfavorable circumstances may be, produce wonders (I, chap. 14, 261–62).

In time, Americans would have to deal with the problem of liberty's survival in a modern nation demanding greater intellectual and

emotional strengths capable of extending the loyalties of local sociability onto its grander canvas. Tocqueville paradoxically located the most
profound challenges to liberty in the very sources of American democratic strength – its mental and emotional commitment to movement.
Market forces and technological transformations were as natural to
society as the changes occurring in the human body, but their scale was
unprecedented. In the early years of America, careful husbandry and
abstemiousness had created wealth. The Weberian linkage of Puritan
religiosity, asceticism, and capital accumulation had been succeeded by
a very different psychological phenomenon – the concomitant rise of
individualism and fascination with financial speculation and the endless
multiplication of desires, corrosive of identity and affection in the setting
of the local community, and potentially destructive of liberty at the
national level of citizen action. Local sociability of an intensely committed nature was harmed, but the injury was not so easily reversed.

The other, more serious, consequence would be the shattering of what
he called a "sort of *consensus universalis*" (I, chap. 18, 437). Tocqueville
did not use this language only to convey the meaning of the "tacit agreement" – "the fundamental principles of the Constitution" – that ensured
a republican form of government, but to stress that without freedom,
republicanism would mean little, while democracy, without the republican elements maintained in place, would overwhelm them. He sketched
a vision of democracy that would not cast aside an old but permanent
problem. The task of determining a democratically just relationship
between authority and liberty remained urgent but as difficult as ever.
Their mutual reinforcement established an authentic popular and democratic sovereignty because it was grounded culturally and politically in
the township and provincial liberties. The Union was less important
than the "republican form of government [which is] . . . the natural state
of the Americans." The Union was, he said, "an accident," enduring only
as long as circumstances favored it; it was "the slow and quiet action of
society upon itself" – here Tocqueville echoed his earlier words from his
first volume: "[W]hen . . . I observe the activity, the information, and the
spirit of enterprise in those American townships . . . I see that society
there is always at work" (I, chap. 5, 95 note 50) – which *was* a necessary part of republican government – a conciliatory government – with
time given over to deliberation. Only then are laws founded on the
enlightened will of the people properly executed (ibid., chap. 18, 433).
If that action were to prevail, American democracy would successfully
challenge the false European republicanism that would give power to

"those who know what is good for the people" – the idea that the will of the state embodied sovereignty. Tocqueville ironically referred to the latter as "a happy distinction which allows men to act in the name of nations without consulting them and to claim their gratitude while their rights are trampled underfoot" (ibid., 434). His appeals to self-worth were meant to test the reverse of this distinction. The individual's ability to look after himself through the use of his reason was matched by the creative principle of the republic. It permeated every aspect of life from family to township, and from township, though various levels, to the Union. Of equal value, the imperatives of *form* (I, chap. 5, 73), the institutional and constitutional frameworks that respected the spaces between rulers and ruled, the powerful and the powerless, and that allowed them the time needed to hear one another, were intended to juxtapose necessary order and thoughtless change (II, Bk. 4, chap. 7). Commitment to the one and a skeptical stance toward the other were the strengths democracy needed.

The Algerian Parallel

That American democratic institutions had secured a polity with room for liberty was a great achievement, but democracy's future in different parts of the world demanded care to encourage a close harmony between the particular constellations of liberty, custom, and law (I, chap. 17, 342). Though liberty was never to be thought of as instrumental, there was no absolute or final model of liberty that could be superimposed upon any society. It had to emerge from socially concrete experience, but at the same time to transcend it. Some societies were better than others in working toward ensuring that freedom was the highest goal they could strive for. If we shift our attention to individual or communal issues of identity to Tocqueville's concept of the differing manifestations of history and geography, we may turn to his ideas on the future of Algeria, since they provide a useful pendant to his views of the American future. His personal experiences in Algeria followed two earlier 1837 articles in which he showed himself to be a staunch supporter of French national aspirations.[8]

---

[8] "Deux Lettres sur l'Algérie," *Oeuvres complètes d'Alexis de Tocqueville*, 18 vols. (Paris: Gallimard, 1950–98), 3 (*Ecrits et discours politiques*), part 1, 129–53. Cited hereafter as OC. These letters were published in *La Presse de Seine-et-Oise* (June 23, August 22, 1837). For an early study of Tocqueville's justification of French rule in Algeria, see Melvin Richter, "Tocqueville on Algeria," *Review of Politics*, 25 (1963), 362–98. See

In the first of these newspaper articles, he wrote that the indigenous Kabyles of Algeria should have been the proper subjects of Rousseau's musings on early human beings, rather than the Caribs and other Indians of America:

You must not imagine . . . that all these Kabyles form one great people subject to a single government. They are still divided into small tribes, as in the first age of the world. These tribes have no power over one another nor even ties among them. They live separately and are often at war; each has its own little independent government that it establishes itself, and its own uncomplicated legislation. If Rousseau . . . would have sought his models in the Atlas . . . he would have found men subject to a sort of social police, yet nonetheless almost as free as the isolated individual who enjoys his savage independence in the heart of the woods. . . . But Rousseau might not have approved so much of several of the Kabyles political axioms. These people have as their fundamental maxim that no foreigner should set foot on their territory. . . . [I]f it pleased you to visit them in their mountains, even if you came with the best intentions in the world, even if you had no aim but to speak about morality, civilization, fine arts, political economy, or philosophy, they would assuredly cut off your head. It is a principle of government they obstinately resolve never to breach.[9]

The entire region that had once been under precarious Roman domination, and later the Ottomans, in his view demanded the application of policies to ensure the success of French sovereignty.[10] Thus, for the Algerian Muslim population, "There is neither usefulness nor obligation to allow [them] an exaggerated idea of their own importance, nor to persuade them that we have a duty to treat them under all circumstances as if they were our fellow citizens and our equals. They know that we have a dominant position in Africa; they expect us to keep it."[11] For Europeans in Algeria, he advised a privileged but highly circumscribed place, not to be fully controlled from the center, yet far from enjoying self-rule. Algerian independence, similar to that which the Anglo-

---

also, Michael Hereth, *Alexis de Tocqueville: Threats to Freedom in Democracy*, trans. George Bogardus (Durham, N.C., Duke University Press, 1986), pp. 157–65; Tzvetan Todorov, "Tocqueville et la doctrine coloniale," in Alexis de Tocqueville, *De la colonie en Algérie*, ed. Tzvetan Todorov (Brussels: Editions Complexe, 1988), 9–34; Stéphane Dion, "Durham et Tocqueville sur la colonisation libérale," *Journal of Canadian Studies*, 25, no. 1 (1990), 60–78.

[9] "Première lettre sur l'Algérie," OC 3 (*Ecrits et discours politiques*) part 1, 131–32.

[10] "Rapports sur l'Algérie 1847," in Alexis de Tocqueville, *Oeuvres*, ed. André Jardin, with the collaboration of Françoise Mélonio and Lise Queffélec, 2 vols. (Paris: Gallimard, 1991), I, 799–809. Cited hereafter as *Oeuvres*.

[11] Ibid., 814.

Americans had carved out for themselves, was not desirable.[12] Not surprisingly, his animus against centralization, which he said was more dangerous once you were further away from Paris, would be especially dangerous in Algeria, which was even more distant. He opposed a rigid centralizing regime directed from Paris for the Europeans who were colonizing the area, counseling instead a self-governing network of villages as the best hope for a sound political life based on independent and individual decisions. It was absurd that no provisions were being considered for a colonial assembly, for municipal government not manned by chosen officials, guarantees of liberty of the press, electoral rights and jury trial – which was an unbelievably shortsighted policy for a colonial power that should instead cultivate independence of mind, but most of all understand that its authority rested on the benefits to be reaped from consolidating local links among the colonists with common interest to cultivate and defend.[13] The indigenous population of Algeria were to be given different treatment. He believed it futile to extend French liberties to them. "Those who have been there [in Africa] know that the Muslim and Christian societies unfortunately have no links, that they form two juxtaposed, but completely separate bodies. They daily know that this condition of affairs tends to grow for reasons which cannot be stopped. . . . The fusion of these two populations is a chimera dreamed of by those who have not been on the spot [to see for themselves]."[14] In Algeria, France should work toward partial colonization and total domination,[15] and encourage the coexistence of two cultures, the existing Muslim one and a future Christian one brought there by French colonists. He did not conceal what for him were obviously distasteful policies that gave greater

---

[12] By a decree of December 9, 1848, the areas of Algeria under civilian as opposed to military control became three *départements*, each divided, as in France, into districts and subdivided into communes, administered by prefects, sub-prefects, and mayors. The former "mixed" and "Arab" territories remained in the hands of the military. This dual system ended in 1858, when a policy of "assimilation" was extended to the Muslim population. The plan ostensibly was to break down the hierarchical social system in which aristocratic landowners exploited sharecroppers. It resulted, however, in the exploitation of the native sharecroppers by the Europeans. After the suppression of an uncoordinated rebellion in 1871, the new French government of the Third Republic caved in to the demands of the *colons* and exacted lands and money for further colonization. For a compact account, see Charles-Robert Ageron, *Modern Algeria*, trans. Michael Brett (London: Hurst & Company, 1991). See also, Douglas Johnson, "The Maghrib," *The Cambridge History of Africa*, vol. 5, c. 1790 to c. 1870, ed. John E. Flint (Cambridge: Cambridge University Press, 1976), 99–124.

[13] "Travail sur l'Algérie (octobre 1841)," *Oeuvres*, I, 725–37.

[14] Ibid., 752.   [15] Ibid., 695–99.

judicial protection to the indigenous populations than to the European civil population. At the same time, he deplored the confiscation of Arab lands for the benefit of Europeans who exploited the former Arab owners as laborers. Tocqueville's concept of civilization was once again put on display:

> In Africa, Muslim society was not uncivilized; it was merely backward and imperfect. . . . [W]e have made Muslim society much more miserable, more disordered, more ignorant, and more barbarous than it was before it came to know us.
>
> It is doubtless a good thing to employ indigenous peoples as agents of the government, but on condition that we provide leadership according to civilized views, sharing our French maxims. This has not always occurred, nor has it occurred everywhere, and we can be accused sometimes less of having civilized the indigenous administration than of having reinforced its barbarism with European forms and intelligence.
>
> Theories are sometimes linked to these actions. In various writings, the professed doctrine is that the indigenous population, having reached the most extreme degree of depravity and vice, is forever incapable of any amendment and of all progress; that, far from enlightening them, we must rather end by depriving them of the knowledge they possess.[16]

There is a slightly schizophrenic cast to these remarks. Ironically, he took advantage of his friend Arthur de Gobineau's stays in various parts of the Near East to deepen his knowledge of Muslim societies, and from this information he strengthened his notions of cultural divisions. He came thus to express his belief in the superiority of Western culture, and turned to Christianity as instrumental in deepening original and modern notions of individual worth, individual conscience, and liberty, lacking, he felt, in other cultures. The French, he went on to say, had no duty – nor would it be useful – to let their Muslim subjects indulge in exaggerated ideas of their own importance. They could not be treated in every circumstance precisely as if they were equals and fellow-citizens. Semi-civilized peoples understood justice, not indulgence. Furthermore, they had the capacity to understand the values of good government. A benign paternalism, designed to encourage the development of their imperfect societies, would not be successful if it imposed European values. He vaguely spoke of helping to revitalize Islam, which he said was not inherently resistant to enlightenment, since Islamic culture had a history of

---

[16] "Rapports sur l'Algérie 1847," ibid., 813.

innovation in the arts and sciences.[17] While Tocqueville conceded that the Muslim religion possessed durable foundations and achievements, he maintained that it had a retrograde notion of liberty. Nor did he predict, as in the case of Native Americans, the extinction of the Kabyles, descendants of Arab women and Turkish soldiers, who formed the most populous group of Berbers and who, though they too had achieved a degree of civilization, seemed to have reached a limit and had failed to advance further. Room had to be made for them. Their survival as an identifiable group was explained by their proximity and continued hostility to the Arabs, the power of their religion, but especially their tribal organization, which the mountainous terrain helped keep intact.[18] Conflict in the Algerian colony appeared to him to engender separate identities. Arabic society was aristocratic, while the Kabyles, in utter contrast, lived in small tribes, fiercely proud of their independence, and were partial to democratic notions of property and government – a feature to which Tocqueville had not given attention ten years earlier. Indeed, he compared the Kabyles to the Swiss of the small cantons of the Middle Ages. Nothing should be done to upset their social and political organization, especially by ill-advised plans to impose military control over them.[19]

Tocqueville asked his friend in the United States, Francis Lieber, to send him materials that would permit a comparative analysis between Algerian and American geography and tribal organization.[20] But he did not complete it. Anglo-American exclusion of both the aboriginal and Afro-American populations paralleled Tocqueville's active, rather than passive, encouragement of French domination of divided and mutually unfriendly, if not totally hostile, cultural groups in Algeria. Underlying both his attitudes toward non-Anglo-Americans and non-European Algerians was his undying belief in the superiority of European civilization.

---

[17] Ibid., 814–15. Seymour Drescher sums up Tocqueville's position well, a viewpoint he shared with Beaumont: "Rejecting the principle of totally dependent individuals, Tocqueville and Beaumont embraced the principle of dependent peoples." *Dilemmas of Democracy, Tocqueville and Modernization* (Pittsburgh: University of Pittsburgh Press, 1968), p. 194.

[18] "Notes du voyage en Algérie de 1841," *Oeuvres*, I, 685–86.

[19] "Rapports sur l'Algérie 1847," ibid., 853–54.

[20] Tocqueville to Lieber, July 22, 1846, OC 7 (*Correspondance étrangère d'Alexis de Tocqueville*), 110–11. Lieber warned against comparisons that diminished the differences between the Arabs and Native Americans, Lieber to Tocqueville, September 25, 1846, 111–12, note 7, ibid. Melvin Richter condemns Tocqueville for "failing to apply to the French action in North Africa ... the sociological insight and ethical awareness he had demonstrated in his study of the United States." See "Tocqueville on Algeria," 363.

Still, if parallels were to be drawn between the Kabyles and the aboriginal Americans, he gave the first much more leeway to develop their future on the ground that they possessed a more highly developed social organization. There was, of course, in indigenous Algeria a population that had not been pushed to the extremities of extermination and desolation experienced by Red Americans, and who asserted their identity in a renascent tribalism – the attribution to one's self and to one's tribe of an essential humanity denied to others. This is matched, of course, by vociferous expressions of competing American tribalisms, and as well by groups ready to do injury and harm in defense of essentialism. At first sight, there appear to be no obvious analogies between French-Arabic culture in Algeria and white-black culture in the United States in the nineteenth century. Yet if we extend our gaze to the period almost a century later, long after Tocqueville's death, when "qualified" Arabs gained civil and political rights, we find a parallel in the Reconstruction period when black Americans gained the franchise, which they then lost for several generations, and regained only in the 1960s.

Tocqueville and Slavery

Was there any possibility of an African-American revolution? Just as Tocqueville thought that revolutions were unlikely to break out in democracies, so in 1840 he did not see how the slaves could mount a revolutionary challenge, a question that I will explore more fully later in this chapter. He was acutely aware of the troubling and, he believed, shameful blot of slavery, but he did not think that even if it were ended, Afro-Americans possessed the resources to become part of the American political community. They had been robbed of and lost, in their servitude, the pride they had once possessed as peoples, and were unable to face their masters who proudly vaunted the superiority of their race. It was hard enough to try to erase the marks of legal inferiority and inequality, sanctioned in a privileged aristocratic society, let alone erase the "visible and indelible signs" of color (I, chap. 18, 372–73). Neither Tocqueville's notion of beginnings, nor American freedom, as it had thus far developed, made provision for them in any realistic future. So the exceptionalism that was born of a new beginning for freedom in America had a vicious side to it.[21] American democracy was impregnated with

---

[21] For the view that Tocqueville's liberalism and racism are indistinguishable, see Curtis Stokes, "Tocqueville and the Problem of Racial Inequality," *Journal of Negro History*, 75 (1990), 1–15.

emotions of deep racism that were unlikely to be lessened or eradicated even under the force of law (I, chap. 18, 390). Moreover, once slavery was abolished – it would not long survive the repugnance felt toward it – it was likely that liberty would be abused, unless the enslaved Americans seized it for themselves (I, chap. 18, 397). The last eventuality was not too remote for Tocqueville to imagine, because of his inclination to think of liberty as an innate and universal human need. In fact, the French Revolution was a compelling example of how the nation, ignoring rank, income, and birth invoked liberty as a unifying force.

But while one form of servility was overthrown in France, the odds against rising above the lasting effects of American slavery to a calm use of liberty were perhaps too great. Still, no other Western nation had to deal with the problem of non-Europeans occupying the same geographical space in quite the same way as did America. American democratic liberty – the very point Tocqueville made at the outset of his theory of beginnings – had nourished a personal pride inseparable from race – the superiority of the white race (I, chap. 18, 389–90). No matter what had been written about slavery that did not take race into account as a major factor, including the fact that during the slave trade Africans enslaved Africans,[22] or Adam Smith's observation that in his day slavery still flourished in eastern Europe, large parts of Asia, and all over Africa,[23]

---

[22] See for instance the examples of slave-owning practices in the Americas examined by Hugh Thomas, *The Slave Trade. The History of the Atlantic Slave Trade, 1440–1870* (London: Macmillan, 1997).

[23] See *The Wealth of Nations*, eds. R.H. Campbell and A.S. Skinner (Indianapolis: Liberty Classics, 1981), III. ii. 8–12. Smith had previously written in his *Lectures on Jurisprudence. Report of 1762–3*, eds. R.L. Meek, D.D. Raphael, and P.G Stein (Indianapolis: Liberty Classics, 1982), iii. 102, that "In a republican government it will scarcely ever happen that it [slavery] should be abolished. The persons who make the laws in that country are persons who have slaves themselves." The republics to which Smith referred were the ancient Greek republics. He then went on to suggest, first, that because North American slaveowners were not all rich, they treated their slaves with some humanity (iii. 107), but more significant was his view that the "more arbitrary the government is in like manner the slaves are in better condition, and the freer the people the more miserable are the slaves; in a democracy they are more miserable than in any other. The greater [the] freedom of the free, the more intollerable (sic) is the slavery of the slaves. Opulence and freedom, the two greatest blessings man can possess, tend greatly to the misery of this body of men, which in most countries where slavery is allowed makes by far the greatest part. A humane man would wish therefore if slavery has to be generally established that these greatest blessing[s], being incompatible with the happiness of the greatest part of mankind, were never to take place" (iii. 110). Smith anticipates Tocqueville's point that the existence of freedom, together with the experience of slaves who had been granted their freedom, psychologically prepared the slaves for it.

by Tocqueville's time the racial divide between Afro-Americans and whites had become the decisive justification for the continuance of slavery. The chosen people – the English Pilgrims who had chosen themselves in solemn covenant – jealously guarded their patrimony against others. It was not simply a narrow theocentric conception that they were defending, but an even narrower one that took as its central justification the superiority of a particular human collective at a certain point in history. Is this how we should interpret Tocqueville's reference to the "superiority" of the white race, "in intelligence, in power, and in enjoyment"? Or, when he said, "[i]f we reason from what passes in the world, we should almost say that the European is to the other races of mankind what man himself is to the lower animals" (I, chap. 18, 344), and then, when unable to subdue them, he destroys them, justifying what we today define as genocide? Or was he simply recording what he thought to be a long-standing, irreducible prejudice, recalling much of the conventional thought of his day? After all we know of his attacks on the cruelty and inhumanity of slavery, it is abundantly clear that race for him was a cultural, not a biological, aspect of the human species.[24] We can also feel secure, though with some reservations, in suggesting that when he took human beings seriously as subjects, he understood that their integrity rested on their freedom, not only to act, but that it is an act of will born from a sense of beginning. His trouble arose from being unable to find a clear passage to a point allowing fruitful beginnings for all human beings. The difficulty could not be resolved by ascribing and finding a solution to it in logic. Rather it stemmed from the twin-sided nature of

---

[24] Montesquieu dealt with the origins of slavery, remarking that "slaves are contrary to the spirit of the constitution," whether of a monarchy, and especially of a democracy "where everyone is equal." *The Spirit of the Laws*, trans. and eds. Ann Cohler et al. (Cambridge: Cambridge University Press, 1989), Part 3, Bk. 15, chap. 1, p. 246. In chap. 5, p. 250, he offers a caricature of the European stereotype of black slavery, before going on to write about its "true origin" in the rest of Bk. 15. On seventeenth-century notions of race, and François Bernier's attempt at racial classification, see Siep Stuurman, "François Bernier and the Invention of Racial Classification," *History Workshop Journal*, no. 50 (2000), 1–21. For French eighteenth-century views, see Michèle Duchet, *Anthropologie et histoire au siècle des lumières* (Paris: Flammarion, 1971). For more recent studies, which go beyond the French world, see Ivan Hannaford, *Race: The History of an Idea in the West* (Washington: Woodrow Wilson Center Press; Baltimore and London: Johns Hopkins University Press, 1996) and Nicholas Hudson, "From 'Nation' to 'Race': The Origin of Racial Classification," *Eighteenth-Century Studies*, 29 (1996), 247–64. Also consult, André Jardin, "Alexis de Tocqueville, Gustave de Beaumont et le problème de l'inégalité des races," in Pierre Guiral and Emile Temime, eds., *L'idée de race dans la pensée politique française contemporaine* (Paris: Editions du CNRS, 1977), pp. 200–19.

American democracy, on the one hand liberating, on the other hand oppressive; the one promising inclusiveness, the other securing its opposite.

Could there not be a time when white Americans might take cognizance of and show respect for those who lived in but did not feel themselves to be part of and were not permitted to share in the American future? If liberty did come to the slaves, without ending at the same time their feelings of misery and ignominy, the ground for a future slave rebellion would indeed be prepared (I, chap. 18, 395). The American slavocracy saw no choice, Tocqueville said, if they wanted to ensure the permanence of their power, but to use "their despotism and their violence against the human mind" (ibid.). Unlike the ancients, who did not restrain the minds of their slaves, the slaveholders acted both on their bodies and minds, yet much more effectively against the mind than the body. We are invited, so to speak, to remember how Tocqueville exclaimed against the tyranny of the majority:

> [T]he civilization of our age has perfected despotism itself, though it seemed to have nothing to learn. Monarchs had, so to speak, materialized oppression; the democratic republics of the present day have rendered it as entirely an affair of the mind as the will which it is intended to coerce. Under the absolute sway of one man the body was attacked in order to subdue the soul; but the soul escaped the blows which were directed against it and rose proudly superior. Such is not the course adopted by tyranny in democratic republics; there the body is left free and the soul is enslaved (I, chap. 15, 274).

Perhaps without fully intending it, Tocqueville drew a parallel between the tyranny of democratic majorities and the tyranny of slaveholders by according to both the doubtful honor of breaking the defenses of the soul. And, as if to make such a point more salient, he claimed that the American slave's physical condition had been improved. He perceived, long before most planters could bring themselves to question the economic advantages of slavery, that its rationale lay in an ethos of pure racialism.[25] However, when he wrote that the slaveholders' fear of "commingling" reduced the slaves to the level of "brutes," he did not, I believe, mean that they had reduced them to total animality, for to have done so would have been to bring down the entire institution, economic and racial. The slaveholders were not intent on destruction

---

[25] *Oeuvres*, I, 117, 132, for instances where the economic costs of slavery were acknowledged by those Southern plantation owners who sold surplus slaves in a declining market.

or elimination (as the Nazis were when they reduced the Jews to almost total animality by snuffing out any hope of survival by the uninterrupted action of the killing machine), but instead sought to exploit the productive labor of their slaves, while ensuring their bondage. Humiliation and shame were constantly present in the lives of the slaves, but they did not suffer them in the ultimate manifestation the Jews endured in the camps where they were put to "work" doing things that were not a means to any end ("other than humiliating and shaming them").[26] As a group, the slaveowners were not guilty of such conduct. By extending to the slaves participation in productive labor, they unintentionally kept before them the hope of freedom. Such was the inevitable dynamic of the master/slave relationship. So long as "The hope of liberty [was] allowed to the slave to cheer the hardships of his condition," the possibility of ending the relationship presented itself to the slaves. Thus, if the slave masters, as Tocqueville argued, believed it necessary to act violently against their minds, the masters paradoxically acknowledged that they were not simply brutes. In their actions, the masters daily let it be known that the

---

[26] Avishai Margalit, "Decent Equality and Freedom: A Postscript," *Social Research*, 64 (1997), 157. See Margalit's *The Decent Society* (Cambridge, Mass., Harvard University Press, 1996) for a fuller treatment of humiliation and the conditions that are needed for maintaining a humane society. See also Avishai Margalit and Gabriel Motzkin, "The Uniqueness of the Holocaust," *Philosophy and Public Affairs*, 25 (1996), 65–83. The idea that "the" Jew was not a simple instrument of labor for the Nazis, and, indeed, that he was regarded not even as an animal, but was debased and degraded in a process leading to the annihilation of a non-being outside the human species, as a heap of material, forces us to look beyond the psychological margins of humiliation. See, in addition, Vladimir Jankélévich's arguments in, "Shall We Pardon Them," trans. Ann Hobart, *Critical Inquiry*, 22 (1996), 552–72. A different view is taken by Giorgio Agamben, *Homo Sacer. Sovereign Power and Bare Life*, trans. Daniel Heller-Roazen (Stanford: Stanford University Press, 1998). His highly original study shows how, especially in our own democratic and totalitarian times, human beings, when reduced to their bare lives (that is, their natural beings), face the full weight of sovereign power, which alone has the right to kill, not because they have surrendered that right to it, but because, as Hobbes puts it, they *leave* but *do not give* that right of punishment to him in a condition of "mere nature." The sovereign thus gains the right to kill, but those killed are not sacrificed. Inspired by Foucault's theory of biopolitics, but going beyond it to discuss the concentration camps, Agamben suggests that it is an error to think of the Jewish victims as sacrificial, for what indeed were they sacrificed to? As non-human beings, "'as lice,' which is to say, as bare life," they could scarcely qualify as victims (p. 114). Agamben's *Remnants of Auschwitz. The Witness and the Archive*. trans. Daniel Heller-Roazen (New York: Zone Books, 1999) explores the different meanings of shame and dignity. For Bernard Williams, *Shame and Necessity* (Berkeley, Los Angeles and London: University of California Press, 1993), p. 220, "The root of shame lies in exposure . . . in being at a disadvantage: in what I shall call, in a very general phrase, a loss of power. The sense of shame is a reaction of the subject to the consciousness of his loss."

truth of their condition lay inscribed not only in the bodies but in the racially inferior minds of the slaves.[27] (The same was true, but much more extremely in Nazi behavior; in their case, it was not the inferior slave mind that had to be kept in check, but the insidious Jewish mind that had to be exterminated.) It was the anxiety about the possibility, the anxiety of freedom, not depression about the permanence of slavery, that kept hopes alive.

Frederick Douglass was later to say that the demand on the part of slaveowners to "annihilate the power of reason of the slave" was coupled with the need to make him [the slave] "feel that slavery is right; and he can be brought to that only when he ceases to be a man."[28] Douglass writes about the infantalization and emasculation of the slave, and does not give enough weight to the fact that freedom was not absent from the minds of the slaves, and that the slaveholders, who knew it, tried to extinguish this thought, but could not wholly succeed. And, as we have seen, Tocqueville did entertain the possibility of a reversal initiated by the slaves themselves, but he set this aside as unlikely on the grounds that a beaten people could not win their own freedom by themselves. The Afro-Americans – even those who were free men – were caught in a double bind: "To induce the whites to abandon the opinion they have conceived of the moral and intellectual inferiority of their former slaves, the Negroes must change; but as long as this opinion persists, they cannot change" (I, chap. 18, 372 note 32).

Tocqueville's condemnation of slavery was unequivocal. It was an "execrable principle," wreaking "unparalleled atrocities," demonstrative of the total perversion of the "laws of humanity" (ibid., 394–95).[29] It was incompatible with the new political world, transformed by democracy, that to be true to itself, should "enable individual man to maintain whatever independence, strength and original power he still possesses" (II, Bk. 4, chap. 7, 347). Tocqueville famously disputed Gobineau's biological determinism and belief in white superiority, and tellingly – in

---

[27] For a brilliant study of how the Greeks tortured slaves to know the truth "buried" in their bodies and minds, see Page duBois, *Torture and Truth* (New York and London: Routledge, 1991), particularly chaps. 4, 6, and 8.

[28] Frederick Douglass, *Narrative of the Life of Frederick Douglass, an American Slave* (New York: Viking Penguin, 1982), p. 135.

[29] Later in 1839, he disputed that slavery had been necessary to human life and the development of industry and therefore justifiable in the past. Free labor, not slavery, was the root of industrial civilization. Slavery, he said was "a horrible abuse of force." See his "Discours improvisé à l'Académie des sciences Morales et Politiques de l'Institut," 20 avril 1839? OC 16 (*Mélanges*), 165–67. The dating is as in the original.

response to the latter's highly speculative philological theories – dismissed them partly on the grounds that written records to plot the stages of human development from its origins were simply not available.[30] He rejected Gobineau's blunt reductionism whereby "the racial question overshadows all other problems of history [and] holds the key to them all," and, in its reductionist mode, assigned the lowest place on the ladder to "the Negroid variety."[31] The term "race" had no basis in theories of biological determinism that formed the foundation of the South's apologetics, which for Gobineau explained the inequality of peoples. Rather beliefs in the racial division of humanity could be traced, however hesitatingly, to cultural causes. And these in turn could not be divorced from stages in societal development, so that, for instance, one could acknowledge differences between primitive and advanced societies. Racial differences were hence not manifestly determining, either in the sense of creating or justifying a hierarchy of primitive and advanced, superior and inferior peoples. Race was, Tocqueville insisted, not to be singled out as the decisive factor determining cultural states. Besides, the comparative study of human cultures was in a state of infancy. What he did say was that:

> There is in every nation, whether as the result of race or prolonged education, something very tenacious, perhaps something permanent that is tied in with all the events of its [a nation's] destiny and may be perceived throughout every turn of chance, in all the epochs of its history. This is especially true of half-civilized nations which have existed apart from others for long periods of time. To clearly discern the particular features which distinguish the physiognomy of the masses making up the human species is a precondition for speaking clearly about them.[32]

Hierarchies among human beings, he admitted, existed, but they were not likely to be nor could they be assumed to be biological. He noted while he was in America that there was indeed no monolithic racial theory, that there were dissident voices who maintained that Afro-Americans were not an inferior portion of the human species, but on the contrary were as enterprising, as intelligent, and as capable of education as whites. The Quaker John Jay Smith the Librarian in Philadelphia, told Tocqueville that the only way to save the South from the disaster of

---

[30] Tocqueville to Gobineau, November 17, 1853, OC 9 (*Correspondance d'Alexis de Tocqueville et d'Arthur de Gobineau*), 202.

[31] Arthur de Gobineau, *Essay on the Inequality of the Human Races* (1853–55), trans. Adrian Collins (London, 1915), pp. 120, 173.

[32] Tocqueville to Beaumont, November 3, 1853, OC 8 (*Correspondance d'Alexis de Tocqueville et de Gustave de Beaumont*) part 3, 164.

unchallenged slavery would be to adapt a form of serfdom as a transition to a state of a more complete liberty.[33]

Neither was a theory of geographical determinism part of Tocqueville's way of understanding changes in human society. He favored a rough conjectural stadial theory of human development, which embraced a view of peoples throughout the globe as living in designated parts of the world in primitive or savage conditions – the hunting and pastoral ages – followed in ascending order, by agricultural and commercial societies.[34] The particular force of geography – the knowledge of the uses by human beings of physical sources on the planet, as well as their distribution – remained a mystery, but Tocqueville was reasonably certain that when more work was devoted to the study of human instincts, habits, and preferences, the influence of environment would be far from negligible, if not in fact decisive.[35] Though there were, he believed, certain constants in human behavior, such as the expression of the entire range of human emotions, he did not embrace a theory of a universal and constant human nature that would, for example, valorize honor in quite the same way in every culture. The notions and practices of honor in aristocratic and democratic societies were indeed different, but notions of honor itself did not disappear from the human psyche. Neither society nor history could be understood in either wholly universal or relative terms. He was not partial to eighteenth-century views that all human groups moved through successive historic states, and which, whatever that state is at any given time, will reach the same point of development, marking the same hour, as it were, though at different times. The stadial view is by definition "progressive," since it does not assume that all societies move from primitive forms of social and economic organization to less primitive and presumably higher states of individual and collective being. There was some engine of adaptation at work, but its mechanisms awaited conceptualization and empirical verification.

Tocqueville's ideas of civilization and the movement of history made ample room for contingency, and thereby reduced the certainty of

---

[33] Conversation with Smith, October 25, 1831, in *Oeuvres*, I, 243–44. See also Pierson, *Tocqueville and Beaumont in America*, p. 513.

[34] For the classic treatment of the stadial theory of history, see Ronald L. Meek, *Social Science and the Ignoble Savage* (Cambridge: Cambridge University Press, 1976).

[35] Tocqueville to Beaumont, October 25, 1829, OC 8 (*Correspondance d'Alexis de Tocqueville et de Gustave de Beaumont*) part 1, pp. 92–94. For a reconstruction of human history that gives primacy of place to geography and environment over the globe and over long spans of time, see Jared Diamond, *Guns, Germs, and Steel: The Fates of Human Societies* (New York: Norton, 1997).

outcomes, whether we look at his considerations on the democratization of Western society, or at his belief that such a transformation, in some respects, was producing a superior form of social organization. He was much less optimistic about the power of reason to move humanity toward perfection. To a large degree, Tocqueville, we remember, thought that Native Americans formed a single culture that would eventually become extinct. But he did not think that other nomadic peoples, such as the Kabyles whom he praised for their simple democratic organization, were inevitably destined to disappear. While respecting historical laws, he was not sure that the laws were so single-"minded." As for the Anglo-Americans, their belief in democracy did indeed give enormous energy and force to their notion of perfectibility. Every advance, technological and otherwise, was taken as evidence for the progressive improvement of life, and was identified with human perfectibility. Belief in perfectibility, however, carried a reasonable idea beyond the limits of reason (II, Bk. I, chap. 8, 34–35). But rather than allying himself with those who would restrict the scope of perfectibility characteristic of an aristocratic age, he equated the belief in freedom with "the perfection of the human species, which is at the head of human creation."[36] But, again, he qualified his enthusiasm. Both the belief in a naive perfectibility and in reason – key Enlightenment concepts – would earn his not entirely unjustified scorn in his study of the Old Regime. Poets in democratic times might possess the vision and imagination to expand the human mind, but only in the sense of enriching their lives by making them more reflective (II, Bk. I, chap. 17, 78).

Like Marx, Tocqueville witnessed the destruction of Europe's traditional order, the triumph of the bourgeois ethos, the struggle of the working classes for political and economic power. At the same time, he was fairly sure of, if not the disappearance, the decline of non-European societies.[37] Individuals could in some instances move from one culture to, and be assimilated into, another, but always by observing existing intricate rules of caste and class formation. Whole collectivities could not. While Tocqueville rejected race as a criterion in determining cultural

---

[36] Tocqueville to Gobineau, January 24, 1857, OC 9 (*Correspondance d'Alexis de Tocqueville et d'Arthur Gobineau*) part 3, 280.

[37] Tocqueville also noted the European and American penetration of China in the 1850s, and predicted that the Chinese would not long survive the absence of "true" spiritual foundations. As it was, he said, they lived lives of self-contented materialism and were steeped in a species of Epicureanism. See Tocqueville to Beckwith, September 7, 1858, in OC 7 (*Correspondance étrangère d'Alexis de Tocqueville*), 235–37.

differences, he supported, we are now justified in saying, a theory of civilization to explain the survival of some cultures and the decline and disappearance of others, as well as attributing superior characteristics of adaptation to the first.

We may now see why Tocqueville could hardly be receptive to ideas such as that which would impose serfdom for slavery as an intermediate stage leading to American advancement. Those who supported it believed in it as one reasonable way to avoid violence. Slower change was preferable. Equally important was the belief that only people capable of creating their own freedom contributed to civilization; and while condemning the authors of their servitude, he placed them below "the superior in intelligence, in power and enjoyment . . . the white, or European, the MAN preeminently so called" (I, chap. 18, 344). Other peoples, he acknowledged, as we saw, had beginnings as well, but they were lost in an undetermined time. The original languages of Afro-Americans had fallen into disuse and their memory of their religion and customs had been almost obliterated. For Ralph Ellison, whom we will meet again in the next chapter, by contrast, this brew of lost memories, lost languages, and the search for something with which to replace them propelled Afro-Americans to become Americans, for once set down in the new land they invented something totally new from the bricolage of their own pasts and the fragments brought to America from Europe by whites.[38]

Yet, Tocqueville saw mainly that because Negroes were tied by slavery to the land, they had become a servile part of an agricultural society. Their beginnings had the earmark of originality, but it was not a fully willed beginning. They remained rootless, living in a half-way house, neither, Tocqueville maintained, African nor American (ibid.). By being fixed on the land, even as slaves, however, they were, by a simple comparison of their condition with that of their free masters, able to yearn for the end of their servitude, and thus to imagine the foundations for a

---

[38] "Indivisible Man," in *The Collected Essays of Ralph Ellison*. Introduced by John F. Callahan (New York: The Modern Library, 1995), p. 368: "We had to learn English. We had, in other words, to create ourselves as a people – and this I take right down to the racial, the bloodlines, the mingling of African blood with the bloodlines indigenous to the New World." He adds that "Culturally, we (black Americans) represent a synthesis of any number of . . . elements": "Indian, Spanish, Irish, part any and every damn thing." In the "Haverford Statement" of May 30–31, 1969, ibid., p. 430, Ellison is even more forceful on this point when he speaks of the "American people united in all their diversity by a bond of language, partially the creation of a voice which found its origins in Africa."

new beginning – thinking of themselves as having the attributes of choice, but not yet with the resources to transform them into acts. If there were examples, as in communities of free Afro-Americans, where the assimilation of the attributes of American civilization including literacy was taking place, Tocqueville observed, they were prevented by hostile local practices from exercising their rights at the polls, to assemble freely, or to bear arms. Even limited forms of political assimilation remained unacceptable to Anglo-Americans. This resistance by no means ended the black assertion of whatever shards of dignity they possessed; and indeed, in cases too numerous to mention, that dignity was not a negligible quality.

For the most part, the dignity remained in the shadows in Tocqueville's account. For one thing, he did not venture into the history of the mingling of the Atlantic African and American worlds. He left unexplored the history of a whole continent. If he believed that the slaves had no memory of their past in Africa, he helped to obscure it by failing to imagine that its preservation was indeed a vital part of the slave experience. For another, he absorbed too readily and rather too quickly the critiques of the slaveholding economy that Northerners were only too eager to present to him to sharpen their sense of the superiority of their own commercial economy based on free white labor and entrepreneurial skills. What remained with him was a portrayal of an indolent slaveholding aristocracy, struggling to keep its agrarian economy alive, and losing out to the market economy of the North – an assessment that reverses the South's real economic strength, which was created by a class of slaveholders acutely responsive to market forces.[39] Along with it came a picture of the black population so oppressed by the demands of sugar, rice, cotton, and tobacco cultivation as to make impossible any semblance of a black culture with a distinct sense of community, language, or family loyalties.[40] He had few if any inklings of how the Afro-American populations lived once they were settled as slave workers in America. He did not think to ask what the structures of a master-slave society looked like, and how they changed as many of the conditions – demographic, economic development, technology, and complex movements of cultural recognition and rejection – changed. But it would be an error to accuse Tocqueville for failing to ask the kinds of questions

[39] Robert W. Fogel, *Without Consent or Contract. The Rise and Fall of American Slavery* (New York and London: W.W. Norton, 1989), chaps. 3–4.

[40] For the classic story of black family relations, see Herbert G. Gutman, *The Black Family in Slavery and Freedom, 1750–1925* (New York: Vintage, 1977).

that have only recently become part of American historiography.[41] He may, however, be criticized for a failure of imagination. The Native American touched his romantic fantasies that found their origin in a literature of imaginary voyages; they gained his empathy; by contrast, transported Africans gained his pity and not a little condescension, though not without some acknowledgment that he might have underestimated their resilience and skills of survival. How they survived was a closed book for Tocqueville, and the degree to which he held it shut cannot be explained without conceding as significant the very weighty cultural baggage that he brought with him to America.

The anti-slavery movement was not given its due either, chiefly because he was unable to imagine how blacks and whites could live together in a free society. So he came to the stark conclusion that the separation of the races, not only biological but geographical, would mark the future of American democracy. An American system of apartheid was what he saw in store for it. That this has not happened was due to the energies and high ideals of evangelical reformers who took the lead in the anti-slavery campaigns and who also participated in the temperance and women's rights movements. They not only wanted to blot slavery out, but to find practical ways to integrate blacks into general society, and they rejected the view that the only alternatives were a racially mixed or a racially separated society, as Tocqueville maintained. Indeed, as Robert Fogel notes, the supporters of William Lloyd Garrison organized campaigns to gain equal civil rights for blacks in the courts, in elections, and in churches, and also worked to forge ties with black abolitionists.[42] As Fogel phrases it, the power of one group of people to have full control over another was seen to be "profoundly evil and corrupting" and originally motivated the religious radicals who initiated the campaign (no matter how overlaid with political expediency it became). Moreover, it served to bring about an egalitarian ethic.[43] The creation of a viable

---

[41] A large and significant part of this aspect of the early history of American slavery may be sampled in Ira Berlin, *Many Thousands Gone. The First Two Centuries of Slavery in North America* (Cambridge, Mass. and London: Belknap Press of Harvard University Press, 1998). Berlin is intent on showing how masters and slaves continually negotiated their relationships, how, "if slavery made *race*, its larger purpose was to make *class*" (p. 5, his italics), and why a linear analysis or a premise of false optimism does an injustice to Afro-Americans who tried "to fashion a world of their own in circumstances not of their own making" (p. 12).

[42] Robert W. Fogel, *Without Consent or Contract*, pp. 265, 276–77.

[43] Robert W. Fogel, *The Fourth Great Awakening and the Future of Egalitarianism* (Chicago and London: University of Chicago Press, 2000), p. 104.

anti-slavery coalition with a real chance to influence politics, however, took more than two decades of work: by the late 1850s, Tocqueville watched the changes from afar and hoped that the rupture of the Union would be avoided.

The project of resettling Afro-Americans in Liberia where, Tocqueville believed, some few thousand were said to have introduced democratic institutions, may have been inspired by fine ideals. He observed ironically that descendants of the slaves brought to America were now, upon settling in Liberia, with the help of the American Colonization Society,[44] introducing free political institutions such as a representative system of government. But recolonization schemes offered no remedy to the black demographic explosion. From 1820 to 1832, the comparative figures showed 2,500 Negroes transported back to Africa as against 700,000 born in the American states. But the most compelling argument against such a policy was that it did not address the morality of slavery: "It [transportation] could not prevent the growth of the evil which is daily increasing in the states. The Negro race will never leave those shores of the American continent to which it was brought by the passions and the vices of Europeans; and it will not disappear from the New World as long as it continues to exist. The inhabitants of the United States may retard the calamities which they apprehend, but they cannot now destroy their efficient cause" (I, chap. 18, 393–94). It was plain that America, in Tocqueville's eyes, had to face this problem by dealing with it at home. It could not be exported either physically or psychologically. The fantasy of " 'getting shut' of Negro America," the fantasy of "a benign amputation" continued long after Liberia came into existence, but had become more insidiously rooted, as Ellison said over a hundred years later.[45]

Tocqueville's denunciation of American slavery, which was published in *The Liberty Bell* in 1856 and reprinted in William Lloyd Garrison's *Liberator*, the most important abolitionist newspaper, starkly pointed to the tragic paradox of the existence of slavery in the most civilized and

[44] The Society, as Robert W. Fogel tells us in *Without Consent or Contract*, pp. 252–53, did the most to revitalize anti-slavery activity, but it did not, in deference to the slaveholders, challenge the legality of slavery, and stressed that it wanted only to remove free Negroes. Despite its cautious program and "despite the many slaveholders who felt that clearing free Negroes from the South would reduce the danger of insurrection, militant leaders of the proslavery bloc, especially in the deep South, viewed the Colonization Society with alarm."

[45] Ralph Ellison, "What America Would be Like Without Blacks," in *Going to the Territory* (New York: Random House, 1986), p. 107.

free society in the world.[46] The paradox was even greater, as Tocqueville reminds us in the *Democracy*, when one realized that Christians in the sixteenth century reestablished slavery, not as a rule embracing the entire human race, but as an exception, "restrict[ing] it to one of the races of mankind" and thus inflicted a "wound . . . upon humanity," which "though less extensive, was far more difficult to cure" (I, chap. 18, p. 371). Thus, in the American experience, Christian acceptance of human bondage rested uneasily alongside Tocqueville's notion of a positive conjunction of religion and liberty. Indeed, he specifically sited the principles of equality within the Christian Gospels, upon which he founded his argument that the United States came closest to furnishing the best example of a modern civil society based on universalist principles. By repeatedly singling out the Gospels, he threw into bold relief the nether side of Christian thought. In defending them, he would go only so far as to support the abolitionist struggle and the Free Soil movement against the expansion of slavery in the western states and territories, while opposing abolition in the original slaveholding states as dangerous and premature. A feeling of unease remains, however, because Tocqueville's theory of beginnings and freedom rests entirely on making room for change. The choice he made rested on his observations that white Americans were not prepared to create an interracial society. He candidly confessed that "if I had the misfortune of living in a country where slavery had been introduced and that if I hold in my hand the liberty of the Blacks I would not open it."[47] Rather than viewing the abolitionists as working with some chance of success toward the eventual integration of the freed slaves in a re-created organic community, he saw them as endangering its fragile supports.[48]

---

[46] OC 7 (*Correspondance étrangère d'Alexis de Tocqueville*), 163–64. Later that year, Tocqueville told Gobineau that the anti-abolitionists had translated the part of his book (*Essai sur l'inégalité des races humaines*) that "tends to prove that the Negroes belong to another, to a different and inferior race, but they suppressed the part which tends to argue that, like every other, the Anglo-Saxon race is also decaying." Tocqueville to Gobineau, July 30, 1856, OC 9 (*Correspondance d'Alexis de Tocqueville et d'Arthur de Gobineau*), 267–68. We should remember that he showed no doubt some twenty years earlier that the whites were the world's superior race.

[47] Cited from Tocqueville's notes to *De la Démocratie en Amérique*. First critical edition, revised and augmented, by Eduardo Nolla, 2 vols. (Paris: Librairie Philosophique J. Vrin, 1990), I, 276 note f.

[48] On the power of the abolitionists to alter minds, Richard Rorty makes the point that sentiment is not enough. Though their condescension was not what Tocqueville found offensive, he would not have, I believe, dissented from Rorty's view that reason is the more powerful instrument of change. Rorty writes, "[I]f we hand our hopes for moral

These qualities of Tocqueville's thought are a good example of the ways he spoke of history and the ways of human beings. The paradox he pointed to so clearly in *The Liberty Bell* finds its beginnings in an earlier paradox rooted in the Puritan sense of individual conscience that sanctioned defiance of unlawful authority, yet failed to prevent the aggressive individualism that had strong roots in Puritanism and strained the integrity of community. Its very foundations excluded the possibility of creating space for, and of thinking about, a new beginning for peoples of non-European cultures within a larger community. For in his fear that democratic peoples might move in ways that were inimical to "the great experiment in Self Government,"[49] Tocqueville saw signs of a possible new meaning being given to barbarism, one that was not only the harbinger of modern despotism as he perceived it and which he, as time has proved, exaggerated, but one that certainly subsisted on hubris born of feelings of racial superiority and national pride. The politics of affection, of neighborly, small associations, which rested on both trust and wariness, could not deal easily with the intrusion of people regarded as foreign.[50] It could not at all encompass those thought to be inferior.

It is worth remarking that Tocqueville also had in mind two things. One was that the narrow circles of sociability evident in the society of aristocratic castes could not extend their sensibility to those outside them. The second may be seen in his ambiguous feelings over the affective aspects of the new democratic social ground. These incoherent feelings seem to reflect a like emotional ambiguity that he discerned in the slavocracy that inflicted great suffering upon, yet could show pity toward, its slaves. Yet why were slave masters not affected by the evil? Despite the extermination of whole sections of humanity in the twentieth century, no one has quite matched Tocqueville's elegance and truth: "[T]he same man who is full of humanity towards his fellow creatures

---

progress over to sentiment, we are in fact handing them over to *condescension*. For we shall be relying on those who have the power to change things – people like the rich New England abolitionists . . . rather than relying on something that has power over *them*." The power he refers to is the power, not of niceness, but the power that obedience to the moral law may exert on those who occupy seats of power. The first kind of power must come, he says, from below. Richard Rorty, *Truth and Progress. Philosophical Papers* (Cambridge: Cambridge University Press, 1998), volume 3 pp. 181–82.

[49] Tocqueville to Beckwith, April 2, 1857, OC 7 (*Correspondance étrangère d'Alexis de Tocqueville*), 193.

[50] The challenges, he said, from the influx of non-British immigrants, especially from Germany with its absolutist traditions, would cause tensions. Tocqueville to Sedgwick, August 15, 1854; September 1, 1856, ibid., 159, 182.

when they are at the same time his equals becomes insensible to their afflictions as soon as that equality ceases. His mildness should therefore be attributed to the equality of conditions rather than to civilization and education" (II, Bk. 3, chap. 1, 176). In 1835, the publication data of the first volume of *Democracy*, he said that the presence of "a black population was the greatest threat to the Union" (I, chap. 18, 370). He then went on to argue that despite the existence of a free black population, racial prejudice and intolerance were, if anything, even stronger (ibid., 373). Five years later, in the second volume, he may have startled his readers by changing the focus from equality to inequality:

> If ever America undergoes great revolutions, they will be brought about by the presence of the black race on the soil of the United States; that is to say, they will owe their origin, not to the equality, but to the inequality of conditions (II, Bk. 3, chap. 21, 270).

The paradox enclosing this judgment highlights the fact, noted by Tocqueville elsewhere, that the existence of equality tends, in the long run, to abhor its opposite, even while efforts are exerted to confine it. Thus the politics of the heart may actually operate in all societies, each imposing its own limits, but what remained uncertain in democratic society was whether the divergence between its principles and its practices would become an acute concern, threatening to tear it apart. There is an understandable ambiguity in predicting such a momentous shift in the life – no less than the death – of a new nation. That only a people conscious of its selfhood could mount effective, and if need be, armed resistance to a dominant culture, continued to be Tocqueville's position.[51] Thus, for the moment, whether the revolution would be due to black action or to the whites who favored their liberation was a question he left open, four years after his conversation in Montgomery with John Roberts Poinsett, an anti-nullificationer and later Van Buren's War Secretary, who told him that a slave revolt would never succeed for, even if it were concerted and well led, it would be overwhelmed by superior white resistance. In Tocqueville's transcription, Poinsett said that there

---

[51] On the obstacles to the creation of black revolutionary power, in spite of the unmistakable signs of rifts in master-slave relationships, including those between privileged and non-privileged slaves, as well as the obdurate fact that the slaves had no real weapons to launch an armed attack, see most notably, Eugene D. Genovese, *From Rebellion to Revolution: Afro-American Slave Revolts in the Making of the Modern World* (Baton Rouge: Louisiana State University Press, 1979). See also, Robert W. Fogel, *Without Consent or Contract*, pp. 196–98, and Orlando Patterson, *Slavery and Social Death: A Comparative Study* (Cambridge: Harvard University Press, 1982).

were few dangers from the slaves; if they were informed enough to make a serious revolt, they also knew that it could not succeed.[52]

Tocqueville made no mention of the slave revolt in South Carolina in 1822, nor of Nat Turner's rebellion in Virginia in 1831; and nowhere does he allude to the more momentous black insurrection in the 1790s led by Toussaint L'Ouverture in Saint Domingue/Haiti, which had long-term effects on the mainland, sharpening, on the one hand, black-white and master-slave antagonisms, while, at the same time, increasing doubt about the legitimacy of slavery and stimulating anti-slavery sentiment and agitation.[53] Yet, he may have had in mind, without giving it the full measure of his analytical powers, the unintentional consolidation of a more conscious sense of black nationhood in the Caribbean and in slave-holding America. He had few doubts that the numerical strength of the blacks in the West Indies would in the end overcome the small numbers of isolated white planters.[54] In the southern United States, the dangers of conflict between whites and blacks were "inevitable, perpetually haunt[ing] the imagination of the Americans, like a painful dream" (I, chap. 18, 391–92). He weighed the variables that might determine white and black survival. Only a united white response from the North to assist the South's slaveholders could save them, but if it came to that it would end in "the destruction, which menaces them (the Negroes); [for] they must be subdued by want or by the sword" (ibid., 391). If, however, the Union were dissolved, the Northern whites would not come to the aid of the white South unless a "positive obligation" ensured such a move.

[52] *Oeuvres*, I, 133 and 193.

[53] For a succinct assessment of the Haitian insurrection, see chap. 6 in Robin Blackburn, *The Overthrow of Colonial Slavery 1776–1848* (London and New York: Verso, 1988). Blackburn makes several points about its repercussions in the West Indies and in the United States. His most cogent is that slavery's overthrow in Haiti "required conscious and dedicated protagonists as well as favorable conditions. Without the emergence of 'Black Jacobins' in 1793–4, and their alliance with revolutionary France, a generalized emancipation would not have been consolidated in St. Domingue . . . [P]art of the grandeur of the great Revolution in St. Domingue/Haiti is that it successfully defended the gains of the French Revolution itself." (p. 259). Tocqueville was aware of the views of John Hazelhurst Latrobe, a Baltimore lawyer, active in the American Colonization Society which favored black resettlement in Liberia. In his conversation, Latrobe referred to "the destruction of Saint-Domingue," which brought French families to the United States. See *Oeuvres*, I, 190.

[54] Tocqueville (I, chap. 18, 393 note 51 and 412 note 61) writes that in 1830, of a total of 2,329,766 Negroes, 2,010,327 were slaves and 319,439 were free. All in all, Negroes made up about a fifth of the total population, which numbered 12,856,165. Tocqueville's figures are based on his reading of the Census of 1830. See also, *Historical Statistics of the United States from Colonial Times to 1957* (Washington, D.C., 1960).

(Tocqueville may have meant something like the Missouri Compromise or a stronger constitutional measure.) The South's superior capacity to wage war would, moreover, not be enough to overcome black "numerical strength and the energy of despair upon their side, . . . powerful resources to men who have taken up arms" (ibid.). Eventually the whites in the South would be forced, like the Moors in Spain, to return to the country of their origins.

Again we see Tocqueville succumbing to an either/or interpretation and conclusion. It was doubtless heavily influenced by the opinions he gathered from Americans in high places, such as Pierre-Etienne Duponceau, a French veteran of the American Revolutionary War, and president of the Philadelphia Philosophical Society when Tocqueville met him. Duponceau, however, while also speaking in apocalyptic tones, was certain that slavery would not last the century, and that during its course the black population would be freed to find their future outside America. The blacks would be driven from America, perhaps exterminated, by a numerically stronger white population, united in every region of the United States.[55] A rather different picture was offered by another informant, Guillemin, who had lived in Savannah and Baltimore before taking up his post in New Orleans in 1816 as French Consul. The white aristocracy was, he told Tocqueville, exposed to dangers on the mainland and almost certainly headed toward destruction in the Antilles. If instead, it had accepted the colored people *gens de couleur* who were biologically close to them and alike in their educational background, it would have gained them for their cause. By default, the blacks would benefit from their intelligence and leadership.[56]

The constitutional foundations of the Union in the 1830s were still far from solid, Tocqueville believed, as did former President John Adams, with whom he shared the fear that its dissolution, brought on by growing South-North economic divisions and western expansion, was not a remote possibility.[57] The doctrine of Nullification, which gathered force in South Carolina's acts of defiance against the federal government's tariff policies, best espoused by Vice-President John Calhoun, threatened to restore "the anarchy from which the Americans were delivered by the act of 1789" (I, chap. 18, 428).[58] Tocqueville remained unconvinced that

---

[55] *Oeuvres*, I, 85.   [56] Ibid., 122–23.   [57] Ibid., 74–77.
[58] Eugene D. Genovese called Calhoun "the Marx of the Master Class" for his defense of the constitutional rights of the States to interfere, in order to protect their reserved interests" in *The World the Slaveholders Made* (New York: Pantheon, 1971), pp. 136, 182.

the Union was safe from the centrifugal force of regional and local loyalties: "General Jackson is the agent of the state jealousies" (ibid., 431); "[s]o far is the Federal government, as it grows old, from acquiring strength and from threatening the sovereignty of the states, that I maintain it to be growing weaker and the sovereignty of the Union alone to be in danger" (ibid., 433). Clay, a planter from Georgia with whom Tocqueville conversed in Boston, saw a future in which a free black population would create their own state in the South from which the whites would withdraw, because, as he said, reversing the conventional prejudice, the blacks would never agree to mix with whites so completely as to form a single people.[59] On the future of black-white relations, his predictive powers were flawed: secessionist and nullifactionist agitation did not lead either to a peaceful separation or to an all-out war against Afro-Americans. Abolitionism and the anti-slavery movement were too deeply rooted and affected too many lives, thousands of whom were too intertwined, to lead to this kind of Armageddon. Beyond his condemnation of slavery, and his hope for a compromise that would mark the way to its eventual but non-violent extinction, Tocqueville all but ignored or was ignorant of pre-Civil War life in the free or slave black communities. He drew the lines between the American black and white worlds too sharply, and did not pursue some of his inquiries to their realities. He was not unaware of the enormous injuries suffered by free blacks in the North who were not recognized as full citizens – for example, in Pennsylvania, where he learned that although blacks had the right to vote, they did not dare do so without being maltreated, or in Ohio, where a young lawyer told him that Negroes could, according to the law, be driven from the state at will, had no political rights, could not testify against whites, or serve on a jury.[60]

Race, Color, and Post-Christian Humanism in Tocqueville's Thought

The question does not end there. Tocqueville has been similarly criticized for failing to ask how the Native American nomads might also be incor-

[59] *Oeuvres*, I, 64. He is not to be confused with Henry Clay. The views expressed here are hardly consistent with the position taken by the latter. As a founding member of the American Colonization Society, Henry Clay defended slavery in Missouri and in the Southwest. See Paul Goodman, *Of One Blood. Abolitionism and the Origins of Racial Equality* (Berkeley, Los Angeles, and London: University of California Press, 1998), pp. 16–18.

[60] *Oeuvres*, I, 93, 113–14, 173.

porated into what has been called "the nomadic element circulating through the ethos of democracy" – the nomadic element being the restless nature of democratic modernity.[61] The few instances he witnessed of how Native American converts to Christianity fared in the United States did not inspire him with the confidence that attempts to integrate them would produce lasting or even beneficial results. The lack of a plan to end the human agony is indeed troubling, not only because he had no concrete solutions, and indeed seemed resigned to the Indians' fate, but because the question was generally pushed to one side by most Americans except, as William Connolly shows, by those few, who, like Henry David Thoreau, could see beyond conventional thinking, but not far enough to advance a political argument capable of rescuing the Native Americans.

How indeed could they have been rescued? Racial mixing was one of the features of life in all sections of the Republic, but it was generally held in abhorrence and dread, as we have seen in Tocqueville's testimony. As a word, miscegenation was not coined until the 1864 election by northern Democrats. Tocqueville momentarily expanded on the possibility of racial mixture in a kind of afterthought. He ventured into dangerous territory. Others had of course been there before him, not only as observers but as participants. It was never far from their minds. He discerned the psychological and social ambiguities for the first time in his brief visit to New Orleans, and later, leaving out almost all of the descriptive detail to be found in his notes, when he gave his ideas a more polished but somewhat more obscure form in the *Democracy*.

In New Orleans, where he was struck by the unmistakable atmosphere of the city's "Frenchness," he felt at home, though at the same time he was puzzled and fascinated by the apparently easy mixture, the hybridity, the creolization of society, the process of *métissage* that he noted when he spoke of the *métis*, of the Native Americans, and the Anglo-Americans who crossed the divide. In the most hybrid city in the United States, so unlike the much more firm patterns of division he found in Boston and Philadelphia, he saw a mixed population, people of all shades of color, speaking French, English, Spanish, and Creole. He felt a sense of unease at the spectacle of the "unique link provided by the immorality between the two races," which created a bazaar-like

---

[61] See William E. Connolly, "Tocqueville, Territory and Violence," *Theory, Culture & Society*, 11 (1994), 19–40, who charges Tocqueville with "slippery language of regret without moral indictment and, more significantly, of the recognition of undeserved suffering without a plan to curtail it in the future" (27).

atmosphere," with women of color devoted, "as it were, by the law, to concubinage." He took as his example the celebration of the New Orleans ball of the quadroons, in which all the men were white, while the women were of color, or at least of African blood. He found it fascinating and "repulsive," using a diction that expressed his disapproval of the "relaxation of morals." The partly open, partly concealed crossing of racial divisions may have evoked the ambiguities of his response. He was informed that white men had the freedom, with the tacit knowledge of their white wives, to father two or more sets of families. The ball brought together mothers, young girls, children – all of mixed blood.[62]

He did not have the full picture of the origins of miscegenation in Louisiana, where, as well as in the Latin Caribbean plantations, a three-caste society had developed and was roughly divided into African and Indian slaves, free people of color, and whites, connected in some instances by intermarriage, but more often, as he called it, by concubinage. Indeed, as he observed, when he spoke in the Chamber of Deputies to report on the Legislative Commission's findings on slavery in the French colonies, it was uncommon for slaves to marry, for "a profound and natural antipathy between the institution of marriage and slavery" was inevitable in circumstances when a man "can never exercise conjugal authority." Given the harsh realities that faced his children, who, by the very fact of being condemned to experience his own miseries as a slave, the father was robbed, because they suffered the same condition as he did, of his capacity to assume responsibility for them, with all its duties, rights, hopes and solicitude.[63] When he visited Louisiana, the enfranchisement of free people of color and the existence of a three-caste society set it apart from the rest of the United States. When Andrew Jackson addressed the free men of color, calling on them in 1814 to enlist to defend America, he promised them equal treatment alongside white

---

[62] *Oeuvres*, I, 180. Gustave de Beaumont's account in *Marie or Slavery in the United States*, trans. Barbara Chapman (Stanford: Stanford University Press, 1958), pp. 64–65, conveys the same feeling of shock. "[T]hese monstrous unions (the open bargaining between white men and mothers for their daughters) have not even the decency of vice, which hides itself in shame, as does virtue for modesty's sake ... When the American from the North has made his fortune, he has achieved his goal. One fine day he leaves New Orleans and never returns. ... Then the girl of color sells herself to another man. And that is the fate of women of the African race in Louisiana."

[63] "Rapport fait au nom de la Commission chargée d'examiner la proposition de M. de Tracy, relative aux esclaves des colonies." (July 23, 1839) in OC 3 (*Ecrits et discours politiques*) part 1, 43.

recruits. Thus, when Tocqueville made his observations, the notions of racial mixture were significantly different as between the former Spanish and French colonies and the states to their north.

Why was there, Tocqueville asked, a multitude of people of color in New Orleans and so small a number in the northern states? For him the answer lay in the difference between the English, who left for the New World to escape religious persecution, and, by coming with their families intact, created a completely new society, while the Spaniards and the French, motivated by the search for quick wealth came alone and easily cohabited with people of other races.[64]

> The mixed race is the true bond of union between the Europeans and Indians; just so, the mulattoes are the true means of transition between the white and the Negro; so that wherever mulattoes abound, the intermixture of the two races is not impossible. In some parts of America the European and the Negro races are so crossed with one another that it is rare to meet with a man who is entirely black or entirely white; when they have arrived at this point, the two races may really be said to be combined, or, rather, to have been absorbed in a third race, which is connected with both without being identical with either (I, chap. 18, 389).[65]

The ambiguities may be traced to the French Code Noir of 1685, applied by the French crown in Louisiana to determine the grounds for enfranchisement as full citizens. It was bestowed on freed slaves, and permitted them to own property, including slaves, which *gens de couleur libre* were able to do while Louisiana was still a French colony and afterward when it became part of the United States. By the time the Code was revised in 1724 to end this practice and to outlaw miscegenation as

---

[64] *Oeuvres*, I, 181.

[65] Tocqueville, a few years later, wrote about the abolition of slavery as inevitable, "When, among free men, races mix and classes grow closer and merge throughout the Christian and civilized world," *OC* 3 (*Ecrits et discours politiques*) part 1, 81. The prediction, minus the psychological tensions that Tocqueville observed in America, appears in a series of six articles, "L'Emancipation des esclaves," in *Le Siècle*, published between October and December 1843. James Baldwin knew what the tensions were: "The Negro [recognizes] that he is a hybrid. . . . In white Americans he finds reflected – repeated as it were, in a higher key – his tensions, his terrors, his tenderness. . . . Now he is bone of their bone, flesh of their flesh. . . . Therefore he cannot deny them, nor can they ever be divorced." *Notes of a Native Son* in *Collected Essays* (New York: The Library of America, 1998), p. 89. Cf. the 1821 views of the Cherokee leader, John Ridge, cited in Thurman Wilkins, *Cherokee Tragedy: The Story of the Ridge Family and the Decimation of a People* (New York: 1970), p. 145. "If an Indian is educated in the sciences, has a good knowledge of the classics, astronomy, mathematics, moral and natural philosophy, and his conduct equally modest and polite, yet he is an Indian, and the most stupid and illiterate white man will disdain and triumph over this worthy individual."

well, neither the one nor the other ended. In fact, the blood of Afro-Americans, Native Americans, and whites had become mixed. This did not deter Andrew Jackson from recruiting *gens de couleur* in the war against Britain. But in the course of the century, free people of color saw their gains fall away, culminating in the Supreme Court's decision in *Plessy v. Ferguson, 163 U.S. 537* (1896) that a distinction must be drawn between "white and colored races – a distinction which is founded in the color of the two races, and which must always exist as long as white men are distinguished from the other race by color."[66] Before Reconstruction, all who were native to Louisiana were known as *Creole*. Afterward, whites imposed their dominance over blacks, as well as other whites who could not trace their roots to colonial times. Today, white Creoles, according to Virginia Dominguez, regard themselves as the only authentic Creoles, while Cajun refers to a purely white descendant of Acadian colonial settlers. These are the only "true" distinctions they acknowledge. "The white side by definition cannot accept the existence of colored Creoles; the colored side, by definition, cannot accept the white conception of Creole."[67]

In the United States, as Barbara Jeanne Fields says, "racial ideology supplied the means of explaining slavery to people whose terrain was a republic founded on radical doctrines of liberty and natural rights." Indeed, slavery had existed "without race as its ideological rationale" for a hundred years. Then race was introduced to explain "why some people could rightly be denied what others took for granted: namely liberty. . . . But there was nothing to explain until most people could, in fact, take liberty for granted."[68]

Tocqueville discerned the penalties, even if mitigated by the advantages, that were suffered by those who crossed the racial divide. Furthermore, the Anglo-Americans justified the dispossession of Native

---

[66] For two recent studies of these complex matters, see Joseph Roach, "Body of Law: The Sun King and the Code Noir," and Elizabeth Colwill, "Sex, Savagery, and Slavery in the Shaping of the French Body Politic," in *From the Royal to the Republican Body. Incorporating the Political in Seventeenth- and Eighteenth-Century France*, eds. Sara E. Melzer and Kathryn Norberg (Berkeley, Los Angeles, and London: University of California Press, 1998), 113–30 and 198–223. The citation from the Supreme Court decision is in Joseph Roach, 129.

[67] Virginia R. Dominguez, *White by Definition: Social Classification in Creole Louisiana* (New Brunswick: Rutgers University Press, 1986), p. 149.

[68] Barbara Jeanne Fields, "Slavery, Race, and Ideology in the United States of America," *New Left Review*, no. 181 (1990), 114. Cited in Elizabeth Colwill, "Sex, Savagery, and Slavery in the Shaping of the French Body Politic," 206, note 30.

Americans by pleading that they were incapable of civilizing themselves, yet at the same time celebrated fraternity as a Christian principle.[69] When it came to the "third race" – the fusion of Afro-Americans and whites – the hybrids could not deny the whites, but the whites, as members of the majority, could try to deny both Native and Afro-Americans. Gustave de Beaumont took up the theme in *Marie*. The heroine looks white, but has colored blood. In New Orleans, she and her brother, George, were thought to be white, but they leave, together with their father, after she rejects a wealthy Spaniard who wants to make her his mistress. Failing to get his way, he reveals that she is of mixed blood. In New Orleans, she has no future; she will always be tainted and considered black. She is in a liminal space, not in society. In Baltimore, a Frenchman, Ludovic, falls in love with her, and persists in his love even after her father reveals her mixed ancestry. They marry, but the entire family has to run the gauntlet of a murderous mob. As the riots die down, the philanthropic society in New York working for black liberation publishes a statement, saying, " 'We never conceived the insane project of mingling the two races; in this regard we could not fail to recognize the dignity of the whites; we respect the laws which uphold slavery in the Southern states.' " The couple finds final refuge in the wilderness of Michigan, where Marie dies, and Ludovic remains, waiting to die in utter loneliness. George, meantime, takes part in and dies in an abortive uprising of slaves and Indians in the South, leaving behind a dire warning: "The black population is doomed to the eternal scorn of the whites; the hatred between us and our enemies is irreconcilable. An inner voice tells me that this enmity will end only with the extermination of one of the two races."[70]

Native Americans were divided in their attitudes toward white civilization – they admired it but could not, Tocqueville thought, capitulate entirely to it. Their inclinations were entirely in opposition to such aspirations. On the frontier, which brought people of different cultures together, skin color, economic differences, ignorance, and enlightenment created agonizing, and, almost always, insurmountable divisions. National prejudices – prejudices due to differences in education and birth – were sources of isolation and division.[71] He reported that Kentucky and Tennessee were quite different from the older Southern slave-owning

[69] *Oeuvres*, I, 364.
[70] Gustave de Beaumont, *Marie or Slavery in the United States*, quotes from pp. 129, 172.
[71] "Quinze jours dans le désert," in *Oeuvres*, I, 405.

societies, because the people who had moved there cultivated small plots
of land, which they worked alongside their slaves. Reliance on a slave
population for its labor on marginal, rather than large, tracts of land,
was economically regressive, but at the same time the leap from the indolence that such patterns of land and labor encouraged to rational and
industrious forms was not an easy matter to manage. For Tocqueville
this was the paradox. Sharing some of the hardship of labor brought
Afro-Americans and whites together, but slavery's roots were so deep
that it could not be simply eradicated, even when economic realities
argued against it. It persisted most savagely in places such as Kentucky
and Tennessee, where the exigencies of economic survival exaggerated
the worst side of white-black relations. Even so, Kentuckians and
Tennesseans were as quick as people in the older states to act like
Americans – that is to say, to inform themselves through the press and
to argue about politics.

Yet such a frame of mind did not mitigate what Tocqueville isolated
as the decisive feature of disadvantage: the conflict between the economically marginal and the slaves at the bottom of the social scale. The
structures of atrophied forms of self-respect, resting on the miseries
of others deemed lesser human beings, increased the levels of frontier
violence.[72] The crossing of racial boundaries under these conditions
occurred, but they were not as smoothly managed as in the relatively
more relaxed and economically confident white society of Louisiana or
South Carolina. Tocqueville touched a raw nerve, for in distinguishing
white-black relations in the different parts of the Union, he laid bare the
much greater assaults on Southern social structure that came from interracial sex than in the North, where the problem of preserving patterns
of patriarchy and racial hierarchy were not absent but far less pressing.
He may have in fact benefited from some knowledge of how far back
these problems could be traced in Northern Anglo-American society,
where mulatto children, while chiefly the offspring of white fathers and
black mothers, were sometimes also the children of white mothers and
black fathers.

In a certain, very important sense, Tocqueville described a fluid
social world in which the very point of being American allowed one to
think of some movement toward new forms of social life. That Afro-
Americans might have some expectation of being able to achieve a notion
of autonomy in a self-defined community, separated from the dominant

[72] *Oeuvres*, I, 283–88.

white one, he did not rule out. But it was a fragile hope. After his visit
to America, he became a member of the Société française pour l'abolition de l'esclavage, and later, as a member of the Chamber of Deputies,
sat on two legislative commissions to determine the future of the blacks
and the question of indemnities for their owners once abolition gained
consent.[73] He appeared to retreat from his earlier support for rapid
general emancipation to a slower and more measured approach, the line
taken by the Broglie Commission's Report of 1843. Two years later,
when the question remained stalled in both Chambers of the National
Assembly, he told his fellow legislators that the United States was a
society with a striking dissonance between its avid hunger for equality
that would not brook any differences in wealth, education, tastes, and
morality, and a ferocious determination to keep the slaves from acquiring the rudiments of literacy while simultaneously supporting a network
of public schools. But it was natural, he added, for those in dominant
positions to exploit their resources to maintain the status quo. Their
privileges – his eyes were on the abolition and extinction of slavery in
the French West Indies – would preferably be ended by a wise government capable of taking the steps to avoid the disasters of revolution by
bringing the interests of the privileged few and the non-privileged many
together in compromise.[74] The French nation, moreover, had a duty to
do so as the double heir of the Revolution and Christianity. Two years
earlier, he had made the same point: "Who has spread these notions of
freedom and equality throughout the world that are weakening and
destroying servitude? . . . We were the ones. . . . Christianity, after having
fought long against egoistical passions, which reestablished slavery in the
sixteenth century, was tired and resigned. . . . We were the ones to give
a determined and practical meaning to this Christian idea that all men
are born equal, and it is we who have applied it to the facts of this
world."[75] He was more explicit when in 1845 he linked the anti-slavery
movement to the revolutionary struggle against "the principle of castes,
classes . . . recovering, as it is said, the rights of human kind which were
lost," declaiming that "it is we who . . . are the true authors of the

[73] See Seymour Drescher, *Dilemmas of Democracy: Tocqueville and Modernization* (Pittsburgh: University of Pittsburgh Press, 1968). See also the new study by Lawrence C. Jennings, *French Anti-Slavery. The Movement for the Abolition of Slavery in France 1802–1848* (Cambridge: Cambridge University Press, 2000).
[74] "Intervention dans la discussion de la loi sur le régime des esclaves dans les colonies," (May 30, 1845), OC 3 (*Ecrits et discours politiques*) part 1, 117–18.
[75] "L'Emancipation des esclaves," ibid., 88.

abolition of slavery."[76] This is a stunning anticipation of the two aspects of Etienne Balibar's theory of "fictitious universality" – "how one great historical 'fiction,' that of the universalistic church, could be substituted by another historical 'fiction,' that of the secular, rational institutions of the state (in practice the nation-state), with equally universalistic aims."[77]

In this hyperbolic mood, Tocqueville went on to say that the Anglo-Americans owed their feelings of humanity to the cardinal principles of a revolutionized Christianity. But he had little to say if or how the subjected portion of America had appropriated Christian principles following the religious awakening that captured masters and slaves alike in a revivalist fundamentalism. Indeed, he did not stop to consider how they too might follow their leaders out of servitude to freedom.[78] In fact, between 1790 and 1830, Christianity, to which they became deeply committed when a full-fledged slave system was consolidated, was revivalist and fundamentalist, not Puritan, and from its teachings they acquired a sense of self undirected toward revolutionary goals.[79] His failure to open up this question leads us to ask if the Puritan faith in the democratic culture he described was as wholesome as he made it out to be. One aspect of the Christian humanist and Enlightenment culture of which he was part espoused universalist values, yet its protagonists also labored frustratingly with the question of transferring them to non-Western peoples who were seen as peoples lacking in selfhood. Autonomy, we recall, is derived from *autonomos*. It is the will that means giving laws to oneself, knowing that one is doing so, and that such law-giving at the same time imposes limits on oneself. It comes into being when those who are suppressed and suffer discrimination act together to end their suffering. Such an achievement would mean gaining "the right to acquire rights," as Hannah Arendt declared, a right that is not yet guaranteed by law.

---

[76] Ibid., 124–25. Following the February 1848 Revolution, steps were hurriedly taken to end slavery, which was officially decreed abolished by the Provisional government on April 27. By then, emancipation and republicanism had become closely identified. The promotion of the second entailed the defense of the first.

[77] Etienne Balibar, "Ambiguous Universality," *differences: A Journal of Feminist Cultural Studies*, 7 (1995), 56–57.

[78] The Christian scriptures, as David Brion Davis writes, possessed a clear message of deliverance for the slaves who dreamed of a new Jerusalem. See *The Problem of Slavery in the Age of Revolution 1770–1823* (Ithaca and London: Cornell University Press, 1975), pp. 555–56. For the different uses of Christianity made by whites and slaves, see Eugene D. Genovese, *Roll, Jordan, Roll* (New York: Pantheon Books, 1974).

[79] For this view of revivalist Christianity's role in offering the slaves a feeling of dignity, see Orlando Patterson, *Slavery and Social Death*, pp. 73–74.

Tocqueville questioned whether the concept of the autonomous self could be effectively taken up by non-Western societies. The difficulty he might have had in transferring to people in other cultures the same kinds of emotional responses he felt, for example, in the pride he took in his family's ancient roots in Normandy, while at the same time he espoused universalist ideals that qualified strict loyalty to parochial identity, never arose. As far as he could fathom, non-Western cultures did not offer any compelling examples or proofs that anything remotely resembling such ideals were even an incipient part of their traditions and values. At least he gave thought to two disturbing aspects of their impact on Native and Afro-Americans. He could not forbear, but nevertheless could not raise, an effective voice against the amputating effects of Anglo-American culture on what he thought was the vanishing culture of Native Americans. Theirs was a pre-modern society mixing divine, human, and natural elements. As for Afro-Americans, they appeared to be in a less indeterminate condition, and once they cast off the incubus of slavery, they might indeed gain the will to assert their political rights. Though silent, as we noted, about the role of Christianity in the lives of American slaves, in the French Antilles the key to acquiring the will to political rights lay, he argued, in emancipation as the first step to the blossoming of a full Christian culture encompassing everyone, including all blacks, for Christianity was a religion uniting free men.[80] So long, moreover, as the men in power – the masters – assumed that inequality was a right, they would have no qualms in exercising their tyranny while believing they were good men. Calling on his knowledge of the United States, Tocqueville captured some of the contradictions of America where, alongside an unbridled equality that refused to tolerate any differences created by wealth, education, taste, and morality – which he attributed to "natural" causes, when in fact they were more than a little cultural – the people who lived by these rules found it "natural" to keep millions of their fellow beings in servitude.[81] Five years later, he looked back and forward:

---

[80] "Rapport fait au nom de la commission chargée d'examiner la proposition de M. de Tracy, relative aux esclaves des colonies (July 23, 1839)," OC 3 (*Ecrits et discours politiques* part 1, 43. In the 1845 report, Tocqueville let his rhetoric gallop out of control when he said that more than a millennium ago, Christianity had destroyed servitude in the world. He was more nearly on the side of truth when he added that as recently as the end of the eighteenth century, Christianity and slavery existed side by side (ibid., 125).

[81] Ibid., 117.

It is self-evident that the waves continue to roll, that the sea rises; that not only have we not seen the end of the immense revolution that began before we were born, but that the infant born today will probably also not see. This is not a question of an alteration, but a transformation, of the social body. To reach what point? In truth, I do not know, and I believe the question surpasses all intelligence. One knows that the old world is ending; but what will the new one be? The greatest minds of our time are no more in a position to say so than those in antiquity were able to predict the end of slavery, the [birth] of Christian society, the barbarian invasions, all those great events that have renewed the face of the earth. They felt that the society of their time was dissolving, that is all.[82]

Tocqueville found himself in retreat, but it was far from being a redoubt. He confined himself to what was for him the all-consuming question of how to create an enlightened, rational, and reflective loyalty to country (I, chap. 14, 251–52). Enlarged patriotic feelings might be cultivated in a society in which, like most others, citizens tended much more readily to locate their identity in what was closer to hand, their "property and the domestic affections, with the recollections of the past, the labors of the present and the hopes of the future" (I, chap. 18, 401–02).[83] In this respect, Americans would, he hoped, find the will to move away from particular and local loyalties – without losing sight of those that nurtured citizenship – to embrace the principles of individual achievement that subordinated cultural or racial origins to the common weal.

This was the nub of his difficulty, and America's as well. The spirit of the American Constitution represented for him the promise of a nation that owed its beginnings to an uneasy, because oscillating, fusion of volition and a felt sense of community. Then the nation, as Tocqueville saw it emerging from the Constitutional debates, might or might not succeed in replicating the moment of its Puritan conception, but at a higher level of consciousness. Having moved beyond America's colonial origins at the end of the eighteenth century, the Union in the 1850s had to struggle with the problem of who could be part of the *consensus universalis*, the tacit agreement by means of which, as we saw, Tocqueville posited the coming into being of a republican polity. As a society elevating will and universalism, America could not on grounds of principle deprive people who were culturally different from taking part in such a *consen-*

---

[82] Tocqueville to Eugène Stoffels, April 28, 1850, *Oeuvres complètes*, ed. Gustave de Beaumont, 9 vols. (Paris: Michel Lévy frères, 1864–66) 6, 461.

[83] On the history and nature of American patriotism and national identity and the arguments questioning their value, see the essays by Martha Nussbaum, Charles Taylor, and Gertrude Himmelfarb in *For Love of Country: Debating the Limits of Patriotism*, ed. Joshua Cohen (Boston: Beacon Press, 1996).

sus. At the same time, because Americans also defined themselves along cultural lines, many of their best minds were presented with stark choices when thinking about how America might open itself up to "others." Even if the Union were to fail, he believed that the principles underlying American republicanism might perhaps prevail, and prove formative of the ideal nation that existed only in the mind, but was for that very reason the only power that kept society together. It was this power that must not be suppressed. "Individuals," Tocqueville said, "have an immense capacity to do *evil,* but rarely to do good." Still, he added, only "by slaving at the oars of independent political action" could "a little bit of good" be achieved.[84]

Here we must remember his distinction between the visible (the institutional, including the distribution of powers) and the invisible (the symbolic, the mythic and remembered) sources of authority, to which he pointed early on in *Democracy in America.* His republicanism took for granted the ineradicability of customs, the mores or *moeurs,* the "habits of the heart . . . the notions and opinions current among men and of the mass of those ideas which constitute their character of mind" (I, chap. 17, 310). The political, if amputated from its roots in *moeurs,* would be subverted by them. Their refractory substance could be determining – indeed, crippling – if the nation could not summon up the intelligence he said was needed to acknowledge, but not to succumb to, the ways in which society's image of itself merely reflected what it wished to see. Within the Union, the instability that threatened derived from this fissure between political will and social habits. He stumbled, as did many well-intentioned Americans.[85] Either the patriotism he praised would

---

[84] OC 6 (*Correspondance anglaise. Correspondance et conversations d'Alexis de Tocqueville et Nassau Senior*) part 2, 415. These thoughts were recorded by Mrs. Simpson on February 18, 1854. He made similar observations in a letter to Kergorlay, July 29, 1856, OC 13 (*Correspondance d'Alexis de Tocqueville et de Louis de Kergorlay*) part 2, 303. Then he spoke of his wish "to utter true and honest things which can signal the name of the writer to the attention of the civilized world, and to serve in some small measure the good cause."

[85] For a discussion of the arguments that defended slavery while espousing liberty, as well as those that challenged the idea that while the ideal of equality was far from being realized in America, the existence of American slavery had to be seen as a relative evil within the context of contemporary Western civilization, see Liah Greenfeld, *Nationalism. Five Roads to Modernity*, pp. 449–84. The power of local customs and values – what some tend today to call "community standards" to ward off dissident opinions – cannot be brushed aside in favor of what pro-slavery advocates called abstract justice and which they saw as socially impracticable. As Judith Shklar points out, southerners claimed that their "republican virtues" depended on slavery. See *The Faces of Injustice* (New Haven and London: Yale University Press, 1990), p. 116.

transcend the confining terms of the Union and successfully identify itself with the republican principle of American politics, or it would prove to be powerless in ending the politics of affliction.

But one may well ask how this appeal to patriotism, which was seen in radically different ways along the North-South divide, could bring forth the kind of response that would prove affection for and loyalty to the existing laws. Patriotism of this sort failed to arouse a common defense of the Union. Instead, what may be called the *national appeals made in each part of the Union* triumphed over a weak sense of identification with it. For Ralph Ellison, the Civil War and the brief Reconstruction period retained the symbolic power to remind America of lost opportunities, of what Darryl Pinckney sees as the "complexity and resilience of black folk . . . capable of a mournful patriotism in spite of everything that had gone wrong since Reconstruction."[86] The symbolism possessed even greater power in Mark Twain's pre-Civil War setting of *Huckleberry Finn*. Pondering Huck's "bid to free himself from the conventionalized evil taken for civilization by the town," Ellison shows how his act represented Twain's acceptance of his own "personal responsibility in the condition of society."[87] After that, the individualism, which Tocqueville had singled out as an original feature of American life whose excesses threatened humanism, triumphed and threatened whatever good might come from the tension between the two. He deplored America's uncritical celebration of individualism as morally and politically injurious to the ethos of a humanist autonomy – that is, to the role of active agents assuming responsibility for themselves in a democratic polity, and he associated that ethos with what for him was an irreducible and inherent religious sensibility, however important its Christian roots once were.[88]

Humanism, separated from its Christian roots, was transformed by Enlightenment rationalism, specifically by the spread of deism and natural religion, both abhorred by theists as leading to skepticism and irreligion. For Tocqueville, the politics of Christianity was indefensible

---

[86] Darryl Pinckney, "The Drama of Ralph Ellison," *New York Review of Books*, 44 (May, 15 1997), p. 56.

[87] Ralph Ellison, "Twentieth-Century Fiction and the Black Mask of Humanity," in *Shadow and Act* (New York: Signet Book, 1966), pp. 48, 50.

[88] See Harvey Mitchell, "Tocqueville's Flight from Doubt and His Search for Certainty: Skepticism in a Democratic Age," in *The Skeptical Tradition around 1800. Skepticism in Philosophy, Science, and Society*, eds. J. van der Zande and R. H. Popkin (Dordrecht, Boston, and London: Kluwer Academic Publishers, 1998), 261–79.

on the grounds that in a modern state, religious intervention in the shaping of political decisions would spell the death knell of religious beliefs. The great number of religious sects, in his opinion, did not convert their religious enthusiasm into political platforms (II, Bk. 1, chap. 3, 28). Rather they bore indirectly on politics by sharing a common belief in the same moral law uttered in God's name. They also reinforced, rather than undermined, democratic and republican institutions. The bedrock of Christian belief was not splintered in America. The sects' benign or even beneficial influence on politics was not questioned by Tocqueville (I, chap. 17, 310–13), but he was not unaware of the presence of fanatical and strange sects and common outbursts of what he called "religious insanity" (II, Bk. 2, chap. 12, 142). In general, a non-sectarian humanism had not yet cracked the crust of the American religious ethos. Neither had it centered itself completely in Tocqueville's psyche. Though no deist, neither was he an observant Christian. Still, his humanism grew out of a commitment to the universalism he saw as fundamental to Christian belief. Those who sought new paths that could include non-Europeans in a civil society had to face the fact that their reading of the Christian message of liberation was not shared by all Christians. Some versions of Christian doctrine, as they came to be asserted by Southern exponents of a revived classical democracy, were, they believed, not inimical to a defense of slavery as a basis for a superior democratic government. This is as important a conclusion to be drawn from the tribulations Americans faced by the threat of Civil War, with persons on either side of the slavery controversy appealing to Christian teachings to support their position, as the fact that there was a vigorous secular undercurrent in America. It still has to be conclusively demonstrated that a deistically inspired, non-Christian humanism had indeed taken strong hold in America. In favor of an interpretation focusing on its strength is that many of the Founding Fathers were more inclined towards deism than to Christian beliefs and the fact that the Constitution makes no reference to God. Against such a view is that however firmly deistic beliefs had been set down in many quarters of America, particularly in the North, the debate was mainly carried out within a Christian matrix, between nominal Christian abolitionists and slaveholders professing to be Christian.

The coexistence of Enlightenment/humanist ideals and Christian beliefs was an indelible feature of America, no matter how much the secularism of the first transformed the second. It would be pointless to dispute the weakening over time of some of the oldest Christian responses to the new peoples found in America, which viewed Native Americans as potentially capable of understanding Christianity, and were therefore truly men – as may be seen in Pope Paul III's *Sublimis Deus* (1537).[89] The drawback to religious conversion was that as it progressed, the distinctions between Europeans and non-Europeans could not be sustained. Philip Curtin argues that the shift to race became the only way to save the notion of European (read American) exceptionalism,[90] the point from which non-Europeans could be categorized and found wanting. A more radical stance is taken by Charles Mills, who challenges the conventional notions of social contract theory on the grounds that it was in fact, despite disclaimers from thinkers ranging from Hobbes to Kant, touched by actual historical events. Instead of universalizing human experience, whether conjecturally or anthropologically, history racialized it, and hence created a politics of privilege. Mills goes on uncompromisingly to claim that racism was not anomalous and "incongruent" with Enlightenment European humanism, but required by the Racial Contract – that is, a contract excluding non-Europeans. This is the only proper way, he tells us, to see the social contract – as part of the terms for the "European appropriation of the world." "The racist 'exception,'" in his assessment, "has really been the rule: what has been taken as the 'rule,' the ideal norm, has really been the exception."[91]

Liberalism and racism are not, however, bedfellows. Mills's position needs some qualification. A firm conception of race was not in place much before the eighteenth century, and was not given fuller scope until the nineteenth. For social contract theorists, race and civilization were not seen as isomorphic; civilization was not seen as a white artifact. What constituted "civilization," and was seen as distinguishing it from "backward" cultures, were levels of economic organization, forms of political order, and a recognizable language. To be sure, when, in justification of the obliteration of Native American cultures, or in defense of slavery on economic grounds, the older ways of distinguishing them were weakened by moral outrage, race became the favorite explanation for the differences between European, Native, and African cultures. Thus, it is true

---

[89] For the citation, see Robert A. Williams Jr., "The Algebra of Federal Union Law: The Hard Trail of Decolonizing and Americanizing the White Man's Indian Jurisprudence," *Wisconsin Law Review* 1986, 230–31, 233.

[90] Philip D. Curtin, Introduction to *Imperialism*, ed. Curtin (New York: Walker, 1971), p. xiii.

[91] Charles W. Mills, *The Racial Contract* (Ithaca and London: Cornell University Press, 1997), p. 122.

that putatively different levels of rationality (Locke) and a combination of rationality and attributed characteristics, not seldom racist (Mills), were used to justify policies of exclusion. Race remains inscribed in and haunts the consciousness of Americans, even while many in the black and white communities strain to see signs of a dulling of racial antagonisms. The presence of this festering sore, so long after the abolition of slavery, reminds us that American society continues to turn its back on those it wishes to exclude. Yet, white critiques of racist exceptionalism, in all their complex modes of frankness and not infrequent obfuscations, were not lacking, and increased in momentum down to the present time. They seem to have a louder volume today as well as a larger audience. The Puritan covenant proved in time not to be as "everlasting" (Genesis 17:7) as those who bound themselves to it believed. Still, the connection between liberalism and racism, however it is measured, cannot be wished away.

The men and women of the generations that followed the first comers were deeply disturbed, perhaps to the point of paranoia, by problems of creating a coherent society that had outside its margins, and sometimes within them, people who were thought strange, literally strangers, culturally different and non-assimilable. Under what conditions could such a society survive? Under what kinds of perverse moral and mental strategies, and in what kinds of civil societies, could such divisions continue to be justified?[92] The short and incomplete answer is that such a society

[92] Hegel's thoughts are interesting in this regard. He was one of the first thinkers to consider that a civil society could not forever bar certain groups on the grounds that "they are not like us." The state, he said, should be intent on preserving the foundations of civil society, and seek to be "prudent and dignified" by recognizing the fact that man as man possesses feelings of selfhood. He chose the Jews to make this point, with the weak qualification that their exclusion from civil rights might be justified if it served some higher right, presumably the right of the state. He was, however, disinclined to sacrifice the benefits to civil society by excluding them. He was prepared to extend the state's narrowest toleration to Quakers and Anabaptists, who served it only passively, and not actively when it needed to be defended in war. Hegel called these examples anomalies. The nomadic peoples were, however, not an anomaly. Neighboring peoples might regard them in the same way as they looked upon Jews and Muslims, whose religious views were such as to justify their exclusion by Christians from sharing a general identity. Indeed, it was justifiable for "civilized" nations to deny nomads, as barbarians, equal rights, and, as well, to treat the autonomy accorded them as nothing but a formality. Not at all a formality was a fact of American life, summed up in Hegel's recollection that the American Congress, in a debate on the slave trade, heard a Southern member declare, "Give us our slaves, and you may keep the Quakers." See *Philosophy of Right*, trans. T.M. Knox (Oxford: Oxford University Press, 1942), paragraph 331, p. 213; paragraph 351, p. 219; paragraph 279, pp. 168–69, note *.

survives by rejecting not just a notion, but a theory of, common humanity. The longer answer is different. If we recall that not only non-democratic but classical democratic societies justified the divisions of humankind on the grounds that these were rooted in nature, it would be remarkable to rule out the fact that natural explanations for difference have been used, and will likely continue to be used, to legitimate discriminations of various kinds, as advocated by Richard Herrnstein, Charles Murray, Dinesh D'Souza, and others.[93] Given these likelihoods, the only way to create a legitimate democratic society is to shift the emphasis, as in fact it is being done, from an over-reliance on alleged scientific proofs of ineradicable differences in the makeup of humankind. If it proves beyond doubt that there are such differences, a democratic society will not use penalties, but rather find the intellectual resources to adjudicate social, economic, and racial conflict on principles of fairness, justice, and decency. These are political solutions. They should take precedence over all others, because they affect all members of a civil society that calls itself democratic.

In that connection, there is much that is compelling in Paul Gilroy's reminder that the contacts in America and elsewhere in the European world between whites and non-whites could not have taken the forms and witnessed the conflicts they did without the presence of both negative and positive responses to the Enlightenment, as well as responses that moved back and forth between the two poles. The experiential interconnectedness of black cultures in America and Britain, as well as the connections between black and white cultures – which should be expanded to include the interconnectedness and connections between red, white, and black cultures – in fact created forms of cultural miscegenation.[94] How effective can it be against racist thought? Doesn't it continue to penetrate the skins of whites, Afro-Americans, and Native Americans alike? It would seem that life experiences have challenged an overly simplistic view of otherness. It is not because they subscribe to the idea that the social contract is a camouflage for a racial contract that excluded them that Afro-Americans are inclined to express racist

---

[93] See Richard J. Herrnstein and Charles A. Murray, *The Bell Curve. Intelligence and Class Structure in American Life* (New York: Free Press, 1994) and Dinesh d'Souza, *The End of Racism. Principles for a Multicultural Society* (New York: Free Press, 1995).

[94] Paul Gilroy, *The Black Atlantic. Modernity and Double Consciousness* (London and New York: Verso, 1993). Seymour Drescher, *Slavery to Freedom: Comparative Studies in the Rise and Fall of Atlantic Slavery* (New York: Macmillan Press, 1999) offers the most recent, dependable, and comprehensive study.

ideas. It is rather because of their past histories. Despite its ambiguities, they have come to share uneasily, to be sure, the promise of the Enlightenment.

It is this question around which the debate about a practical democratic society is already focused. For to be driven to the extremes of black, white, or any other color is to fragment further whatever remains of a belief in a national force with the power to give Americans a sense of themselves as they participate in a common endeavor. Let us remind ourselves of Tocqueville's insistence that a nation must not only know how to distribute power among its political institutions, but also that such power must necessarily be deployed to assure the best distribution of equality without sacrificing liberty, and conversely, that freedom, to retain its purposes and versatility, has to be regulated on rational, and hence impartial, grounds. What others after him have taken up, especially at the end of the twentieth century, is whether there is sufficient energy in the associational life that he admired as the touchstone of American democracy. This is the subject of Chapter 8.

PART III

AMERICAN DEMOCRACY ON TRIAL

7

Difference, Race, and Color in America

The Indians will perish in the same isolated condition in which they have lived, but the destiny of the Negroes is in some measure interwoven with that of the Europeans. These two races are fastened to each other without intermingling; and they are alike unable to separate entirely or to combine.[1]

We began as a nation not through the accidents of race or religion or geography ... but when a group of men, *some* of them political philosophers, put down, upon we now recognize as being quite sacred papers, their conception of the nation which they intended to establish on these shores. They described, as we know, the obligations of the state to the citizen, of the citizen to the state; they committed themselves to certain ideas of justice, just as they committed us to a system which would guarantee all of its citizens equality of opportunity.

I need not describe the problems which have arisen from these beginnings. I need only remind you that the contradiction between these noble ideals and the actualities of our conduct generated guilt, an unease of spirit, from the very beginning.[2]

America has long lived with the psychological scars inflicted by conflicts over color and race. The changing uses of the term "race" have exercised and occupied the minds of all Americans in the past, and do so to this day. That they have been so long-lasting may be seen in the opening passages of this chapter, which form its leitmotif. Tocqueville records in the opening extract the efforts of the three racial groups of America to find psychological sites for their historical survival. His understanding of the relationship between different moments of civilization and the conditions for the creation of American civil society, from which slaves

[1] Alexis de Tocqueville, *Democracy in America*, I, chap. 18, 370.
[2] Ralph Ellison, "Hidden Name and Complex Fate," in *Shadow and Act* (New York: A Signet Book, 1966), p. 165.

and aboriginals were to be kept out, continues to serve as a valuable prologue to continuing manifestations of racial prejudice. In the epigraph
taken from Ralph Ellison's writings, we see two major racial groups of
America juxtaposed once again. They took each other's measure, according to their predispositions, in a double watchfulness of one another.
Tocqueville, always excepting the descendants of the earliest Anglo-
American settlers, distinguished the first settlers from the later "inferior"
non-settled adventurers who wanted to leave everything behind them in
Europe, ready to plunder and scatter all resistance (I, chap. 18, 412). He
remarkably grasped two features of America, an expansiveness driven
by a dream of starting anew, and also the harsh realities imposed by
racism that created frontiers within a moving frontier. In the early twentieth century, the new territories still included Oklahoma, where Ellison
learned as a child and as a young man how Europeans, Afro-Americans,
and Native Americans were living in various postures of estrangement
from one another, even when they mingled.[3]

In Chapter 4, we looked at how Tocqueville dealt with the future of
the conquered Native Americans. In their earliest encounters, the question of identity and difference appeared most direfully and most fatefully. The beginnings of Anglo-American civilization exposed to view not
only existing aboriginal peoples. The forced transport of various African
peoples created a constantly changing backdrop in which all three played
out their interlocked roles. What ought to be kept in mind, as we move
forward in time, is the underlying chronic tension produced by the claims
of the Anglo-Americans to set in place a new vision of humankind that
extended its privileges to some deemed to be worthy of them, while with-
holding them from others in the name of European and Christian-
centered notions of civilization. Those pretensions were themselves
challenged soon enough, lending them an unintended and paradoxical
poignancy. Underneath the search for democratic fairness and justice can
be heard ominous cries for retribution.

A sense of deep hurt lies at the very heart of American society. It
creates bitter debate on how to call upon and command the resources of

---

[3] See Ralph Ellison, *Going to the Territory* (New York: Random House, 1986), p. 133.
Ellison qualified the notion that "geography is fate" by adding (p. 134) that "[I]t is not
geography alone which determines the quality of life and culture. These depend upon
the courage and personal culture of the individuals who make their homes in any given
locality." His lifelong devotion to and recollections of Oklahoma shaped his outlook,
but both were transmuted, as the second epigraph shows, by his need to experience, not
only the separate peoples or bits of geography, but all of America and Europe.

American democracy to deal with the grievance. Two broad currents are at work. Those who make up the first have transformed the undeniably inhumane experiences of marginalized groups into an ideology of permanent victimhood. The partisans of the second endeavor to heal the wounds of the victims by appealing to the Enlightenment ideals of the Founding Fathers. But the Constitution's reading the aboriginals and the slaves out of the social contract stained these ideals. The greatest difficulty facing the advocates of these ideals is finding a basis for giving them new urgency.

Native Americans have behind them a long history of decimation and forced flight, squalor, and death. The 1887 Allotment Act, which effectively dispossessed them of their land, was ended in 1933, but it was then too late to reverse the minute parcelization of reservation lands. Policy then shifted toward the improvement of life on the reservations, but the results were scandalously unimpressive. Then came the Relocation Program implemented to hasten integration by encouraging individual Native Americans to take city jobs. The failures were mixed; the successes imperceptible. Extreme protests of aggressive defiance began to sound loudly in favor of apartness, as in 1961 when the National Indian Youth Conference announced its support of tribalism as the best way for Indians to survive.[4] In 1968, President Lyndon Johnson told Congress that Native Americans had rights both as Native Americans and as Americans. His message marked another step away from the politics of assimilation toward a politics of identity. Assimilation, as a solution to the future of Native Americans, had been on the minds of some white Americans for generations, but was ultimately rejected by many Indians as undesirable. The American Indian Movement was founded the same year as a vehicle for the mobilization of militant protest in favor of tribal autonomy. The Movement defied federal agents at Wounded Knee in South Dakota. In the last two decades, a more confident Native American presence in American politics, together with a changing demography (the 1990 Census revealed that almost nine million Americans listed themselves as having Indian ancestry – an increase of two million since 1980), has changed much in America. The largest change, it is suggested, may be seen in the ways a not insignificant number of white Americans seem to prefer to find an escape for

---

[4] See Alvin Josephy, Jr., Joane Nagel, and Troy Johnson, eds. *Red Power: The American Indians' Fight for Freedom*, 2nd ed. (Lincoln: University of Nebraska Press, 1999), pp. 13ff.

their racial identity as a legacy from a shameful past, yet feel uneasy as non-white Americans seek to identify themselves more assuredly as Native Americans or Afro-Americans who labor to re-create positive racial pasts. At the same time, when, as it now seems increasingly to be the case, Native Americans straddle both their own and the white worlds, and as more white Americans look for Indian ancestry, the blurring of racial lines tends to challenge the basis of separatism, whoever espouses it.[5]

A seemingly single register of complaint has not drowned out discordant voices among Native Americans. They do not see their plight inside a monochromatic hue, as we discover from the novels and essays of writers who are called Native Americans, and who, like the characters they write about, are the descendants of several generations of mixed marriages. Together, as subjects and writers, they know that they are heirs to scores, even hundreds, of different cultures and language groups. Differences, as well, of upbringing, whether on reservations or in cities, form their backgrounds and shape but do not always determine what they choose to do. If their worlds are oriented toward the past, there is an unmistakable push away from the ambiguities of present isolation and incomprehension to a keen desire for a more satisfying future. The works of such "Native" American writers as N. Scott Momaday, Sherman Alexie, Louise Erdrich, and Michael Dorris tell of the sacredness and sacrifices of the past, preserved in vibrant oral cultures countless centuries old, but also they tell the stories of the more recent past, of individuals trying to secure the ties of family, even as they loosen under the pressures of dispersal from reservation to city, and back again. But what everyone dimly knows is that the culture of deprivation and neglect is not shared in the same way by all Native Americans. There is dignity to be found in remembering the past and in seeking community. They seek a sense of self-worth by seeking to distinguish notions of ancient Native American time and history from Western ideas of how to speak about and how to derive value from the past. But there is dignity as well, as Momaday, Alexie, Erdrich, Dorris, and others attest, in knowing and coming to share in the foundations of Western culture, as much theirs

---

[5] For this view, and a consideration of the causes lying behind this shift in thinking, at least among liberals in the universities and the media, see Scott L. Malcomson, *One Drop of Blood. The American Misadventure of Race* (New York: Farrar Straus Giroux, 2000), pp. 373–388, who is also the source for the information about events since 1961 and the 1980 and 1990 Census figures, pp. 111–14. For the challenges to the exclusivity of race, see pp. 115–19.

as their "own." It is a gift they have fought for. The gift is not matched on the other side of the divide between whites and reds. White Americans perceived in red America nothing that they wanted. There is another kind of dignity, in short, arising from a feeling of belonging to more than one culture. Ironically, Native Americans may in fact be the gainers in the centuries-long contact of cultures, but only if the opportunities for sharing in the dominant culture improve. It is impossible to read these writers without being impressed by the power of this double pull, the pull of the past and the pull of a common culture, in which Native Americans can move with fewer burdens of inequality and find the ways do so more freely than before. Momaday, whose belief in the sacred past and present of the multiple Native Americas is fierce and noble, writes, "It is imperative that the Indian defines himself, that he finds the strength to do so, that he refuses to let others define him. Children are at the greatest risk. We, Native Americans in particular, *but all of us*, need to restore the sacred to our children."[6]

Because of this varied response, the pull toward an ideology of victimhood should not be seen as inevitable. It needs critical scrutiny if it is not to become hardened and destructive. One of the best hopes for Native Americans may be found in what Native American writers say about themselves, and how they enable readers to see how the characters in their books reveal their uniqueness, yet not their total apartness from "Others." By trying to enter the worlds of those Others through imaginative literature, non-Native Americans, however they come to identify themselves in a society that can often no longer recognize visible differences, may come to see how those Others perceive non-Native Americans as the Others. In *Reservation Blues*, Sherman Alexie's novel about Spokane Indians and their Flathead Indian girlfriends, who form a rock band and try their luck in New York, a telling encounter takes place between Thomas and Chess and a restaurant waitress, who is startled to find that she is speaking with Indians:

> "Hey," Chess said, "you ain't seen two Indian men come in here, have you?"
> "What?" the waitress asked. "What do you mean? From India?"
> "No," Chess said. "Not that kind of Indian. We mean American Indians, you know? Bows and arrows Indians. Cowboys-and-Indians."

[6] N. Scott Momaday, *The Man Made of Words* (New York: St. Martin's Press, 1997), p. 76. My emphasis.

"Oh, "the waitress said, "that kind. Shoot, I ain't ever seen that kind of Indian."

"We're that kind of Indian."

"Really?"

"Really."[7]

In a related but different accent, Louise Erdrich says that her life in the United States as a writer finds its salient markers in Western as much as in non-Western culture:

> Of course. I am ambivalent, I am human. There are times I wish that I were one thing or the other, but I am a mixed-blood. *Psychically doomed*, another mixed-blood friend once joked. The truth is that my background is such a rich mixed bag I'd be crazy to want to be anything else. Nor would any Native writer who understands that through the difficulty of embracing our own contradictions we gain sympathy for the range of ordinary failures and marvels.[8]

And there is in Michael Dorris's attitude to American policies toward Indian land claims an easy familiarity with the kinds of practical deals that can be negotiated when all the cards are on the table:

> None of the treaties was kept by the government to the letter of the law. Those treaties provided for a continuing political identity for Indian nations which has not been supported by the kinds of prerogatives that should have come as a result of treaties. So unlike any other ethnic group in the country, when Indians look at the government, they don't say change things. They say, keep the laws that were made in the nineteenth century. . . . They're looking to uphold the laws that exist. . . . You have to believe in American ideals if you're an Indian, because those ideals set up treaties that recognized Indian sovereignty, and if ever Americans lived up to those ideals, it would be a good day for Indians.[9]

In today's United States, Native Americans are among groups that single themselves out or have been singled out as having special claims to be designated as historically and morally ignored others. Does Will Kymlicka, who has written deeply on the subject of Canadian Native peoples, help to clarify the needed distinctions between the fact of victimization and the ideology of victimhood? Kymlicka also deals with Native politics in the United States. He argues for policies of special concern; he writes of the need to draft creative provisions to give Native peoples special political status. Such steps, if carefully managed, need

[7] Sherman Alexie, *Reservation Blues* (New York: Atlantic Monthly Press, 1995), pp. 238–39.

[8] *Conversations with Louise Erdrich and Michael Dorris*, eds. Allan Chavkin and Nancy Feyl Chavkin (Jackson: University Press of Mississippi, 1994), p. 238.

[9] Ibid., pp. 142–43.

not, he asserts, be seen as a contravention of democratic equality. Calling both on John Rawls and Ronald Dworkin to support his view that inequalities in cultural membership should be a source of concern for defenders of a liberal egalitarian theory, Kymlicka advocates "special rights for national minorities if there actually is a disadvantage with respect to cultural membership, and if the rights actually serve to rectify the disadvantage." So, for instance, because in North America the indigenous people of Canada suffer more greatly the unmitigated power of the majority will than the Québecois – or the Puerto Ricans in the United States who suffer from greater disabilities than Hispanics from Latin America – means must be found to ensure "group-differentiated self-government rights [to] compensate for unequal circumstances which put members of minority cultures at a systemic disadvantage in the cultural market-place, regardless of their personal choices in life."[10] In advocating such measures, which he believes will "protect the context within which [basic civil and political rights] have their meaning and efficacy," he quickly adds that a distinction should be made between group rights and the rights of groups that are not designated as culturally distinct – that is to say, groups that are defined by gender, color, and, we might add, immigrant groups that seek to become part of the mainstream.[11]

As I read him, Kymlicka blurs the distinction between the history of oppressors and their victims and the protest of victimhood. By introducing scales of differentiation among groups each of whom believes its grievances are as worthy as any other, he might in fact be inviting each to enter into a competitive game in a calculus of suffering. Even if some scheme could be worked out to make such differentiations work, what might its consequences be? Inadvertent or cynical exploitation or a rough measure of justice? It is hard to say. If the policies will act to nurture self-worth in people, the endeavors are worth supporting. But if they act instead to prolong feelings of helplessness and woundedness, the sense of wrongs righted is not likely to encourage feelings of autonomy – the capacity to enlarge the vision of choice. Will the compensation for the inequality of circumstances, which Kymlicka proposes, work to the detriment of individual choice or work in its favor? Will the policies that are

---

[10] Will Kymlicka, *Multicultural Citizenship. A Liberal Theory of Minority Rights* (Oxford: Clarendon Press, 1995), pp. 109–10, 113. Also see his earlier study, *Liberalism, Community and Culture* (Oxford: Oxford University Press, 1991).

[11] Will Kymlicka, "The Good, the Bad, and the Intolerable: Minority Group Rights," *Dissent* (Summer 1996), 24–25.

being introduced to return or give lands to Native peoples bring them
rights as individuals, and not only the rights derived from belonging to
groups Kymlicka calls culturally distinct? Compensation to the group in
all likelihood will enhance its identity, but to ensure that such a measure
amounts to individual freedom and a fair notion of equality shared with
others – not an unenforceable idea of egalitarianism – more thought
must be given to avoid locking individual identity into the grid of group
identity.

The sharpness of the conflict between individual and collective rights
seems to be more marked in the United States than in Canada, which is
Kymlicka's major cultural focus. It is not that the individual is less important in Canada and that group rights count for nothing in the United
States, but that, as Kymlicka and others argue, American rights culture
favors the first rather than the second, and are more attuned to redress-
ing individual wrongs. It is not likely that Americans would approach
and receive the land and self-government claims of Native peoples,
for example, with the same patience and equanimity as the citizens of
Canada, where significant modifications in conventional notions of sovereignty have been introduced. Of course, affirmative action, whether
designed to be more forthright or less confrontational, is meant in the
United States to make up for or reverse past injustices. Much more
radical is the new interest in seeking forms of compensation for the
wrongs of slavery, a campaign which may or may not be short-lived. The
point in making these contrasts between the two rights cultures is that
neither can be said to look exclusively in one direction, and that the two
have important points of contact. In both, moreover, as we have seen,
individuals have found and continue to explore means of exiting from
the loyalties that particular groups command and transfer them to those
of the dominant culture without feeling they are betraying either.[12]

In time, the exploitative uses of victimhood may diminish in importance, but until and if they do, those who seek its protective comforts
may do so at the cost of infantilizing themselves. Believing that they represent a radical challenge, they in fact help to prolong the ties that bind
them to their parents. In that respect, the solace of the familiar is the
mirror image of the appeal that sameness has for whites, who also share
with Native and Afro-Americans deeply ambiguous feelings about racial
mixing. Perhaps, even more dangerously, they will try to use victimhood

---

[12] See Michael Ignatieff, *The Rights Revolution*. CBC Massey Lectures Series (Toronto:
House of Anansi Press, 2000), for a fine analysis of Canada's rights culture.

as an aggressive weapon against whom they see as symbols of a dominant and alien culture. Indeed, so deeply are Native Indian grievances felt that, for example, in Québec, the Kahnawake Mohawk band in 1994 expelled members whose pure blood lineage could not be traced for several generations. The act was intended to preserve the band's "genetic quality."[13] It was not likely to have gained approval from Erdrich, Dorris, and Momaday. Whether the Mohawk band's pronouncement is an egregious piece of rhetoric, or is devoutly and passionately believed, the declaration reinforces the genetic argument from the other side of the divide. Some members of the "oppressed" (remember Pericles' use of the word) and some of the "oppressors" appear to be joining forces on the basis of the mighty gene, but disagree on who constitutes the superior and inferior members of the human race.

Thus, race continues to occupy a major place in the cultural and political consciousness of Americans, whatever has been said about its weak or strong conceptual basis on either biological or cultural grounds. Just recognizing this is to admit how versatile a term it is. It won't go away for three reasons. First, because it continues to define for many an inextinguishable dividing line between whites, reds, and blacks. Second, because of the political and economic gains expected by those who claim to be its victims. Third, because there are those who deeply feel that some form of compensation is justified to mitigate past inequalities, and that such a historically necessary process requires, at the very least, a politically expedient notion of race to sanction policies designed to create a level playing field. There has come into being a coalition of interests that engages in the politics of disadvantage seemingly in order to extend advantage to all. Such a posture flows from the belief that by following certain paths, an age of equality will be introduced and lie within the reach of the dispossessed, and finally wipe out the inequities of the past.

This species of politics is more marked, and indeed is not the same, in the culture of Native America as it is in the culture of Afro-America. It is associated with the more highly charged identity of race with blackness, and both are identified with slavery. Each was superimposed on the other, without any clear evidence that any one of them came first. The

---

[13] *Toronto Globe and Mail*, March 17, 1994. Cited in Katherine Fierlbeck, *Globalizing Democracy. Power, Legitimacy and the Interpretation of Democratic Ideas* (Manchester and New York: Manchester University Press, 1998), pp. 83–84. It should be noted that to safeguard civic equality, the Canadian Charter of Rights forbids the use of blood, ethnic, and racial principles for establishing group membership.

redness or whiteness of Native Americans does not seem to be so crucial a sign of difference as the blackness or whiteness of Afro-Americans. All who are part of this coalition embrace – but especially Afro-Americans, for whom color is the critical point of difference – the notion that unless the paths of recognition and compensation are explored, the unpleasantnesses of the past, based on a belief in inequality founded on difference, will become even more unpleasant in the future. In other words, they invoke affirmative action on the grounds that color-blindness is not only a species of blindness itself, but that it is futile to make appeals to it as a practical way to deal with injustice in societies where color-blindness is not the norm. Together with this position, another is advocated – namely, that color-consciousness cannot and should not be ignored, for without acknowledging its power past injuries will not be rectified. "The conundrum of color," James Baldwin wrote late in life, "is the inheritance of every American, be he/she legally or actually Black or White." Rightly he saw it as an inescapable feature of American society, not made anymore tolerable, he said, by the fact that a black underclass had become a permanent feature of the American economy.[14]

The catch, as others see it, is that such an approach will fail in its purpose to use color-consciousness as a bridge towards social solidarity, because it continues to rest on a notion of race. It is also argued that those who cling to it, as an instrument of racial solidarity, separate themselves out from a notion of the mainstream to which peoples from diverse cultures contribute. They thus deny the opportunity of forming themselves as part of a larger whole.[15] Taking one of his cues from Charles Taylor, Anthony Appiah argues, first, that identity is constituted by dialogue with others, and second, that it relies on concepts and practices shaped by religion, society, school, and the state, all four of which are mediated by the family. In *Sources of the Self*, Taylor located the self within what he called "webs of interlocution." As he put it, "The full definition of someone's identity . . . usually involves not only his stand on moral and spiritual matters but also some reference to a defining com-

---

[14] James Baldwin, "Introduction to *Notes of a Native Son*, 1984," *Collected Essays* (New York: The Library of America, 1998), pp. 810–11.

[15] See Anthony Appiah and Amy Gutmann, *Color-Conscious: The Political Morality of Race* (Princeton: Princeton University Press, 1997). For an impassioned plea against white liberals and Afro-Americans alike, the first for trading on shame and guilt, the second, for cashing in on the material rewards to be gained from exploiting the ideology of victimhood, see Shelby Steele, *A Dream Deferred. The Second Betrayal of Black Freedom in America* (New York: Harper Collins, 1998).

munity." For Taylor, the richness of identity is considerably reduced by Western culture's – most dramatically and now traditionally by America's – headlong rush from community to an unqualified individualism.[16] He seeks to round out this definition of identity by speaking in favor of "a recognition of the need for difference, . . . felt viscerally as a matter of dignity, in which one's self-worth is engaged."[17] One can see why Taylor's insistence on dignity for those who see themselves as different might underline even more firmly the position Appiah chooses to defend. Appiah wants much the same thing – recognition of Afro-American dignity – but it should not, he strongly believes, be sacrificed for something equally precious: the idea that the Afro-American self is not constructed solely within the black community. Just as gender, ethnicity, nationality, and sexuality should not be distinguishing features of identity, so should race not be considered its absolute mark, especially as no real argument can be made for elevating it above all others and making it the single determining factor in social relationships and political action.[18] Appiah rejects what he calls the imperialism of identity – that is, making people shape their individual identities by the very stereotypes from which they wish to escape, including being taken as representative of and belonging to a group that is said to be "racially" of lower intelligence.

But aloofness is not an option, for the prospect of conflict between individual freedom and identity politics cannot be ignored. In urging government policies to combat racism, Appiah writes that "government can't be color blind because society isn't – people and institutions treat citizens differently according to whether they are black or white, yellow or brown."[19] In fact, color may continue as a defining sign of difference for more people than they themselves are likely to admit. "To argue," Orlando Patterson writes in agreement, "that we should begin to solve the problem of 'racial' exclusion by assuming a color-blind world is to assume away the very problem we are trying to solve . . . The simple

---

[16] Charles Taylor, *Sources of the Self. The Making of the Modern Identity* (Cambridge, Mass., Harvard University Press, 1989), pp. 36, 40.

[17] Charles Taylor, "Nationalism and Modernity," in *The State of the Nation. Ernst Gellner and the Theory of Nationalism*, ed. John A. Hall (Cambridge: Cambridge University Press, 1998), 191–218, citation from 207.

[18] Anthony Appiah and Amy Gutmann, *Color-Conscious*, pp. 37, 38, 55–56, 92–99. For more on Taylor's argument, see his *Multiculturalism and the "Politics of Recognition"* (Princeton: Princeton University Press, 1994).

[19] Anthony Appiah and Amy Gutmann, *Color-Conscious*, pp. 99, 179–80, 71–74, 102–03.

truth, the simple reality, is that 'racial' categorization is a fact of American life, one that we can do away with only by first acknowledging it." He is concerned about the ways in which what he regards as the overracialization of all issues relating to Afro-Americans has blurred the issues and diminished the opportunities for clear thinking about their place in American society. This tendency gives those who stigmatize them another arrow in their quiver – that of a highly suspect scientific valorization. "Having abolished the ontological basis of 'race' in biology, American social scientists vie with each other to reestablish the ontological essence as social fact. And this, in turn, has led to the idea of 'race' creeping back into natural science."[20] He faults, at the same time, large sections of the Afro-American leadership who have, by embracing separatism, given up on integration in the belief that Afro-American identity and achievements can be secured only by abandoning the common American path toward success.[21]

The pressing problem is whether democracy can live with some concessions to cultural inequalities, however these are defined, and, on their foundations, adopt in recompense, measures to ensure that they are not discriminatory or disabling. The terrain, though rocky, has not been unexplored. Such measures are now introduced principally in the context of cultural or identity politics – of ethnicity and gender – which critics say renders the professed goals of an achievement-oriented democratic culture nugatory. Cultural, or identity, or status politics, being other-directed, asks us to see ourselves in the eyes of the other, and these may or may not include what "scientific" findings may tell us about the varieties of human beings. On this account of the human condition, differences are explained and expressed within a notion of politics meant to throw a protective mantle over some sections of the population. At best, they only grudgingly admit the advantages of wider social and political solidarities. Even more questionable is the expectation that the stress on identity/difference can marshal effective weapons against the profound sources of inequality.

There is in Appiah's defiance a strong echo of Ralph Ellison's powerful plea to be taken as an individual for whom race and the color of skin do not carry a person's total worth. In the decades when Ellison made

---

[20] Orlando Patterson, *The Ordeal of Integration: Progress and Resentment in America's "Racial" Crisis* (Washington, DC: Counterpoint, 1997). The first quotation is on p. 163, the second on pp. 3–4.

[21] Ibid., pp. 85–86, 125–45, 171–203.

his greatest mark, race was not seen as the overwhelmingly sole determinant of the individual and the only distinguishing marker of a people's identity, as it, unexpectedly and often perversely, seemed to have become in the final years of the twentieth century. This is bloody territory indeed, for color-consciousness is not easily obliterated by appeals to the putative power of universal rationality and to an all-embracing humanity. The creation of boundaries is centuries-old and can accommodate several degrees of exclusiveness. Democracy is supposed to make visible the invisible. It is supposed to make us equal, or as nearly equal as possible. But the view that visible bodily marks, which are often hypothetically related to invisible marks of intelligence, and which are said to reside in our genetic structures, has become one of the highly charged currencies of democratic exchange, and promises to make the subject of inclusion-exclusion one of interminable debate.

Deprivation, degradation, and shame combine to make Afro-American protest almost overwhelmingly color-conscious. By folding class consciousness into color-consciousness, it identifies the first as a function of the second and obscures the nature of economic disparities. Reductionism in the opposite direction, of course, has self-limiting consequences, because it paralyzes efforts to deal effectively with the problems of improving the chances for greater egalitarianism while doing little or nothing to preserve the belief in distinctiveness as a valuable aspect of a democratic civil society. Thus, remedies that recognized severe economic inequality could prove effective in realizing both a juster redistribution of resources and in enhancing the respect sought by minorities, while reducing their feelings of obligation and resentment. The shortcomings of public policies that stress first one approach, and then – in an effort to correct its unintended consequences – the other, are well known, as may be seen in the backlash against affirmative action. For this reason, the attempt to find a middle ground that would do justice to the complexities of class and race formation, and a parallel effort to see the first not exclusively as an economic phenomenon, nor the second as exclusively a cultural one, is to be welcomed.[22] The myth of America as a "classless" society remains powerful, however, so much so that priority is given to the question of identity, rather than focusing more

---

[22] Nancy Fraser offers a spirited argument for such an approach in "Social Justice in an Age of Identity Politics: Redistribution, Recognition, and Participation," *The Tanner Lectures on Human Values*, 19 (1998) (Salt Lake City: University of Utah Press, 1998), 1–67.

centrally on such economic and social questions as employment, housing, and education. Centuries of white hostility are certainly responsible for radical racial solidarity, but it in turn reinforces the belief among racists that color is the decisive carrier of inferiority on all levels, just as it is taken to be a badge of superiority by black extremists.

Humiliation and shame certainly feed those feelings of psychic revenge. We have been asked to consider whether reducing the power of humiliation and shame to deepen social divisions may be more important than seeking identical rights for people. What would this look like? Citizens would be persuaded to lower their ideological sights in exchange for a society with modest expectations on its institutions and citizens to refrain from humiliating one another. Such acts of humiliation and shaming, which lead to collective de-individuation, would in time be reduced. De-individuation means the singling out of a population for separate and inhumane treatment, but paradoxically gives it a "greater," but a perverse, because illusory, kind of individuality. Humiliation thus deprives people of their individuality, and identifies them wholly as members of a group in which they are told to seek their authentic selves.[23] There is a double dynamic at work. The negative sources of identification – that is, identity imposed by others – shows us one side of a double mirror. The other side is the presumed positive, sometimes verging on the superior, working out of self-identity, which at first might be used as a tactical ploy but then settles in as an unquestioned virtue, a residual effect, as we know from the experience of building power on the basis of false premises and disingenuous postures.

Iris Young is impatient with a certain kind of liberal bias that assumes the superiority of a set of assimilationist ideologies, because, as she puts it, they constitute an unquestioned initial premise. It was only "after the rules and standards [had] already been met," that the right of particular groups to enter the political world was recognized. Jacques Derrida's notion of the "metaphysics of presence" strongly influenced her contention that the liberal idea of identity "reduce[s] differences to unity."[24] She is banking a great deal on another premise, that a wider solidarity and a plurality of social perspectives will be achieved by encouraging people of diverse social and racial backgrounds to acknowledge their sep-

[23] See Avishai Margalit, *The Decent Society* (Cambridge, Mass.: Harvard University Press, 1996).
[24] Iris Marion Young, *Justice and the Politics of Difference* (Princeton: Princeton University Press, 1990), pp. 97, 166–67.

arateness, find the resources to differentiate it from a narrowly conceived identity based on self-interest and preference, and subsume it to the largest notions of justice.[25] The liberal notion of identity politics that she deplanes, moreover, overlooks the realities of group differences determined by culture, practices, power, and privilege that provides "a resource for democratic communication," while recognizing that it may, by making room for all social groups, make it harder to reach decisions.[26] Inclusion is, in this view, a worthy goal, and must not be eschewed because it might make democratic politics less efficient. Young's premise is that people can still lend coherency to their lives while shifting their ground in a great variety of social and political interactions, that they are various, rather than one-dimensional, in their identities. To be ascribed one identity is reductive. In its fatal misunderstanding and intolerance of individuality, it is opposed to Tocqueville's plea for diversity. Whatever its shortcomings and its blighted hopes, the Enlightenment may still hold out the best prospects for human beings, and remain the best assurance against the elevation of cultural identity that, as a foundation for political and civil life, diverts attention from what Kant declared as its hallmark: "*Enlightenment is man's emergence from his self-incurred immaturity. Immaturity is the inability to use one's own understanding without the guidance of another.*"[27] He meant the emergence to maturity to apply to all humankind. He made no distinction between "mature" and "immature" cultures. This is clear from his claim that the idea of humanity, if it is to carry weight in an argument about moral freedom, must be free of content, as for example, in his characterization of the civil state: "[R]egarded as a lawful state, [it] is based on the following *a priori* principles: 1. the *freedom* of every member of society as a *human being*. 2. the *equality* of each with all the others as a *subject*. 3. the *independence* of each member of a commonwealth as a *citizen*."[28] Kant enables us to see a little more clearly how this moral

[25] Iris Marion Young, "Difference as a Resource for Democratic Communication," in *Deliberative Democracy. Essays on Reason and Politics*, eds. James Bohman and William Rehg (Cambridge, Mass. and London: MIT Press, 1997), 383–406, esp. 393–98.

[26] Iris Marion Young, *Inclusion and Democracy* (Oxford: Oxford University Press, 2000), pp. 90, 119.

[27] Immanuel Kant, "An Answer to the Question: What Is Enlightenment?" *Kant's Political Writings*, trans. H.B. Nisbet, ed. Hans Reiss (Cambridge: Cambridge University Press, 1991), p. 54. My emphasis.

[28] Immanuel Kant, "On the Common Saying: 'This May be True in Theory, But It Does Not Apply in Practice,'" ibid., p. 74.

universalism may be reasserted by refusing any culture a superior place in a hierarchy of cultures.

The absence of content in Kant's notion of the autonomous citizen deprives us of the capacity to envision him as a living reality. That is why the forces in communities marshaled in defense of or against either the familiar and the known, for or against notions of superiority and ineradicable difference, and how society and politics were affected by supporters and resisters of school desegregration, which were depicted powerfully by J. Anthony Lukas more than a decade ago, can have such an immediate appeal. His account of three families and how their lives touched one another remains compelling, because of its gritty portrayal of people struggling to make sense of what was happening to them and their communities. No theoretical analysis can capture this. *Common Ground* is Lukas's day-to-day account of people affected by, and how they in turn affected the outcomes of, busing policies introduced to create a racially integrated system of education in Boston in the 1970s. Within the city's neighborhoods, solidarities had been created and local interests had the self-assurance of immunity from hostile change. Resistance to it was predicated on the primacy of community wishes bolstered by a belief that in protecting them they were expressing and giving full life to democratic values. These were also invoked by the other side, but on different premises. Democracy, for the first group of embattled citizens, did not so much mean equality as it did community, or what was conceived to be a community of equals. Implicit in this attitude was that no infringement of justice was in play when it came to others who were thought to be undesirable because of their differences. For the second group, justice was denied if no provision were made for equal access to the city's schools, no matter what parts of Boston the children lived in. Busing meant disturbing both black and white communities, and the turmoil was anguishing enough to cast a heavy shadow on the intentions of those who believed the changes were needed and demanded the support of the law and the police. There were additional sources of conflict. Three of the most important were appeals to the meanings of the Constitution, calls within the Irish Catholic community to the Christian ideal that demanded respect from and for all God's children, and finally the divisions within the black community between those who believed that integration would reveal the extent to which the poor in both the white and black communities were engaged in a futile struggle against each other, and those who wanted to fight for recognition on the basis of black power. Lukas sets the enormous stresses felt in Boston against

Tocqueville's recognition that two political systems existed in America, "the one," as Tocqueville said, "fulfilling the ordinary duties and responding to the daily and infinite calls of a community; the other circumscribed within certain limits and exercising an exceptional authority over the general interests of the country."[29]

The most striking of Lukas's findings is that deprivation was the major source of the conflict and that it turned people inwards to a defense of what they knew and took solace from. They are not likely to turn toward others until they feel secure enough to see, if we accept Richard Rorty's conclusion, that "difference from others [is] inessential to one's self-respect, one's sense of worth." Without feeling sufficiently free from risk, they will, in addition, lack the resources for the sympathy needed to see others in plight or find it hard to identify with them.[30] If only it were so simple, might be William Connolly's rejoinder. The problem of identity/difference is not only one of economic inequality. It is embedded in a paradox, discerned by Nietzsche, Heidegger, and Foucault, not mired, as their critics contend, in incoherence. The difficulty of providing either teleological and transcendental foundations for an unambiguous identity highlights the unalterable fact that the very texture of social life confers privilege upon a certain set of identities and conceals "the element of arbitrary conquest in the differences they create and negate."[31] Historical perspective, of course, permits us to see how they change over time. There exists, so to speak, a dynamic of differentiation that alters them. The notion of an unchanging identity, resistant to change, on the slender theory of essentialism, creates illusions at both ideological extremes, capturing the creators of the stereotype and the differentiated and alienated object of the stereotype in a monolithic vision of individuals and groups.[32] It is against such reductive ideas that Henry Louis Gates, Jr., also rebels, for it freezes rather than opens up the opportunities for dialogue, and fails to recognize that identities are nothing in

---

[29] J. Anthony Lukas, *Common Ground. A Turbulent Decade in the Lives of Three Amercan Families* (New York: Alfred A. Knopf, 1985). This is a quotation from Tocqueville and is found on p. 207.

[30] Richard Rorty, *Truth and Progress. Philosophical Papers* (Cambridge: Cambridge University Press, 1998), vol. 3, p. 180.

[31] William E. Connolly, *Identity/Difference. Democratic Negotiations of Political Paradox* (Ithaca and London, Cornell University Press, 1991), pp. 67–68. For a brief treatment of "the politics of difference," see Jean Bethke Elshtain, *Democracy on Trial. The CBC Massey Lecture Series* (Concord, Ontario: Anansi, 1993), pp. 63–91.

[32] See Joan W. Scott, "Multiculturalism and the Politics of Identity," *October* 61 (1992), 19.

fact but recognitions and therefore "like everything else, sites of contest and negotiation."[33]

Lukas's immensely affecting studies of men, women, and teenagers living in a charged atmosphere of social and racial tensions helps us to see how a "site of contest" in a critical period of school desegregation did not lead to an unqualified success in negotiating change. It is a peerless account that sets it conspicuously beside the book Robert Bellah and his colleagues published in the same year (1985). Among the many points of common observation and concern between them was the negative response of citizens of Suffolk, a suburb of Boston, to the proposal to make room for low-cost housing for Afro-Americans and Hispanics – a good because not untypical instance of the tyranny of small groups that trades in communitarian values to the disadvantage of larger ones. Bellah and his associates concluded that "One gets involved in public life only to the extent to protect one's hearth and home and one's decent friends and neighbors from the evils of a mysterious, threatening, complicated society composed of shadowy, sinister, immoral strangers. There is no rationale here for developing public institutions that would tolerate the diversity of a large heterogeneous society and nurture common standards of justice and civility among its members."[34] Lukas and Bellah and his fellow authors capture the tensions of American society, caught in a vice of internal divisions and against a background of vast international economic change in hitherto underdeveloped parts of the world. To counteract some of the worst effects of such change at the more tractable first-story level where individuals lead their lives, Bellah calls on a spirit of mutual generosity that would pay one's debts to society and renew the moral virtue that inspired America's original founders, while acknowledging its short supply. Indeed these exhortations are sounded again and again. Noble sentiments, without doubt, but how are they expected to sprout in the hearts of those who feel aggrieved and ignored?

And, why, as well, believe that those who do not have a past of deprivation will feel generous? The fear of the unknown, charted by Lukas, may be measured, if not scientifically, at least impressionistically, by

[33] Henry Louis Gates, Jr., "Beyond the Culture Wars: Identities in Dialogue," *Profession* 93 (New York: Modern Language Association, 1994), 11.

[34] Robert N. Bellah et al., *Habits of the Heart. Individualism and Commitment in American Life* (Berkeley, Los Angeles and London: University of California Press, 1985), p. 185.

sounds of resistance from people who feel themselves beleaguered in a hostile modern world. In the same year that Lukas's book was published, the *New York Times* carried a story of the reaction of Jonathan F. Fanton, then president of the New School for Social Research, to small-town America. It differs from the Boston area's turmoil over busing only in its seemingly single-minded and undivided community solidarity against the outside world. To Fanton, "sections of Middle America seem to have become refuges for a new know-nothingism." The *Time's* reporter went on to quote Fanton as decrying small-town America, not only for its provincialism, but for having deliberately chosen to embrace it. Jean Bethke Elshtain, who cites this snippet in her book, comments that there are many ways to interpret it, including the residues of Tocqueville's perception of the truths of community life and association.[35] There is much nostalgia and myth-making in this wish to return to a supposed Arcadia. As we saw, Tocqueville was one of the progenitors of the myth, and founded it on the basis of the "creation story" he said was engraved in the hearts of the first colonists in New England, who spoke of being chosen to create a new society in the wilderness.

Like Anthony Appiah after him, Ralph Ellison, more than two generations ago, rejected the idea that race should be ultimately defining, on the grounds that the concept of race was deployed by whites as emotional and epistemological grounds for establishing two identities, that of their own dominant culture and that of subordinate ones, which existed along parallel lines of superiority and inferiority. Ellison, resisting the notion of fixing his identity along one axis, believed in a common humanity. He writes, in his introduction to his *Invisible Man*, that he thought of his book "as a raft of hope, perception and entertainment that might help keep us afloat as we tried to negotiate the snags and whirlpools that mark our nation's vacillating course toward and away from the democratic idea."[36]

Tocqueville, even longer ago, as we saw, could not always get over the barriers of race, as he perceived them at work in American society that espoused enlightened ideals, but that in significantly decisive areas, practiced a politics at variance with them. When he considered differences and the ways in which allowances should be made for them in an

---

[35] Jean Bethke Elshtain, *Real Politics at the Center of Everyday Life* (Baltimore and London: Johns Hopkins University Press, 1997), pp. 340–41. The excerpt from the *New York Times* is dated December 4, 1984.

[36] Ralph Ellison, *Invisible Man* (New York: Random House, 1993), pp. xxiv–xxv.

egalitarian society, without injuring the ideal or the substance of equality, he invoked the principle of merit. In one of his earliest efforts to define the various meanings of American equality, he envisioned American social mobility as the decisive outcome of the accumulation of wealth, because in America wealth was fluid and not permanently the preserve of one group. Hence, Americans in the aggregate would come to share in a rough but never a complete equality, and they would do so without attributing superiority to any one. What he thought was missing in America, and which he seems to have given exaggerated status in France, was the high respect shown intellectual life and mental gifts that for him legitimately and rationally made up the basis for distinctions among human beings.[37] As we also saw, he took up the notion of capacities, of the qualities that were needed to fulfill the role of the autonomous citizen, and maintained that political apprenticeship and practice deepened them, but at the same time he did not think that even because these were not equally distributed, a politically just democratic society was not possible. The question of how to weigh capacities in a democracy has not disappeared, and indeed is thought to be central to any discussion of how these might be enhanced in American society without damage to the principle of equality.[38]

It remains to be seen how such variations on the older concepts of equality have substantially changed the ways in which it is perceived. Already perceptions were changing almost from the time Gunnar Myrdal was thought to have had the last word on this question.[39] Ellison early took exception to Myrdal's unexamined starting point that Afro-Americans are "simply the creation of white men." Didn't they (Afro-Americans), he asked, "at least help to create themselves out of which they found around them?"[40] He drove home the point more mordantly, yet not entirely pessimistically, by describing the American dilemma as emerging from "the pathology of social hierarchy, a reaction to certain

[37] Alexis de Tocqueville, *Oeuvres*, ed. André Jardin with the collaboration of Françoise Mélonio and Lise Queffélec, 2 vols. (Paris: Gallimard, 1991), I, "De l'égalité en Amérique," 276–78.

[38] See the essays by James Bohman, "Deliberative Democracy and Effective Social Freedom: Capabilities, Resources and Opportunities," and Jack Knight and James Johnson, "What Sort of Equality does Deliberative Democracy Require?" in *Deliberative Democracy. Essays on Reason and Politics*, eds. James Bohman and William Rehg (Cambridge, Mass., and London: MIT Press, 1997), 321–48, 279–320.

[39] Gunnar Myrdal, *An American Dilemma: The Negro Problem and Modern Democracy* (New York: Harper and Brothers, 1944).

[40] Ralph Ellison, "An American Dilemma: A Review," in *Shadow and Act*, p. 301.

built-in conditions of our democracy that are capable of amelioration but impossible to cure."[41] In the 1990s, Andrew Hacker compared what he believed to be Myrdal's misreading of American ideals with Tocqueville's predictions of deeply ingrained racial hostilities.[42] Ellison approached the dilemma as a novelist, who, while writing about the black experience, never divorced or amputated it from the larger American one. Tocqueville chose the history of civilization as the point from which to view the significance of social stress, violence, and change, which, as different parts of the globe touched one another with unprecedented technological power, upset the boundaries of the past and mixed peoples together, bringing questions of racial and cultural difference into the historical equation.

When we recall Tocqueville's slim hope that American literature might one day possess transforming power, and his even less sanguine reflections and more disconsolate mood that black and Native Americans faced enormous, indeed, almost insuperable, barriers in the struggle to assert their humanity, Ellison's gifts as an American writer appear to have realized Tocqueville's cautionary prediction in a most paradoxical way, even for a thinker who schematized life's paradoxes so masterfully. For Ellison, the novel was not a simple instrument or means for assembling the pieces of the American puzzle. He reached back to and considered himself the equal of Hawthorne, Melville, and Poe, writers who were contemporaneous with Tocqueville but of whom the Frenchman had no knowledge. Of Ellison's commitments as a writer, he said of *Invisible Man* that "I wrote it in an attempt to give meaningful form to a body of experience which is much more chaotic and complex and tragically human and real than most of the solutions that are offered to deal with it . . . I believe the picture presented in *Invisible Man* is a true one and that its statement about human life transcends (and was meant to transcend) mere racial experience. That on the broader level of its meaning it says something about the experience of being an American and that this includes all Americans white or black."[43] Ellison saw the early pre-Civil War novel as the beginning of the spiritual process by means of

[41] Ralph Ellison, "The Little Man at Chehaw Station," in *Going to the Territory*, pp. 19, 20.

[42] Andrew Hacker, *Two Nations. Black and White, Separate, Hostile, Unequal* (New York: Ballantine Books, 1995), pp. xii, 225–26.

[43] Ellison to Sydney Spiegel, December, 13, 1959, John F. Callahan, "'American Culture is of a Whole': From the Letters of Ralph Ellison," *The New Republic* 220 (March 1, 1999), 40.

which Americans of all origins used fragmentary visions of Europe to create the American dream without dispelling the mystery of how, coming from different regions, and as diverse as they were in their social, cultural, and religious backgrounds, they came to be and are each American. He writes of how each tries "to snatch from the whirling chaos of history" a "share of reality" that "belongs not to [each] group alone but to all of us."[44] Tocqueville, a century and more earlier tried to entrap this "whirling chaos of history," to stop it long enough to comprehend how Europeans, Afro-Americans, and aboriginal peoples came to be together, yet existed apart.

Ellison, like Tocqueville, accepted the historical significance of the political ideals of the eighteenth century as they took form in America with its particularities of race, religion, and geography. Neither the one nor the other, however, succumbed to the spurious notion that a search, no matter how thorough, for the elements of race, religion, and geography would exhaust their meaning, nor that taken singly or in combination they could be so placed as to yield final truth, not only about persons, but also of the nature of history in general, the heterogeneity of American society, and the power of the state. Ellison, springing from a singular minority, sought to raise his head above the cultural periphery by embracing universality and making liberty, solidarity, and emancipation work for him. While etching out both the sharp and the indistinct boundaries that separated the races, he also sought out evidence for, and argued on behalf of, cultural interpenetrability without any illusions whatever that the racial conflicts in America would quickly disappear. A serious effort had to be made to bring the experience and history of Afro-Americans into white consciousness.[45] Since then the projects of restoration have multiplied.

The mounting radicalization of black American politics and the deterioration of economic expectations made Ellison a unique if not a wholly lonely figure as long ago as the 1960s and 1970s. His hope for a reflective rather than a violent assertiveness of black rights, his appeals to Americans of all backgrounds, and not least Afro-Americans whose specific regional and particular backgrounds he reminded them made up the

---

[44] Ralph Ellison, "Hidden Name and Complex Fate," in *Shadow and Act*, pp. 166–67.

[45] Ralph Ellison, "The Uses of History in Fiction: Ralph Ellison, William Styron, Robert Penn Warren, C. Van Woodward, Southern Historical Association 1968," *Conversations with Ralph Ellison*, eds. Maryemma Graham and Amritijit Singh (Jackson: University Press of Mississippi, 1995), pp. 153–55.

several textures of the American experience, received polite but almost dismissive response from new generations of younger black men and women. There are signs that his stature is returning to full tide.[46] Something much more subtle and mysterious was at work in America both in Tocqueville's and Ellison's time. They came very close to catching its substance. How it could be what it was became Tocqueville's major concern in America. Ellison's despair – not his surprise – is enfolded in what might be seen as an ironic celebratory mood of America in ways that Tocqueville could only have faintly, if at all, imagined. Nevertheless it seems to flow from a similar conviction that democracy created problems as well as opportunities. Curiously Ellison summoned up Tocqueville's name only once, and that one time in an essay devoted in part to the contest of wills between Melville's Bartleby's negativism and the genteel lawyer. I suspect that his brief allusion to Tocqueville's aristocratic stance in democratic America attracted him precisely because of his own need and taste for a life led in a kind of aristocratic aloofness.[47]

There is both celebration and lament in the ambiguities of America's early belief, reiterated over the generations, in its exceptionalism. It inspired the first comers and, in successive years, it became for many Americans the measuring stick by means of which to understand themselves. It also acted as a stimulus to British and European observers of colonial and post-colonial America, who, right down to the present, try to understand them. Tocqueville's observations rested on those made by earlier visitors, and departed from them only in his fair confidence that a new political science was needed to capture the uniqueness of America. This sense of exceptionalism seems to require continual renewal. Even in an age that turns an ambivalent eye on sacred beginnings, the need to affirm them remains strong, as George Armstrong Kelly writes in his probing study of America's political and religious foundations, adding

---

[46] One may glimpse Ellison's hurt, which he expressed in 1982: "All of the new attention [that he was receiving] is somewhat bewildering but nevertheless satisfying when I consider all of the crap I had to take from some of the so-called Black Radicals during the late '60s and most of the '30s." Letter to James Randolph, May 2, 1982, John F. Callahan, "'American Culture is of a Whole': From the Letters of Ralph Ellison," *The New Republic*, 220 (March, 1999), 45. See also, "Indivisible Man," a collage or a collaboration between Ellison and James Alan McPherson on Ellison's craft, goals, and determination to keep his vision of America alive in the face of growing Afro-American alienation and black power. In *The Collected Essays of Ralph Ellison*. Introduction by John F. Callahan (New York: The Modern Library, 1995), pp. 355–95.

[47] Ralph Ellison, "Perspective of Literature," in *Going to the Territory*, p. 328.

that this thirst is "characteristic of a disillusioned nation that has come of age, not only because of world power, responsibility, and empire but also because of a loss of unquenchable faith in its own uniqueness. In other words, America has been inquiring, probably for the last time, whether it is *sui generis* and how this might be shown."[48] In this mood of skepticism and dejection, he takes shots at Robert Bellah's attempt to trace the twentieth-century's manifestations of America's civil religion to their beginnings,[49] reducing it to evidence of "a fiction if not quite an 'idolatry' " that had only a transient place in the American creed.[50] When Americans speak of themselves as the American people, or when in times of crisis the "American people" are rhetorically invoked by politicians, either to seek sanction for a policy or to proffer solutions in a time of crisis, they speak as if Americans, holding on to their memories, can once more regain a belief in their country's departure from the bad kinds of history enacted only in other countries, and can once more declare a new beginning.

Americans want to hold on to some belief that their problems over race and how differences divide them will be overcome in ways that will be uniquely American. As Daniel Bell fervently puts it, America is "an *exempt* nation," "an exemplary nation," lying outside the "laws of decadence or the laws of history."[51] Such a feeling of a distinctive ethos can be invigorating, but also heavily self-deceptive. In his review of the scholarly debate on the truths and fictions of American exceptionalism, especially in its latest phase, Michael Kammen rightly stresses the different (from the histories of European nation-states), rather than the exceptional, aspects of the American past, including "variations in racial attitudes." Thus, while what it means to be American continues to be a legitimate question, he concludes that "while the United States has retained a great many differences, over time those differences have gradually become notably less exceptional."[52]

[48] George Armstrong Kelly, *Politics and Religious Consciousness in America* (New Brunswick and London: Transaction Books, 1984), p. 233.
[49] Robert Bellah pursued the concept of America's civil religion first in his article, "The American Civil Religion," *Daedalus* 96 (Winter 1967), 1–21. He followed it up with *The Broken Covenant: American Civil Religion* (New York: Seabury Press, 1975).
[50] George Armstrong Kelly, *Politics and Religious Consciousness in America*, p. 242.
[51] Daniel Bell, " 'The Hegelian Secret': Civil Society and American Exceptionalism," in *Is America Different? A New Look at American Exceptionalism*, ed. Byron E. Shafer (Oxford: Oxford University Press, 1991), 51.
[52] Michael Kammen, *In the Past Lane. Historical Perspectives on American Culture* (New York and Oxford: Oxford University Press, 1997), pp. 189, 197.

A sense of loneliness, not uniqueness, is achingly etched in Wallace Stevens's poem, "The Sick Man," written in 1949, scant years before Ellison's *Invisible Man* was published. The ache was still there some fifty years later in Philip Roth's *American Pastoral.*[53] Stevens, of Anglo-American stock, and Philip Roth, a secular Jew, speak to us from a place of sorrow, of regret, of nostalgia, of anger, and, in Roth's case, of devastation, that is not, as in his earliest works, lessened by irony or made bittersweet by humor. What they lament is the end, as they imagine it, of the American dream, so permanent a theme in the drawing of the American landscape and its promise. No matter that Stevens died before the brutal experiences of the last three decades. His poem loses none of its sense of hope against hope even when set against the background of the destruction of Roth's American family, shattered by the war in Vietnam, racial violence, and incomprehension.

The strivings of the past have no way of regenerating themselves, but the right words may yet be found. Listen to "The Sick Man":

Bands of black men seem to be drifting in the air,
In the South, bands of thousands of black men.
Playing mouth-organs in the night or, now, guitars.

Here in the North, late, late, there are voices of men,
Voices in chorus, singing without words, remote and deep,
Drifting choirs, long movements and turnings of sounds.

And in a bed in one room, alone, a listener
Waits for the unison of the music of the drifting bands
And the dissolving chorals, waits for it and imagines

The words of winter in which these two will come together,
In the ceiling of the distant room, in which he lies,
The listener, listening to the shadows, seeing them,

Choosing out of himself, out of everything within him,
Speech for the quiet, good hail of himself, good hail, good hail,

The peaceful, blissful words, well-tuned, well-sung, well-spoken.[54]

Philip Roth's novel brings together four generations of American Jews, uneasily enjoying the fruits of their labors and struggling with the assaults that global technological change has brought to the industrial superiority of America. It is set against the recklessness and brutality of

[53] Philip Roth, *American Pastoral* (Boston: Houghton Mifflin, 1997).
[54] Wallace Stevens, *Collected Poetry and Prose*. Library of America (New York: Penguin Books, 1997), p. 455.

the Vietnam War, racial riots, and a misunderstood notion of assimilation in a small town dating its origins to the American Revolution or before, where the descendants of Anglo-Americans play self-regarding games in the belief that while they will be challenged, they will never lose their dominance. And smeared across this emotional storm is an even more desperate persona, the daughter of the novel's protagonist, who, despite her stammering voice, perhaps has the words as Moses the stammerer did, but does not have anyone who will hear her. She resorts in the end to gestures to express her need for self-destruction as the only way to meet the destructive urges of American society. Roth's anti-hero, Swede, mouths words, but they tell him only of the emptiness he feels in the void around himself.

Stevens's "The Sick Man," and Roth's "Swede" thus have their wordlessness to unite them. They describe a society of conflict and chaos, arising from a diminishing belief in its capacity to renew itself, as if the beginnings of that society would forever be re-represented without change in the present. John Edgar Wideman's *The Lynchers*[55] shows once again the destruction of a sense of community of hope, but this time from the perspective of young black men who seek common purpose in a plan to lynch white men to avenge the injustices their ancestors had suffered.

Even greater depths of racial hatred are chronicled in Toni Morrison's *Paradise*,[56] the novel she sets in Ruby, Oklahoma, whose founding fathers, leaving hundreds of years of persecution in the south behind them, try to create a Utopian community – a racially pure black town. The town is in fact racist, and those who depart from the principles of its first foundations are put in mortal danger. The town reenacts the Disallowance of the black pilgrims as they made their way to Oklahoma, at first seeking but being denied shelter in Fairly, a town of light-colored Afro-Americans. In Ruby, the founding elders keep an eye on those among them who dare to violate the iron racial law – they become the new Disallowers. This marks the first step toward keeping the community in an iron vice and turning it into a prison. The last step ends in a lynching party, ironically registering the triumph of revenge, the antithesis of justice, the opposite of the attempt to undo social wrongs in a

[55] John Edgar Wideman, *The Lynchers* in *Identities. Three Novels* (New York: Henry Holt and Company, 1994).
[56] Toni Morrison, *Paradise* (New York: Penguin Books, 1997).

civil society, itself the ancestor to democratic public life that strives to find means to circumscribe and confine the passions that injure individuals and society both.

Still, Morrison bids us to reflect on the meaning of Patricia's repudiation of a lifetime's dedication to the genealogy of the founders of Ruby; not only was it obsessive, but a myth-making artifact. She burns all her papers. The mythology of blood and race is also exposed in Sherman Alexie's *Reservation Blues*, but he brings to it a very different twist. Chess, the strongest woman in the novel – except for Big Mom, the deity with human features, the spiritual beacon and historical repository of Indian woes, the carekeeper of musical lament, and, above all, the black American blues – sees no end to the trail of suffering. Indeed, she dwells on the double turn of inheritance:

> *All you can do is breed the Indian out of your family . . . All you can do is make sure your son marries a white woman and their children marry white people. The fractions will take over. Your half-blood son will have quarter-blood children and eighth-blood grandchildren, and they won't be Indians anymore. They won't hardly be Indian, and they can sleep better at night.*

She closes her meditation on a much more despairing note:

> *Don't you see? . . . Those quarter-blood and eighth-blood grandchildren will find out they're Indian and torment the rest of us real Indians. They'll come out to the reservation, come to our powwows, in their nice clothes and nice cars, and remind the real Indians how much we don't have. Those quarter-bloods and eighth-bloods will get all the Indian jobs, all the Indian chances, because they look white. Because they're safer.*[57]

In July 1998, at the last televised forum of Clinton's national "dialogue" on race, Alexie firmly took exception to the President's sudden outburst that his grandmother had been one-quarter Cherokee. As reported in Christopher Hitchens's book, Alexie replied that people "are always talking about race in coded language. What they will do is come up to me and say they're Cherokee."[58] With an American President donning the mantle of a Native American to glorify himself, and disingenuously identifying himself with them, an awful irony may be drawn. Many Americans talk about the possibility of a post-racist America.

---

[57] Sherman Alexie, *Reservation Blues*, p. 283. Italics in the original.
[58] Christopher Hitchens, *No One Left to Lie To. The Triangulations of William Jefferson Clinton* (London and New York: Verso, 1999), p. 52.

Ralph Ellison was one of them. James Baldwin was not optimistic, but yet he retained a hope in the power of memory. Time would not be out-witted, as if what happened never took place, he wrote years ago.[59] If what remains of the American principles of equality and liberty still possess power to convince and sway people, Ellison's vision and Baldwin's warning may have some effect.

[59] James Baldwin, "Introduction to Notes of a Native Son, 1984," *Collected Essays*, p. 810.

8

Maintaining American Democracy

I'd rather live in a civil society than a political society . . . What we have . . . is a deconstructing of government, a roll back of politicization. In a civil society you feel a desire to fit into a community and satisfy your neighbors. In a political society, under the heavy hand of government, you expect your neighbors to satisfy you.[1]

How is American democracy faring 160 years after Tocqueville completed *Democracy in America*? How does it deal with the practical problems Americans face when they think about how to make the practices of justice and human rights work for them? How many believe that voluntary associations, conventional politics, and public policy continue to shape their life's desires? Broad sections of the American public doubtless believe that all serve them well, but sometimes they question whether consensus will always lie in wait for them so long as they are reasoning and well-intentioned individuals. My purpose in this chapter is to see how politics in America is generally perceived and to make some suggestions about how it really has been working in this century. The liberal view is that America benefits from a commitment to consensus politics, to a politics that avoids extremes and seeks agreement, to a politics that avoids conflict and yearns after peace. The reality of how consensus is reached, however, is captured only with difficulty. It is generally defined as accord and harmony, by contrast with discord and turmoil. The Latin

---

[1] Cited in Jenny Diski's review of Andrew Ross, *The Celebration Chronicles: Life, Liberty and the Pursuit of Property Values in Disney's New Town* (London: Verso: 2000) and Douglas Frantz and Catherine Collins, *Celebration, USA: Living in Disney's Brave New Town* (New York: Holt, 1999), *London Review Of Books*, 22, no. 16 (August 24, 2000).

consensus gentium adds people to the definition, thus making consensus popular agreement. As soon as we ask how agreement is reached, we introduce the problem of how to measure and how to perceive it. When we do so, we find that a strong element of appearance lurks within the seeming innocence of agreement achieved in practice in a variety of ways. The appearances of consensus, or the actual political world of consensus – agreement to avoid disagreement – may in fact be mistaken for consensus itself. The political institutions through which the consensus-creating processes may thus be quite different from, and opposed to, the deservedly praised, but conceptually and practically difficult, promise of consensus as an "authentic" process and desirable goal of meaningful democratic dialogue. It will, however, not do to build it up as a monolithic entity reached by accurate understanding, or break it down as dissensus if the majority do not agree, or to seek some middle ground whereby the majority either agree or think they do not, or disagree and think they agree, to find grounds to dismiss it entirely on *pis-aller* grounds. Support for the "authentic" view preserves belief in the possibility of achieving wide areas of agreement, but it is powerless without acknowledgment of the politics of dissent, of the search for a means to break through and challenge the circle of conventional dialogue leading to consensus, which would then oppose itself to the politics of consensus as it is commonly practiced.

To be sure, many Americans gain their immediate experience of the virtues of consensus and derive their sense of civic participation from sharing a common life with neighbors in voluntary organizations, spreading their memberships and expending their energies across self-contained groups. It may be, though, that their identification with problems and causes that are closer to hand has actually stood in the way of perceiving the importance of larger issues. A vicious circle is in play. Seeking to find in local concerns a substitute for the frustrations of large-scale politics, which has increasingly shut them out of the political forum, they cannot easily find their way back to it. The effort to do so has become fraught with frustration and disappointment for many.

On matters that are more crucial and divisive, they are more likely to be aware that they share conflict, rather than consensus. They are attuned, on the one hand, to the myth that America is uniquely able to resolve social and economic conflict through political institutions that heal the wounds of inequality and indignity. The myth certainly plays a powerful part in keeping serious political discussion at rest, shrouding the sources of conflict. On the other hand, the wounds do not disappear.

They have been reopened, and new ones inflicted, at various times in the past. One need only think of some of the more acute instances of conflict, such as the Civil War, Reconstruction, labor's war against an unregulated market, the struggle for civil rights for Afro-Americans, and more recently the expansion of rights to women and gays. At the end of these periods of discord, areas of agreement are found and peace is restored. Thus Americans are by turn simultaneously riven by divisions and brought together by a tolerable measure of consensus. The great divisions shown by these examples succeed in marshaling political participation, because they are divorced from the promise of false consensus. But Americans, though rarely free from lesser sources of disagreement, often regard these as the more important, expend their energies in supporting very particular interests, and refuse to see how they fit into society's concerns as a whole. The real sources of the divide are thus sharpened by this failure.

We should bear in mind that Tocqueville praised American political associations because, by providing a free and common forum for like-minded citizens, they ensured liberty and diminished the risks of radical change. He did not discern profound ideological differences between the political parties of the kind that were endemic in France. In a sense, then, the freedom of political associations was freedom from the disruptive politics of Europe, a distinctively a priori American premise. Indeed, he thought – perhaps he deluded himself – that with the exception of divisions over the extension of popular authority (I, chap. 10, 185–86), only the slightest of differences divided American parties (ibid., 204). With a remarkable dismissal of the realities, America, he said, was free from religious strife, class conflict, and poverty – all sources of animosity in Europe. For most Americans, therefore, the overwhelming wish was to be left undisturbed in their enjoyment of the equality of their conditions and the sameness of their lives. The broad spectrum of agreement in all sections of American society depended on the notion that a majority view was not only the foundation of political action, but that competition among contending groups for majority support eliminated harsh political and social confrontations. "In a country like the United States," he declared, "in which the differences of opinion are mere differences of hue, the right of association may remain unrestrained without evil consequences" (I, chap. 12, 203–04). How then, if having left behind the great divisions that tore European society apart, might modern democratic people embrace the political, while remaining on the safe side of the ideological abyss? Only by deliberately acting in the public forum,

Tocqueville declares. Why they should so act remains, however, a puzzle if democratic people had so little to question, so little to discuss, so little to challenge. Are political differences as trivial today as they were when Tocqueville purported, or have they become deeper? Was his conception of American politics permeated by a species of wishful thinking, predicated on the belief that political conflict was not an American phenomenon, or did he look askance at, or away from, the political brokerage of power?

Is standard liberal democratic ideology capable of producing a coherent view of the possibilities of civic engagement? The question that those liberals, who want to move on from sentiment about, and abstract formulations of, the good democratic life, must answer is how the foundations of the civil society they so much want to see blossom, may be given a new lease through the civic associations that would not only acknowledge, but do something about, the complex problems created by the pressures that inequalities of income place on civil society. Why is it assumed that an increase in the numbers of civic associations will by themselves bring to light the sources of, and provide solutions to, economic inequality, and, at the same time, stabilize democratic political life? Is it the case that democratic citizens have the opportunity and possess the will to reach beyond their isolation when they commit their energies to the furtherance of their special interests? Special interest and pressure groups express some of the sharp divisions of opinion that Tocqueville believed melted away in the search for majority support. Indeed, do they, rather than neighborhood or church associations, not catch the spirit of associational life insofar as they represent the cleavages of American life where it counts – in delivering votes and in forcing policy decisions that alter the social and economic distribution of power?

Confidence in Voluntary Associations

Confidence in voluntary associations has not diminished. It has taken on a new glow among many who see in them the key elements of a civil society. Let me recall briefly the central points that Tocqueville made in his praise of civic or voluntary associations. First, it is within these small associations that people learn the value of collective effort. Second, the absence of political associations or politics itself, in which large numbers of people take an active part, is traceable to the absence of civic life. The strength of the one depends on the strength of the other. Finally, assembled in voluntary associations, persons achieve a form of consensus or agreement. But it is in the larger undertakings of national life that individuals, having learned the art of compromise in smaller ones, learn what he called the "general theory of association" (II, Bk. 2, chap. 5, 126). Tocqueville prized the one and the other, because citizens engaged in both needed peace to do so and are not tempted for that reason to upset the order of government. The struggle for power was thus regulated, and was not likely to escape well-established limits. This was, Tocqueville maintained, the essence of democratic power.

Do voluntary associations have the power to attract American participation and good will? Can they be counted on as the vital arena of public life in which Americans wish to exchange ideas, take heed of each other's needs, and tolerate each other's differences? Are the modern proponents of voluntary associations right in expecting the transformation of American democratic politics once they are strengthened? How accurate is the counter-claim that the agencies of the state are the crucial vehicles for a democracy that prides itself on realizing greater equality and expanding the boundaries of liberty, while respecting difference?[2] Are the thousands of these associations the instruments that show democratic people how their private interests are tied to the general interest, and enable them to see how their self-interest might be rightfully bound by useful restraints, restraints that would not injure their sense of independence, but are necessary to ensure their political liberty? Are these associations a form of personal fulfillment, because those who are part of them seize the opportunity to calculate, with a mixture of reason and intuition, the probable outcomes of common actions? What exact link exists between the expression of difference in an egalitarian society and its tendency to gravitate toward the known, the tried, and the familiar? Democratic individuals might satisfy themselves and those closest to them on what is important to their lives, but are they increasingly failing to know or show any sense of common purpose beyond their own concerns? Where the insistence on difference as a way to assert dignity and to demand recognition could be considered a natural, even a good, thing, will civic and political participation and deliberation prevent it from being transformed into a protective shield against and the rejection of others? Is American democracy's greatest value to be found, not in anything governments do as much as in what energetic Americans do to

---

[2] Why Americans regard the government as a powerful, hence unwanted, intrusion in their lives, yet look to it as the dispenser of the goods they desire and believe are necessary to their security, will be taken up at greater length in the next chapter.

move society? Do Americans believe they have equal opportunities and do they believe they have equal political rights, in the sense of being able to exercise them in order to have a chance of fulfilling the objects of their opportunities? Moreover, do they share a belief in what has been called a "reciprocity of perspectives, which goes beyond the limits of one's own view and makes possible the establishment of a shared point of view, as well as an explicit understanding of differences in point of view"?[3] One of the compelling reasons for such participation is that it may arguably be the crucial arena where the relentless and unquenchable drive for equality can be debated. While the traditional expressions of inequality had been hard to break, the newer, more powerful forms of class and racial inequality, however, might be even harder to shatter.

Robert Putnam adduces the same reasons as Tocqueville in his praise of voluntary associations as the foundation of American democracy's health. Much that is familiar in the American civic and political land-scape is due to the work of their members who gathered together in pursuit of like-minded goals and educated themselves and others in the process of cooperating with one another. Through their common activities, individuals, civic organizations, and communities created what he terms the "social capital" and trust that are necessary to ensure an energetic democracy, now at risk because of the smaller number of people taking an interest in their collective lives as communities. His statistical survey of the ups and downs of civic participation show that both have diminished for the last thirty years. His figures surprisingly do not show a high level during the economic depression of the 1930s. For a while, during economic prosperity, beginning in the World War II period and lasting into the 1960s, social capital and trust were on the rise, thereafter declining steadily, until by the mid-1990s, only about half the number of people who had worked for a political party at the beginning of the 1970s were still involved. The economic euphoria of the 1990s does not, however, appear to have buoyed up civic engagement as the prosperity of the earlier middle and late-middle period appears to have done. Neither of these two periods in America's economic development, however, proves conclusively Tocqueville's fear that near-total concentration on economic affairs would distract citizens from their civic responsibilities. It did not in an earlier one; it appears to be important in the later one, though we should remember that the decline began in

---

[3] Carol C. Gould, *Rethinking Democracy* (Cambridge: Cambridge University Press, 1988), p. 293. Gould regards reciprocity as an aspect of democratic personality that will be cultivated in open association with others.

the seventies.[4] Ronald Inglehart claims that America, like other post-industrialist societies – an America basking in economic growth – fosters newer forms of political participation based on improving the quality of life and individual freedom, for example, and that existing political institutions of all kinds are unable to accommodate the new needs and desires of younger generations of Americans. He calls this a post-materialist America, but he prudently avoids suggesting that America is experiencing a spiritual renewal.[5] The end of scarcity economics points neither to the end of the materialist mentality that Tocqueville accepted as natural to human beings, yet deplored at the same time, nor is it a certain marker of a greater interest in public life.

In an earlier article that introduced his research and concerns, Putnam clearly took a position alongside the proponents of deliberative democracy. "Deliberative democracy is not merely about expressing opinions, and it is undermined by anonymity and incivility.... An adequate stock of social capital is an important prerequisite for deliberative democracy."[6] How may the latter be fostered? Claus Offe, who has looked at the prospects of enhancing citizen "competence," is not optimistic. Recalling Tocqueville's analysis of the institutional factors, such as the experience of local governments and the Protestant conscience that led to the creation of the civic spirit, he comments that Tocqueville was:

aware of the ambiguities of some of these background conditions that would subvert, as he feared, rather than maintain these aristocratic virtues within a democratic setting. But today, within urban, open, highly stratified, mass-mediated bureaucratic modern (or "post-modern") societies we have even less of a tested answer than Tocqueville had as to what structural and institutional conditions provide the most fertile ground for the habits of the heart and mind that would provide for a mass base of the democratic form of government.[7]

---

[4] Robert D. Putnam, *Bowling Alone. The Collapse and Revival of American Community* (New York: Simon & Schuster, 2000).

[5] Ronald Inglehart, "Postmodernization Erodes Respect for Authority, but Increases Support for Democracy," in *Critical Citizens. Global Support for Democratic Government*, ed. Pippa Norris (New York: Oxford University Press, 1999), 23–56.

[6] Robert D. Putnam, "Democracy in America at Century's End," in *Democracy's Victory and Crisis*, ed. Axel Hadenius (Cambridge: Cambridge University Press, 1997), 27–70. Quotation from p. 62. This is an expanded version of Putnam's article in the *Journal of Democracy*, 6 (1995), 65–78.

[7] Claus Offe, "Micro-Aspects of Democratic Theory. What Makes For the Deliberative Competence of Citizens," in *Democracy's Victory and Crisis*, ed. Axel Hadenuis (Cambridge: Cambridge University Press), 81–104. Quotation from p. 102. Cf. Seymour Drescher's comment that ahistorical representations of a decline in public spirit in the United States rely on anecdote and "d'une nostalgie romantique pour l'âge d'or'" in "L'Amérique vue par les tocquevilliens," *Raisons politiques*, no. 1 (February 2001), 63–76. Citation from p. 73.

The idea that public argument can be a genuinely deliberative process leading to mutual agreement is advanced to see how the power of the democratic majority and the rights of individuals might be reconciled, but the conditions in which the desired reconciliation is to take place are largely described in ideal and abstract terms with few, if any, hints of how real disagreements might be brought to resolution.[8]

Putnam asks – indeed, he exhorts – Americans to bring a new vision to their lives by reviving their trust in each other, to do what past generations supposedly achieved, to stem the tide of complacency and indifference, to further decentralize government, to let local groups and institutions do the job of distributing resources and enhancing equality. Can this be achieved, and is this the way to proceed? The question cannot be answered unless we also ask if individuals, civic associations, and communities can create the trust that cuts across parochial interests. Can we take it for granted that the existence of trust in its simple forms (between neighbors) or complex forms (between and among neighborhoods), and in associations dedicated to the achievement of commonly but narrowly held goals, extends beyond the immediate interests of discrete groups?[9] Moreover, a larger point may be obscured by focusing on the question of trust. Well-established associations, by their sheer weight of experience and longevity, may make it hard for fledgling associations to gain support and make their mark. For example, groups that dissent from established and traditional approaches to education may find their voices drowned out by well-financed and highly organized associations. Trust may, in such a case, not be extended, and existing associational life may well rest in the hands of the powerful. In that event, they may claim to speak for the majority against an upstart minority. This picture of associational life would be incomplete, moreover, if we fail to take note of some important features of dissenting groups. One group of dissenters, who may be said to support democratic goals, radically favors their extension to groups with little or no power, while other dissenting groups are in fundamental disagreement, not only with such schemes, but call democracy itself into question, foster distrust in its goals, and proclaim authoritarian beliefs. Both groups of dissenters, however, may

---

[8] See the essays in *Deliberative Democracy*, ed. Jon Elster (Cambridge: Cambridge University Press, 1998).

[9] Cf. Martin Hollis's discussion of the relationship between trust and rationality, and his hope that by viewing the latter in a non-instrumental way, a common cooperative effort might be forged to make collective life rich and rewarding. See *Trust Within Reason* (Cambridge: Cambridge University Press, 1998).

in fact call into question existing patterns of trust, and both may be ready to flout the law. Thus, if one of the cardinal democratic beliefs is that room must be found for, and support given to, all associations in the expectation that democratic political life will be the ultimate beneficiary of an open forum, we must probe further and ask if voluntary associations by themselves will ensure the enhancement of democratic virtues, let alone guarantee general support for democracy. To the spontaneity of civic life is attributed the fountainhead of all that works in the United States. Corruption comes, it is said, from big government, which impedes the vigor of civil society. Each of these views is, of course, a caricature, the first perhaps less so than the second. Since each of these positions is not lacking support, what needs to be discussed further is where the best prospects for democracy may be found.

Some Theoretical Background

First, let us see how a few prominent thinkers deal with these problems. The thinkers I shall first focus on start out from a theoretical framework, and are removed, it seems to me, from the daily odors of political practices. I begin with John Dewey who, some seventy years ago, spoke out against the experts and in favor of the "vitality and depth of close and direct intercourse and attachment." Then, as if he had in mind Tocqueville's enthusiasm for a multiplicity of associations, he said that sorting out, by some form of agreement "what transactions should be left as far as possible to voluntary initiative and agreement and what should come under the regulation of the public is a question of time, place, and concrete conditions that can be known only by careful observation."[10] Obviously, empirical work had to be done.

There seems to be little to distinguish Dewey's position from those declared by theoreticians closer to us in time. Rawls theorized that consensus was the medium through which a well-ordered, stable, feasible, or juridically just, rather than a desired, society may come into being. An overlapping consensus, by marginalizing, indeed, holding at bay and excluding, social and other differences, should be the goal of a democratic society. Such a society would be benign, not coercive, and open to a plurality of ends.[11] Since then, Rawls seems less enamored of

---

[10] John Dewey, *The Public and its Problems* (New York: Henry Holt, 1927), pp. 193, 213.
[11] John Rawls, "The Domain of the Political and Overlapping Consensus," *New York University Law Review*, 64 (1989), 233–55.

consensus. To be sure, he wishes to smooth the way to political engagement, and is prepared to consider the benefits to democratic society from
the power of comprehensive commitments – which he characterizes as
the personal deliberations and reflections, be they religious, philosophical or moral, that are a part of the larger cultural background – once the
presumed advantages of such commitments are transferred from associational groups to the political realm where the tests of public reason (the
hallmark, in his view, of a democratic society) operate. From his earlier
advocacy of a rather strict division between the loyalties developed in
associations and the kinds of loyalty demanded of citizens in a well-
ordered and legitimate society – namely, to a constitution "the essential
of which all citizens may reasonably be expected to endorse in the light
of principles and ideals acceptable to them as reasonable and rational"
– Rawls has gone on to say that such boundaries are too artificial and
hence politically unrealistic. It is salient that he develops his argument
with examples taken from the abolitionist campaigns against slavery in
the United States before the Civil War and the civil rights struggles a
century later. In the first case, challenges did ultimate violence to the
boundaries between the comprehensive beliefs espoused by the abolitionists and the pre-Civil War political system that failed to maintain a
well-ordered society. In the case of the civil rights campaign, many could
legitimately ask if America retained the features of a well-ordered society
that Rawls puts great stock in.[12] Nevertheless, in both instances, reciprocity, civic friendship, and civility must be seen as the foundations
for its very existence, for unless citizens recognize each other as equally
reasonable, rational, and sincere, there is little hope that either their
comprehensive views or their political values will flourish. On the most
contentious issues dividing a democratic citizenry – and these will not
fade away – the vitality of public reason will rest on how particular cases
– for instance, controversies arising from different attitudes toward ethnicity, race, and gender, are dealt with. It is then that a difficult balancing act will be performed to see how far the particular, highly specific
views of citizens may be allowed to intrude into political decisions.

Thus, there is legitimate debate around the range and depth of human
rights to be secured. Fixation on any one of them may violate a democratic civil society's values and let its advocates seek to triumph in an

[12] John Rawls, "The Idea of Public Reason and Postscript," in *Deliberative Democracy.
Essays on Reason and Politics*, eds. James Bohman and William Rehg (Cambridge,
Mass., and London: MIT Press, 1997), 96, 121, 135–36.

atmosphere of illegitimate coercion. The problem, as ever, for liberals like Rawls, remains how cooperation can be induced on terms that all can find acceptable without exerting a huge strain, not only on reserves of rationality and impartiality, but on the core of consensus itself.[13] Democracy makes room for passionately held opinions, and even the kind of passionate intensity that can be construed as a bid to smite one's enemies figurally, and, in the past, literally as well. Then, it did not find the toleration of deliberate appeals to racism difficult. At the best of times, it is said, democracy enlists passions, not to destroy, but to advocate, not to injure, but to reason. This may, however, result in a harmless form of dialogue, in banality and false sentiment, or in a kind of hypocrisy that, *pace* Judith Shklar, is highly unlikely to soften the hard edges of social discourse once people, as she argues, overlook their social standings.[14]

Though his terms are not identical, Jürgen Habermas expresses views that are similar to Rawls's:

[T]he common good substantially consists in the success of [the community's] endeavor to define, establish, effectuate and sustain the set of rights (less tendentiously laws) best suited to the condition and mores of that community.

Politics is seen, not surprisingly as a dialogic process, but a field of: contestation over questions of value and not simply questions of preference . . . [P]olitics [is] a process of reason and not just of will, of persuasion, not just of power, directed toward agreement regarding a good or just, or at any rate acceptable, way to order those aspects of life that involve people's social relations and social natures.[15]

---

[13] For Rawls' earlier treatment of what constitutes the well-ordered society, see *Political Liberalism* (New York: Columbia University Press, 1993), especially pp. 16–17, 50. I should note that even before his essay on an overlapping consensus, Rawls favored the "principle of toleration" as ensuring the inclusion of conflicting views. See "Justice as Fairness: Political not Metaphysical," *Philosophy and Public Affairs*, 14 (1985), 223–51.

[14] See chap. 2, Judith Shklar, *Ordinary Vices* (Cambridge, Mass., and London: Harvard University Press, 1984, especially p. 77: "Hypocrisy can do as much for equality as it does for inequality. It may be indispensable if we are ever going to fully accept human diversity in all its individual manifestations." Nancy Rosenblum, following in Shklar's footsteps, talks about the need to develop a thick skin: "The alternative to the politics of recognition in everyday life is not license to express one's opinions or prejudices but treating everyone identically and with easy spontaneity." See *Membership and Morals. The Personal Uses of Pluralism in America* (Princeton: Princeton University Press, 1998), pp. 348–63. Quote from p. 356. Rosenblum moves from Shklar's seemingly benign uses of hypocrisy to an equally untroubled, but almost totally unrealistic notion of how spontaneity works in situations of conflict, whether personal or collective.

[15] Jürgen Habermas, *Facts and Norms: Contributions to a Discourse Theory of Law and Democracy*, trans. William Rehg (Cambridge, Mass.: MIT Press, 1996), quotes from pp. 268–74.

The attributes of a dialogue that moves unerringly and clearly, reasonably, and uncoercively, seems more like an ideal description than the
kind of exchange that can be managed in a public forum, whether it
takes place in a voluntary or a political association. A similar criticism
may be directed at Frank Michelman, for whom democratic politics
ought ideally, and as much as possible in practice, to broaden the opportunities for discourse and dialogue among citizens, not only within
formal forums, such as legislatures and city councils, but "in the town
meetings and local government agencies, civic and voluntary associations; social and recreational clubs; schools public and private; manage-
ments, directorates and leadership groups of organizations of all kinds,
workplaces and shopfloors, public events and street life." Of equal
importance for a vital democracy, Michelman says, is the expansion of
political freedom through the law's "constant reach of inclusion of the
other, of the hitherto excluded – which in practice means bringing to
legal-doctrinal presence the hitherto absent voices of emergently self-
conscious social groups."[16]

William Connolly is also worried about the stresses imposed by an
undisciplined tendency of citizens in democratic society to express their
dismay or anger over real or perceived threats to their identities and
differences. The best way to explore the greatest range of their needs,
without imperiling society and organized political institutions, including
the state, is, he contends, to adopt the foundations of what he calls agonistic democracy. Cultivation of its tenets would ensure the incorpora-
tion of "strife into interdependence and care into strife." He posits, as
do the others we are canvassing, a hypothetical model of democracy
where inequalities – but, most urgently, economic inequality – are
reduced. Everyone then will be able to take part in the common life and
"engage in the mysteries of identity and difference." If the limits are set
unrealistically, for example, by recycling the "politics of resentment," the
democracy of the possible turns into a nightmare, in which all will lose.
Society will then be plunged into degradation and sickness. Agonistic
democracy is productive only if citizens know how to exercise responsibility toward one another and can learn to tell the difference, however
hard it may be, between genuine sources of deprivation and the hyper-
developed propensity to indulge all kinds of lesser resentments. Connolly
is aware of the tension between the bureaucratic definition of what

---

[16] Frank I. Michelman, "Law's Republic," *Yale Law Journal*, 97 (1988), 1529, 1531. Cited
in ibid., pp. 275, 547.

is normal identity and the opposition to it from groups that assert their right to be heard. He seems readier than Rawls to think of the ways democratic political institutions might deal with and absorb the conflicts focused around the claims to equality and the right to preserve difference.[17]

Surely what must be asked, however, is if the principle of social action from the ground up is the only way to think about democratic civil society, in short, if there is more than sentiment to support the principle. So far, the evidence points to an almost total focus on a refurbishing of the principle, though there are some signs that the dread in which the state is held may be losing its edge. Michael Walzer, who has written with illumination about the incommensurability of value systems and experiences, and on the diverse ways of evaluating them, asks us to acknowledge conditions of "complex equality." In his view, the latter carries a more meaningful reality than identity.[18] When it comes to evaluating civic organizations, he tends to concentrate, not on any of their narrowing characteristics, but rather on their lack of sustainable organization and funds as the source of their weakness.[19] If only groups would improve their ability to defend themselves in a society in which each pursues its discrete goals, civil society would be healthier. But would this be enough? More is needed, he says. It is the state that is "the necessary instrument of justice," because it is more "fully inclusive and democratic than any of the groups whose activity it regulates." Similar abstract principles – perhaps utopian is an apter word – follow:

> Its [the state's] citizens must be citizens in the fullest sense: politically educated, competent, and informed; possessed of the complete set of civil rights and liberties; and, most important of all, organized in the widest possible range of parties, unions, movements, circles, schools, groupings, and so on.[20]

And again, "[t]he singular, universal political community requires a particularistic associational life"; "the one [the state] depends on the many, the many on the one." This is not, Walzer claims, "a vicious circle," because "it is the deep structure of democratic politics itself."[21] He tries to give greater depth to his conviction that associational life

[17] William E. Connolly, *Identity/Difference* (Ithaca and London: Cornell University Press, 1991), pp. 212, 84–85.
[18] Michael Walzer, *Spheres of Justice* (New York: Basic Books, 1983).
[19] Michael Walzer, "Multiculturalism and Individualism," *Dissent*, (Spring 1994), 187.
[20] Michael Walzer, "Pluralism and Social Democracy," *Dissent*, (Winter 1998), 52–53.
[21] Ibid.

must be strengthened, arguing that there are two kinds of plurality in the United States – one of groups and one of individuals – but that while individualism can be the vehicle of personal advancement for some, it does not work for many. To save those who are at the margins of society, where they are condemned and often condemn themselves to futile, because powerless, gestures of protest, organizations capable of generating self-confidence remain the single most effective way to extend citizenship and improve civil society. Walzer seems at times not to be too sure of his ground. On the one hand, he celebrates the state as autonomous and neutral among groups. This suggests a hands-off, rather than an interventionist, state, and seems to endorse a nineteenth-century liberal version of the night watchman state. On the other hand, he abandons the notion of the state as a detached observer when he calls upon it to introduce policies that would lift up minority and disadvantaged groups and break the cycle of dependence and economic inequality.[22] The state he favors is thus not a morally indifferent state. Holding both views, he feels, entitles him to conclude that he is advocating a species of social democracy, or what he says is or might be called left liberalism in the United States.[23]

There is something to be said for the expectation that such measures will constitute, in Walzer's words, "a defense of group differences and an attack on class differences."[24] He acknowledges the importance of the latter, but he veers away from any analysis of their origins and consequences in American society. Indeed, social mobility is for him a much more favored basis for the analysis of economic inequality than social

[22] See the Epilogue to Michael Walzer, *On Tolerance* (New Haven and London: Yale University Press, 1997).

[23] Ibid., p. 112. In "Rescuing Civil Society," *Dissent* (Winter 1999), 62–67, Walzer asks whether associational life might not be strengthened by subsistence pay, supported by the state, for activist individuals in organized groups working to keep civil society alive. He is far from hopeful. For an earlier proposal to have the state give financial support to associations that would enlarge the level of democratic debate and deliberation, see Joshua Cohen and Joel Rogers, "Associations and Democracy," *Social Philosophy and Policy*, 10 (1993), 282–312. In his essay, "Procedure and Substance in Deliberative Democracy," in *Deliberative Democracy. Essays on Reason and Politics*, eds., James Bohman and William Rehg (Cambridge, Mass., MIT Press, 1997), 407–37, citation 429, Cohen attempts to set out the foundations for a vital associational life that would enhance the deliberative element in democratic decision-making and create greater opportunities for organizations pursuing goals geared, in his description, "to issues that are decidedly more sprawling and open-ended – as in . . . urban poverty or regional economic development."

[24] Michael Walzer, *On Tolerance*, p. 111.

class. What Walzer does not say – and this certainly must be the crux of the matter – is that group differences can also be expressions of class distinctions. It is hard, moreover, to measure how the reciprocal actions of the state and civic associations will affect outcomes – in other words, affect the reaction of some comparatively advantaged competing groups to policies they believe improve the conditions of groups close to them in the wage earning population, while disadvantaging their own. It is taken as self-evident that class-based groups exist and pit themselves against the interests of the larger political community.[25] It is more accurate to say, however, that they wish to enlarge it to make it work for them.

Judith Shklar appears to take a harder look at some of these questions. She expresses unease with what she says is Walzer's unrealistic version of citizen participation, and his reluctance to face the unpleasant facts of hatreds forged in the name of parochial solidarities. In her view, the state must intervene, not occasionally but often, and with lawful force, to settle differences among mutually hostile groups.[26] Shklar herself wavers over the role of the state, which she brands as paternalistic and arrogant when it shows itself too eager to assume the mantle of omniscience.[27] With a keen sense of the difficulty, indeed, the near-impossibility of making people "behave" and erasing such basic feelings as a sense of injustice, revenge, resentment, and envy, she counsels instead a retreat from the notion that sound public policies can be achieved without leaving behind them a trail of pain. "The best way," she proposes, "to bridge the gap between settled expectations and demands for public change may be a system of effective and continuous citizen participation in which no one wins or loses all the time."[28] She offers no ideas on how such a delicate balance could be achieved. What kinds of institutions, for example, could be devised and set in place to keep score? On the broader issue of preventing harsh conflict, Albert Hirschman agrees with Shklar. Conflicts in advanced democratic market societies are more likely to be solved, he argues, by taking a more-or-less rather than an either-or approach, the first being subject from the beginning

---

[25] For example, by Daniel A. Bell, "Civil Society versus Civic Virtue," in *Freedom of Association*, ed. Amy Gutmann (Princeton: Princeton University Press, 1998), 239–72.

[26] Judith N. Shklar, *Political Thought and Political Thinkers*, ed. Stanley Hoffman (Chicago and London: University of Chicago Press, 1998), pp. 376–85.

[27] Judith N. Shklar, *The Faces of Injustice* (New Haven and London, Yale University Press: 1990), pp. 116–20.

[28] Ibid., p. 121.

to a spirit of compromise, in contrast to the mistaken second premise
that agreements to resolve issues are reached once and for all. Still,
Hirschman wonders whether the revitalization of a community spirit will
alone be able to weather the storms let loose by the kinds of conflicts
that have become so prominent – namely, abortion and multiculturalism.[29] Again, however, one senses a feeling of resignation and tired acceptance. We all have, Shklar and Hirschman tell us, reservoirs of feelings
ready to be disturbed by conflict.

There is nothing very much mistaken in these obvious reminders. The
way to lessen conflict or to channel it so that it does not rip society apart
is at stake. For many, the search for electoral support from a broad
middle group of voters resulted in the formations of coalitions of interests in each of the major parties, and served both them and the public.
That route was deemed to be better than any movement toward the
polarization of opinion, and it had the advantage of safely leaving out
sections of American society considered to be dispensable because they
were lacking in power. They barely survived in a series of third parties.
The Democrats were for a time a party that brought together conservative Southerners and North-Eastern liberals in an uneasy alliance, but
was nevertheless thought to be a stable one permitting a sharing of power
that did not impede important New Deal policies. The same attempts to
preserve alliances within the major parties continue. The question that
is not taken seriously enough is how people might come to regard as
desirable a fuller and franker airing of the sources of conflict, and the
costs they might be prepared to bear in reducing some of the injustices
the conflicts express.

Do the sources of conflict have to be blunted to deal with them? So
it seems to David Hollinger. He places his bets on a post-ethnic America,
in which not one but several identities are recognized within singly bound
ethnic groups. He sees the United States becoming a society of people
who come together in voluntary associations that overlap and transcend
group identities.[30]

For Richard Rorty, the democratic story is the story of the Left in
America – the America he admires – a story that has been punctuated

[29] Albert O. Hirschman, *A Propensity of Self-Subversion* (Cambridge, Mass., and London:
Harvard University Press, 1995), pp. 231–48, especially pp. 242–48.

[30] David A. Hollinger, *Postethnic America: Beyond Multiculturalism* (New York: Basic
Books, 1995).

by strength and failure.[31] He expands his earlier belief that democratic solidarity may be "thought of as the ability to see more and more traditional differences (of tribe, religion, race, customs, and the like) as unimportant when compared with similarities with respect to pain and humiliation – the ability to think of people widely different from ourselves as included in the range of 'us'."[32] He wants to make a new case for the argument that individuals and groups who have been caught up in ethnic and religious hostilities (and in the debates about sexual mores) are blind to more pressing economic issues and to the way in which, if these were acknowledged as crucial, the cultural Left in the United States might begin to know the extent to which the super-rich determine economic policies and keep the rest of the population engaged in futile endeavors.

What might be done to change the direction of America? Rorty suggests, first, a re-creation of the Left based on an alliance between the cultural Left (mainly the Left as it developed in the universities when it did good work in raising the level of awareness of differences in American society); the remnants of what he labels the old reformist Left, which changed the balance of economic power over several decades, until the sixties, when it went into hibernation; and the labor unions, which kept Americans alive to the need to redress social injustice. Second, he asks the cultural Left to stop its theorizing, especially around the subject of individualism versus communitarianism. He then invokes the pragmatism of Dewey and the democratic dreams of Whitman as correctives to the abstractions produced by such theorizing. Finally, he expects that if the constrictive ideologization of a half-century ago is set aside, the universities will be enabled to begin the proper education of politically responsible citizens. At the moment, however, it is hard to see in any detailed way how each of these three parts of a refurbished Left will revitalize itself. The unions, for example, seem to be looking for support and gaining more from employees in the public service and among professionals, in short, from people who think of themselves as middle class, and who are salaried as such.[33] They may, however, it must be said, add

[31] Richard Rorty, *Achieving Our Country. Leftist Thought in Twentieth-Century America* (Cambridge, Mass.: Harvard University Press, 1998).

[32] Richard Rorty, *Contingency, Irony, and Solidarity* (Cambridge: Cambridge University Press, 1989), p. 192.

[33] For a review of the present state of union membership; the assault on unions by corporations that know how to work the case law that information on the kinds of union

some luster to the notion of dignity in work, and so give some impetus to awakening the old reformist Left. Rorty puts his ultimate hope in those who have hope, for they are the only people who will build a cooperative society, a social democratic society that will revive the fervor of the old Left in America – a coalition of men and women who were liberals and socialists campaigning to bring about piecemeal reform. But he steers clear of those who would renew the notion of the "movement," which marks, he is sure, a descent into apocalyptic politics with its belief in historical certainty that is bound, as in the past, to lead people, both those who believe in their own purity and those who would follow them, astray. Better finite campaigns than belief in one grand thing.[34] Rorty espouses pragmatic politics and rejects revolutionary rhetoric.[35]

The Promise and Limits of Civic Action

To register the fullness of changing morality and contemporary popular views of politics, we may recall Tocqueville's belief that Americans, driven by their mores, were able to acknowledge some common concerns that they would not subordinate to physical gratification:

In democratic society the sensuality of the public has taken a moderate and tranquil course, to which all are bound to conform: it is as difficult to depart

---

activities permitted under the National Labor Relations Act; and the remarkable change in the demographics and composition of the labor force that today finds its strength in unions, see Andrew Hacker, "Who's Sticking to the Union?" *New York Review of Books*, 46, no. 3 (February 18, 1999), 45–48. As Hacker sums up the latter development, especially in California, "to the extent that unions are representing more and more members of the middle class, they may find themselves able to gain wider support" (p. 48).

[34] Richard Rorty, *Achieving Our Country*, pp. 111–25. Robert Bellah et al., *Habits of the Heart. Individualism and Commitment in American Life* (Berkeley, Los Angeles, and London: University of California Press, 1985) pp. 212–13, would most likely agree. When Bellah speaks of social movements as the alternative to the power of business leaders and technical experts, he has in mind the traditions of democratic reform, which range over time from working-class response to industrial capitalism, through the periods of agrarian protest, the socialism of industrial workers, some aspects of Progressivism, to the Civil Rights campaigns of the 1950s and 1960s. See John Keane's critique of Rorty's earlier work. He treats it sympathetically, agreeing with Rorty's anti-foundationalism, but faulting him for an exaggerated anti-historical and pre-political bent. *Civil Society. Old Images, New Visions* (Cambridge: Polity Press, 1998), pp. 59–60. Keane's book sums up the arguments of his earlier works.

[35] On Rorty's admiration for Havel, see his essay, "The End of Leninism, Havel and Social Hope," in *Truth and Progress* (Cambridge: Cambridge University Press, 1998), vol. 3, pp. 228–46.

from the common rule by one's vices as by one's virtues. Rich men . . . gratify a number of petty desires without indulging in any great irregularities of passion; thus they are more apt to become enervated than debauched. . . . The reproach I address to the principle of equality is not that it leads men away in the pursuit of forbidden enjoyments, but that it absorbs them wholly in quest of those which are allowed (II, Bk. 2, chap. 11, 140–41).

In any case, moderation, if it ever were as Tocqueville described it, is no longer the name of the game. Will people continue to pile up preferences they have so far sought, or will they seek alternative ones? To argue that the range of choices must be widened if democratic civil society is to flourish may be construed as a cautiously optimistic assessment of the deepest wishes of its members as conscientious citizens. Yoneji Masuda, who argued this way some twenty years ago, spoke naively of voluntary communities and a classless society, liberated from the power of the state and the market.[36] The lack of realism in such prophecies supports a posture of prudent retreat from the challenge of determining orders of preferences. The seemingly insoluble problem may be rejected as a challenge to the existing social fabric, or it may be greeted as a legitimate criticism of the interchangeability of the market and the political forum. Both the challenge and the criticism remain without any visible way around either. People may not believe that their sensual pleasures are corrupting. They may also say that they are not at all passive recipients of the world's goods, that they in fact participate actively and democratically when they consume them, or some may insist that they can also pay heed to those who tell them that the gratifications they seek on the Internet yields a virtual, not a real, democracy – in short, that they are not misguided.

What Americans will do with a more equal distribution of Internet technology, if indeed there is a realistic possibility that they will be given such power, is thus not certain. (This is not uniquely an American phenomenon.) In the electronic age, some of the hopes and visions of the utopian dreamers of a new world seem to have been revived. Cyberspace, not more than a few years ago, was thought of as a community-building process. Discrete communities would function alongside one another, not unlike the real or visualized communities described by Tocqueville. Just as he perceived that there were opportunities to expand the vision of his New England townships beyond their local loyalties, so

---

[36] Yoneji Masdua, *The Information Society as Post-Industrial Society* (Washington: World Future Society, 1980).

too would the electronically isolated communities of cyberspace shed their insularity in search of larger horizons. May we expect information technologies to alter the dynamic of group affiliations so radically as to make them unrecognizable? It does not seem likely. Each civic group will obviously continue to defend its choices as no less valuable than those preferred by others. Fragile and precarious though democracy is, there is nothing to say that its demise is inevitable, and one way to find out is to test human invention, to challenge existing democratic institutions to find the means to deal with, and perhaps, even infiltrate, the "capillary-like network of microdecisions" spun out by professionals who manage bodies of knowledge that are transforming the post-national corporate world and the state itself. The next step is either to accept the view that professional experts effectively subvert democracy by commandeering choices, or to find proofs that ordinary citizens can expand their capacity to make them by hard intellectual effort.[37] As the situation now stands, there is an abyss of difference between the power available to individual and small group users and the power exercised by corporate capital, and governments, and the media.

The Internet has caught the attention of plebiscitary democrats as a sure-fire method for tapping the popular will. Except for the instantaneous and mercurial delivery of information, the product is not different from the information that polling for electoral purposes delivered before the information revolution. It is after all the popular pulse that is supposedly still being measured. It cannot know how to conduct its own polls, nor does it have the resources to do it. Those who do conduct them define the issues for public discussion. The importance of information-gathering is what political uses can be made of it. All sorts of civic and political associations, parties, and pressure groups will use it. And, of course, so will government. This is borne out by the research of several scholars versed in the intricacies of political polling, who tell us, for example, about polling manipulation of strategic rhetorical language to deter people from giving direct answers to questions,[38] or, more obviously, how clients who fund survey research "exercise at least

[37] Jean-Marie Guéhenno, *The End of the Nation-State*, trans. Victoria Elliott (Minneapolis: University of Minnesota Press, 1995), pp. 140–41.

[38] Leon H. Mayhew, *The New Public: Professional Communication and the Means of Social Influence* (Cambridge: Cambridge University Press, 1997), pp. 236–40, cited in Slavko Splichal, *Public Opinion, Developments and Controversies in the Twentieth Century* (New York and Oxford: Rowman and Littlefield, 1999), p. 249.

de facto control over what research gets done and how it is conducted."³⁹ Is there, nevertheless, something to be said about the possibility, through the new technology, of a new kind of direct democracy, the democracy that gives political parties, governments, and corporations, for example, immediate information about popular wishes? Or may it instead encourage them to act on what may be called "permissive consensus," the idea that V.O. Key long ago originated, which simply put, means giving these institutions permission to move in one direction as opposed to another, to act rather not to act, but takes no account of differences in individual response, knowledgeable and non-knowledgeable people, and, most of all, gives us no information about those who direct politics, governments, and corporations.⁴⁰ Of course, political institutions evolve as do technologies, but the relationship between the two, now that they have entered cyberspace, is still imperfectly understood. There is a mode of acquiring technology that, we are told, may be more appropriate to public institutions than to firms in the corporate world. In the latter, new entrepreneurs aggressively push older firms to one side and preferably into the corporate grave. In other institutions, including political ones, something else is said to occur. By making bits of new technologies their own, they may upset the balance of the existing order and may clear the ground for a new one. Thus, there is agreement on some of the ways in which technology has reinforced what we have always known about the older means of influencing people, and some agreement, too, about the instantaneous accumulation and distribution of information, but less than is needed for a coherent theory of the immediate and long-range impact of technology upon democracy.⁴¹

What may be safely said is that the mass media, omniscient and irresistible, have indeed become the Ur-power. What it is not safe to say is that it should be seen as the ultimate fallout of the homogenization of society, or that it contributes decisively to it. It is more prudent to say that until a theory of information technology – a theory of the internal operations of the technology itself is available – we will not be able to

³⁹ Peter V. Miller, "The Industry of Public Opinion," in *Public Opinion and the Communication of Consent*, eds. T.L. Glasser and C.T. Salmon (New York: Guilford, 1995), 109, cited in ibid., p. 250.
⁴⁰ V.O. Key, Jr., *Public Opinion and American Democracy* (New York: Alfred Knopf, [1961], 1967), p. 536, cited in ibid., pp. 250–51.
⁴¹ Philip E. Agre, "Yesterday's Tomorrow. The Advance of Law and Order into the Utopian Wilderness of Cyberspace," *Times Literary Supplement*, July 3, 1998.

contemplate how we will have to shift our thinking away from the familiar dialogic exchanges to unfamiliar and uncharted kinds of exchange in which we think we are engaged in the first but don't perceive how they have been subtly changed. An instrumentalist view of technology, by placing the observer in a privileged position, conceals the fact that the media define the ways human agents seek to define themselves, and not how they define themselves outside them.[42] This is as true of a post-print as of a print culture. It remains a problem crucially important in a society that believes itself to be uniquely dedicated to the ideally unimpeded access to knowledge and information needed to form serious views on the issues affecting everyone. If the technologies of communication overwhelmingly give us more of the same, and just the minutest amount of what might be truly startling or different, they also more importantly obscure the real changes occurring in areas over which individuals and groups possess little or no control. A more cynical view is that the information networks give us what we want, and that what we want much of the time is for others to make decisions.

Tocqueville's genius for paradox makes room both for the possibility of democracy's failure, and, much more marginally, for its success. It may be that the best that can be done is to find within democracy's hidden corners the way to undermine a development that tends to make citizens passive consumers of everything technology can produce, and enable them to find the necessary critical powers to reassert the active part of human experience. Again, what should be kept in mind is that just as in the transfer of the kinds of energies between political and civil life, a reciprocal action exists, so the power of the media rests on the continued support of the public, while it shapes and manipulates it in turn. Today's information organs not only induce people, as in the early days of the United States, to want the same things, but also to reduce politics to a commodity like any other. Two of American democracy's critics on the neo-Marxist Left, Michael Hardt and Antonio Negri, see a link between the communications industry and the degradation of democratic politics, and say so in extravagant language:

If political representation continues to function while lacking any solid foundation in society, the void must be covered over by the construction of an artificial world that substitutes for the dynamics of civil society. The new communi-

---

[42] For a penetrating analysis of a difficult subject, see Geoffrey Winthrop-Young, "Silicon Sociology, or, Two Kings on Hegel's Throne? Kittler, Luhmann, and the Posthuman Merger of German Media Theory," *Yale Journal of Criticism*, 13 (2000), 391–420.

cations processes of the so-called information industry contributes to this end. A mechanism familiar to the development of democratic society is repeated here: the passage from the democratic representation of the masses to the representatives' production of their own voters. Through the mediatic manipulation of society, conducted through enhanced polling techniques, social mechanisms of surveillance and control, and so forth, power tries to prefigure its social base. Society is made aseptic through mediatic and communicative operations designed to dominate the dynamic of transformation and simplify the complexity of reality.[43]

Public opinion, thus transformed, is more than ever obsessed with the average. While it is hard to imagine electoral politics without survey research, its measurement is not only scientifically dubious, it feeds on itself and sustains the notion that it meets the criteria of democratic consensus. While there is no clear or certain answer, opinion polls, conducted without regard for centered public debate, have a specious quality, designed more to influence opinion than they are to gain a fair measure of it. Such opinion by polling is nearly always taken as authoritative, at least until the next sound bite. It can be, and is, invoked in highly partisan ways. It would be surprising if it were not. Occasionally, more stringent regulations have been suggested to remove its more suspect aspects, for example, its cloak of scientific neutrality under which polling agencies – the media foremost among them – say they operate but in fact have the effect of inducing in people the belief that their opinions count in some disembodied and almost-error free way in the democratic process.

Afro-Americans and Civic Action

There now seems to be no lessening in the tempo of withdrawal by large sections of the middle class from the voluntary associations that once appeared to be part of American civil and political life. A more aggressive form of withdrawal is to be found from large sections of the Afro-American community. This was not the case a generation ago. As a result of the civil rights movement, decisive moments of executive action on the part of successive administrations, a host of Congressional enactments, and, not least, judicial decisions appealing to the Constitution, the very people whom Tocqueville believed were fated to a dangerous future instead found openings in it. This could not have happened

---

[43] Michael Hardt and Antonio Negri, *Labor of Dionysus. A Critique of the State-Form* (Minneapolis and London: University of Minnesota Press, 1994), p. 271.

without the older forms of civic engagement that mobilized sections of
the black and white communities, and, in the case of the black community, the National Association for the Advancement of Colored People
Legal Defense Fund has worked tirelessly in its briefs to the Supreme
Court, which has over the years overturned some of the most egregious
judicial decisions and extended rights to black Americans. But the expectations of an integrated America have not been met. For this diminution
of hopes, various reasons have been suggested. The two major arguments
are reverse images of one another. Indeed, we may be tangled up in a
cause and effect relationship, with one substituting for the other. Thus
it is claimed that Afro-Americans actually prefer to go their own way
and that they are unduly influenced by those who spearhead beliefs
in black superiority. The reverse of this argument is that while white
America may speak in favor of integration, its level of tolerance and its
capacity for generosity is in fact low. Black perception and experience is
that once a substantial number of blacks move into the suburbs, for
example, whites desert them in large numbers.

In public education, the attempts to create integrated schools have
similarly not been a great success. Some would say that it is failing. As
for post-secondary education, the evidence from a new study by two
educators, Derek Bok and William Bowen, is that affirmative action over
the past twenty years has been a success. Their contention is that black
graduates from elite universities have moved forward to post-graduate
and professional studies that have taken them up the economic ladder.
This in turn has created a more solid foundation for the growth of a
black middle class, not entirely apart from and at least marginally part
of a wider non-segregated community.[44] Yet, as the black middle class,
buoyed up by economic success, has grown in size, the status of its
members cannot be said to have automatically improved, if the opposition to affirmative action is kept in mind. The debate over affirmative
action is far from over in education. Orlando Patterson is a proponent,
while Ward Connerly, former Regent of the University of California
and chairman of the California ballot initiative to end racial preferences
under affirmative action, including university admission policies, is a
staunch opponent on the grounds that it perpetuates racial divisions
by raising resentments among whites without strengthening the self-

---

[44] Derek Bok and William G. Bowen, *The Shape of the River. Long-Term Consequences
of Considering Race in College and University Admissions* (Princeton: Princeton University Press, 1998).

image of Afro-Americans who must live with the accusation that their admission was not earned but granted.[45] William Julius Wilson also predicts the sharpening of differences between black Americans and economically disadvantaged whites if an unmodified policy of affirmative action is pursued. He favors political action based on a coalition of Americans of all races working together to advance policies of "affirmative opportunity" to undermine and supersede the notion of merit that relies so heavily on the tests administered by the Education Testing Service.[46]

The most persuasive endorsement of affirmative action is Ronald Dworkin's. It does work and it is fair, he declares, and in its aim to widen the diversity of student classes it answers America's deepest commitment to improve the opportunities for people to know one another as a group sharing in and debating social values.[47] While in the workplace, movement toward integration has been registered in some large corporations, such as IBM, AT&T, and Levi Strauss, gains appear to be even smaller. There is little comfort to be taken from stories, gathered by a *New York Times* group of reporters, told by whites and blacks, across a wide range of occupations, including the army, film, the Internet, and the slaughterhouse industry, who express feelings of disquiet, deep anger, defiance, and not a small degree of resignation as many face dead-end jobs,

---

[45] On the need to keep it in place as an instrument to achieve less inequality, but not misapplying it and therefore injuring the principle of merit, see Orlando Patterson, *The Ordeal of Integration. Progress and Resentment in America's "Racial" Crisis* (Washington, DC: Counterpoint, 1997), p. 166. If firm measures were introduced, he argues, to break the cycle of poverty and discrimination, the various sections of the disadvantaged population, not only Afro-Americans, would move forward and become part of the main American stream and make affirmative action unnecessary in fifteen years. On Ward Connerly's position and a wider range of opinions, see the PBS website, which explores the issues discussed in the December 4, 1998 television airing. George M. Fredrickson, *Black Liberation. A Comparative History of Black Ideologies in the United States and South Africa* (New York and Oxford: Oxford University Press, 1996), pp. 321–22, recommends policies of affirmative action to narrow the gap between "privileged whites and underprivileged blacks," and does not rule out the possibility of a "Third Reconstruction." California's Proposition 209, approved in a 1996 referendum, made admissions policies in public colleges illegal if they took race and ethnicity into account. On the origins and now nearly impregnable fortress of the Education Testing Service, which now determines the rules and standards for admission to the institutions of higher education, see Nicholas Lemann, *The Big Test: The Secret History of the American Meritocracy* (New York: Farrar Straus Giroux, 1999).

[46] William Julius Wilson, *The Bridge over the Racial Divide: Rising Inequality and Coalition Politics* (Berkeley: University of California Press, 1999).

[47] Ronald Dworkin, *Sovereign Virtue. The Theory and Practice of Equality* (Cambridge, Mass. and London: Harvard University Press, 2000), especially pp. 403–08 and 423–26.

differential wage sales, and crude and subtle forms of discrimination.[48] Finally, the disproportionately high numbers of blacks who make up the prison population remains a stain on American society. Quite extraordinary, but an undeniable feature of the treatment of Afro-Americans is the fact that they constitute by far the largest pool of the male population who have been sentenced to death and face execution, especially and overwhelmingly in the South. Some go so far as to argue that the state death penalty now stands in for the lynchings of some generations ago. Calls for the abolition of capital punishment have replaced the calls for the abolition of slavery. It is, however, retained as "a ritual assertion of a communal moral order,"[49] and it is used as a reinforcement of the practice of exclusion, while pretending otherwise. Thus, while some of the rigid stereotypes do not, as in the past, take up the center of conflict, they are not entirely absent from some of the explanations offered for black unemployment, criminal behavior, and slow educational progress. The conservatism of Americans on these questions is underscored by a Gallup survey of April 25–28, 1996, which showed that 83 per cent of those polled opposed racial preferences in jobs and schools, and 79 per cent approved of the death penalty.

In response to white resistance, large numbers of Afro-Americans have chosen to remain outside existing boundaries of civic and political life. Inner city blacks have decisively chosen to turn their backs on it. The older forms of coercive disenfranchisement have thus been replaced by voluntary ones. Just as significantly, civic and political disenfranchisement, at one time challenged and seemingly overcome, is no longer the issue. These sections of African-America no longer see disenfranchisement in these terms. They see it as operative on all levels of life. They

---

[48] See *New York Times* website: http://www.nytimes.com/library/national/race/060400. For examples, see Charles Le Duff, "At a Slaughterhouse, Some Things Never Die," *NY Times*, June 15, 2000. Wade Baker, a black slaughterhouse worker attributes the economic decline to the Mexican workforce, which fears unionization and is paid more. The slaughterhouse is described as a "plantation with a roof on it." A liberal white perspective is available in the report by Janny Scott, "A White Journalist Wrote It. A Black Director Fought to Own It," *NY Times*, June 11, 2000. There was no love lost between the white writer, a man of great good will, and the black director, who feared that his independence would be compromised by acceding to the former's judgment.

[49] See Thomas Laqueur's insightful "Festival of Punishment," *London Review of Books*, 22 (October 5, 2000), 17–24. Quote from p. 18. In this assessment of the death penalty in the United States, Laqueur cites the statistics of death by race, notes the overwhelming use of the death penalty in the South, and accounts for the procedural innovations that delay executions for years, while failing to mitigate the fact that race and capital punishment are twisted together in a macabre death play that defies the values of a civilized society.

see themselves as inhabiting a different world altogether, a subculture with the most tenuous social links to the more settled sections of society. Disorder and crime are most often their only decisive connections with them. While there continues to be controversy around the question of how income differentials are the cause of Afro-American disadvantage, or whether the disadvantages are due, in the view of some, to hereditary factors, the debate itself does not question the exacerbating effect of low income on educational opportunities and expectations of success in modes that are acceptable to the majority.[50] It is not only sheer economic disadvantage that is a source of inequality and discontent; it is all that accompanies or flows from these conditions. Deprivation becomes a textured part of an authentically degraded existence that removes from the people living it any sense of what Amartya Sen calls capabilities, those qualities that make participation in the life of the community possible – "appearing in public without shame."[51]

Thus, on one side of the color divide are to be found voluntary organizations devoted to the promotion of racial solidarity as a foundation for economic justice and enhanced political power, while on the other side are to be found groups that look at such measures as proof that Afro-Americans cannot succeed because they are inherently inferior, and if they nevertheless do, their success will never be anything but marginal. The Nation of Islam movement is the most powerful exponent of racial division, and it is matched in its difference-unfriendly world only by that of the white supremacists. It is committed to a celebration of racial difference, not on the view of the mutual gains delivered by a sense of the diversity of peoples, but on the basis of total separateness and hatred. On the other side, the stigmatizing white supremacists operate on the lunatic fringe and advocate and carry out acts of violent terror. Both rely on the narrowest definition of racial solidarity. Difference for them is community making. Louis Farrakhan is at the head of an organization that has gained a measure of respect from many quarters in the

---

[50] Andrew Hacker, "Grand Illusion," *New York Review of Books*, 45 (June 11, 1998), 26–30.

[51] Amartya Sen, *Inequality Reexamined* (Cambridge, Mass.: Harvard University Press, 1992), pp. 114–16. Sen quotes from Smith, who discusses the necessaries indispensable for what he calls "the support of life." "Under necessaries . . . I comprehend not only those things which nature, but those things which the established rules of decency have rendered necessary to the lowest ranks of people." The quotation is to be found in V. ii. k. 869, *The Wealth of Nations*, eds. R. H. Campbell and A. S. Skinner (Indianapolis: Liberty Classics, 1979). Sen insists that poverty and the inequality it creates will be better understood once thinking about it is shifted from an income-centered to a capability-centered concept.

Afro-American population. As well, it represents a much larger part of that population than do white supremacists, who believe that they are articulating the deepest feelings of all whites. The followers of Farrakhan, of course, also say that they democratically reflect the wishes and goals of every member of a stigmatized and neglected minority. Their presence is a rebuke and challenge to the democratic ethos as it has been realized in the United States and how it is imagined by those who have hope in its capacity to grow.

The belief that voluntary associations will fulfill their role as a bridge between peoples of diverse origins, social class, and interests, by accustoming them, through trials of mutual discussion, to the virtues of consensus and compromise is yet another instance of how well-intentioned Americans permit their ideals to get the better of cool analysis. Such organizations as parent-teacher groups, church groups, athletic groups, circles and movements of various persuasions, womens' groups, housing groups, and so on are valuable and needed, and doubtless generate the enthusiasm to give their participants feelings of good will and common purpose. Yet they are far from being able to influence the centers of power. Their presence may in fact serve a quite unintentional purpose – to give Americans the impression that conflict and division are an unusual and aberrant feature of American life, so far are they in time and mentality from the crucial periods of conflicts of power in their history. The makers of the American Constitution did not believe that conflict could be thrust to one side as something left over from pre-Enlightenment times. They had a much livelier sense of the workings of power. They did not innocently believe that it would vanish. Instead, they crafted a constitution ringed with provisions to ensure (while hoping for the best) that power was contained, so aware were they of its disruptive force if it fell into the wrong hands. The Federalists were involved very soon in party struggles with the Jeffersonian Republicans, and both were unafraid to speak of the use of power to gain support from the people. There is, in fact, a great distance from that time to this, and between Tocqueville's and Putnam's ideal voluntary associations, acting for the common good, and special interest groups that do have the power to command attention from politicians.[52]

[52] That interest groups, despite their many shortcomings, including most glaringly their pursuit of narrow interests, are more important than civic associations in representing citizens by speaking for them in national politics in Washington, is a conclusion reached by Jeffrey M. Berry, *The New Liberalism. The Rising Power of Citizen Groups* (Washington: Brookings Institution Press, 1999).

Open acknowledgment of the intricate web of relations linking special pressure groups, government, and corporate giants could at the very least tell Americans that even if class is not the sole mark of identity and division in their lives, it cannot be wished away through feelings of good will. The facades of political institutions stand, but the decisive work that makes markets and the state run is initiated by experts in these conglomerates of power, the professional specialists who, each working for different and immediate ends, are at their command information posts, and, by controlling them, constitute a new voice in politics and shape it in new ways. Neither market nor forum can do without them. The intricate and complex tasks they perform furnish ample proof that the concentrations of power they control are a function of their ability to satisfy the need among voluntary associations and private citizens to believe that they, too, have a share in exercising power. More often than not, how they achieve and maintain their hegemony is invisible to most people, who are mostly left in the dark. The more visible that hegemony becomes, the greater the chance of establishing the foundations of a genuine forum of debate on, first, the present lack of opportunities to enhance equality, and, second, the ways in which it might be reaffirmed as a democratic goal. One aspect of the challenge would be to accomplish some part of this project without resorting to a false, because coercive, rhetoric of consensus, and to replace it with a much less conforming kind of consensus based on debate and negotiation. The other aspect would be to reject a reading of equality that would attempt to erase all traces of difference as if they violated it.

9

The State, Authority, and the People

As we have seen in the last chapter, and earlier in Chapter 3, liberal and democratic thinking places civil society at the very center of democracy and the state at its margins, as if an opposition between them forges the dynamic that ensures its health and survival. There is a long theoretical history, we may also remember, behind these suppositions, much of it brought to life for Americans by the end of the dictatorship-regimes of east and east-central Europe in and after 1989, earliest in Czechoslovakia, Hungary, Poland, and more recently in the former Yugoslavia.[1] But American pluralistic resistance against the power of the state has its own paternity, notably through the action, as Tocqueville believed, of its voluntary associations, and the implementation of the constitutional division of powers, which he saw as the liberal institutionalization of the intermediary powers needed to check the sovereign state. There is some hint in this Tocquevillian formulation, a formulation that is *de rigueur* among conservative liberals, that a different picture might arise through a theory that fused civil society and state and ended the dichotomy. While Tocqueville spent some time on the possibility of a decline in the effectiveness of the tripartite separation of powers, and gave even less time to the power of organized interests, his concentration was on how the contradictory impulses of Americans who cherished liberty but demonstrated an equal need for guidance could almost involuntarily create the conditions for democratic despotism. Thus, while voluntary associations cultivated liberty, which consolidated the habits and affections of civil society, the centralization of power by a regulatory administrative regime

[1] For Vaclav Havel's ideas on the opposition, see his *Open Letters. Selected Writings 1965-1990* (New York: Alfred A. Knopf, 1991), and "The State of the Republic," *New York Review of Books*, 45 (March 5, 1998), 42–46.

– the power that government has to keep them under control – was a harbinger of a democracy wrenched from its pristine moorings, ending in a new kind of despotism where choices would become illusory. Inveighing against its possible onset, Tocqueville singled out the state as the dominant player usurping the institutions of civil society and manipulating them for its own purposes. It should be clear, however, that he spoke of the state, not only as a political power but as an administrative and social power that would infantilize people, keeping them happy in the way a school teacher benevolently treats his pupils, rather than as a parent who uses his authority to prepare "men for manhood" (II, Bk. 4, chap. 6, 336). Being kept happy as children, democratic people lose their capacity to think as responsible adults and take as benefits what are in fact their opposite. The supreme power of the state "does not destroy, but it prevents existence; it does not tyrannize, but it compresses, enervates, extinguishes, and stupefies a people" (ibid., 337).

Before Tocqueville made the prediction that the modern administrative state might become in time the expression of both the substance and forms of democracy, he considered the nature of an imaginary authority, which he painted in non-conflictual colors. His contrasts between a society of distinctive classes, concentration of power, and custom hallowed by ignorance, and a democratic society where power was shared, intellectual awareness diffused widely, and equality was on the rise, make it plain that at the very outset of his study, he is imagining a flourishing American republican democracy in which authority would be largely unproblematic. "I can conceive of a society," he wrote:

in which all men would feel an equal love and respect for the laws of which they consider themselves the authors; *in which the authority of the government would be respected as necessary, and not divine*; and in which the loyalty of the subject to the chief magistrate would not be a passion, but a quiet and rational persuasion. With every individual in the possession of rights which he is sure to retain, a kind of manly confidence and reciprocal courtesy would arise between all classes, removed alike from pride and servility. The people, well acquainted with their own true interests, would understand that, in order to profit from the advantages of the state, it is necessary to satisfy its requirements. The *voluntary association of the citizens* might then take the place of the nobles, and the community would be protected from tyranny and license (I, Introduction, 9–10, emphasis mine).[2]

---

[2] The limits of the state as a voluntary association binding citizens and imposing political obligation on them and that they have obligations only to their common authority is a question taken up by Carol C. Gould, *Rethinking Democracy* (Cambridge: Cambridge University Press, 1988), chap. 8.

Tocqueville was satisfied that a judicious distribution of powers among several administrative bodies, together with a respect for order and law, would render authority acceptable. The right balance between regulation and freedom would thus not only be achieved but would just as critically form a safeguard against "a vague and ill-defined craving for independence" – the opposite of what he called a preference for mature freedom (I, chap. 5, 73). In fact, he described a transformation in the American psyche once it made the mental leap and no longer had any reason to dispute the power of authority to determine its own duties and rights. "The notion they all form of government is that of a sole, simple, providential, and creative power" (II, Bk. 4, chap. 2, 309). By transforming it thus, he rendered its exercise highly problematic. In its new form, it has to sustain, and people must believe that it sustains, a commitment to equality, while in fact authority, as it is seen and experienced in real life, may be called on to support various conditions of inequality, and, if not negating, at least compromising those of equality. Appeals made in its name are notoriously unstable, since they arise from disputes over changing notions of equality as the process of democratization includes more and more people.

Like others before him, Tocqueville distinguished both between authority and power and between a constituted and a non-constituted authority's use of power. He did not consider the question theoretically, and might have had some difficulty had he done so, if only because the distinctions are not always clear. One of his intellectual heroes, Pascal, who lived through some of the most tempestuous times that led to the birth of the absolutist state and the concept of an unchallengeable sovereignty, considered the relationship between justice and force, or right and might, and concluded that only an ideal religious community could reveal and make their true nature manifest. The voice of the people was not negligible in the juxtaposition he drew. Through the activities of their ordinary daily lives, replete with the values of custom, convention, and diversion, they bestowed actual authority on their rulers. Even if the mental effort to achieve this act of transfer was not rationally founded, and even if the origins of authority continue to remain obscure, in the real world it was assumed to be reasonable and authentic, and in terms familiar to ourselves it expresses the notion of bestowing tacit consent to authority: Both its reasonableness and authenticity might even be thought of as the reverse side of the idea that the modern state came into being without reference to the people at all. Pascal thus avoids the strict notion of sheer power in the governance of human beings, whereby force is constantly used or is threatened to be used,[3] though of course there are examples where it has so been exercised, and justifications for it, as, when in Carl Schmitt's distinction between friend and foe, "the Machstaat overrides the Rechtstaat," the supreme example of the triumph of sovereignty.[4]

This leaves us with a notion of legitimate authority that is based on how human beings value themselves and others and how it responds to these values. In a democracy, nothing is supposed to stand in the way of the implementation of the people's will. Tocqueville wrestled with the extraordinary newness of how legitimate and constituted authority was created and asserted in democratic politics, and found that he could best do so by treating the disturbing question of the presence of error in democratic decision-making (either in a series of steps transmitted from below to the top, or at the top itself when the state acts as the legitimate voice of the people's will). Democratic laws express the majority's will, and though they are subject to error, they cannot in the end "have an interest opposed to their own advantage." Moreover, a properly consti-tuted community is able to support bad laws in the knowledge that they can be changed. It can also survive the people whom they elect, because, he said, anticipating his principle of self-interest rightly understood to which he gave too generous a reading, democratic citizens are enlight-ened and aware of their rights. In fact, democracies prosper when the virtues and talents of the men who are elected do not rise above or fall below the interests of the community, though a total congruence between them is improbable. Despite its errors and its vices, the community is served by people who bring it good without necessarily intending it. The allusions to error clearly show that Tocqueville was impatient with the concept of a Rousseauian general will, free of error, waiting to be born. For Rousseau, it was not to be simply identified with the majority will, because private interests always seek their own advantage and thus subvert its "constan[cy], unalterab[ility], and pur[ity]"; or with the idea that serious and important questions preferably need unani-mous approval before a decision is passed.[5] For Tocqueville, what the

---

[3] I discuss this matter in, "Reclaiming the Self: The Pascal-Rousseau Connection," *Journal of the History of Ideas*, 54 (1993), 637–58.

[4] Quoted by Rune Slagstad, "Liberal Constitutionalism and Its Critics," in Jon Elster and Rune Slagstad, eds. *Constitutionalism and Democracy* (Cambridge: Cambridge Univer-sity Press, 1988), 116.

[5] Cf. Rousseau, *Social Contract*, ed. and trans. Victor Gourevitch (Cambridge: Cambridge University Press, 1997), Bk. 4, chap. 1.

majority decides must be understood as a practical question. Legitimacy is conferred upon whom it confers authority (I, chap. 14, citation from 247).

According to the rules of a constitutionally created democracy, the vested authority is not only carrying out its will, but a will that acknowledges only itself, and can only acknowledge itself, for it lacks the power to know itself in the way that Rousseau thought it ideally might in a polity capable of eliciting from its citizens responses free of partisanship. Hence Tocqueville did not accept an imaginary general will that must be satisfied. Rather he was committed to a political science that pragmatically accepts human weaknesses and makes the best of them, including the folly of thinking that agreement is a sign of infallible reason and virtuous sentiment: "[I]n a nation where democratic institutions exist, organized like those of the United States," he stated, "there is but one authority, one element of strength and success, with nothing beyond it (the people). . . . The smallest reproach irritates its sensibility. . . . The majority lives in the perpetual utterance of self-applause. . . . This irresistible authority is a constant fact, and its judicious exercise is only an accident" (I, chap. 15, 274–76).[6] To understand how this irresistible authority is treated in the United States, I will discuss, first, the way in

---

[6] As if paraphrasing Tocqueville – "The people reign in the American political world as the Deity does in the universe. They are the cause and the aim of all things; everything comes from them, and everything is absorbed in them" (I, chap. 4, 60) – Carl Schmitt declared that "in democratic thought the people hover above the entire political life of the state, as God does above the world, as the cause and end of all things, as the point from which everything emanates and to which everything returns." See *Political Theology: Four Chapters on the Concept of Sovereignty*, trans. George Schwab (Cambridge: MIT Press, 1985), p. 49. Tocqueville, he was to say after the Second World War, lacked the courage to think of "historical salvation that would have saved him from the despair of his historic vision of Europe." See "Historiographia in Nuce. Alexis de Tocqueville," *Revista de Estudios Politicos*, no. xliii (1949), 109–14. At the same time, Schmitt interpreted democratization, and its location in the legislature, as the end of the dichotomy between society and state. In another place, Schmitt disputes the notion that democracy speaks as the voice of humanity, rather than, as he says, the voice of the people, who make up a consensual, homogeneous culture, which is the foundation of a constitutional state. See *Die Diktatur: von den Anfängen des modernen Souveränitätsgedankens bis zum proletarischen Klassenkampf . . . Die Diktatur des Reichspräsidenten nach Art. 48 der Weimerar Verfassung* (Munich and Leipzig: Duncker and Humblot, 1928), cited in Jürgen Habermas, *The Inclusion of the Other. Studies in Political Theory*, trans. Ciaran Cronin (Cambridge, Mass.: MIT Press, 1998), pp. 134–38. Also, according to Schmitt, the granting of emergency powers under the terms of the Weimar Constitution represented the triumph of the democratic will. As he saw it, the Nazi seizure of power was not only the fulfillment of the popular will, but also a supreme instance of the "decision" that tests the hidden power of sovereign action.

which the role of the state is perceived; second, how difficult it is to make accessible to modern sensibilities the very notion of authority; and, finally, how intractable is the nature of the people's will and intentions.

The Democratic State

In the United States, charges against the unlawful exercise of authority are raised all the time. We will return to this question after taking up the problem of the ways in which and for what purposes power among the three branches of government is exercised and contested in and by the modern democratic state. The Federalists thought that the legislative, rather than the executive branch, because of its closeness to the people, needed most scrutiny, since by directing the "wealth of the society" it was susceptible and made its constituents more susceptible to the influence of money, including the question of taxes, and so on.[7] Uppermost in many minds today is the executive power, but it is not the sword that is feared as much as a seemingly mindless and thoughtless bureaucracy. When Americans, whether professional politicians or ordinary citizens, speak of government they mean, not a specific administration headed by a Democrat or a Republican, but most emphatically the federal government. The charges, almost overwhelmingly hostile, are heavily tilted against the executive branch of government and its administrative bureaucracy. However hard-pressed citizens might be to offer a coherent account of it, they tend to see it as unified and autonomous, standing above them and beyond their control. It is branded as bloated with usurped power, inflexible in its dealings with citizens, and untrustworthy. Many of the accusations come from congressional representatives, even as they themselves utilize a vast bureaucratic machine as a counterpoise to the power of the White House. Suspicion of government is largely a synonym for suspicion of the ominous state and the President as Head of State. Thus, despite the care that was taken to balance and separate powers 200 years ago, the tradition of hostility to the executive powers of government remains firm.

The state has been looked at with distrust at least since the American Revolution. It was against the illegitimate use of power by the British imperial government that many Americans, nurtured on the Bible, raised their injured voices. The British monarch had abused his authority and

---

[7] *Federalist* No. 78, *The Federalist*. From the Original Text of Alexander Hamilton, John Jay, and James Madison (New York: Modern Library, n.d.), p. 504.

put his subjects in a state of infanthood, when in fact they had come to regard themselves as responsible adults. By attacking the ancient covenant as well as the Lockean view of contract, the British crown placed free-born Americans in mortal danger. They were also bred on Montesquieu and Thomas Paine, drawing from them arguments against illegitimately constituted authority, and declaring that since they had no representation in the British Parliament, the crown ought to be directly responsible to them. When the War of Independence came to an end, quarrels broke out over what branch of government possessed sovereignty. But it was the legislative branch of government that Thomas Paine said needed restraint in the mid-1780s, and he turned not to the executive branch but to the judiciary to end what he thought was an abuse of authority.[8] Yet he did not question the principle that government was needed to make up "the deficit of virtue."[9] Alexander Hamilton believed that the judiciary alone was capable of keeping the correct balance of powers between the legislative and executive arms of government.[10] Ever since, Americans have found themselves in an ambiguous relationship to the state, which they don't name as such, preferring the less imposing term – the administration – which they understand as the repository of Presidential power. They look to it in extremity, as during the Great Depression or in wartime, but for the most part, over the past two decades or so, they have turned away from it as a positive force in their lives. Its detractors see in it the threat of bigger government and interference with individual lives and choices. They do not normally view it as an overarching institution, acting authoritatively, protecting polity and society, nor consistently as an umpire in conflict-laden situations and as the instrument encouraging dialogue among people confused about and ready to fight over their differences. Instead, increasingly, the courts in the United States are called upon to adjudicate disputes over civil and political liberty. The state fails to speak forcefully, as it did as a welfare state, about assuming the largest part of the burden in determining policy

---

[8] See John Keane, *Tom Paine: A Political Life* (London: Bloomsbury Pub., 1995).

[9] Thomas Paine, *Common Sense*, ed. Isaac Kramnick (London: Penguin, 1976). Cited in Judith Shklar, *Redeeming American Political Thought*, eds. Stanley Hoffman and Dennis F. Thompson (Chicago: University of Chicago Press, 1998), p. 135.

[10] In *Federalist* No. 78, Hamilton declared that the judiciary, having neither the power of the sword of the Executive, nor the power over the purse of the legislature, had merely its power of judgment to determine the constitutionality of the laws, but more significantly, it could never, because of its comparative weakness, be a source of injury to the "general liberty of the people." We know, of course, that some of its judgments did indeed endanger liberty.

in education and health, and in racial and other forms of discrimination – while at the same avoiding any actions that would appear to oppress citizens – and in creating a high regard for all of them by cultivating in them a due concern for one another. Even if such a description of the grounds for the state's legitimacy may sound out of place in this century, I invoke it to stress its present spirit of comparative defensiveness and indecisiveness on these questions, which expresses the suspicion of big, and the preference for, small government.

Let us see how Frank Ankersmit deals – in the main, theoretically – with the role of the state, not only in its function as the crucial determinant of policy on social and economic issues, but also as the organ that has two sides to it. One is the outside, which is presented to the public and is constitutionally accessible to it; the other is the inside, which commands, not hierarchically but in diffused patterns, its own impetus, and is rarely seen by the public that has consequently no means of controlling it through constitutional means. The state is a complex set of instruments wielded by persons, whose loyalties are determined by criteria that are not always attuned, and may hence be opposed, to the differing and conflicting perceptions of a many-minded public that cannot, because of its divisions and loyalties, agree on its own needs. What matters in Ankersmit's account is his plea that the state must be restored to the center of political philosophy as the chief means to ensure that it will continue to be an active, though not the preponderant, partner in democratic society. He is mindful of the fact that modern democracy had its origins in the framework of the sovereign state (at least in France), and that its best chances of surviving in the United States, as well as elsewhere, lie within the state. He is not therefore against endowing the state with power, but it must be, he says, the right kind of power, and that will not be forthcoming until there is clear thinking about it. For the present, thought about the state is mired in the notion that it is an "insurance company," with gifts to dispense to the public that is only too eager to accept entitlements, and avoids the task of devising the means to find them for itself, while the state itself turns all politics into economic problems.

The state, of course, has grown enormously in strength since the end of the eighteenth century. Its enhanced power was rightly seen by Tocqueville as one of the greatest threats to individual freedom and civic associations. When Ankersmit tells us how the state can dispense gifts to a public eager for handouts, he reminds one of Tocqueville's distaste for the expanding role of the state: "The state almost exclusively undertakes to supply bread to the hungry, assistance and shelter to the sick, work to the idle, and to act as the sole reliever of all kinds of misery (II, Bk. 4, chap. 5, 323). Ankersmit deplores, as does Tocqueville, the conversion of political questions into economic ones.[11] Once so reduced, politics disappears; nothing is then left for the citizen to worry about except ensuring his equal (as he sees them) share of material goods. For Tocqueville, the choice was between "a democracy in which people are forced to be happy, [and] one in which the people learned to discern all the conditions for their happiness."[12] Taking it for granted that the future state will gain even more strength, Ankersmit asks political philosophers to think about "[h]ow to create a stronger state within the parameters of democracies."[13] He supposes the not unlikely situation that may indeed place the delicate relationship between state and civil society in jeopardy under the economic pressures of preserving elements of the welfare state. Under such a strain, he posits an opposition between the state that insists on using the *available* means for financing welfare, and the self-governing institutions of civil society that contend that all means should be used to bolster and expand them. The public, given its distrust of politicians and its suspicions of the state's power, is likely to lose its trust in representative democracy and will turn wearily, perhaps eagerly, away from democratic and toward autocratic government. On this account, Ankersmit agrees with Tocqueville's pessimistic analysis of how democratic people may fall into "servitude." Such a turn of events would thus spell doom for democracy. Instead of counseling a strengthening of civil society by supporting voluntary associations, Ankersmit remains attached to the need to reconceptualize the democratic state's purpose. But it is to political parties that he looks to strengthen the state and reinforce the public's confidence in it and them. Because, however, most parties in the West have long since been depoliticized, they must present

---

[11] In his critique of liberal concepts which "typically move between ethics . . . and economics," Carl Schmitt saw an "attempt to annihilate the political as a domain of conquering power and repression." See *The Concept of the Political*, trans. George Schwab (New Brunswick: Rutgers University Press, 1976), p. 68.

[12] Cited in Harvey Mitchell, *Individual Choice and the Structures of History. Alexis de Tocqueville as Historian Reappraised* (Cambridge: Cambridge University Press, 1996), p. 146.

[13] Frank R. Ankersmit, *Aesthetic Politics. Political Philosophy Beyond Fact and Value* (Stanford: Stanford University Press, 1996), pp. 188, 209. His arguments are mainly laid out in chap. 4, the principal lines of which may be found in Sections 5 to 8, pp. 186–211, and again in the final pages of the conclusion, pp. 354–72.

themselves to the public as capable of representing a comprehensive view of the range of problems it must face. Whether they can or will, he concludes, remains uncertain.[14]

There is a close connection between how one might think about the state's expanded role, including how one might deny it opportunities to satisfy its inordinate desire to take over, absorb and subsume civil society, and how one might reasonably think about the question of human rights. As I argued in the previous chapter, it is shortsighted and wrongheaded to think of the state in permanent opposition to civil society, just as it is foolish to neglect the fact that not all voluntary associations are committed to democracy. As for the demand for and recognition of new rights, they may be a product of different stages in economic productivity, expanding as it increases, but not easily contracting when society experiences economic decline. They do not, because, just as the question of the lawful and legitimate role of the state in a democracy is related to the contested uses of authority, so is the distribution of economic goods a question of regulatory justice – when the legitimacy of the range of the state's actions is determined – and a question of distributive justice, when the question of how economic resources, capabilities, and end-products are to be shared is considered. Thus, the dilemma of allocating resources available for social services touches everyone and everything.

The dilemma centers on the notion and the practice of founding and expanding human rights, the signature of a democratic society, so different Tocqueville said, from the absolutist societies of pre-revolutionary Europe, "where never was there less political activity among the people" (I, chap. 2, 44). Tocqueville's definition of democracy as political activity was never so sharp. It was through their political rights, as we have seen, that he believed Americans could protect their other rights, particularly their rights to property. At the same time,

---

[14] Harvey C. Mansfield, Jr., and Delba Winthrop agree with both Ankersmit and Tocqueville that big government, by relegating politics to a process of delivering benefits, paradoxically "takes a low view" of it. See "Liberalism and Big Government: Tocqueville's Analysis," *Tyranny and Liberty. Big Government and the Individual in Tocqueville's Science of Politics* (London: The Institute of United States Studies, University of London, 1999), p. 19. Mansfield offers a more extended treatment of the risks of entitlements in *America's Constitutional Soul* (Baltimore and London: Johns Hopkins University Press, 1991), esp. pp. 74–75, where he criticizes intellectuals for showing scant regard for the intellect and indulging in unreflective compassion for the disadvantaged.

in a world that had forsaken faith and sentiment for calculation and reasoning, the idea of and the need to link rights and private interest – "the only immutable point in the human heart," was the sole barrier against a government that exploited its authority through fear (I, chap. 14, 255). Private rights had, on the one hand, to be protected against the democratic urge to satisfy the rights of society (II, Bk. 4, chap. 7, 344–45). On the other hand, there was in Tocqueville's delineation of rights a commitment to political participation that commands citizens to act together, for it best serves both their individual and common interests. He thus stands for negative and positive liberty: both are required if citizens are to feel secure as private persons and engaged as public citizens.

Appeals to the authority of the Constitution are constantly uttered, sometimes as one of the rituals of American politics, but sometimes, as well, in efforts to recover the original intentions of the Founding Fathers and the meaning of the Bill of Rights. Will Americans be able to distinguish between issues, such as "rights" owing to nature, gender, and human difference, and issues that were once the kernel of political debate – that is, debate focused on the authority of the state and the liberty of the individual to oppose it? Will they find the ways that take account of the differences that have long clamored to be acknowledged and have to some degree been recognized. At the same time, will they know how to give proper weight and balance to those "rights?" Historically how these questions surrounding rights came to be central to a consideration of the respective roles of authority and liberty is far from clear, whether we turn to the Greeks, who were concerned about them (Antigone who challenged Creon), or to John Locke, who advocated an unprecedented measure of religious freedom. Norberto Bobbio, who has studied these matters over a lifetime, has never wavered in his belief that the only society that deserves to be called a democracy is a society that recognizes that its citizens have fundamental rights, but that however fundamental they are, they arise from specific historical conditions. For him, to cite only one, but a highly critical, example, the French Declaration of the Rights of Man and the Citizen was a revolutionary point in the history of the expansion of human rights, while some of the latest, still controversial ones, such as the rights to a protected environment, and others, still vague and undetermined, such as biological rights, cannot be understood or considered apart from their historical context. "They are established, not all at the same time, and not forever. It would appear that philosophers are asked to pass sentence on the fundamental nature of human rights, and even to demonstrate that they are absolute, inevitable and incontrovertible, but the question should not be posed in these terms."[15]

Rights, our intuitive experience tells us, and empirical observation confirms, clash, producing competing claims that justice, for example, is denied if total freedom of association is ever challenged. Only the most doctrinaire libertarian can suppose that there are never issues that override the rights of associations to do as they wish at all times. In the United States, the battle over human rights remains hotly contested between those whose view of the Constitution is rigidly set in the mold of past adherence to the preservation – well into a good part of the twentieth century, for example – of the right of industry as a private person in *Lochner v. New York* (1905) and those who favored legislation limiting the length of the working day. A half-century later, the decision remained startling and offensive, and strengthens the conclusion that rights are interpreted and determined by the concerns of a particular time frame and a particular social and economic structure. Specifically it was not until long after labor unions gained rights that the Supreme Court decided that if union membership was a fair condition of employment, members were nevertheless not required to support a union's political agenda. In this case, a determination was made on the negative impact of coerced association on a person's liberty. Thus, Nancy Rosenblum makes a valid distinction – and is clearly hopeful that future rulings in the courts and in legislatures will bear her out – between the activities of associations that are congruent with the goals of liberal democracy, and thus help to expand, or at least to protect equality and freedom, and such other associations that compromise or negate them.[16] She vigorously questions the wisdom of legislation and court rulings that intrude on a person's right to associate with like-minded people seeking to satisfy their sentiments, religious or ethnic preferences, and so on, and set themselves finite means to meet specific goals (but she sets limits on conspiratorial and paramilitary groups). At the same time, she justifies "[g]overnment-mandated membership policies when exclusion from an association denotes second-class citizenship." The case that came before the Supreme Court, which determined that women who were denied full and voting membership in the Junior Chambers of Commerce, would

[15] Norberto Bobbio, *The Age of Rights*, trans. Allan Cameron (Cambridge: Polity Press, 1996), p. xi. Some of these same points are made as well by Harvey Mansfield, *America's Constitutional Soul*, pp. 184–85, 198.

[16] Nancy L. Rosenblum, *Membership and Morals. The Personal Uses of Pluralism in America* (Princeton: Princeton University Press, 1998), chap. 5.

henceforth be assured of it. In Justice William Brennan's majority opinion in *Roberts v. Jaycees*, not only was second-class citizenship for women judged to be unwelcome, but so were the "stigma, degradation, unequal status, injury to personal dignity and self-respect," which their membership rules tolerated.[17] Rights are now a supreme matter for litigation. Every individual or group, Afro- and Native Americans, women and others, can argue that their particular condition is proof of universality in fact and action. Some would put an essentialist cast on their grievances, but this compromises the notion of universality at its root and seriously calls into doubt the belief, more often expressed as an unexamined hope, that all rights can be equally satisfied in the real world, rather than working through the political process, such as it has become, to approve of the changes needed to expand rights and hence ensure greater equality.

Charles L. Black contends that much good will come from the expansion of rights that were not enumerated by the Founding Fathers. They are not for that reason to be ruled out, and are, indeed, left open for present and future generations of Americans to determine, by taking their cues from the "Pursuit of Happiness" clause of the Declaration of Independence, and the Ninth Amendment provision that the enumeration of rights does not preclude the rights "retained by the people."[18] To what extent, however, may rights be considered as foundational to politics? They change, as Black recognizes – and, as we saw, Bobbio takes a similar stand on the evolution of rights – as perspectives on notions of well-being change. There is, to be sure, a bottom line below which we may recognize inhumane treatment, clearly recognized as a violation of well-being, such as slavery. The struggle over rights then may be viewed as an important feature of civil society. What a civil society achieves is a working relationship between and among the various groups that struggle and sometimes cooperate with one another over differing ways

---

[17] Ibid., p. 162. George Kateb, "The Value of Association," in *Freedom of Association*, ed. Amy Gutmann (Princeton: Princeton University Press, 1998), 35–64, challenges the majority decision as giving a green signal to government to invade the notion that "one is one's expression, [that] one lives to express, [that] one lives by expressing." Citation from p. 53. Admitting the difficulty of distinguishing between what he calls selfhood and personhood, he thinks of the latter as that element of human dignity that is shared equally by all, while the former speaks to a person's sense of himself as a unique being. Thus, for Kateb, the Roberts decision encroaches on and instrumentalizes selfhood, and therefore pays too high a price for trying to advance the notion of personhood.

[18] Charles L. Black, Jr., *A New Birth of Freedom: Human Rights Named and Unnamed* (New York: Grosset/Putnam, 1998).

by means of which they come to understand the purpose of coming together in the public sphere. They come together to debate issues such as the right of women to determine their "rights" as against the "rights" of the fetus; homosexual "rights"; the virtues and flaws of affirmative action; the meaning of equal pay for work of equal value; the "rights" of aboriginals to claim their ancestral lands, as well as claims for compensation for past injuries.

Authority in the Modern Democratic State

It is hard to deny that the complex negotiations between citizens and their representatives leading to the making of decisions are not a trifling point when political parties, organized groups representing various interests, the multiple branches and levels of government, and the great corporations take part in the making of laws, though their participation is crucially determined by unequal distributions of power. Consequently, the laws may not satisfy all who seek to establish what we may say is a deep notion of authority that expresses the will of the people. "[A]uthority has vanished from the modern world," Hannah Arendt said in a famous essay.[19] She speaks of the founding political act as an affirmation of authority, incomparably embodied in the Declaration of Independence ("We hold these truths to be self-evident") and in the Constitution. She links this with the exercise of power, and adds that political communities die when they lose the will to act. "Power is actualized only where word and deed have not parted company, where words are not empty and deeds are not brutal."[20] As did the framers of the Constitution, she understood that once appeals to traditional authority would no longer be exercised in a democracy, politics would not eliminate conflict but rather have to find the means to deal with it. Support for legitimate authority no longer rested on garlanding it with a notion of the sacred. The point is that the authority of democracy resides in democracy itself, conceived, as I have been describing it, as a series of deliberate steps leading away from the particular needs of a host of groups, each pursuing its narrow interests, to a consensus expressing the will of the people based on a common understanding achieved through

---

[19] Hannah Arendt, "What is Authority?" in *Between Past and Future. Six Exercises in Political Thought* (Cleveland and New York: Meridian Books, 1963), p. 91.
[20] Hannah Arendt, *The Human Condition* (Chicago: University of Chicago Press, 1958), p. 200.

communication.[21] But it is precisely on the grounds of establishing the distinguishing features of democratic authority that there is real disagreement. It remains, on the whole, more than half-concealed.

Arendt made the question of authority a significant part of her political theory, and asked how a secularized version could take its proper place in a democratic society. For Arendt, the genius of America was to have laid the foundations of a polity that brought authority and freedom together in a fruitful embrace. That genius shaped a revolution that had as a starting point a belief in a new kind of political participation. We find her arguing that politics cannot be understood if those who practice it ignore authority, however distant its origins lie in the largely mythologized lives of ancient lawgivers. She was impatient at the thought of having "to live in a political realm with neither authority nor the concomitant awareness that the source of authority transcends power and those who are in power." It meant having "to be confronted anew, without the religious trust in a sacred beginning and without the protection of traditional and therefore self-evident standards of behavior, by the elementary problems of human living-together."[22] She could not accept the narrowing opportunities for political participation in a depoliticized world. It is true that when she said that "the loss of permanence and reliability – which politically is identified with the loss of authority – does not entail, at least not necessarily the loss of the human capacity for building, preserving, and caring for a world that can survive us and remain a place fit to live in for those who come after us,"[23] she tended to look back nostalgically to an idealized Greek *polis*. But she had too good a grasp of the realities of modern political life to make this the whole of her concept of politics.

For Arendt, the voice of the Founding Fathers is the voice of authority. She valued them as political theorists. In loyalty to her republicanism, she had a certain contempt for the politicians who came after them, but she did not repudiate them totally. Politics she understood as the realm of conflict and not of the search for one truth. Such a misplaced endeavor had no place in politics. Unfortunately, the promises, the backtracking, and the shifty, as well as the shifting, alliances that create the world of mass democratic politics also manipulate facts and opinions,

---

[21] That consensus is no longer the central aspect of social relationships, because they have been transformed by a globalized economy, is the position that Jean-François Lyotard took more than two decades ago, *La condition postmoderne* (Paris: Minuit, 1979).
[22] Hannah Arendt, *Between Past and Future*, pp. 140–41.   [23] Ibid., p. 95.

and do so, not only by deception of the kind Tocqueville took for granted, but also by the self-deceptions of the deceivers who end by believing the lies they create and mobilize. Only a free and uncorrupted press, Arendt said more than twenty-five years ago, could ensure the flow of factual information without which opinion cannot be deemed free. That she should have concluded her remarks by thinking about the press as the major source of information, even while electronic forms were already transforming it, puts her closer to Tocqueville than to the Madison Avenue managers she speaks about.[24]

Arendt also quite strongly argues that the defining narrative of the self is an exercise in authority, and seeks to strengthen her argument by moving to the world of the classroom where children are made aware of their heritage. "The world into which children are introduced, even in America, is an old world, that is a pre-existing world constructed by the living and the dead, and it is only new for those who have newly entered it by immigration. But here illusion is stronger than reality because it springs directly from a basic American experience, the experience that a new order can be founded." What is more, she said, it was "founded upon a full consciousness of a historical continuum, for the phrase 'New World' gains its meaning from the Old World, which, however admirable on other scores, was rejected because it could find no solution to poverty and oppression."[25] The authority of the teacher rested on what Arendt called taking responsibility for the world when he speaks of knowing its meaning – a metaphysical notion. After the teacher has completed his work, and adults have left their childhood behind them, they will, if properly educated, learn to love the world to enable them to take responsibility for it to ensure its survival.[26] This conception of responsibility is quintessentially American, for it stems from the notion of the individual as the sole judge of his actions.

Like Arendt, John Rawls considers how the family acts as a moral authority, encouraging self-esteem in children, making obedience to reasonable requests unonerous.[27] Harry Eckstein similarly goes back to the experience of family life; he asks us to focus on the poor of America,

---

[24] Hannah Arendt, "Truth and Politics," in *Philosophy, Politics and Society*, Third Series, eds. Peter Laslett and W. G. Runciman (Oxford: Basil Blackwell, 1967), 104–33 and "Lying in Politics," in *Crises of the Republic* (New York: Harcourt Brace Jovanovich, Inc., 1972), 1–48.

[25] Hannah Arendt, *Between Past and Future*, pp. 177–78.   [26] Ibid., p. 190.

[27] John Rawls, *A Theory of Justice* (Cambridge, Mass.: Harvard University Press, 1971), pp. 463–65.

who live in a culture of authoritarianism, and fail to deal effectively with associational life and political conflict.[28] For Americans, Tocqueville reminds us, however, concern for others was acceptable only if it was reconciled with a notion of self-interest rightly understood. Utility, rather than the display of virtuous motives – not that they are not invoked – is the real springboard of actions undertaken for a common purpose. Doing so, Americans believe that they are preserving their belief in individual conscience and action, without doing violence to the principle of utility as a basis for authority. When, however, the priority that they give to their belief in their own judgment tends to destroy confidence in such or such a person, but more importantly in authority itself, utility as a standard of conduct begins to lose its power to convince. It can be argued, of course, that this appeal to utility was a way for Tocqueville to reintroduce virtue, at least in its negative version.[29] This is, however, not the same as the republican virtue and the "political economy of citizenship" called for by Sandel, who thinks that Tocqueville saw in the politics of American democracy the uncomplex exercise of virtue.[30] Rather, he cautioned that if those who live by the utilitarian principle see nothing to gain from self-denial in concrete situations, their readiness for sacrifice will not come into play. Similarly, appeals to the forging of a common understanding, on the basis of finding "a shared political and normative vocabulary," without which, "a democratic society cannot sustain itself over time,"[31] fail to pay heed to Tocqueville's sober analysis.

When the springs of democratic authority are more concretely considered – for example, in the support for, or the rejection of, a notion of authority based on religion and tradition – Americans give quite different answers. We may turn to the ranks of today's religious Right for

[28] Harry Eckstein, "Civic Inclusion and Its Discontents," in *Regarding Politics: Essays on Political Theory, Stability, and Change* (Berkeley: University of California Press, 1992), pp. 343–77.

[29] Cf. Harvey C. Mansfield, Jr., and Delba Winthrop, "Liberalism and Big Government: Tocqueville's Analysis," p. 23: "Tocqueville believes that the working of institutions requires virtue, not lofty virtue but the virtue available in a democracy ranging from raw intractability to active self-interest to moderate ambition."

[30] Michael J. Sandel, *Democracy's Discontent. America in Search of a Public Philosophy* (Cambridge and London: The Belknap Press of Harvard University Press, 1996), especially pp. 333, 348, mistakenly argues that Tocqueville makes a direct appeal to the exercise of virtue.

[31] Jean Bethke Elshtain, *Democratic Authority at Century's End* (London: The Institute of United States Studies, University of London, 1998), pp. 13, 16, 18. Tocqueville's notion that the unrestrained sovereign and prideful self leads to the desiccation of the humanist civic ideal finds echoes in Elshtain's observations.

an illustration. Traditionalists and fundamentalists, in defending religion and authority, do not appeal to the kind of utilitarian arguments Tocqueville used. They also conveniently overlook the secular past of the Founding Fathers. Most of all, they link their highly distorted notion of eighteenth-century Anglo-American religiosity to a populist notion of democracy. The undiminished appeal of populism, with its roots in localism and mandated democracy, is found in many parts of the United States, but nowhere is its hold more tenacious than in the Bible Belt. The authority the religious Right seeks is the authority of small groups working to preserve the self-centeredness of parochial institutions and organizations. The democratic structure of small groups, it is also obvious, is not incompatible with this vision. The religious Right invokes the authority of religious family values and traditional sexual morality, which, on these and related issues, is calculated to keep order and maintain the primacy of small groups. It does not place economic equality at the head or the middle of its concerns. The Right is publicly anti-elitist, and makes a virtue of saying that it is as much at home in the small nooks and crannies of American society as in large corporations. It disingenuously parades its hatred of big government, but never hesitates to make it work for its national objectives.

In the past, the Left put much of its hopes on direct democracy, as when it spearheaded the agitation for referenda, initiative, and recall. Smallness was the Left's way to dodge the issue of elitism, which it saw as an invasion of the unmediated popular will, but for almost fifty years from the time of the New Deal it transferred its loyalty to the welfare state to counteract the depredations of the corporate world. The modern activist state, though born then, remains a reluctant one, providing fewer social services than other major advanced states, and not questioning, moreover, the power of state and local levels of government to deliver them. In the generations since the New Deal, the Left has had to deal with the fact that a large segment of the American population is curiously less fearful of the corporate world than it is of the state, unmindful of the fact that the American state has hardly been inhospitable to business, no matter how impatient business can be with federal regulatory practices. Today, the Left is on the defensive, and cannot quite decide on how to mobilize the public to take an active role in politics.

There is another way to look at the divisions in American society. According to James Hunter, America has always been divided along a basic fault line. It is the troubled heir to two major claimants that speak as if each represents the true source of authority. One owes its origins to the secular, urban, and national legacy of the Enlightenment, and the other to the agrarian, local, and clerical legacy of Reformed Protestantism. Each carries in its bosom a belief in it own moral authority over the most vital questions troubling modern and postmodern citizens. They are locked together in a culture war: "What we have in the contemporary American culture war are competing understandings of the sacred, competing faiths – in reality, competing parochialisms."[32] A culture war of the kind Hunter describes is one way to discern the fissures in American democracy. It ignores the history of social violence that did not bypass the United States. It was present from the very beginnings of America's wars against Native Americans, and slavery could not have been enforced without it. It was next used by a repressive state and corporate groups against working-class protest, minorities, and parties and organizations on the Left – and no more so than in the twentieth century. When the state enforces its monopoly of violence, it does so to a fanfare of legitimacy and authority. Many Americans choose to give bad and good marks to the use of authority in a highly selective way. It may be true that they accept the authority of the state more often than they reject it, but they also believe they are betraying a sacred principle if they say they trust it completely, even in emergencies such as war. That violence on the different sides of the American political spectrum is endemic may be a function of an inability to come to terms with the exercise of authority about which people have deeply ambiguous feelings. Can the fervor shown by the heirs of the Enlightenment and by the religious Right be distinguished from one another? Do the protagonists of the one and of the other not harbor a stubborn Manicheanism, each of them claiming that the other is impelled by evil intent? Can we, with perfect equanimity and with a straight face, speak about two kinds of democratic authority, a pure one and a flawed one?

Neither Left nor Right, the first the heirs of the Enlightenment, the second the distant heirs of Reformed Protestantism, has been able to present a persuasive notion of how and for what purposes authority works in a democracy beyond the sovereign functioning of the voluntary organizations themselves. Michael Sandel, who does not see himself as either a man of the Left or Right, sees the work of these associations as a healthy rebuke to the moral impoverishment of a strictly indivi-

---

[32] James Davison Hunter, "The American Culture War," in *The Limits of Social Cohesion. Conflict and Mediation in Pluralist Societies.* A Report of the Bertelsmann Foundation to the Club of Rome, ed. Peter L. Berger (Boulder, Colorado: Westview Press, 1998), 8.

dualistic notion of freedom. While appealing to Aristotle's notion of self-government, he wants to transform it so that it can meet the problems of the wider world without supplanting – because he is confident that it cannot supplant – the local and most abiding roots of human relationships. He would have Americans be at home in three public spaces: their small communities, the nation, and the world. Only in this way can politics be restored to the fabric of America. The return to the small, to local initiatives, to civic consciousness is the path Americans should follow, he believes, to revive the principles of civic virtue. These principles will, he asserts, be capable of restoring a sense of identity enhancing moral commitment to a collectively shared notion of an American public philosophy that will give fuller scope to the opposing demands of private and public life. Such an endeavor is more important, he contends, than collective concern for distributive justice, and it is, in addition, he says, a salubrious example of the benefits of the dispersal and diffusion of sovereignty.[33]

But the citizens upon whom such hopes are centered may in fact not care to be so engaged, as Tocqueville had earlier told his readers. Many of them indeed long ago seem to have given up. A substantial number may retreat, as Richard Rorty speculates, into the camp of the right-wing fundamentalist populists for whom debate is a foreign idea. If Americans were to embrace fascism, Rorty adds, it will be because they are experiencing globalization without having set up a welfare state.[34] From a non-Left perspective, Edward Luttwack expresses similar anxieties. Americans may be on the high road to the kind of future in which blue- and white-collar workers are set against one another in a battle for higher wages and declining social benefits, while tax levels remain low. At the same time, the gains made by Afro-Americans and other visible minorities, by women and homosexuals, could be challenged and reversed.[35]

So where should Americans look to for guidance? Many Americans refer to the judiciary in hushed tones, and maintain that economic, social,

[33] Michael J. Sandel, *Democracy's Discontent*, passim.
[34] Richard Rorty, "Emancipating our Culture," in *Debating the State of Philosophy. Habermas, Rorty, and Kolakowski*, eds. Jozef Niznik and John T. Sanders (Westport, Conn.: Praeger, 1998), 58–66.
[35] Edward N. Luttwak, *The Endangered American Dream* (New York: Simon and Schuster, 1993). See especially p. 159. "With its 246 million all-out individualists, diverse and sometimes clashing races, and a long history of violence, America could never be compared to famously law-abiding Japan, cohesive Finland, strict Switzerland, or indeed any First World country at all. Of late, however, it cannot even be compared with itself."

and political confrontations are perfectly well dealt with through the courts, and furthermore that such processes are the best way to establish the authoritative judgments that they say society requires. We may turn to Alexander Hamilton once again to grasp to what lengths he was prepared to go to ensure that the hallowed bosom of the judiciary should serve as a protective shield both of the constitution, against the other branches of government, but most of all against "the effects of those ill humors which the arts of designing men, or the influence of particular conjunctures, sometimes disseminate among the people themselves, and which though they speedily give place to better information, and more deliberate reflection, have a tendency, in the meantime, to occasion dangerous innovations in the government, and serious oppressions of the minor party in the community":

> The interpretation of the laws is the proper and peculiar province of the courts. A constitution is, in fact, and must be regarded by the judges, as a fundamental law. It therefore belongs to them to ascertain its meaning, as well as the meaning of any particular act proceeding from the legislative body. If there should happen to be an irreconcilable variance between the two, that which has the superior obligation and validity ought, of course, to be preferred; or, in other words, the Constitution ought to be preferred to the statute, the intention of the people to the intention of their agents.
>
> Nor does this conclusion by any means suppose a superiority of the judicial to the legislative power. It only supposes that the power of the people is superior to both; and that where the will of the legislature, declared in its statutes, stands in opposition to that of the people, declared in the Constitution, the judges ought to be governed by the latter rather than the former. They ought to regulate their decisions by the fundamental laws, rather than by those which are not fundamental.

Thus, Hamilton not only supported a framework for judicial review, but more significantly favored a system of judicial supremacy – a more controversial idea. Hamilton bids Americans to put their trust in the small number of qualified men "who unite the requisite integrity with the requisite knowledge" to combat "the ordinary depravity of human nature,"[36] revealing that his appeal to the people was a subterfuge intended to conceal his contempt for them. This characterization of an aristocratic few armed with superior wit against the masses is a dubious notion of how democratic politics, with its unequal mixes of rational and irrational behavior, really works. Even more to the point is that such a notion would unquestioningly vest in judges the power to make the

[36] *Federalist* No. 78, pp. 506–11.

kinds of rationally objective decisions that will command authority, as if they unerringly possessed a larger capacity to stand above and outside the society in which they live. It may be stretching the argument dangerously to suppose that this vision of their role as custodians of the rule of law makes their judgments authoritative rather than merely legal.[37]

Tocqueville not only agreed with Hamilton, and sought to soften the sharp and stark realities of pure majority rule as the ultimate source of democratic authority. The independent judiciary, in the course of obliging the people to be consistent with themselves by obeying their own laws, he said, helps citizens to preserve the republican form of government. For many who wrote the Constitution, as well as for their political heirs, the judiciary is the ideal voice that creates, through its decisions, the circumstances in which citizens will become more fully aware of the choices that are open, as well as those that are closed to them, and avoid, as well as correct, as far as possible, the errors they might otherwise be only too likely to commit. Was Tocqueville's judgment clouded by a superbly idealized notion of how in everyday life the courts and its lawyers decide matters?

We the People

Tocqueville had a low opinion of the people's capacity to make proper choices in selecting their public figures:

> The people have neither the time nor the means for an investigation of this kind (to form a reasonable judgment of the character of a single individual standing for public office). Their conclusions are hastily formed from a superficial inspection of the more prominent features of a question. Hence it often happens that mountebanks of all sorts are able to please the people, while their truest friends frequently fail to gain their confidence (I, chap. 13, 208).

Thus, if not for the political skills of America's educated classes, American political institutions would have fallen prey to the ill-considered wishes of the popular classes. Americans are, in addition, prosaic and share homely tastes; while they love or say they love change, they protect their conservative interests. They are, it is true, constantly agitated, but the agitation they feel, and the zeal they show for

---

[37] For a critical assessment of the problematic ways in which the rule of law has been incorporated into different notions of the law and politics, see Judith N. Shklar, "Political Theory and the Rule of Law," in *Political Thought and Political Thinkers*, ed. Stanley Hoffman (Chicago: University of Chicago Press, 1998), pp. 21–37.

commerce, are not the same as enthusiasm for new ideas: "Even when the confidence of a democratic people has been won, it is still no easy matter to gain their attention. It is extremely difficult to obtain a hearing from men living in democracies, unless it is to speak to them of themselves"(II, Bk. 3, chap. 21, 269–70, 271–72, 274).

Just as Tocqueville looked back at the politics of the Founding Fathers, who established the foundations of a national voice, registering a new start in America's development as a distinct society, so have observers since then been impressed by the grave nature of key crises that marked American democracy. The debates that ended with the adoption of the Constitution ended one crisis. The decision to preserve the Union in 1861 was another, as were the Reconstruction period and the New Deal. On these occasions, it was in the name of the people that the crises were met and confirmed. The patricians of 1787 prefaced their remarks and constantly interspersed their arguments with allusions to the voice of the people, but they looked upon them with a fearful eye, and made sure that republicanism rather than democracy was the animating spirit of the Constitution. We should remember as well that for all that Madison invoked the will of the people, the Constitutional Convention was not a popularly elected assembly. Indeed, if there were serious misgivings about the absence and disregard of popular participation, the chief actors were not overly concerned.

Hannah Arendt's thoughts on revolution and political freedom may be seen as a model for the relationship between constitutional crisis and renewal. Liberation and political freedom are not to be confused, she argues, nor should the object of political freedom be forgotten. Its purpose is "not how to reconcile freedom and equality, but how to reconcile equality and authority."[38] Revolution was the prelude to liberation, and was not necessarily followed by an opening to political freedom. Indeed, they could, as historians of revolutions have demonstrated, be disjoined by the very act of constitution-making. Indeed, the word constitution means both the act of constituting and the laws that are constituted, and there is in Arendt's interpretation the strong implication that the two exist in a state of opposition. There is "an enormous difference in power and authority between a constitution imposed by a government upon a people and the constitution by which a people constitutes its own government."[39] Sieyès' "famous distinction between a

---

[38] Hannah Arendt, *On Revolution* (New York: Viking, 1963), p. 283.
[39] Ibid., p. 144.

pouvoir constituant (constituent power) and a *pouvoir constitué*" put the "nation into a perpetual 'state of nature.'" While, to be sure, the French Constituent Assembly's power resided in "the will of the nation," however that was defined, and stood "above all government and all laws,"[40] and hence was the source of authority and power for government and law, the dichotomy did not exist in America, because the American Constitution embodied both beginning and principle. It was, in Arendt's mind, meant to be a perpetual engine of newness: it was, in her words, both *constitutio libertatis* (the foundation of freedom) and *novus ordo saeclorum* (a new order). The American Constitution was preserved from arbitrariness. The men who made it had a heightened sense of the necessary distinction between reflection and choice, which they achieved through common deliberation and the exercise of power dictated by chance and force. Social and economic questions, scientific and technological expertise, she argued, were not properly political questions. Such concerns and such knowledge must not be permitted to intrude in the political realm, where decisions had to be made in favor of the common interest and against particular interests. She endowed the makers of the Constitution with heroic intellectual prowess and political genius, and resigned herself to the decline of politics, as if the legacy of post-Federalist politics in the last two centuries had nothing to do with how the Constitution makers achieved their miracle.

While hardly building his arguments on Tocqueville's reservations about the reasoning powers and wisdom of the broad masses, Bruce Ackerman notes that "We the people" are for the most part:

> absent from the scene, and . . . there can be no hope of capturing, in some simple snapshot, what the citizenry thinks about an issue. Nobody can plausibly predict what the People would say if they devoted a lot of time and energy to scrutinizing their received opinions in the process of hammering out a new collective judgment about the 'rights of citizens and the permanent interest of the community.' Normally the People just aren't spending the time and energy; and we had better design our normal lawmaking system with this in mind.[41]

This call has something of the ring of Tocqueville's ironic but ambiguous distinction between great and small political parties, which recognizes in the first a vast and principled endeavor to deal with revolutionary situations, as in the debates on the provisions of the American

---

[40] Ibid., pp. 161–63.
[41] Bruce Ackerman, *We the People. Foundations* (Cambridge, Mass. and London: The Belknap Press of Harvard University Press, 1991), p. 242.

Constitution, and, in the second, the plodding work of parties obsessed
with immediate, particular, and selfish interests: "Society is convulsed by
great parties, it is only agitated by minor ones; it is torn by the former,
by the latter it is degraded; and if the first sometimes saves it by salutary
perturbation, the last invariably disturb it to no good end" (I, chap. 10,
182).[42] As one of the central points of his thesis of extraordinary
and ordinary moments in American history, Ackerman argues that
Americans live for the most part in a political atmosphere that does not
call upon their ongoing participation. They have better things to do,
and hardly question what government bodies at all levels normally do.
In times of crisis, however, a political transformation occurs. Revolutionary reformers – Ackerman's conjunction – initiate a movement away
from the normal course of politics and bring about profound changes in
the Constitution and the national substance. They are active in the public
interest and create an organizational presence in the public consciousness and legislative scene to rise above narrow concerns. They work their
wonder through a varied group of political and non-political bodies, and
crucially through elections, and the various levels of government – the
Supreme Court, as well as the President and Congress – to set in place
the authority of the popular will. Their acts "engage the prophetic voice"
and constitute a "spiritual renewal."[43] The useful fiction of the sacred is
rekindled in these words. About these crises in America, Ackerman
writes that "Only after the reformers carry their initiative repeatedly in
deliberative assemblies and popular elections has our constitution finally
awarded them the solid authority to revise the foundations of our polity
in the name of We the People."[44] A "bandwagon effect" comes into play,
by which the revolutionary reformers gain more and more solid support.
Their revisionary plans constitute the achievement of a higher consensus
hitherto lacking in the course of normal politics. The people have, he
asserts, little to do with the creative moves for change, even when, as he
expects, they will once again, as at the time of the Constitutional Convention and the Depression crisis of the New Deal, no longer consign to
a distant part of their consciousness matters that demand urgent attention, but instead bring them forward in a burst of active citizenship and
assert the virtues of democratic authority. The model for future ruptures

[42] Ackerman alludes to this passage in ibid., p. 354 note 26 to substantiate his theory of
the dynamic of normal politics.
[43] Bruce Ackerman, *We the People. Transformations* (Cambridge, Mass. and London: The
Belknap Press of Harvard University Press, 1998), p. 4.
[44] Ibid.

in the constitutional and political institutions are the Federalists' understanding of popular participation and ratification: *"legitimation through
a deepening institutional dialogue* between *political elites and ordinary
citizens."*[45]

Appeals for spiritual renewal and to the prophetic voice are made by
writers with very different political beliefs. Robert Fogel declares himself
to be the "secular child" of what he calls the "Third Great Awakening"
– "Awakenings" are yet another way of defining critical points in
America's history – which lasted from 1930 to 1970, when big business
was reigned in, and union, civil, and women's rights were expanded. He
seeks, in a Fourth Great Awakening, to link prospects for greater egalitarianism with an adoption of the main planks of the Christian Coalition. Americans, including Afro-Americans, will come to recognize that
its programs to reinforce family values and rescue alienated young people
from the ravages of drugs and crime will bring them greater self-
realization, a heightened sense of opportunity, and give more meaning
to their lives. A respiritualization of American life is expected to enhance
equality: "spiritual equity" will act to supplement the Third Great
Awakening's concentration on achieving greater economic equality.[46]
In view is a new alignment of politics comparable to the post-Civil War
formation of the Republican Party.[47]

The rhetoric of expectation is to be found on the other side of the
spectrum as well, as may be seen in Antonio Negri's vision of the future
of democracy. It brings him closer to Tocqueville, Arendt, and Ackerman
than to Fogel, but his anarchist thrust is not only opposed to theirs but
also to Marxism, which he claims he is reviving to answer to this era's
conditions. Constituent power resides in the people, and for that reason
is a living thing, always present, always threatening to reassert itself.
"[D]emocracy, a real democracy of right and appropriation, equal distribution of wealth, and equal participation in production" is what the
"multitude" strives for. "[T]he republican genius will never succeed in
subduing democracy." The people are only apparently absent from the
republic, another instance of the liberal failure to acknowledge their

[45] Ibid., p. 85. Italics in original. A few pages later (p. 87), we find the words, "I hardly
wish to deny that the Federalists fell far short of the ideal of popular sovereignty, even
as it was understood in the eighteenth century. When judged in modern terms, the
Founding looks even worse."
[46] Robert W. Fogel, *The Fourth Great Awakening and the Future of Egalitarianism*
(Chicago and London: University of Chicago Press, 2000), pp. 14, 28, 176–81.
[47] Ibid., pp. 26–27.

strength, which it confuses with absolute unity. The confusion, for example, led to the transformation by the French revolutionaries of Rousseau's abstract and enigmatic general will into the will of the nation, which, again, is not to be identified with democracy. And Negri believes that another distinction is necessary – the distinction between the *potentia* (power) of the multitude and the *potestas* (Power) of the state. The first is to be found in the "many that is, in the strength of singularities and differences."[48] It (*potentia*) constitutes democracy. Forever inhabiting power, it forever challenges constituted power. Constituent power (remember Arendt's borrowing of the concept from Sièyes, which Negri acknowledges) is by definition foundational. Constituted power is, on the contrary, not, and therefore cannot be considered legitimate. Legitimacy resides only in the power of the multitude, the people. We may see the corner into which his logic, overcoming the reality of experience, drives him. He reluctantly concedes the serious existence of the dilemma. "[M]any have tried but few have had any success in attempting to ground democracy absolutely on these principles," principles of the "absolute equality of rights and duties, and on the effectiveness of rights."[49] The solution lies in a new theory, a theory that conceptualizes constituent power as crisis,[50] transforming it presumably from an inert to a living state, from a non-revolutionary to a revolutionary situation, the exact thing that Tocqueville said was not only undesirable, but unlikely because in America "to live at variance with the multitude is, as it were, not to live. The multitude requires no laws to coerce those who do not think like themselves: public disapprobation is enough; a sense of their loneliness and impotence overtakes them and drives them to despair" (II, Bk. 3, chap. 21, 275). The people do not want violent change, and guard against it by seeking to be like everyone. Negri does not see equality as leading to a flattening out of differences; he sees it as an ideal that would recognize and nurture them. So for him, Tocqueville's termination of revolution is a "tragic nonsense," resulting in a final blow to democratization. Americans had their beginning once upon a time. They are not destined, in Tocqueville's theory, to have another, if beginnings mean radical and violent political change, the only meaning Negri is eager to assert.[51] The

---

[48] Antonio Negri, *Insurgencies. Constitutional Power and the Modern State*, trans. Maurizia Boscagli (Minneapolis and London: University of Minnesota Press, 1999). Citations in the text are from pp. 305, 155, 166, 201–03, 307.

[49] Michael Hardt and Antonio Negri, *Labor of Dionysus. A Critique of the State-Form* (Minneapolis and London: University of Minnesota Press, 1991), pp. 283, 310.

[50] Antonio Negri, *Insurgencies*, p. 318.   [51] Ibid., pp. 180, 246.

liberal/democratic split is summed up in these two concepts of constituting and constituted power, both admitting the distinction between
the two kinds of power. Tocqueville sees only a limited theoretical and
political advantage in posing a permanent dichotomy between the two,
while Negri welcomes the dichotomy as the only way to test and expand
democracy.

Democratization is not, Cornelius Castoriadis declares, the achievement of the reign of law or of right or of equality, but rather the questioning of the law by and through the community, an inherently political
act that signifies the liberty of a historically rooted society to shape itself.
This is its "instituting" power, but it is not, he warned, to be confused
with the delusion that there is a real constituting power. It is entirely
imaginary.[52] As if giving new voice to both Tocqueville and Schmitt, we
are told that:

> The sole genuine limitation that democracy can bear is self-limitation, which
> in the last analysis can only be the task and the work of individuals (and of
> citizens) educated through and for democracy. Such an education is impossible
> without acceptance of the fact that the institutions we give ourselves are neither
> absolutely necessary nor totally contingent. This signifies that no meaning is
> given to us as a gift, any more than there is any guarantor or guarantee of
> meaning; it signifies that there is no other meaning than the one we create in and
> through history. And this amounts to saying that democracy, like philosophy,
> necessarily sets aside the sacred. In still other terms, democracy requires that
> human beings accept in their actual behavior what until now they almost have
> never truly wanted to accept, namely, that they are mortal. It is only starting
> from this unsurpassable – and almost impossible – conviction of the mortality
> of each one of us and of all that we do, that people can live as autonomous
> beings, see in others autonomous beings, and render possible an autonomous
> society.[53]

Not surprisingly, Antonio Negri seeks to expose even more radically
the flaws in such categories as the welfare state, the institutions of representative liberal democracy, and the perilous condition of society itself.
His critique of the limits that the post-modern state has imposed on civil
society has, in his words, subsumed it to the point that neither the first
nor the second can find its bearings. As he describes it, the post-modern

---

[52] Cornelius Castoriadis, "Power, Politics, Autonomy," in *Cultural-Political Interventions
in the Unfinished Project of the Enlightenment*, eds. Axel Honneth et al. (Boston: MIT
Press, 1992), 288, 292.
[53] Cited by David A. Curtis, "Cornelius Castoriadis: An Obituary," *Salmagundi*, (Spring-
Summer 1998), nos. 118–19, 60.

state is "paroxysmal," ostensibly acting on behalf of society, but actually separating itself from it:

In effect, the very figure of the law is being modified, as the supremacy of the executive and administrative procedure is imposed on the guarantist, general, and abstract definition of the norm. From two different perspectives we can see how the action of parliaments is limited while the action of executive organisms is expanded. First, we can note the dependence or subordination of representative decision making with respect to political, economic, and military powers. The new rules dictated by technocratic authorities and the police force of the new world order dominate the internal workings of the communitary groups. Second, governmental systems are increasingly open to administrative and executive intervention of specific issues and in particular cases, marginalizing the production of abstract and general norms. The organs of popular representation are thus continually more restricted and subordinated by two increasing pressures: one that comes from outside, from the new world order, and another that comes from inside, from the administrative demands. In the case of the United States, of course, the two coincide.[54]

Never before, Negri asserts again and again, has there been such a total rupture between state and society. Never before has there been such dissimulation to disguise this fact. Never before has civil society been so weak and unable to respond. Whereas during the heyday of the welfare state the state was forced to recognize organized collective interests, some of which were opposed to it, such a dialectic no longer exists. And it no longer exists, because "the parasitic organization of capitalism [is] no longer able to organize labor, [is] no longer able to engage and discipline labor through the institutions of civil society."[55] Negri proposes an alternative to the dialectic, one that would open a fresh political methodology, one that, he says, shares with liberal political theory the belief in the will of citizens to explore alternative ends.[56] Beyond their doubts about the future of contemporary politics, liberal theory and Negri's utopianism with its faith in a kind of redemptive anarchism fail to meet. The notion that a renewed natural law would somehow revitalize civil society is a chimera, because for him civil society no longer exists. "Neither Madisonian pluralism nor even Jeffersonian populism have (sic) ever succeeded in proposing an effective resistance to Hamiltonian centralism."[57] Negri's apocalyptic appeal to the raw power of the multitude places him in a theoretical place all his own, despite his grudging admiration for Tocqueville and Arendt.

---

[54] Michael Hardt and Antonio Negri, *Labor of Dionysus*, pp. 297–98. The term paroxysmal appears on p. 295.
[55] Ibid., p. 282.   [56] Ibid., p. 285.   [57] Ibid., p. 306.

The refusal to be counted in the conservative, liberal, let alone radical camp, marks Harvey Mansfield's efforts to find in the Constitution the fountainhead and mainstay of America's peculiar democracy. As if in passing, he refers to the question of authority in terms reminiscent of Arendt, noting that the Constitution's call on Americans is a call from a human, not a divine, authority, but then he proceeds to argue a more practical point as he sees it, but not before pausing to support Madison's in *Federalist* 49 that government, originating in the people, cannot recur to them; and similarly that, because the Constitution originates with the people, its authority must be elevated above them if it is to retain its authority over them and elicit "reverence" and "veneration" from them (a point on which we paused in Chapter 2). The alternative is a release of popular passion, which only a properly constituted government can control, an absolute requirement if order is to be maintained, and, in the absence of which, authority and power would be returned to the people again, just the kind of reversion to the constituent power that Negri regards with such abandon. Mansfield's thesis rests as well on Hamilton's *Federalist* 78, which we discussed earlier, and contemplates with misgivings any arguments that would restore authority directly to the people. Between the people and the implementation of their will there must always be a supervening power with the obligation and responsibility of understanding their intentions in difficult constitutional matters, just as Hamilton said, and, in such a manner that will soften partisan quarrels.[58] But what happens when judicial review, instead of ending them, contributes to them by a majority decision that is itself heavily impassioned? Judicial review, of course, allows for different arguments and split decisions, and the majority rules there as it does in settling elections. That is not an issue. However, if we keep in mind Hamilton's position, that "the Constitution ought to be preferred to the statutes, the intention of the people to the intention of their agents," and that the courts are instituted to "ascertain its [the Constitution's] meaning" (*Federalist* 78), the challenge is to produce a decision that will satisfy people that their intentions have been accurately discerned. When such a situation does arise, as in the instance of the contested presidential election of 2000, the majority on the United States Supreme Court demonstrated extraordinary shortsightedness. Its 5 to 4 decision on December 12, 2000, to question and overthrow the Florida Supreme Court's decision on electoral procedures on grounds that it unconstitutionally

---

[58] Harvey C. Mansfield, Jr., *America's Constitutional Soul*, pp. 179–82.

changed the Florida Legislature's electoral laws raises the authority of judicial review once again, but perhaps never more acutely, especially when the majority's argument focused on the difficulty of establishing the intentions of voters. Members of the minority dissented, declaring that the majority's decision put a stop to the procedures that might indeed have ascertained the people's will.[59]

A more acceptable decision might stress Hamilton's distinction between intention and will – the first being more settled, the second momentary. By focusing on the first, the notion that the rule of law was being upheld might have a more solid footing. The issue is delicate and critical. Arguments are made that the Court must be above the fray. It has been attacked throughout its history for being in it, while many have advanced views about how it might reaffirm (or affirm) its authority. Hamilton conceded that there would be times when the people acted to change the Constitution, and immediately added that the judiciary, which had the duty and right to intervene bravely and decisively, had to face the difficulty of reading the authoritative voice in a republican democracy:

> [u]ntil the people have, by some solemn and authoritative act, annulled or changed the established form, it is binding upon themselves collectively as well as individually; and no presumption, or even knowledge, of their sentiments, can warrant their representatives in a departure from it, prior to such an act. But it

---

[59] From the Supreme Court of the United States: George W. Bush et al., Petitioners v. Albert Gore, Jr., et al. On writ of certiorari to the Florida Supreme Court (December 12, 2000). Per Curiam: J. Stevens, dissenting: "What must underlie petitioners' entire federal assault on the Florida election procedures is an unstated lack of confidence in the impartiality and capacity of the state judges who would make the critical decisions if the vote count were to proceed. Otherwise, their position is entirely without merit. The endorsement of that position by the majority of this Court can only lend credence to the most cynical appraisal of the work of judges throughout the land. It is confidence in the men and women who administer the judicial system that is the true backbone of the rule of law. Time will one day heal the wound to that confidence that will be inflicted by today's decision. One thing, however, is certain. Although we may never know with complete certainty the identity of the winner of this year's presidential election, the identity of the loser is perfectly clear. It is the Nation's confidence in the judge as an impartial guardian of the rule of law." J. Ginsburg, also dissenting: "[T]he court's reluctance to let the recount go forward, despite its suggestion that [t]he search for intent can be confined by specific rules designed to ensure uniform treatment . . . ultimately turns on its own judgment about the practical realities of implementing a recount, not the judgment of those much closer to the process. . . . In sum, the Court's conclusion that a constitutionally adequate recount is impractical is a prophecy the Court's own judgment will not allow to be tested. Such an untested prophecy should not decide the Presidency of the United States."

is easy to see, that it would require an uncommon portion of fortitude in the judges to do their duty as faithful guardians of the Constitution, where legislative invasions of it had been instigated by the major voice of the community.[60]

The menace of pure majoritarianism may be seen as a permanent feature of the debate, one that lasts to this day. Perhaps, at this point, we might recall, first, Tocqueville's belief that the democratic will cannot in the long run err, and second, his mixed message that Americans, during elections of all kinds, do not strain their differences and those of the parties to whom they give their allegiance to the breaking point. So far there was no danger that this might happen, but "[s]till the epoch of the election of the President of the United States may be considered as a crisis in the affairs of the nation" (I, chap. 8, 140). The warning expressed the fear that the full fabric of the constituted power might be ripped apart.[61]

Once again, Rousseau, who is too easily dismissed, is the figure who will not silently slip away. In the first place, he held as sacred "the simple right of voting in every act of sovereignty – a right which nothing can take away from the citizens – and on that of speaking, proposing, dividing, and discussing, which the government is always very careful to leave to its members only . . ."[62] Notwithstanding the difficulty moderns have with his Spartan demand that only virtuous citizens could be counted members of a real community, he lurks in the shadows, stubbornly clinging to the notion that democratic sovereignty, in its total embraciveness, serves to obscure the presence of the people, and that when the people are absent, they still manage to make themselves felt. When, and as this happens, the problem of who is equal and free emerges in all its political complexity. Two observations flow from this insight, both of which are implied in Mansfield's argument that being free and equal does not constitute the central issue of democracy. First, he attacks both populists and intellectuals for sharing, he thinks naively and disingenuously, an uncommon belief in a simple equality. "So," he says, "we suppose that pluralism is the consequence of indulging equal rights rather than a forthright admission of the inevitability of inequality."[63] One need not, however, pace Mansfield, support the notion, first, of a totally socially

---

[60] *Federalist* No. 78, p. 509.
[61] Jürgen Habermas, *The Inclusion of the Other*, p. 249, considers elections, on what he defines as the liberal view, meeting "the function of *legitimating* the exercise of political power, and on what he defines on the republican side, as a "function of *constituting* society as a political community and keeps this founding act alive." Emphasis is his.
[62] Rousseau, *Social Contract*, Bk. 4, chap. 1.
[63] Harvey C. Mansfield, *America's Constitutional Soul*, p. 11.

constructed self, or a second notion that equality of opportunity is an absolute assurance against inequality to claim that democracy means in some true sense striving for greater equality, and that such an endeavor does not lead inexorably to the rule of an unthinking majority cajoled into submission by government. Second, he welcomes the absence of the people. In a constitutional democracy:

> the essential character of the Constitution is that, whereas all its parts are *derived* from the people, none of them is the people. Indeed, the people that ratified the Constitution in 1787–88, the sovereign people, has disappeared from view except for an occasional appearance to make an amendment (which is not a fully sovereign act because amendments are made under the procedures of the Constitution). The sovereign people has been replaced by the constitutional people, the highest authority to be sure, but highest *under the Constitution*.[64]

In deference to the Federalists and to Tocqueville, Mansfield asks us to recognize that when the institutions of constitutional government, by being separate from the people, oblige government to control itself, government may be enabled to control the people, appealing to their reason against their tempestuous will. In his judgment, finally, the Constitution *"consitutionalize[s] necessities,"* the necessities of diverse human beings, their interests and ambitions, living in a large territory. The plea he makes is for popular self-restraint to moderate individualism, and for an end to what is viewed as democracy's craving for state intervention, the desire to see government do for people what they should be choosing and doing for themselves.

The distance between the making of the laws and agreeing to be obedient to them has lengthened, the ties that bind people in democracies to the laws and to one another have been loosened, and whatever responsibility and judgment citizens once believed they had for helping make them has been diminished. If the bands of obligation are not tightened, and the judgment that citizens have to exert their will through the political institutions they have available is not exercised, there are those ready to do so to the disadvantage of democracy. They seek to pass off their authoritarian agenda as legitimate authority. They are the Americans who say that they are among the select few with the qualifications to appreciate the authentic voice of political philosophy. They represent the oligarchic, not the republican, mode of thought. Playing to the crowd's fears, they inflate the following of populist leaders

---

[64] Ibid., p. 210.

who have a stake in religious and other kinds of fundamentalism.[65] There is no certainty or guarantee that Americans will not mistake authoritarianism for authority, nor that they will be able to escape the confusion that will follow, nor that they will avoid making and justifying nondemocratic decisions.

[65] For a guide to and critique of authoritarianism in America, see Shadia B. Drury, *Leo Strauss and the American Right* (New York: St. Martin's Press, 1997).

10

Conclusion

Throughout this book, I have tried to find the right distance between our own time and Tocqueville's to reach a proper reckoning of the intellectual power of his theory and the accuracy of his observations. And, as I suggested at the beginning, democracy and modernity came to be uniquely identified with one another in America. Modernity embraces more than the forces of the capitalist market place. It rests on a scientific and technological edifice kept in place by bureaucracies of experts, in both government and in private corporations, who are dependent on networks of information and communication for even the simplest of exchanges. The broad and specific features of that edifice were in an infant stage in Tocqueville's time.

The economics of capitalism was, if not fully developed in Tocqueville's work, not an unimportant part of it. The close connection that he saw between individualism, self-interest, the hunger for material success, and the power of the state, on the one hand, and the combined forces of commerce and the expanding frontier that opened up opportunities and concentrated energies in unprecedented ways, on the other, did not yield a full-bodied critique of capitalism. He did not offer a systematic analysis capable of grasping its strong and fragile points. He had no broad economic vision of what was taking place and what might happen as it made its advance in the Western world. He did, however, capture American fascination with practical science and technology that remains perhaps one of America's enduring fantasies. But theoretically more important than either the mechanisms of the market or the power of science or the processes of technology were the psychic, moral, and political consequences of the pursuit and acquisition of wealth. The pursuit of wealth – the materialization of mind, as he put it – exposed the shortcomings and the saving graces of American democracy. Because the equality of conditions propelled people into industry and commerce to improve their well-being, democracy itself was as much the source of the commercialization of society as it was its result. It accounted for American ingenuity in the market. Great moneyed classes, of course, helped to found some of the elements of a new caste society. Yet, nearly as significant was the volatility, not the permanence, of money, encouraging the hope among large sections of the people that wealth was not out of their reach. The easy slide into and out of money in turn became the great democratizer. Thus the wealthy did not constitute a distinct class. If wealth was in fact the great divider, it was not perceived in the United States as the foundation of a permanent structure of inequality.

Tocqueville did not dwell on equal opportunity when he described America's equality of conditions, but he implied that it did in fact exist because of the great mobility of wealth. At the same time, the booms and busts of early industrial capitalism already had the effect of wreaking financial collapse, which he, as an investor in America's railways, nervously watched in 1857, a year of financial collapse. Economic equality was, however, not a goal to be realistically pursued: The iron laws of political economy dictated wage and employment levels. The educated and the property-owning had a greater right and responsibility to determine the contents and limits of public debate. At the same time, citizens, who valued excellence and merit, apart from wealth, had fewer resources available to them to challenge the majority. In reality, the possession of all three was hard to separate in America, so quickly had the identification of the three become part of the prevailing ethos. But it was not without its profound ambiguities. Such economic and social divisions were considered natural, and all of society, moreover, benefited when the educated and the propertied shared the available positions of power among themselves. Just as well in a society that in its irrepressible democratization through franchise extension, tried to assert itself against its leading citizens.[1] Moreover, there had been no opposition from the "higher orders" who were moved by fear, but also by a greater fear that they would lose the goodwill of the lower (I, chap. 58–59). Materialism

---

[1] "De l'Egalité en Amérique," in Alexis de Tocqueville, *Oeuvres*, ed. André Jardin with the collaboration of Françoise Mélonio and Lise Queffélec, 2 vols. (Paris: Gallimard, 1991), I, 276.

could in fact not be halted; its worst effects could be only mitigated. More important was the state's power. In the new economic conditions, it would dominate people's lives by taking over and commanding society's economic resources, the resources that filled lives with endless and not wholly imaginary abundance: "Governments . . . appropriate to themselves and convert to their own purposes the greater part of this new power which manufacturing interests have in our time brought into the world. Manufactures govern us, they govern manufactures" (II, Bk. 4, chap. 5, 331). Thus, Tocqueville's description of the double hook. Material goods lulled people into complaisance, and before they knew it, the state stepped in to reinforce these irresistible desires, and the rigors of public life, in which they might test and strengthen their liberty, faded from view. The egregious individualism that produced desire challenged the democratic foundations of citizenship. It must, he said, be stoked up.

The bloated state is one of the great American fears, so much so, that it has become a cherished shibboleth. The concept of an empty state, responding to the impersonal forces of the economy and technology, is in one respect the inflated state's power opposite, and in another a close twin. In the first version, government is a passive recipient. In that version, government is given the role of a business or management agent for corporate international capital. It tries to conceal its powerlessness, but then, in its inflated version, it paradoxically and enigmatically establishes its authority, or more accurately, re-establishes it by answering to the impersonal forces of the economy and technology. Even if the paradox does not hold, the two versions of the state's role may have the same consequences, or, as Tocqueville was fond of saying in other instances, amount to the same thing: However you look at the source of its power the state, autonomous or dependent, is a force in modern life that places it far beyond the centralizers of the pre-industrial and industrial periods.[2] Plainly, a reductive theory of how economic power and political authority are wielded fails to do justice to the entanglement of political and economic forces. Yet the almost overwhelming tendency to stretch such an explanatory point, especially by attributing either to the economic or political sphere a dominant role, is based on a circular argument that gives power exclusively to the first or to the second. One way

[2] See Jacques Rancière, *Disagreement. Politics and Philosophy*, trans. Julie Rose (Minneapolis: University of Minnesota Press, 1999), p. 113-14, for the notion of the state as manager of the Gross National Product.

to assess how the changes in economic and political life affect people is to conclude that they recognize and appear to accept the changed nature of the political process, one in which politicians, while claiming to exercise power as in the past, have in fact seen it pass from their hands to others, and more often than not play a dumb or passive role. The other is to conclude just the opposite: Government and politicians have the decisive voice, and their power must be severely curtailed. From these opposed starting posts, the public occasionally glimpses some of the processes by means of which economic and political power has been transferred. It takes on the role of spectator, and willingly relinquishes whatever roles it once had in the political process. Its passivity in the face of, and growing disregard of, the new realities may be seen at some level as a protest against its own powerlessness.

This is not quite the same reaction that Tocqueville had in mind when he spoke of the numbing effects that excessive concern for money had upon public life. Further changes had to take place, not only in the politics and institutions of American life, but in their more subterranean regions. Max Weber's travels in America in 1904 took him to many of the same places Tocqueville visited in a land that was still in many parts in wilderness, but which now exhibited even more dramatically the restlessness of spirit and enterprise that had so impressed the earlier traveler. He approached the question of power in modern democracy from the perspectives of legitimacy, rationality, and above all, the bureaucratic forms of a capitalist industrial society. His categories replaced the categories of centralization and democratic despotism that Tocqueville developed as the salient features of modern society. His language fitted more closely and clearly the forces of modern society, which had not only to be reckoned with, but demanded fresh conceptualization. For Weber, then, Tocqueville's fears of a listless and complacent democracy of equals were still pressing, but in a different way. The electoral mechanisms, which Tocqueville had lightly touched, were hardly the place to look for the symbols of thoughtful citizenship. They had in fact become a cynical arena in which party bosses superbly managed the electorate, even tolerating candidates who were ready to stand against electoral and other kinds of corruption as long as it did not disturb their hegemony.

"When American workers were asked," Weber wrote, after World War I, why they allowed themselves to be governed by politicians whom they admitted they despised, the answer was, "We prefer having people in office whom we can spit upon, rather than a caste of officials who spit upon us, as is the case with you."[3] The illustration is a wonderful evocation of the same contempt for caste and class that Tocqueville had witnessed. While the hardy disdain had not disappeared, Weber saw something new. Tammany Hall politics was a relic of past political behavior in which personalities still counted, but the balance of power between political parties and a highly organized professional bureaucracy remained unstable and was yet to be determined. What was urgent in this new constellation was how the exercise of power would gain legitimacy – by what means, in other words, democracy and bureaucracy could each be seen as occupying legitimate grounds. But while he saw the urgency, he was not optimistic. Inequality would grow, while the bureaucratic model of public control and market forces would dominate society. A new servitude was in the making. Tocqueville had already seen it pretty clearly, but it had not yet reached the mature levels that became evident by the early twentieth century. Whereas he maintained that the tyranny of a democratic despotism and centralized government could emerge from an avowed or unconscious complicit pact between individuals, and between individuals and the state – thus giving greater weight to politics than economics – Weber, who also saw the emergence of such a docile population, gave stronger emphasis to the linkages between the market, "the governmentalization of economic activities," and the inevitable emergence of a new mandarinate, a new caste, a new aristocracy. Against its power, freedom and democracy were helpless in the deep sense that both were the products of specifically unique historical forces, and would not likely survive in their older forms. What was happening now was irreversible. But though Weber lived in a time of triumphant bureaucratic capitalism, he also appealed to the human will to intervene and, if not to stop the process, to take an active part in shaping it to human needs, not excluding the needs of the spirit. This appeal was a shot in the dark, if we also recall that Weber doubted whether American political institutions and practices promised either the best road to democracy or to enlightened government.[4]

Ever the seeker of the means to keep the spirit alive, John Dewey, for a time a contemporary of Weber, but longer-lived, spoke toward the end of his life of the "imagination [as] the chief instrument of the good . . .

---

[3] "Politics as a Vocation," in *From Max Weber*, eds. H. H. Gerth and C. Wright Mills (New York: Oxford University Press, 1958), pp. 110–11.

[4] John P. Diggins, *Max Weber. Politics and the Spirit of Tragedy* (New York: Basic Books, 1996), pp. 207–12.

art is more moral than moralities. For the latter either are, or tend to become consecrations of the status quo ... The moral prophets of humanity have always been poets even though they spoke in free verse or by parable."[5] The idea that art could take the place of Christianity for moderns may in fact have also been what Dewey meant.[6] This is close to Tocqueville's prediction that future democratic poets were likely to speak for humanity's religious aspirations and longings, and indeed become the moralists of the modern age. In his respect for a foundationalist morality, he would not have agreed with the more confident pragmatist. His belief in the contingencies of life in an uncertain universe deeply colored his view of human nature and its capacity, not only for error, but for wrongdoing. "Man," Tocqueville said:

> with his vices, weaknesses, that muddled mixture of good and bad, low and high, honesty and depravity, is still, on the whole the worthiest object of examination, interest, compassion, affection, and admiration to be found on earth, and since angels are missing [from the world we inhabit], we can attach ourselves to nothing that is greater and worthier of our attention than our fellow beings.[7]

And, again:

> God has permitted us to distinguish between [good and evil] and given us the liberty of choosing; but beyond these clear notions, everything that moves beyond the boundaries of this world seems to me to be shrouded in overpowering darkness.[8]

In their thoughts on human destiny, however, concern shown by both Tocqueville and Dewey for freedom shines out, even if the light it throws is feeble. Earlier in his life, Dewey spoke of the fruitful and necessary links between freedom and equality:

> Liberty is that secure release and fulfillment of personal potentialities which takes place only in rich and manifold association with others ... Equality denotes the unhampered share which each individual member of the community has in the consequences of associated action. ... It denotes effective regard for what is

[5] John Dewey, *Art as Experience* (New York: Capricorn Books, 1957), p. 348. Cited in Richard Rorty, *Contingency, Irony, and Solidarity* (Cambridge: Cambridge University Press, 1989), p. 69.
[6] Alan Ryan, *John Dewey and the High Tide of American Liberalism* (W. W. Norton: New York, 1995), p. 265.
[7] Tocqueville to Eugène Stoffels, January 3, 1843, *Oeuvres complètes de Tocqueville*, ed. Gustave de Beaumont, 9 vols. (Paris: Michel Lévy frères, 1864–66), 5, 447–48.
[8] Tocqueville to Mme. Swetchine, February 26, 1857, OC 15 (*Correspondance d'Alexis de Tocqueville et de Madame Swetchine*) part 2, 315.

distinctive and unique in each, irrespective of physical and psychological inequalities. It is not a natural possession but is a fruit of the community when its action
is directed by its character as a community.[9]

Dewey went a step further. He asserted that every individual has "the
intelligence, under the operation of self-interest, to engage in public
affairs."[10] He did not, however, entirely trust the inner self. By seeking
security from the opinion of others, the inner self unintentionally and
sadly jeopardized his own individuality and freedom. Nevertheless, like
Tocqueville, he retained the conviction that individual freedom remained
the central question for the modern self and still lay on the drawing
boards for the foreseeable future. Dewey did not neglect to address the
assault of technology on traditional values, and placed his hope on a
critical interaction between the politician and the expert – the problem
addressed by Weber – a process that would incorporate the citizen body's
input through democratic public discussion.

About such speculations, Jürgen Habermas remains of two minds.
Like all heirs of the Enlightenment, even if they agonize over its ultimate
consequences, he sees the value of freedom as freedom from external
constraints, which is the prerequisite of autonomy and legitimacy in a
democratic society. But the loci of power – if they had not entirely shifted
from the nation-state, as the major determinant in making decisions, to
other constituted bodies – have become so complexly interwoven with
the dynamics of advanced capitalism, technology, and expertise that the
citizen has become effectively marginalized. Elections have become pro
forma acts, registering only a plebiscitary function, testifying not least to
the immense power of bureaucratic control – a process Habermas calls
the scientization of politics.[11]

In itself this need not be fatally determining, if there is a way of ensuring that the political will is enlightened. But is this a likely outcome
of a historical process that has witnessed the depoliticization of the
population effectively confined to a public space in which theater and
acclamation have become a substitute for public discussion. The
alternative to what Habermas calls "domination-free communication,"
– communication that is not entirely mediated – is, he says, "a self-
controlled learning process." How does this translate into practice? What

[9] John Dewey, *The Public and its Problems* (New York: Swallow, 1927), pp. 150–51.
[10] Ibid., p. 157.
[11] Jürgen Habermas, *Toward a Rational Society* (Boston: Beacon Press, 1970), especially
chap. 5: "The Scientization of Politics and Public Opinion."

instruments do modern Americans have to achieve such a goal in a world that, as he describes it, has its politics of theater, its bureaucracies, and its system of rationality? His response is that democracy has not reached a point of stasis. It is something more than theater, a place of mime in which everyone plays a part and can know no other part to play. The hope of an unobstructed public sphere is not entirely utopian if two conditions can be met. First, the ability of opinion-forming associations (unions and revitalized political parties, for example) to change values, and, second, the cultivation of "a liberal-egalitarian political culture . . . to [deal with] problems affecting society as a whole."[12] If they are to be full citizens, persons will have to ask themselves if they are willing to accept the burden of their own authority, or, as Habermas states, with his characteristic faith in virtue, to stretch their capacity to "achieve autonomy only by both understanding themselves as, and acting as, *authors* (my emphasis) of the rights they submit to." He expands Tocqueville's distinction between political and human rights, but at the same time he demands much more. Habermas's own criteria for a democratic citizenry as an "association of consociates under law," who participate in opinion- and will-making, and, not least, possess the social, technological, and ecological resources to make use of basic rights, do not add up to a likely scenario. "The prior convergence of settled ethical convictions," he contends, is not the best source of political legitimacy. Rather it is to be found when two tests are met. The first is the safeguarding of the resources that would make equality real within nations, regions, and communities where debates are conducted on how to treat one another and how to treat minorities and marginal groups. The second is to recognize that the founding of norms is an issue of justice, "subject to principles that state what is equally good for all," and that these norms must be "compatible with moral standards that claim universal validity beyond the legal community."[13] These dicta are delivered as ineffable principles, but they trip off the tongue a little too easily.

Are an egalitarian mass culture and the banalization of everyday affairs an effective weapon against class pretensions and sophisticated

---

[12] The consecutive quotes come from "Legitimationsprobleme in modernen Staat," in *Zur Rekonstruktion des Historischen Materialismus* (Frankfurt: Suhrkamp, 1976), p. 279; *Between Facts and Norms. Contributions to a Discourse Theory of Law and Democracy*, trans. William Rehg (Cambridge, Mass.: MIT Press, 1996), pp. 488, 490.

[13] Jürgen Habermas, *Between Facts and Norms*, The quoted passages in the order in which they appear in the text are from pp. 126, 123, 122, 278, 282.

information technology? It is through its channels that, for instance, Foucault's theory of the close fit between power and knowledge is relayed. How is a creative response to these altered facts of political life to be nurtured? In Tocqueville's opinion, the science and art of politics was crucial, but it could only be properly cultivated if it were studied with its practical, not its theoretical, features in mind (which recalls Aristotle's *phronēsis* – the quality possessed by individuals who show wisdom in practical matters). Daily solutions had constantly to be worked on to preserve a workable authority of equals with their individual wills and choices remaining intact. The challenge since those relatively innocent days has been pushed a multitude of notches up. Taking a less forgiving and harder line, Foucault will be remembered for arguing that power is acceptable only when a substantial part of itself is disguised; it can hardly work openly and ironically. It is inseparable from juridical systems introduced and refined at different points of history, first, as monarchical sovereignty, and, second, when, under the mantle of democratic sovereignty, the supremacy of a public collective right is enunciated.[14] Foucault asks us to disabuse ourselves of any ideal notion of a democratic civil society: There is no such thing as a power-free civil society, and there never will be one.

The inertias and inequalities of modernity are, as we saw, a permanent source, doubtless a growing one, of resistance to many notions of democracy, perhaps even more so than the obdurate voices of tradition that sometimes find refuge in a conservative form of communitarianism. Some theorists of civil society tend to surround it with an aura of virtue and innocence. They view its constituent parts as miniature democracies. We should be mindful of the point that Tocqueville made when he spoke of civic and political associations, assigning to the latter the key role in keeping democracy alive. By sharp contrast, these theorists are not able to find a place for those in civil society who are neither at the top nor the middle nor among the lower classes (the latter term now safely expunged from the political vocabulary), but at the very bottom. There, indeed, equality is not even considered for peoples who are regarded as having none of the recognizable qualities and qualifications for inclusion within society. Like his present followers, Tocqueville gave insufficient attention to the narrow foundations on which many well-established associations stood, and which, by their very nature, appealed to single

---

[14] Michel Foucault, *Power/Knowledge*, ed. Colin Gordon (New York: Pantheon Books, 1980), pp. 103–04.

causes, as many of their present-day heirs still do. At the same time, the capacity of voluntary associations to assert their will has been significantly reduced, and must be contrasted with the resources available to the powerful divisions commanded by special interest, pressure, and lobbying groups operating at the national level and on whom the government and business world alike must respond and call on to determine policies. How could it be otherwise? In the belief that local citizen involvement quickens the democratic pulse and that it never beats so firmly as when it identifies power as a gift of the citizenry to itself, partisans of civic associations pass over the difficulties too quickly. It remains a mystery why the advocates of volunteer civic groups in American society believe that their work to stimulate interest in local and particular affairs will make a mark on the procedures of a mass democracy. I do not contest their value, but I do question the extent and depth of their power. In the conditions facing Americans today, the confidence placed in them may be a mirage.

This brings me to make the point – the very reverse of Tocqueville's famous equality of conditions – that conditions do differ and differentiate people. Those who enjoy more of them decisively determine the rules of political democracy, while those who lack equality of opportunity, do not. Tocqueville was satisfied that the criteria of equal opportunity had already been met by the grant of constitutional protection to *all* Americans, including their participation in the political as well as the civic life of the community. It is doubtful that the greatest number of Americans – who, in fact, do not vote in national elections, as has been noted repeatedly – would agree today that their franchise counted as much in controlling democratic institutions as the advantage enjoyed by the rich who run for and acquire office and gain financial support from wealthy private and corporate sources. But Tocqueville believed that the trade-off in his own day was real, especially because of the vitality of democratic life in the voluntary organizations.

Though Tocqueville placed too much faith in locally organized groups as a haven for the heart and the mind, he did not discount the fact that while creating community, they might also stifle dissent. The equality of conditions that he said was not the minimal, but rather the only, equality to be realistically concerned about, could not totally erase the differences created by education, income, and taste. The need for privacy in democracies was intensified by the cultivation of these differences. In their desire for private space, a refuge for their pride, individuals were surely going to seek ways of being different and to "form somewhere an inequality to their own advantage" (II, Bk. 3, chap. 13, 227). Even a democratic society with a mature view of how the common interest was to be served would find it difficult, it seems, to agree on how it was to be achieved. This need for maintaining or finding legitimate forms of difference, for expressing a form of inequality within an egalitarian society could not be suppressed.

Recent thought on the prospects of democracy has shifted away from Tocqueville's concern about the tyranny of a majority of equals that imposes its will and power to worries about the imposition of the authority of a new class of well-placed groups, who, with greater resources at their command, exercise impressive power through the market place of public opinion on the democratic citizen. The anxieties are multiplied by a sense of how willingly people in all walks of life, not only succumb to what they are asked to believe, but also want nothing more than to do so, either from a sense of resignation or cynicism, but perhaps most of all, because they no longer know what to believe or to what public institutions they ought to give their loyalties. Joseph Schumpeter noted this with unsurpassed acuity some time ago:

> [Citizen] ignorance will persist in the face of masses of information however complete and correct. It persists even in the face of the meritorious efforts that are being made to go beyond presenting information and to teach the use of it by means of lectures, classes, discussion groups. Results are not zero. But they are small. People cannot be carried up the ladder. Thus the typical citizen drops down to a lower level of mental performance as soon as he enters the political field. He argues and analyzes in a way which he would readily recognize as infantile within the sphere of his real interests. He becomes a primitive again. His thinking becomes associative and affective.[15]

It used to be said that a pluralist democracy, just because it made room for differing conceptions of the good, created the best environment for a fruitful exchange of ideas about it. This claim cannot be entertained so blithely any longer, at least without qualification. The much-vaunted plurality of values may be more transparent than real. While a many-sided public does indeed exhibit a range of opinions, its members must not only be adequately enlightened to permit or acknowledge distinctions among them but find the best means to translate their values into actions. They may find it difficult to escape the urge to focus on the average, the mean, and the center, to what Tocqueville said was a safe point that

---

[15] Joseph Schumpeter, *Capitalism, Socialism, and Democracy*, 3rd ed. (New York: Harper and Row, 1950), p. 262.

looks askance at raw conflict. This, of course, is what he approved: An active and lively sense of the public good would keep revolutionary violence at bay in America. For him this was a welcome departure from the divisions of a traditional hierarchical society with its threat of violent conflict and the consolidation of social peace that was America's most prominent feature, a peace that was ensured by the wishes of the vast majority of its people. This has been translated into an ideology of consensus that works to keep from the many who do not engage in public life the fact that it is achieved only under the pretense that public life is not political at all, and should not be. The subterfuge may respond to the public's abhorrence of what they deem to be dirty politics, and its conviction that politics cannot be other than a public exhibition of power-sharing within but not outside the political class. The latter takes its own manipulations as the essence of politics, and slights, indeed repudiates, the choices the citizenry made, more robustly in the past, to be sure, but not entirely missing today. From it, the public, however it is divided on normative and practical grounds, tries to gain recognition for its needs and, with some skepticism, believes that it will get some of what it wants through the bargaining that transpires within the political class after elections. Perhaps this kind of consensus is what most Americans want after all. Perhaps this is the way they want to see and practice politics, and are prepared to accept, as the price they pay for it, both the demagoguery of politicians and the endless pleasures of the market place. Contrary to Plato's fear of democratic turbulence, Tocqueville remarked on the deep conservatism of normal politics in America, which was one of its distinguishing features. Despite the political apathy, complacency, and somnolence that an egalitarian society might fatefully breed, resistance to great change remained for him one of its saving graces, for it acted as a positive insurance against revolution. It was not that there could not be legitimate reasons for revolution in democratic times, but so dangerous a moment might be prudently avoided (II, Bk. 4, chap. 7, 346). As Tocqueville also said, the likelihood was that the self-concerned inclinations of Americans, or, what was more likely, the praise heaped on the habits of political self-denial, vaunted as a barrier against political enthusiasm, might, unintentionally and not improbably, lead to the very "evil" of revolution they wanted to avoid. Indeed, the danger was the consolidation of a "stationary" society, or what we might call an immobile one, in which endless debate on how to assess the consequences of introducing variations to save old principles obscured the possibility of creating and acting on new ones. Then, as history so far had shown, the authority of a name would effect the changes in opinion that preferably should have been wrought by genuine intellectual effort, a near impossibility in America, where the equality of intellect, not individual difference, was celebrated. One may easily discern the regret Tocqueville felt for the times of the "enthusiasm that flings the minds of men out of the beaten track and effects the great revolutions of the intellect as well as the great revolutions of the political world" (II, Bk. 3, chap. 21, 269–75). Still, however slight the chances were that such a change would occur, and however imperfect democracy was, it remained alive and well. Even if the complete equality that he deplored as depraved – because its aim was to bring the strong down to the level of the weak (I, chap. 3, 56) – was to be America's fate, it was "better to be leveled by free institutions than by a despot" (I, chap. 17, 341).

Great revolutions of the intellect are hardly an absent feature of America. But the appeal Tocqueville makes for political enthusiasm is rarely heard today. For many, the political landscape is arid, the political has no meaning, even the study of political theory is on trial,[16] and there seems little that can be done about the relentless forces of the market, either in individual countries or on a global scale. Indeed, in a time when the nation-state is said to have surrendered itself to the multinational corporate world, individuals show less and less interest in deepening their commitments to democratic community and more and more eager to give their consent, nay, their obedience, to forces that guarantee efficiency and promise no fuss.[17] Tocqueville's warnings against the insidious growth of soft despotism may now be seen as a global phenomenon. But there is a difference. Economics dominates politics on a scale that was unimaginable in the nineteenth century. The first seems to have driven the second from the scene of purposeful action.

This appears to be the conclusion reached by some critics of the modern democratic state. In John Dunn's searching account of the elusive meanings of politics in modern democracies, these critics claim that politics has neatly adjusted itself (to the dynamics of capitalism), and not

---

[16] For a critique of the state of political theory, see Jeffrey C. Isaac, *Democracy in Dark Times* (Ithaca and London: Cornell University Press, 1998), especially, in his view, its remoteness from actual political problems.

[17] See Jean-Marie Guéhenno, *The End of the Nation-State*, trans. Victoria Elliott (Minneapolis: University of Minnesota Press, 1995), especially pp. 58, 99. Guéhenno expects, but without demonstrating how (p. 127), that the restoration of politics will "start from the bottom, from local democracy and the account that a community will give of itself, and proceed upward."

only "reinforces, rather than mitigates, the harm which they do."[18] There is a more significant conclusion to be drawn, however, Dunn tells us. While he reminds us of the spiritual devastations and degradations of capitalism, he resolutely refuses to indulge in self-righteous judgment. The most urgent reality of modern economics and politics, is, as I have already noted many times, how markets severely challenge the power of citizens and the democratic state itself to chart their own course. It is this knowledge that the citizens of modern democracies must, Dunn argues, come to terms with, while ridding themselves of the illusion that the state has the capacity or the obligation to enrich people's spiritual lives, or that it has been responsible for human despiritualization.[19] It is not, for that reason, to be done away with, as if that were a practical choice. Rather, even while recognizing its capacity for abuse – if left free to do as it wishes – Dunn accepts it on the grounds that in its good forms it gives "their political participants clear and reliably structured incentives to act on balance for the collective better, rather than for the worse," even if this means reducing the power of or replacing human agents with self-enforcing mechanisms.[20] Alongside his counsel of modest expectations stands the somewhat bitter, though not unsurprising, conclusion that greater political understanding of the nature of politics and economics in a triumphant capitalist democratic society may simply be another instance of *tout comprendre c'est tout pardonner* (to understand everything is to forgive everything).[21] Capitalism is the best we have, and we shall have to wait and see, he says, if the state form that best suits it will continue to do its work to reduce human degradation and vulnerability.[22]

No more movements; no pie in the sky promises: Such false enthusiasms, and the errors flowing from them, are best set aside. Caution and consensus, Richard Rorty also argues, will serve humanity's fragile condition best. A secular democratic America may, according to Richard Rorty, be producing a "new sort of individual . . . [who] will take nothing as authoritative save free consensus between as diverse a variety of citizens as can possibly be produced."[23] In this formulation, the democratic roots of authority are in every important respect presumably iden-

---

[18] John Dunn, *The Cunning of Unreason. Making Sense of Politics* (New York: Basic Books, 2000), p. 230.
[19] Ibid., pp. 253–55. [20] Ibid., p. 264.
[21] Ibid., pp. 329, 331. [22] Ibid., pp. 359–63.
[23] Richard Rorty, *Achieving Our Country: Leftist Thought in Twentieth-Century America* (Cambridge, Mass.: Harvard University Press, 1998), p. 31.

tical with the most expansive reading that may be given to a notion of *free* consensus, left, however, undefined. If the consensus Rorty has in mind is meant to restore politics to democracy, it needs to be rethought. Such a consensus has little value without a heightened sense of the inner voice each individual possesses and that we respect in others, and which must have a foundation more solid than emotional affinity with others. This kind of recognition of others is undeniably difficult and more often than not, unsurprisingly, remains unrealized. Nevertheless, it need not be dismissed as impractical. It is not only a question of describing unfamiliar people and redescribing ourselves. It also depends on government to fulfill one of its key functions: The fusion of reason and a robust political will to widen the circle of human goods, as, for example, it did so dramatically in its enforcement of desegregation in the American South. No such measures can be deployed without coercion. Another notion of government sees it as fulfilling its principal function by enforcing its own interest, above all, and, in addition, maintaining and extending the conditions of inequality. In trying to desegregate America, coercion was needed, but it arose from meeting the first, and not the second, notion of government's role. That work must be continued to fortify devalued identities. America celebrates its past and its memorable occasions by telling stories about itself in the public schools, which continue to be, though with great difficulty, the sites where children may find an escape from the tight embrace of single-focused ethnic and religious community.[24] But the likelihood that the American public school system, starved for funds and good teachers, can create a sense of self-worth and a sense of authority seems small indeed at this moment.

So while there is important evidence today that where they exist in America, social divisions have deepened, the deep conservatism that exists alongside them is a barrier to policies of social improvement. How to think about the distribution of human resources, or human capacities, or capabilities, is of crucial importance. It may be of no small consequence whether resources or capacities or capabilities should be the term to be used to determine the degree to which equality and the freedom to take part in decision-making is achieved. Political liberties are guaranteed, Rawls contends, or come to have full or near-full meaning for all, when they are "approximately equal, or at least suffi-

[24] Cf. James Tully, *Strange Multiplicity* (Cambridge: Cambridge University Press, 1995), p. 26: "By listening to the different stories others tell, and giving their own in exchange, the participants come to see their common and interwoven histories together form a multiplicity of paths."

ciently equal, in the sense that everyone has a fair opportunity to hold public office and to influence the outcome of political decisions."[25] An essential part of the qualifications is not only a just distribution of goods, but the intellectual, moral, and physical capacities to be political members of society more fully than at present. The connection between resource distribution and the capacity to grasp it must be made. The primary goods notion of equality – an ideal equality of income, wealth, power, and position – is not, for Amartya Sen, an adequate basis for an analysis of the unequal weight of individuals – that is, an analysis taking the differences in their abilities into account. Such differences matter, and they will play a large part in determining how citizens realize their objectives quite apart from the other causes of the unequal distribution of a society's goods. Once again, but from an outlook radically opposed to the pre-democratic notion of quality, which was treated in Chapter 2, we encounter the question of how measuring equality may be affected by assessing differing personal qualities.[26] Neither in every instance, nor in every context, do people need the same things. Measures have been taken against the stigmas that are the source of unfair and unequal treatment. Other kinds of measures, however, may also be required to make up for such unrecognized differences in capacity as diminish the opportunities for fair and equal treatment. In both instances, the policies adopted will affect the nature and outcome of political decision-making because it unblocks impediments to fuller participation.

These practical questions add weight to the importance of gauging how participants can be effective agents.[27] At the same time, Sen does not insist that to be effective, one must have actual control. No principle of justice or equality is breached if human beings, not faced by barriers to the uses of their freedom, waste their chances and consequently find themselves disadvantaged. Thus individual action is the focus, as he thinks, it should be: It is at the outset rather than at the end of an action that individuals should know how to exercise their freedom to achieve what they wish.[28] If they fail, they have not acted rationally and have no

[25] John Rawls, *Political Liberalism* (New York: Columbia University Press, 1993), p. 327.
[26] See Amartya Sen's paper in *The Quality of Life*, eds. Martha Nussbaum and Amartya Sen (Oxford: Clarendon Press, 1993), 30–53.
[27] Amartya Sen, *Inequality Reexamined* (Cambridge, Mass.: Harvard University Press, 1992), pp. 148–49.
[28] Ibid., pp. 64–65. Sen's emphasis. Sen notes (pp. 121–22) that Marx believed that treating workers only as workers diminished them as persons. Yet Marx, while speaking of needs, Sen says, did not go beyond a class analysis to consider other sources of disparity, such as race and color.

one to blame but themselves. In this respect, we may remind ourselves that Tocqueville did not accept the idea that all citizens have equal capacities, nor that society is obliged to step in to alter such conditions. But his major point was that democratic equality tended to draw them apart from one another and left them weakened. The mystery of capacity was a question of social conditions as well as individual difference. Thus, like Tocqueville, Sen stresses "[f]reedom to achieve," rather than "actual achievements" to mark rationality and hence responsibility. This dictum is double-edged. It rests, on the one hand, on acknowledging that abilities and access to knowledge differ, and, on the other, on not according sufficient recognition to the sources of different abilities and the unequal access to knowledge. It also says little about how the individualism associated with the Puritan conscience became the hyperindividualism of a full-blown market society that cannot be so easily identified with freedom of choice – the individualism that Tocqueville said was a close companion of democracy and was an ever-present threat to public life.[29]

I began this book by speaking of the ceremonial tributes made to democracy, and explored its realities and exposed its myths. I have questioned the arguments of political and social theorists, past and present, who have made democracy's tribulations their life work. Tocqueville's perceptions as a political psychologist, sociologist, and historian nourished much of their thought, even if they did not share all of them, and his remarkable mind continues to do so. Tocqueville believed that crisis was inherent in democracy itself, reflecting the severe strains America experienced when the balance between equality and freedom was tested at key periods in its history. But we should also remember, as we close, Tocqueville's ideal that "men will be perfectly free because they are all

---

[29] In *Development as Freedom* (Oxford: Oxford University Press, 1999), Sen argues that development throughout the world is the foundation of freedom, that economic and political freedoms, rather than being opposed to one another, help to reinforce each other, and that public policies to increase opportunities for education and health complement individual efforts. The stress on the individual as arbiter of all that surrounds him fails to confront the reality of the market's power to vest concentrated control in the private information industry, hence setting the paramaters of debate and the freedom to make rational choices. It also fails to deal with two sets of inequalities, arising from the flows of capital in search of optimum conditions – one deprives labor in advanced economies of some of its bargaining power, the other raises labor's hope in less developed countries but also makes it highly vulnerable to the market. Each of these sets off a cycle of inequalities.

entirely equal; and they will all be perfectly equal because they are entirely free (II, Bk. 2, chap. 1, 99).

In this search for equipoise, the indelible stain of slavery and the destruction of the American Native population remain for many Americans memories of shame and neglect. The vocabulary of crisis has deepened and is now found on all sides, on the Left and the Right (however the limits of the two sides of the spectrum are stretched), and for those who take up positions on the margins of a middle band that gives these matters little reflection. Although Tocqueville was not always right, either in his thoughts about the future of the races in America or the extent and depth of America's democracy, his incomparable observations unerringly captured many of the realities of the American mind. He understood power mainly as a political force, and overwhelmingly as a fatal intrusion by government. He gave insufficient thought to the question of how, apart from pursuing specific and well-defined civic goals, the institutions of civil society could gather the resources to affect the power of the centralized state. It was as if, for him, the two realms of public life existed alongside, but did not touch, one another, with power emanating wholly from the second. He was much more impressed by another kind of power, the power of a dull and uncomprehending worship of egalitarianism that blurred the richness of human diversity. The American movement toward greater and greater equality was, to be sure, irresistible. Its less appealing face was that in the compulsion to extend it, the useful distinctions – useful both for individuals and for society as a whole – that are made among human capacities might be overlooked and lost. Would the search for an elusive and never-satiated thirst for increasing shares of the world's goods absorb and exhaust Americans to the exclusion of all else? There are less obvious goods that society might gain from granting a place for individuals of unequal qualities and for dissenting voices. The urgency of the question has not been dimmed by time. As Americans continue to negotiate the lines connecting authority and liberty – on one scale of measurement, equality and authority – on another, and equality and difference – on yet a third, they may be ready to take steps to imagine and find new and startling ways to see how all six are woven together. They may find, however, that such a struggle will be too burdensome. The choices they could in reality make, depended, Tocqueville believed, on how they would use the familiar signposts of everyday life and the political institutions that were in place to ensure legitimate authority and liberty. Without them, people might experience only a sense of loss and deprivation, which he detected lay deep in the American psyche and expressed itself in restlessness and dissatisfaction. Paradoxically, that restlessness, if not overtaken by forgetfulness, might be the source of new beginnings.

We are emotionally in a place not so different from Tocqueville's. He set out to ponder the future. It was a future he could not contemplate without human agency. A fatal circle keeps human beings within bounds, but it does not keep them from exercising power and shaping the future, he said in his conclusion to *Democracy in America*: Human beings alone have the power of ensuring that equality will exist alongside freedom, knowledge, and prosperity, instead of servitude, misery, and barbarism. The chances were, on balance, not entirely on the side of human blindness, and may still be so.

Works Cited

Ackerman, Bruce. *We the People. Transformations* (Cambridge, Mass. and London: Belknap Press of the Harvard University Press, 1998).
  We the People. Foundations (Cambridge, Mass. and London: The Belknap Press of Harvard University Press, 1991).
Agamben, Giorgio. *Remnants of Auschwitz.The Witness and the Archive*, trans. Daniel Heller-Roazen (New York: Zone Books, 1999).
  Homo Sacer. Sovereign Power and Bare Life, trans. Daniel Heller-Roazen (Stanford: Stanford University Press, 1998).
Ageron, Charles-Robert. *Modern Algeria*, trans. Michael Brett (London: Hurst & Company, 1991).
Agre, Philip E. "Yesterday's Tomorrow. The Advance of Law and Order into the Utopian Wilderness of Cyberspace," *Times Literary Supplement*, July 3, 1998.
Alexie, Sherman. *Reservation Blues* (New York: Atlantic Monthly Press, 1995).
Allen, Theodore W. *The Invention of the White Race*. Vol. 1: *Racial Oppression and Social Control* (London and New York: Verso Press, 1994).
Anderson, Benedict. *Imagined Communities: Reflections on the Origin and Spread of Nationalism*, 2d edition (London and New York: Verso, 1991).
Ankersmit, Frank R. *Aesthetic Politics. Political Philosophy Beyond Fact and Value* (Stanford: Stanford University Press, 1996).
  "Tocqueville and the Sublimity of Democracy, Part I: "Content," *La Revue Tocqueville/The Tocqueville Review*, 14 (1993), 173–200; Part II: "Form," ibid., 15 (1994), 193–217.
Appiah, Anthony and Amy Gutmann. *Color-Conscious: The Political Morality of Race* (Princeton: Princeton University Press, 1997).
Arendt, Hannah. "Lying in Politics," in *Crises of the Republic* (New York: Harcourt Brace Jovanovich, Inc., 1972), 1–48.
  "Truth and Politics," in *Philosophy, Politics and Society*, Third Series, eds. Peter Laslett and W. G. Runciman (Oxford: Basil Blackwell, 1967), 104–33.

Between Past and Future. Six Exercises in Political Thought (Cleveland and New York: Meridian Books, 1963).

On Revolution (New York: The Viking Press, 1963).

The Human Condition (Chicago: University of Chicago Press, 1958).

Baldwin, James. *Notes of a Native Son* in *Collected Essays* (New York: The Library of America, 1998).

Balibar, Etienne. "Ambiguous Universality," *differences: A Journal of Feminist Cultural Studies*, 7.1 (1995), 48–74.

Beaumont, Gustave de. *Marie or Slavery in the United States*, trans. Barbara Chapman (Stanford: Stanford University Press, 1958).

Bell, Daniel. "Civil Society versus Civic Virtue," *Freedom of Association*, ed. Amy Gutmann (Princeton: Princeton University Press, 1998), 239–72.

"'The Hegelian Secret': Civil Society and American Exceptionalism,"*Is America Different? A New Look at American Exceptionalism*, ed. Byron E. Shafer (Oxford: Oxford University Press, 1991), 46–70.

Bellah, Robert N. et al. *Habits of the Heart: Individualism and Commitment in American Life* (Berkeley, Los Angeles, and London: University of California Press, 1985).

The Broken Covenant: American Civil Religion (New York: Seabury Press, 1975).

"The American Civil Religion," *Daedalus*, 96 (Winter 1967), 1–21.

Berlin, Ira. *Many Thousands Gone. The First Two Centuries of Slavery in North America* (Cambridge, Mass. and London: Belknap Press of Harvard University Press, 1998).

Berlin, Isaiah. *The Proper Study of Mankind*, eds. Henry Hardy and Roger Hausheer (London: Chatto and Windus, 1997).

Berry, Jeffrey M.*The New Liberalism. The Rising Power of Citizen Groups* (Washington: Brookings Institution Press, 1999).

Black, Jr., Charles L. *A New Birth of Freedom: Human Rights Named and Unnamed* (New York: Grosset/Putnam, 1998).

Blackburn, Robin. *The Overthrow of Colonial Slavery 1776–1848* (London and New York: Verso, 1988).

Blosseville, Viscount Ernest. Translator of John Tanner, *A Narrative of the Captivity and Adventures of John Tanner, during the Thirty Years Residence among the Indians in the Interior of North America* (New York: G. & C. & H. Carvill, 1830). The title of the translation is *Mémoires de John Tanner; ou, Trente Années dans les déserts de l'Amérique du Nord* (Paris: A. Bertrand, 1831)

Bobbio, Norberto. *The Age of Rights*, trans. Allan Cameron (Cambridge: Polity Press, 1996).

The Future of Democracy: A Defence of the Rules of the Game, trans. Roger Griffith (Minneapolis: University of Minnesota Press, 1988).

Which Socialism? trans. Roger Griffin, ed. Richard Bellamy (Minneapolis: University of Minnesota Press, 1987).

Bohman, James. "Deliberative Democracy and Effective Social Freedom: Capabilities, Resources and Opportunities," in *Deliberative Democracy.*

Essays on Reason and Politics, eds. James Bohman and William Rehg (Cambridge, Mass. and London: MIT Press, 1997), 321–48.

Bok, Derek and William G. Bowen. *The Shape of the River. Long-Term Consequences of Considering Race in College and University Admissions* (Princeton: Princeton University Press, 1998).

Callahan, John F. " 'American Culture is of a Whole': From the Letters of Ralph Ellison," *The New Republic*, 220 (March 1, 1999), 34–48.

Carter III, Samuel. *Cherokee Sunset* (New York: Doubleday & Company, 1976).

Castoriadis, Cornelius. "Power, Politics, Autonomy," in *Cultural-Political Interventions in the Unfinished Project of the Enlightenment*, eds. Axel Honneth et al. (Boston: MIT Press, 1992), 269–97.

Philosophy, Politics, Autonomy: Essays in Political Philosophy (Oxford: Oxford University Press, 1991).

Chateaubriand, François-René de. *Atala, René* (Paris: Garnier-Flammarion, 1964).

Chavkin, Allan and Nancy Feyl Chavkin, eds. *Conversations with Louise Erdrich and Michael Dorris* (Jackson: University Press of Mississippi, 1994).

Clastres, Pierre. *Chronicle of the Guayaki Indians*, trans. Paul Auster (Cambridge, Mass.: Zone Books, 1998).

Cohen, Jean and Andrew Arato. "Politics and the Reconstruction of Civil Society," in *Cultural-Political Interventions in the Unfinished Project of the Enlightenment*, eds. Axel Honneth et al. (Cambridge, Mass. and London: MIT Press, 1992), 121–44.

Cohen, Joshua. "Procedure and Substance in Deliberative Democracy," *Deliberative Democracy. Essays on Reason and Politics*, eds. James Bohman and William Rehg (Cambridge, Mass.: MIT Press, 1997), 407–37.

Cohen, Joshua ed. *For Love of Country: Debating the Limits of Patriotism*, (Boston: Beacon Press, 1996).

Cohen, Joshua and Joel Rogers. "Associations and Democracy," *Social Philosophy and Policy*, 10 (1993), 282–312.

Colwill, Elizabeth. "Sex, Savagery, and Slavery in the Shaping of the French Body Politic," in *From the Royal to the Republican Body. Incorporating the Political in Seventeenth- and Eighteenth-Century France*, eds. Sara E. Melzer and Kathryn Norberg (Berkeley, Los Angeles, and London: University of California Press, 1998), 198–223.

Connolly, William E. "Tocqueville, Territory and Violence," *Theory, Culture & Society*, 11 (1994), 19–40.

Identity/Difference. Democratic Negotiations of Political Paradox (Ithaca and London: Cornell University Press, 1991).

Conseil, L.P. *Mélanges politiques et philosophiques extraits des mémoires et de la correspondance de Thomas Jefferson*, 2 vols. (Paris: Paulin, 1833).

Curtin, Philip D. ed. *Imperialism* (New York: Walker, 1971).

D'Souza, Dinesh. *The End of Racism. Principles for a Multicultural Society* (New York: Free Press, 1995).

Davis, David Brion. *The Problem of Slavery in the Age of Revolution 1770–1823* (Ithaca and London: Cornell University Press, 1975).

Dewey, John. *The Public and its Problems* (New York: Swallow, 1927).

Diamond, Jared. *Guns, Germs, and Steel: The Fates of Human Societies* (New York: Norton, 1997).

Diggins, John P. *Max Weber. Politics and the Spirit of Tragedy* (New York: Basic Books, 1996).

Dion, Stéphane. "Durham et Tocqueville sur la colonisation libérale," *Journal of Canadian Studies*, 25, no. 1 (1990), 60–78.

Dominguez, Virginia R. *White by Definition: Social Classification in Creole Louisiana* (New Brunswick: Rutgers University Press, 1986).

Doran, Eva. "Two Men and a Forest: Chateaubriand, Tocqueville and the American Wilderness," *Essays in French Literature*, no. 13 (1976), 44–61.

Douglass, Frederick. *Narrative of the Life of Frederick Douglass, an American Slave* (New York: Viking Penguin, 1982).

Drescher, Seymour. "L'Amérique vue par les tocquevilliens," *Raisons politiques*, no. 1 (February 2001), 63–76.

Slavery to Freedom: Comparative Studies in the Rise and Fall of Atlantic Slavery (New York: Macmillan Press, 1999).

Dilemmas of Democracy: Tocqueville and Modernization (Pittsburgh: University of Pittsburgh Press, 1968).

Drinnon, Richard. *Facing West: The Metaphysics of Indian-Hating and Empire-Building* (New York: Meridian, 1980).

Drury, Shadia B. *Leo Strauss and the American Right* (New York: St. Martin's Press, 1997).

DuBois, Page. *Torture and Truth* (New York and London: Routledge, 1991).

Duchet, Michèle. *Anthropologie et histoire au siècle des lumières* (Paris: Flammarion, 1971).

Dunn, John. *The Cunning of Unreason. Making Sense of Politics* (New York: Basic Books, 2000).

Dworkin, Ronald. *Sovereign Virtue. The Theory and Practice of Equality* (Cambridge, Mass. and London: Harvard University Press, 2000).

Eckstein, Harry. "Civic Inclusion and Its Discontents," in *Regarding Politics: Essays on Political Theory, Stability, and Change* (Berkeley: University of California Press, 1992), 343–77.

Ellison, Ralph. *The Collected Essays.* Introduced by John F. Callahan (New York: The Modern Library, 1995).

Invisible Man (New York: Random House, 1993).

Going to the Territory, (New York: Random House, 1986).

Shadow and Act (New York: A Signet Book, 1966).

Elshtain, Jean Bethke. *Democratic Authority at Century's End* (London: The Institute of United States Studies, University of London, 1998).

Real Politics at the Center of Everyday Life (Baltimore and London: Johns Hopkins University Press, 1997).

Democracy on Trial. The CBC Massey Lecture Series (Concord, Ontario: Anansi, 1993).

Elster, Jon. "Deliberation and Constitution Making," in *Deliberative Democracy*, ed. Jon Elster (Cambridge: Cambridge University Press, 1998), 97–122.

"Ways of Constitution-Making," in *Democracy's Victory and Crisis*, ed. Axel Hadenius (Cambridge: Cambridge University Press, 1997), 123–42.

Engerman, Stanley L. and Robert E. Gallman, eds. *The Cambridge Economic History of the United States*, 3 vols. (Cambridge: Cambridge University Press, 1997). Vol. 1: *The Colonial Era*.

The Federalist. From the original text of Alexander Hamilton, John Jay, and James Madison (New York: The Modern Library, n.d.).

Fields, Barbara Jeanne. "Slavery, Race, and Ideology in the United States of America," *New Left Review*, no. 181 (1990), 95–118.

Fierlbeck, Katherine. *Globalizing Democracy. Power, Legitimacy and the Interpretation of Democratic Ideas* (Manchester and New York: Manchester University Press, 1998).

Fogel, Robert W. *The Fourth Great Awakening and the Future of Egalitarianism* (Chicago and London: University of Chicago Press, 2000).

Without Consent or Contract. The Rise and Fall of American Slavery (New York and London: W.W. Norton, 1989).

Foucault, Michel. *Power/Knowledge*, ed. Colin Gordon (New York: Pantheon Books, 1980).

Fraser, Nancy. "Social Justice in An Age of Identity Politics: Redistribution, Recognition, and Participation," *The Tanner Lectures on Human Values*, 19 (1998) (Salt Lake City: University of Utah Press, 1998), 1–67.

Fredrickson, George M. *Black Liberation. A Comparative History of Black Ideologies in the United States and South Africa* (New York and Oxford: Oxford University Press, 1996).

Furet, François. "The Conceptual System of 'Democracy in America'," in *The Workshop of History*, trans. Jonathan Mandelbaum (Chicago and London: University of Chicago Press, 1984), 182–84.

Interpreting the French Revolution, trans. Elborg Forster (Cambridge and Paris: Cambridge University Press and Editions de la Maison des Sciences de l'Homme, 1981).

Gadamer, Hans-Georg. *Truth and Method*, trans. of 2d edition, eds. Garrett Barden and John Cumming (New York: The Seabury Press, 1975).

Gates, Jr., Henry Louis. "Beyond the Culture Wars: Identities in Dialogue," *Profession*, 93 (New York: Modern Language Association, 1994), 6–11.

Genovese, Eugene D. *From Rebellion to Revolution: Afro-American Slave Revolts in the Making of the Modern World* (Baton Rouge: Louisiana State University Press, 1979).

Roll, Jordan, Roll (New York: Pantheon Books, 1974).

The World the Slaveholders Made (New York: Pantheon, 1971).

Geyer, Michael. "The Place of the Second World War in German Memory and History," *New German Critique*, no. 71 (Spring-Summer 1997), 5–40.

Gibson, Alan. "Impartial Representation and the Extended Republic. Towards a Comprehensive and Balanced Reading of the Tenth Federalist Paper," *"History of Political Thought*, 12 (1991), 263–304.

Gilroy, Paul. *The Black Atlantic. Modernity and Double Consciousness* (London and New York: Verso, 1993).

Gobineau, Arthur de. *Essay on the Inequality of the Human Races.* (1853–55). trans. Adrian Collins (London, 1915).

Goodman, Paul. *Of One Blood. Abolitionism and the Origins of Racial Equality* (Berkeley, Los Angeles, and London: University of California Press, 1998).

Gould, Carol C. *Rethinking Democracy* (Cambridge: Cambridge University Press, 1988).

Graham, Marryemma and Amritijit Singh, eds. *Conversations with Ralph Ellison* (Jackson: University Press of Mississippi, 1995).

Greene, Jack P. *The Intellectual Construction of America. Exceptionalism and Identity from 1492 to 1800* (Chapel Hill and London: University of North Carolina Press, 1993).

Greenfeld, Liah. *Nationalism. Five Roads to Modernity* (Cambridge, Mass. and London: Harvard University Press, 1992).

Gross, Irena Grudzinska. *The Scar of Revolution. Custine, Tocqueville and the Romantic Imagination* (Berkeley, Los Angeles, Oxford: University of California Press, 1991).

Guéhenno, Jean-Marie. *The End of the Nation-State,* trans. Victoria Elliott (Minneapolis: University of Minnesota Press, 1995).

Gutman, Herbert G. *The Black Family in Slavery and Freedom, 1750–1925* (New York: Vintage, 1977).

Habermas, Jürgen. *The Inclusion of the Other. Studies in Political Theory,* trans. Ciaran Cronin (Cambridge, Mass.: MIT Press, 1998).

Between Facts and Norms. Contributions to a Discourse Theory of Law and Democracy, trans. William Rehg (Cambridge, Mass.: MIT Press, 1996).

"Legitimationsprobleme in modernen Staat," in *Zur Rekonstruktion des Historischen Materialismus* (Frankfurt: Suhrkamp, 1976).

Toward a Rational Society (Boston: Beacon Press, 1970).

Hacker, Andrew. "Who's Sticking to the Union?" *New York Review of Books,* 46, no. 3 (February 18, 1999), 45–48.

"Grand Illusion," *New York Review of Books,* 45 (June 11, 1998), 26–30.

Two Nations. Black and White, Separate, Hostile, Unequal (New York: Ballantine Books, 1995).

Hannaford, Ivan. *Race: The History of an Idea in the West* (Washington: Woodrow Wilson Center Press, Baltimore and London: Johns Hopkins University Press, 1996).

Hardt, Michael and Antonio Negri. *Labor of Dionysus. A Critique of the State-Form* (Minneapolis and London: University of Minnesota Press, 1994).

Hartz, Louis. *The Liberal Tradition in America: An Interpretation of American Political Thought since the Revolution* (New York: Harcourt, Brace and World, 1955).

Havel, Vaclav. "The State of the Republic," *New York Review of Books,* 45 (March 5, 1998), 42–46.

Open Letters. Selected Writings 1965–1990 (New York: Alfred A. Knopf, 1991).

Hegel, G.W.F. *Philosophy of Right,* trans. T.M. Knox (Oxford: Oxford University Press, 1942).

Herrnstein, Richard J. and Charles A. Murray. *The Bell Curve. Intelligence and Class Structure in American Life* (New York: Free Press, 1994).

Hereth, Michael. *Alexis de Tocqueville: Threats to Freedom in Democracy*, trans. George Bogardus (Durham, N.C.: Duke University Press, 1986).

Hirschman, Albert O. *A Propensity of Self-Subversion* (Cambridge, Mass., and London: Harvard University Press, 1995).

The Passions and the Interests. Political Arguments for Capitalism Before Its Triumph (Princeton: Princeton University Press, 1977).

Historical Statistics of the United States from Colonial Times to 1957 (Washington, D.C., 1960).

Hitchens, Christopher. *No One Left to Lie To. The Triangulations of William Jefferson Clinton* (London and New York: Verso, 1999).

Hollinger, David A. *Postethnic America: Beyond Multiculturalism* (New York: Basic Books, 1995).

Hollis, Martin. *Trust Within Reason* (Cambridge: Cambridge University Press, 1998).

Hont, Istvan. "The Language of Sociability and Commerce: Samuel Pufendorf and the Theoretical Foundations of the 'Four-Stages Theory,'" in *The Languages of Political Theory in Early Modern Europe*, ed. Anthony Pagden (Cambridge: Cambridge University Press), pp. 253–76.

Hudson, Nicholas. "From 'Nation' to 'Race': The Origin of Racial Classification,"*Eighteenth-Century Studies*, 29 (1996), 247–64.

Hunter, James Davison. *Culture Wars: The Struggle to Define America* (New York: Basic Books, 1991).

"The American Culture War," in *The Limits of Social Cohesion. Conflict and Mediation in Pluralist Societies*. A Report of the Bertelsmann Foundation to the Club of Rome, ed. Peter L. Berger (Boulder, Colorado: Westview Press, 1998), 1–37.

Ignatieff, Michael. *The Rights Revolution*. CBC Massey Lectures Series (Toronto: House of Anansi Press, 2000).

Inglehart, Ronald. "Postmodernization Erodes Respect for Authority, but Increases Support for Democracy," in *Critical Citizens. Global Support for Democratic Government*, ed. Pippa Norris (New York: Oxford University Press, 1999), 23–56.

Isaac, Jeffrey C. *Democracy in Dark Times* (Ithaca and London: Cornell University Press, 1998).

Jankélévich, Vladimir. "Shall We Pardon Them," trans. Ann Hobart, *Critical Inquiry*, 22 (1996), 552–72.

Jardin, André. *Alexis de Tocqueville, 1805–1859* (Paris: Hachette, 1984).

"Alexis de Tocqueville, Gustave de Beaumont et le problème de l'inégalité des races," in Pierre Guiral and Emile Temime, eds. *L'idée de race dans la pensée politique française contemporaine* (Paris: Editions du CNRS, 1977), 200–19.

Jefferson, Thomas. *Notes on the State of Virginia*, ed. W. Peden (Chapel Hill: University of North Carolina Press, 1955).

Notes on the State of Virginia, in *The Complete Thomas Jefferson*, ed. Saul K. Padover (New York: Duell, Sloan & Pearce, 1943).

Jennings, Lawrence C. *French Anti-Slavery. The Movement for the Abolition of Slavery in France 1802–1848* (Cambridge: Cambridge University Press, 2000).

Johnson, Douglas. "The Maghrib," *The Cambridge History of Africa*, vol. 5, c. 1790 to c. 1870, ed. John E. Flint (Cambridge: Cambridge University Press, 1976), 99–124.

Josephy, Jr., Alvin, Joane Nagel, and Troy Johnson, eds. *Red Power: The American Indians' Fight for Freedom*, 2d ed. (Lincoln: University of Nebraska Press, 1999).

Kammen, Michael. *In the Past Lane. Historical Perspectives on American Culture* (New York and Oxford: Oxford University Press, 1997).

Kant, Immanuel. *Political Writings*, trans. H.B. Nisbet, ed. Hans Reiss (Cambridge: Cambridge University Press, 1991).

Kateb, George. "The Value of Association," in *Freedom of Association*, ed. Amy Gutmann (Princeton: Princeton University Press, 1998), 35–64.

Keane, John. *Civil Society. Old Images, New Visions* (Cambridge: Polity Press, 1998).

Tom Paine: A Political Life (London: Bloomsbury Pub., 1995).

Kelly, George Armstrong. *Politics and Religious Consciousness in America* (New Brunswick and London: Transaction Books, 1984).

Kiernan, V. J. *The Lords of Human Kind: Black Man, Yellow Man, and White Man in an Age of Empire* (1969; reprint New York: Columbia University Press, 1986).

Knight, Jack and James Johnson. "What Sort of Equality does Deliberative Democracy Require?" in *Deliberative Democracy. Essays on Reason and Politics*, eds. James Bohman and William Rehg (Cambridge, Mass. and London: MIT Press, 1997), 279–320.

Kymlicka, Will. "The Good, the Bad, and the Intolerable: Minority Group Rights," *Dissent* (Summer 1996), 22–30.

Multicultural Citizenship. A Liberal Theory of Minority Rights (Oxford: Clarendon Press, 1995).

Liberalism, Community and Culture (Oxford: Oxford University Press, 1991).

Laqueur, Thomas. "Festival of Punishment," *London Review of Books*, 22 (October 5, 2000), 17–24.

Las Casas, Bartolomé. *The Devastation of the Indies: A Brief Account*, trans. Herman Briffault (New York: Seabury Press, 1974).

Le Duff, Charles. "At a Slaughterhouse, Some Things Never Die," *New York Times*, June 15, 2000.

Lemann, Nicholas. *The Big Test: The Secret History of the American Meritocracy* (New York: Farrar Straus Giroux, 1999).

Lévi-Strauss, Claude. *Structural Anthropology*. Vol. 2, trans. Monique Layton (New York: Basic Books, 1976).

Tristes Tropiques, trans. John and Doreen Weightman (New York: Athenaeum, 1973).

Liebersohn, Harry. "Discovering Indigenous Nobility: Tocqueville, Chamisso, and Romantic Travel Writing," *American Historical Review*, 99 (1994), 746–66.

Locke, John. *A Letter Concerning Toleration* (Buffalo, NY: Prometheus Books, 1990).

Lukas, J. Anthony. *Common Ground. A Turbulent Decade in the Lives of Three American Families* (New York: Alfred A. Knopf, 1985).

Luttwak, Edward N. *The Endangered American Dream* (New York: Simon and Schuster, 1993).

Lyotard, Jean-François. *La condition postmoderne* (Paris: Minuit, 1979).

Malcomson, Scott L. *One Drop of Blood. The American Misadventure of Race* (New York: Farrar Straus Giroux, 2000).

Mansfield, Jr., Harvey C. and Delba Winthrop. "Liberalism and Big Government: Tocqueville's Analysis," *Tyranny and Liberty. Big Government and the Individual in Tocqueville's Science of Politics* (London: The Institute of United States Studies, University of London, 1999).

Mansfield, Jr., Harvey C. *America's Constitutional Soul* (Baltimore and London: The Johns Hopkins University Press, 1991).

Margalit, Avishai. "Decent Equality and Freedom: A Postscript," *Social Research*, 64 (1997), 147–60.

The Decent Society (Cambridge, Mass., Harvard University Press, 1996).

Margalit, Avishai and Gabriel Motzkin. "The Uniqueness of the Holocaust," *Philosophy and Public Affairs*, 25 (1996), 65–83.

Masdua, Yoneji. *The Information Society as Post-Industrial Society* (Washington: World Future Society, 1980).

McLoughlin, William G. *Cherokee Renascence in the New Republic* (Princeton: Princeton University Press, 1986).

Meek, Ronald L. *Social Science and the Ignoble Savage* (Cambridge: Cambridge University Press, 1976).

Mélonio, Françoise. "Tocqueville et les malheurs de la démocratie américaine (1831–1859)," *Commentaire*, 10 (1987), 381–89.

Michel, Pierre. *Un mythe romantique. Les barbares 1789–1848* (Lyon: Presses Universitaires de Lyon, 1981).

Miles, Jack. *God. A Biography* (New York: Vintage Books, 1996).

Mill, John Stuart. *Autobiography* (New York: Columbia University Press, 1960).

On Liberty (Indianapolis and New York: Bobbs-Merrill, 1956).

Mills, Charles W. *The Racial Contract* (Ithaca and London: Cornell University Press, 1997).

Mitchell, Harvey. "Tocqueville's Flight from Doubt and His Search for Certainty: Skepticism in a Democratic Age," *The Skeptical Tradition around 1800. Skepticism in Philosophy, Science, and Society*, eds. J. van der Zande and R. H. Popkin (Dordrecht, Boston, and London: Kluwer Academic Publishers, 1998), 261–79.

Individual Choice and the Structures of History. Alexis de Tocqueville as Historian Reappraised (Cambridge: Cambridge University Press, 1996).

"Reclaiming the Self: The Pascal-Rousseau Connection," *Journal of the History of Ideas*, 54 (1993), 637–58.

Momaday, N. Scott. *The Man Made of Words* (New York: St. Martin's Press, 1997).

Montesquieu, Charles-Louis de Secondat, Baron de. *The Spirit of the Laws*, eds. and trans. Ann Cohler, Basia Miller, and Harold Stone (Cambridge: Cambridge University Press, 1989).

Morrison, Toni. *Paradise* (New York: Penguin Books, 1997).

Morse, Jedediah O. *The History of America*, 2d ed. (Philadelphia, 1795).

Myrdal, Gunnar. *An American Dilemma: The Negro Problem and Modern Democracy* (New York: Harper and Brothers, 1944).

Nandy, Ashis. "History's Forgotten Doubles," *History and Theory. Studies in the Philosophy of History*. Theme Issue 34, no. 2 (1995), 44–66.

Traditions, Tyranny and Utopias (Delhi: Oxford University Press, 1987).

Negri, Antonio. *Insurgencies. Constitutional Power and the Modern State*, trans. Maurizia Boscagli (Minneapolis and London: University of Minnesota Press, 1999).

The Savage Anomaly. The Power of Spinoza's Metaphysics and Politics (Minneapolis and Oxford: University of Minnesota Press, 1991).

Negro, Dalmacio. "Virtue and Politics in Tocqueville," in *Liberty, Equality, Democracy*, ed. Eduardo Nolla (New York: New York University Press, 1992), 55–74.

New York Times website:http://www.nytimes.com/library/national/race/060400.

Nisbet, Robert. "Tocqueville's Ideal Types," in *Reconsidering Tocqueville's "Democracy in America"*, ed. Abraham S. Eisenstadt (New Brunswick, N.J.: Rutgers University Press, 1988), 171–91.

Nolla, Eduardo. *Autour de l'autre démocratie*, Instituto Suor Orsola Benincasa (Naples, 1994).

Nolla, Eduardo, ed. *Liberty, Equality, Democracy* (New York and London: New York University Press, 1992).

Nussbaum, Martha. *Cultivating Humanity. A Classical Definition of Reform in Liberal Education* (Cambridge, Mass.: Harvard University Press, 1997).

Nussbaum, Martha and Amartya Sen, eds. *The Quality of Life* (New York: Oxford University Press, 1993).

O'Brien, Conor Cruise. *The Long Affair: Thomas Jefferson and the French Revolution, 1785–1800* (London: Sinclair-Stevenson, 1996).

Ober, J. *Mass and Elite in Democratic Athens* (Princeton: Princeton University Press, 1989).

Offe, Claus. "Micro-Aspects of Democratic Theory. What Makes For the Deliberative Competence of Citizens," in *Democracy's Victory and Crisis*, eds. Axel Hadenius (Cambridge: Cambridge University Press, 1997), 81–104.

Pagden, Anthony. *Lords of all the World: Ideologies of Empire in Spain, Britain and France c. 1500–c. 1800* (New Haven: Yale University Press, 1995).

"Dispossessing the Barbarians: The Language of Spanish Thomism and the Debate over the Property Rights of the American Indians," *The Languages of Political Theory in Early-Modern Europe*, ed. Anthony Pagden (Cambridge: Cambridge University Press, 1987), 79–98.

Patterson, Orlando. *The Ordeal of Integration: Progress and Resentment in America's "Racial" Crisis* (Washington, DC: Counterpoint, 1997).

Slavery and Social Death: A Comparative Study (Cambridge: Harvard University Press, 1982).

Pharr, Susan J. and Robert D. Putnam, eds. *Disaffected Democracies. What's Troubling the Trilateral Countries?* (Princeton: Princeton University Press, 2000).

Pierson, George W. *Tocqueville and Beaumont in America* (New York: Oxford University Press, 1938).

Pietersen, Jan Nederveen. *White on Black: Images of Blacks and Americans in Western Popular Culture* (1990; reprint, New Haven: Yale University Press, 1992).

Pinckney, Darryl. "The Drama of Ralph Ellison," *New York Review of Books*, 44 (May 15, 1997), 522–56.

Plato. *The Republic*, trans. Francis M. Cornford (London: Oxford University Press, 1941).

Putnam, Robert D. *Bowling Alone. The Collapse and Revival of American Community* (New York: Simon & Schuster, 2000).

"Democracy in America at Century's End," in *Democracy's Victory and Crisis*, ed. Axel Hadenius (Cambridge: Cambridge University Press, 1997), 27–70.

"Bowling Alone: America's Declining Social Capital," *Journal of Democracy*, 6 (1995), 65–78.

Rancière, Jacques. *Disagreement. Politics and Philosophy*, trans. Julie Rose (Minneapolis: University of Minnesota Press, 1999).

Rawls, John. "The Idea of Public Reason and Postscript," in *Deliberative Democracy. Essays on Reason and Politics*, eds. James Bohman and William Rehg (Cambridge, Mass. and London: MIT Press, 1997).

Political Liberalism (New York: Columbia University Press, 1993).

"The Domain of the Political and Overlapping Consensus," *New York University Law Review*, 64 (1989), 233–55.

"Justice as Fairness: Political not Metaphysical," *Philosophy and Public Affairs*, 14 (1985), 223–51.

A Theory of Justice (Oxford: Oxford University Press, 1971).

Richter, Melvin. "Tocqueville on Algeria," *Review of Politics*, 25 (1963), 362–98.

Roach, Joseph. "Body of Law: The Sun King and the Code Noir," *From the Royal to the Republican Body. Incorporating the Political in Seventeenth- and Eighteenth-century France*, eds. Sara E. Melzer and Kathryn Norberg (Berkeley, Los Angeles, and London: University of California Press, 1998), 113–30.

Rogin, Michael. "The Two Declarations of Independence," *Representations*, no. 55 (1996), 13–30.

Fathers and Children: Andrew Jackson and the Subjugation of the American Indian (New York: Alfred Knopf, 1975).

Rorty, Richard. "Emancipating our Culture," in *Debating the State of Philosophy. Habermas, Rorty, and Kolakowski*, eds. Jozef Niznik and John T. Sanders (Westport, Conn.: Praeger, 1998), 58–66.

Achieving Our Country. Leftist Thought in Twentieth-Century America (Cambridge, Mass.: Harvard University Press, 1998).

Truth and Progress. Philosophical Papers. Vol. 3 (Cambridge: Cambridge University Press, 1998).

Contingency, Irony, and Solidarity (Cambridge: Cambridge University Press, 1989).

Rosanvallon, Pierre. *Le moment Guizot* (Paris: Gallimard, 1985).

Rosenblum, Nancy. *Membership and Morals. The Personal Uses of Pluralism in America* (Princeton: Princeton University Press, 1998).

Roth, Philip. *American Pastoral* (Boston: Houghton Mifflin, 1997).

Rousseau, Jean-Jacques. *On the Origin of Language,* trans. John H. Moran and Alexander Gode (Chicago and London: University of Chicago Press, 1986).

The Social Contract, ed. and trans. Victor Gourevitch (Cambridge: Cambridge University Press, 1997).

Discourse on the Origin and the Foundations of Inequality Among Men, ed. and trans. Victor Gourevitch (New York: Harper and Row, 1986).

Russett, Bruce with William Antholis. "The Imperfect Democratic Peace of Ancient Greece," in Bruce Russett, ed., *Grasping the Democratic Peace. Principles for a Post-Cold War World* (Princeton: Princeton University Press, 1993).

Ryan, Alan. *John Dewey and the High Tide of American Liberalism* (W. W. Norton: New York, 1995).

Sandel, Michael J. *Democracy's Discontent. America in Search of a Public Philosophy* (Cambridge and London: The Belknap Press of Harvard University Press, 1996).

Sanders, Ronald. *Lost Tribes and Promised Lands: The Origins of American Racism* (Boston: Little Brown, 1978).

Schleifer, James T. *The Making of Tocqueville's Democracy in America* (Chapel Hill: University of North Carolina Press, 1980).

Schmitt, Carl. *Political Theology: Four Chapters on the Concept of Sovereignty,* trans. George Schwab (Cambridge: MIT Press, 1985).

The Concept of the Political, trans. George Schwab (New Brunswick: Rutgers University Press, 1976).

"Historiographia in Nuce. Alexis de Tocqueville," *Revista de Estudios Politicos,* no. 43 (1949), 109–14.

Schneck, Stephen F. "Habits of the Head. Tocqueville's America and Jazz," *Political Theory,* 17 (1989), 638–62.

Schudson, Michael. *The Good Citizen: A History of American Civic Life* (New York: The Free Press, 1998).

Schumpeter, Joseph. *Capitalism, Socialism, and Democracy,* 3rd ed. (New York: Harper and Row, 1950).

Scott, Janny. "A White Journalist Wrote It. A Black Director Fought to Own It," *New York Times,* June 11, 2000.

Scott, Joan W. "Multiculturalism and the Politics of Identity," *October,* 61 (1992), 12–19,

Seed, Patricia. *Ceremonies of Possession in Europe's Conquest of the New World, 1492–1640* (Cambridge: Cambridge University Press, 1995).

Sen, Amartya. *Development as Freedom* (Oxford: Oxford University Press, 1999).

Inequality Reexamined (Cambridge, Mass.: Harvard University Press, 1992).

Sewell, Jr., William H. *A Rhetoric of Bourgeois Revolution. The Abbé Sieyès and "What is the Third Estate"?* (Durham and London: Duke University Press, 1994).

Shain, Barry A. *The Myth of American Individualism. The Protestant Origins of American Political Thought* (Princeton: Princeton University Press, 1994).

Shklar, Judith N. *Political Thought and Political Thinkers*, ed. Stanley Hoffman (Chicago: University of Chicago Press, 1998).

Redeeming American Political Thought, eds. Stanley Hoffman and Dennis F. Thompson (Chicago: University of Chicago Press, 1998).

The Faces of Injustice (New Haven and London, Yale University Press, 1990).

Ordinary Vices (Cambridge, Mass., and London: Harvard University Press, 1984).

Shoemaker, Nancy. "How Indians Got to Be Red," *American Historical Review*, 102 (1997), 625–44.

Sièyes, Emannuel-Joseph. *Ecrits politiques*, ed. Roberto Zapperi (Paris: Editions des Archives Contemporaines, 1985).

Qu'est-ce que le tiers état, ed. Roberto Zapperi (Geneva: Librairie Droz, 1970).

Singer, Brian C.J. "Cultural Versus Contractual Nations: Rethinking Their Opposition," *History and Theory*, 35 (1996), 309–37.

Slagstad, Rune. "Liberal Constitutionalism and Its Critics," in Jon Elster and Rune Slagstad, eds., *Constitutionalism and Democracy* (Cambridge: Cambridge University Press, 1988), 103–30.

Smith, Adam. *Lectures on Jurisprudence. Report of 1762–3*, eds. R.L. Meek, D.D. Raphael and P.G. Stein (Indianapolis: Liberty Classics, 1982).

The Wealth of Nations, eds. R.H. Campbell and A.S. Skinner, 2 vols. (Indianapolis: Liberty Classics, 1981).

Smith, Bruce James. *Politics and Remembrance. Republican Themes in Machiavelli, Burke, and Tocqueville* (Princeton: Princeton University Press, 1985).

Splichal, Slavko. *Public Opinion, Developments and Controversies in the Twentieth Century* (New York and Oxford: Rowman and Littlefield, 1999).

Starobinski, Jean. *Blessings in Disguise; Or, the Morality of Evil*, trans. Arthur Goldhammer (Cambridge, Mass.: Harvard University Press, 1993).

Jean-Jacques Rousseau. Transparency and Obstruction, trans. Arthur Goldhammer (Chicago: University of Chicago Press, 1988).

Steele, Shelby. *A Dream Deferred. The Second Betrayal of Black Freedom in America* (New York: Harper Collins, 1998).

Stokes, Curtis. "Tocqueville and the Problem of Racial Inequality," *Journal of Negro History*, 75 (1990), 1–15.

Stuurman, Siep. "François Bernier and the Invention of Racial Classification," *History Workshop Journal*, no. 50 (2000), 1–21.

Switzer, Richard, trans. *Chateaubriand's Travels in America* (1827), (Lexington: University of Kentucky Press, 1969).

Taylor, Charles. "Nationalism and Modernity," in *The State of the Nation. Ernst Gellner and the Theory of Nationalism*, ed. John A. Hall (Cambridge: Cambridge University Press, 1998).

Multiculturalism and the "Politics of Recognition" (Princeton: Princeton University Press, 1994).

Sources of the Self. The Making of the Modern Identity (Cambridge, Mass.: Harvard University Press, 1989).

Hegel and Modern Society (Cambridge: Cambridge University Press, 1979).

Thom, Martin. *Republics, Nations and Tribes* (London and New York: Verso, 1995).

Thomas, Hugh. *The Slave Trade. The History of the Atlantic Slave Trade, 1440–1870* (London: Macmillan, 1997).

Thucydides, *The Peloponnesian War*, trans. Walter Blanco (New York: W.W. Norton, 1998).

Tocqueville, Alexis de. *Oeuvres complètes*, 18 vols. (Paris: Gallimard, 1950–98).

Oeuvres, ed. André Jardin with the collaboration of Françoise Mélonio and Lise Queffélec, 2 vols. (Paris: Gallimard, 1991).

De la Démocratie en Amérique, ed. Eduardo Nolla, 2 vols. (Paris: Librairie Vrin, 1990).

Democracy in America, trans. Henry Reeve, ed. Phillips Bradley, 2 vols. (New York: Vintage Books, 1945).

Oeuvres complètes, ed. Gustave de Beaumont, 9 vols. (Paris: Michel-Lévy frères, 1864–66).

Todorov, Tzvetan. "Tocqueville et la doctrine coloniale," in Alexis de Tocqueville, *De la colonie en Algérie*, ed. Tzvetan Todorov (Brussels: Editions Complexe, 1988).

The Conquest of America: The Question of the Other (New York: Harper and Row, 1984).

Touraine, Alain. *What is Democracy*, trans. David Macey (Boulder and Oxford: Westview Press, 1997).

Tully, James. *Strange Multiplicity* (Cambridge: Cambridge University Press, 1995).

Vaughan, Alden T. "From White Man to Redskin: Changing Anglo-American Perceptions of the American Indian," *American Historical Review*, 87 (1982), 917–53.

Vidal, Gore. "Reel History. Why John Quincy Adams Was the Hero of the Amistad Affair," *New Yorker*, November 10, 1997.

Walzer, Michael. "Rescuing Civil Society," *Dissent* (Winter 1999), 62–67.

"Pluralism and Social Democracy, *Dissent* (Winter 1998), 47–53.

On Tolerance (New Haven and London: Yale University Press, 1997).

"Multiculturalism and Individualism," *Dissent* (Spring 1994), 185–91.

Spheres of Justice (New York: Basic Books, 1983).

Watt, Ian. *Myths of Modern Individualism* (Cambridge: Cambridge University Press, 1996).

Weber, Max. "Politics as a Vocation," in *From Max Weber*, eds. H. H. Gerth and C. Wright Mills (New York: Oxford University Press, 1958), 77–128.

White, Richard and William Cronon. "Ecological Change and Indian-White Relations," in *Handbook of North American Indians*, 4, 417–29.

Wideman, John Edgar. *The Lynchers* in *Identities. Three Novels* (New York: Henry Holt and Company, 1994).

Wilkins, Thurman. *Cherokee Tragedy: The Story of the Ridge Family and the Decimation of a People* (New York: 1970).

Williams Jr., Robert A. "The Algebra of Federal Indian Law: The Hard Trail of Decolonizing and Americanizing the White Man's Indian Jurisprudence," *Wisconsin Law Review,* no. 2 (1986), 219–99.

Williams, Bernard. *Shame and Necessity* (Berkeley, Los Angeles, and London: University of California Press, 1993).

Wilson, William Julius. *The Bridge over the Racial Divide: Rising Inequality and Coalition Politics* (Berkeley: University of California Press, 1999).

Winthrop-Young, Geoffrey. "Silicon Sociology, or, Two Kings on Hegel's Throne? Kittler, Luhmann, and the Posthuman Merger of German Media Theory," *Yale Journal of Criticism,* 13 (2000), 391–420.

Young, Iris Marion. *Inclusion and Democracy* (Oxford: Oxford University Press, 2000).

"Difference as a Resource for Democratic Communication," in *Deliberative Democracy. Essays on Reason and Politics,* eds. James Bohman and William Rehg (Cambridge, Mass. and London: MIT Press, 1997), 383–406.

Justice and the Politics of Difference (Princeton: Princeton University Press, 1990).

Index

abolitionism, 164, 222

aboriginal people, 16, 21, 81, 83, 85, 89, 91–93, 98–99, 106, 110–11, 146, 186

abortion, 228

Ackerman, Bruce, 9 n.4, 133, 133 n.5, 265–67, 267 n.45

Adams, John, 30, 163

Adams, John Quincy, 30–31

affirmative action, 192, 194, 197, 236–37, 292

Africa, 143–44, 147, 158

Afro-Americans, 5, 8–9, 15, 21, 69, 86, 135, 145, 155, 180, 186, 188, 204, 254

  affirmative action and, 192, 194, 197, 236–37

  and assimilation, 187

  and civil rights, 222, 235–36

  and color blindness and class consciousness, 194–97

  and intelligence testing, 180, 196, 239

  and racism, 72, 160, 179–80, 185–86, 193, 202–03, 209–11, 223

  and segregation, 236

  and victimhood, 187

  assimilation and, 156

  crime and, 238, 267

  desegregation and, 202, 212, 290

  differences among, 16, 201

  discrimination and economic deprivation of, 197, 201–02, 237–39, 249

  disenfranchisement of, 238–39

  humiliation and shame among, 150–51, 198

  identity politics and, 8–9, 14–15, 69, 188, 198, 194–99, 201–02, 224–25

  integration and, 200–02, 210–11, 236–38

  middle class, 236

  radicalization of, 206

  success and, 239

  withdrawal from public life, 235, 238

Agamben, Giorgio, 150 n.26

Ageron, Charles-Robert, 143 n.12

Alexie, Sherman, 188–89, 211

Algeria, 141–46

alienness, 5, 98

Allotment Act of 1887, 187

American Civil War, 86, 164, 176, 177, 205, 215, 222, 267

American Colonization Society, 158

American democracy

  appearance in, 4

American democracy (*cont.*)
 authority in, 22
 capitalism and, 5, 276. *See also*
  capitalism
 communalism and, 49, 119–20,
  127, 200
 conflict in, 4, 213, 215–16, 223,
  227–28, 240, 248, 256, 287
 conformity in, 47
 consensus in, 4, 16, 21–22,
  213–16, 221–23, 233, 234,
  240–41, 255, 287, 289–90
 conservatism of, 263–64, 287,
  290
 consumerism in, 71, 231, 234
 crises in, 264–66, 268, 273,
  292–93
 decision-making in, 8, 21, 255,
  291
 difference in, 9, 27, 41, 69, *see
  also* difference
 dissent in, 220, 286
 envy and resentment in, 6, 15, 138,
  224, 227
 excellence and, 14, 40, 42, 46–47,
  204, 293
 exceptionalism of, 128, 146, 178,
  179, 207–08
 identity in, 8, 14–15, 69, 188,
  194–99, 201–02, 224–25
 individualism and, 11, 14, 32, 71,
  119–20, 226, 229, 261, 274,
  276, 278, 292
 localism in, 137, 140, 174, 214,
  220, 225, 227, 285
 materialism and, 7, 45, 47, 54, 62,
  85, 127, 277, 293
 modernity and, 3, 48, 135, 165,
  276, 284
 racism in, 72, 147, 160–62,
  179–80, 185–86, 193–95,
  202–03, 209–11, 223
 religion and, 49. *See also* authority;
  liberty; New England township;
  Tocqueville
 self-interest in, 7, 28, 63, 217, 245,
  258, 276, 282
 special interest groups in, 68, 216,
  232, 240–41
 universality and, 8–9, 11, 14, 283
 violence in, 260, 268, 287
 voluntary associations in, 8–9,
  21–22, 63–64, 119, 139,
  213–14, 216–18, 221, 224, 231,
  235, 239
 worship of success in, 5–6
American Indian Movement, 187
American Left, 226, 228–30, 234,
 259–60, 261, 293
American Pastoral, 209–10
American Revolution, 3, 28, 65, 122,
 210, 247, 256
American Right, 259–60, 261, 293
L'Ancien Régime et la Révolution,
 75–76
Anderson, Benedict, 117
Anglo-Americans, 16, 23, 47, 62, 80,
 82, 84, 94, 101, 113, 145, 154,
 156, 165, 168, 172–73, 186,
 210
Ankersmit, Frank, 88, 88 n.27,
 249–50, 250 n.13
anti-slavery movement, *see* slavery
Appiah, Anthony, 194–96, 203
Arabs, 144–46
Arendt, Hannah, 121 n.16
 and American Constitution, 255,
  264–65, 267, 268, 270, 271
 and authority, 29, 255–56, 257,
  264
 and depoliticization, 255
 and Founding Fathers, 256
 and majoritarianism, 28–29
 and power, 28–29, 255–56, 264
 and rights, 172
 and the political, 256
 and the self, 257
 on beginnings, 28–29, 256
 on distinctions between liberation
  and freedom, 264–65
 on revolution, 256, 264
aristocratic society, 20, 36–40, 43,
 47, 59, 69, 122, 146, 153, 154,
 160, 163

Aristotle, 261, 284
Articles of Confederation, 132
Asia, 17, 147
Athenian democracy, 10–12, 35, 46, 180
Athens, 10, 11, 12, 27, 32, 54, 121
authoritarianism, 258, 274–75
authority
  and civil society, 42
  and independence, 124, 127, 129
  and judiciary, 261–63, 272–73
  and justice, 244, 247
  and liberty, 13, 19, 49, 50, 75, 134, 256
  and power, 19, 244, 255–56
  and religion, 116–17, 119–25, 128, 244, 256, 259, 271
  and self-interest, 245, 258
  and the people, 133, 263–74
  and the self, 255–57
  and the state, 133, 242–43
  and the U.S. Constitution, 255, 264–65, 267, 268, 270, 271
  and tradition, 255, 258
  constituted, 29, 33, 244–45
  crisis in, 264–66, 268
  democratic, 19, 22, 50–51, 67, 133, 243, 246, 255–56, 258, 260, 266–68, 271, 283, 289
  justification for, 244–45
  legitimate and illegitimate, 75, 127, 245–48, 255, 260
  moral, 257, 260, 268
Aztecs, 96

Bacon, Francis, 42
Balboa, Núñez de, 105
Baldwin, James, 167 n.65, 194, 212
Balibar, Etienne, 53–54 n.7, 71, 172
Barbeyrac, Jean, 104
Beaumont, Gustave de, 80–81, 81 n.14, 166 n.62, 169
Bell, Daniel, 208
Bell, John, 92
Bellah, Robert, 117, 202, 208, 208 n.49, 230 n.34
Benton, Thomas Hart, 90 n.33

Berbers, 145
Berlin, Ira, 157 n.41
Berlin, Isaiah, 53 n.7
Bill of Rights, 252
black Americans, *see* Afro-Americans
Black, Charles L., 254
Blackburn, Robin, 162 n.53
Blosseville, Ernest de, 92
Bobbio, Norberto, 118 n.6, 252, 254
Bok, Derek, 236
Bonaparte, Louis-Napoleon, 35
Bowen, William, 236
Brennan, William, 254
British Parliament, 23
Broglie, Achille-Léon-Victor, duc de, 171
Burke, Edmund, 31
Bush, George W., 272 n.59
busing policy (Boston), 200–03
Byron, George Gordon, 48

Calhoun, John, 163, 163 n.58
Calvinism, 118
Canada, 18, 191–92
Canadian Charter of Rights, 193 n.13
capacities, 12–16, 38, 40–41, 204, 289, 291–92
capitalism, 4–5, 22, 60, 270, 276–79
  and bureaucracy, 276, 279–80
  and consumerism, 231, 293
  and democracy, 269–70, 289
  and information technology, 276, 282
  and market society, 3–4, 8, 10, 58, 60, 66, 71, 227, 241, 276, 289
  commercial, 277–78
  corporate, 232, 241, 276, 278, 288
  economics of, trumps politics, 288–89
  global, 10, 19, 22, 288
  industrial, 277–78
  post-industrial, 282
Caribbean colonies, 17, 162, 166
Cass, Lewis, 92
castes, 19, 36–37, 39, 48, 122, 154, 166, 171, 277, 280

Castoriadis, Cornelius, 84, 84 n.20, 269
Census of 1830, 162 n.54
Census of 1990, 187
centralization, 128–30, 133, 137, 143, 242, 279–90
Charlevoix, François-Xavier de, 90
Chateaubriand, François-René de, 48, 78, 91, 107 n.67
Cherokee Nation v. State of Georgia, 30 U.S., 1831, 97 n.9
Cherokees, 95–100, 110
Chippewayans, 81
Choctaws, 94–95
Christian Coalition, 267
Christianity, 10–11, 87, 93, 106, 116, 125, 127, 143–44, 159, 165, 171–74, 176–78, 186, 200, 281
civic merit, 55
civil associations, *see* voluntary associations
civil religion, 208
civil rights struggle, 222, 235
civil society, 3, 4, 7, 20, 33, 39, 49, 52–53, 55–56, 58–60, 68–69, 71, 76, 106, 115, 122, 139, 179–80, 197, 213, 216, 221, 225, 231, 234, 242–43, 250–51, 254, 269–70, 283–84, 293
civility, 222
Clark, William, 92
Clastres, Pierre, 102 n.56
Clay (Georgian planter), 164
Clay, Henry, 164 n.59
Clinton, William Jefferson, 211
Code Noir, 167
Cohen, Joshua, 226 n.23
communitarianism, 229, 284
Connerly, Ward, 236, 237 n.45
Connolly, William E., 165, 165 n.61, 201, 224
consensus, *see* American democracy
consensus gentium, 214
consensus universalis, 140, 174–75
Constant, Benjamin, 35, 76
Constitution of 1791 (France), 39

Constitutional Convention, 264, 266
Cooper, James Fenimore, 78, 91, 107 n.67
corporate America, *see* capitalism
courts, *see* judiciary
Crees, 97
creolization, 168
culture war, 260
Curtin, Philip, 178
Cyberspace, *see* information technology

Davis, David Brion, 172 n.78
Declaration of Independence, 35, 135, 254, 255
Declaration of the Rights of Man and the Citizen, 35–36, 252
Delgamuukw v. British Columbia, 1010, 101 n.54
democracy
  agonistic, 224
  and difference, *see* difference
  and modernity, 3, 48
  and universality, 8–9
  authority and, 50, 67, 133, 243, 246, 255–56, 258, 260, 266–68, 271, 283, 289
  capitalist, 269–70, 277, 289
  constitutional, 246
  deliberative, 4, 12–13, 219–20, 224
  direct, 233, 259
  electoral, 9
  liberal, 13, 33–34, 47, 216, 223, 253, 267, 269, 270, 273
  majoritarian, 26–31, 134, 273, 286
  mandated, 259
  participatory, 215, 218, 227
  plebiscitary, 232, 282
  pluralistic, 13–14, 226, 273, 286
  populist, 34, 69, 259, 261, 270, 273
  pure, 26–27
  representative, 25, 33, 34, 235, 250, 269–70

democratic despotism, *see* Tocqueville

Democratic Party, 228

democratization, 4–5, 69, 71, 154, 244, 256, 268–69, 277

depoliticization, 8, 250–51, 256, 265, 277, 282

Derrida, Jacques, 198

Descartes, René, 42–43

determinism

biological, 152, 154, 162–63, 190, 196

geographical, 153, 186

Dewey, John, 221, 229, 280–82

Diamond, Jared, 153 n.35

Diderot, Denis, 104

difference, 8, 13–14, 21, 27, 33, 55, 59, 70–72, 178, 203, 205, 217, 226–27, 229, 237, 268, 284

and capacities, 12–16, 38, 40–41, 204, 289, 291–92, 299–301

and culture, 72, 77–80, 83–84, 89, 96, 108, 152, 178–79

and equality, 13–15, 55, 71, 282, 285, 291–93

and identity, 8, 14–15, 69, 150, 188–90, 194–99, 201–02, 206, 224–25, 228, 239–41, 251

and inequality, 14, 71, 238–39, 263

and quality, 291–92

and resemblance, 6, 14

and rights, 252

economic sources of, 5, 169–70, 173, 197, 237, 285, 291

difference principle, 15–16

dissensus, 214

dissent, 220, 286

dissenting Protestant sects, 19

Dominguez, Virginia, 168

Dorris, Michael, 188, 190, 193

Douglass, Frederick, 151

Drescher, Seymour, 219 n.7

D'Souza, Dinesh, 180

duBois, Page, 151 n.27

Dunn, John, 288–89

Duponceau, Pierre-Etienne, 163

Dworkin, Ronald, 191, 237

Eckstein, Harry, 257

Education Testing Service, 237

elections, 2, 9–10, 31, 34, 60, 76, 126, 228, 266, 273, 279–80, 282, 285

Ellison, Ralph, 130 n.25, 155, 155 n.38, 158, 176, 186, 186 n.3, 196–97, 203–07, 207 n.46, 209, 212, 235

Elshtain, Jean Bethke, 203

Elster, Jon, 53 n.6, 107, 107 n.68

Engels, Friedrich, 59

England, 49, 60, 122

Enlightenment, 3, 9, 26, 31, 69–70, 77, 86, 101, 119, 123, 154, 172, 176, 180–81, 187, 199, 240

equality

and authority, 244, 264

and democracy, 123, 216

and difference, 1, 8, 13–15, 46, 51, 55–56, 69, 71–72, 217–18, 225–26, 241, 268, 282, 285, 291–93

and inequality, 36, 189, 191, 197, 224, 226, 239, 244, 274, 280

and justice, 45–46

and liberty, 49, 52–53, 56, 181, 192, 217, 253–54, 264, 273, 281–83, 292–93

and quality, 36–43

and respiritualization, 267

and rights, 123, 251–52, 268

and universality, 14

and utilitarianism, 42

Christian roots of, 171

economic, 36, 216, 267, 277, 280, 285, 291

excesses of, 10, 43–45, 64, 231

human dignity and, 36

ideal, 40, 43, 45

imaginary equality, 6, 44–45

imperfect, 56

legal, 52–53, 269

moeurs and, 35, 122

natural, 37

equality (*cont.*)
  of condition, 6–8, 35–36, 44, 120,
    122, 138, 161, 277, 285
  of opportunity, 6, 218, 241, 274,
    277, 285, 291
  simple, 27, 38, 273
Erdrich, Louise, 188, 190, 193
essentialism, 201, 254
Everett, Edward, 92

family, 114–16, 188–89, 200, 210,
  257
Fanton, Jonathan F., 203
Farrakhan, Louis, 239–40
fascism, 261
federal government, 33, 95, 133, 247
Federalist, The, 24, 25, 29, 271
Federalists, 20, 22, 23, 28, 29, 133,
  240, 247, 265, 267, 274
Federal Union, 21, 57, 95, 133,
  136–37, 140, 161–64, 170,
  174–76, 264
feudalism, 105–06, 122
Fields, Barbara Jeanne, 168
First Nations (Canada), 190
Florence, 112
Fogel, Robert W., 63 n.18, 157,
  158 n.44, 267
Foucault, Michel, 126 n.19, 128,
  150 n.26, 201, 284
Founding Fathers, 20, 34, 35, 177,
  187, 252, 254, 259, 264
Fourteenth Amendment, 13
France, 7, 16–18, 28, 60, 105, 129,
  143, 147, 204, 215, 249
Fraser, Nancy, 197 n.22
Fredrickson, George M., 237 n.45
Free Soil Movement, 159
French Chamber of Deputies, 166,
  171
French Constituent Assembly, 265
French Restoration, 76–77
French Revolution, 31, 75–76, 147,
  171
French West Indies, 171
fundamentalists, 172, 259, 275
Furet, François, 75–76 n.1, 86

Gadamer, Hans-Georg, 69
Garaudy, Roger, 103 n.58
Garrison, William Lloyd, 157–58
Gates, Jr., Henry Louis, 201
Genesis, 100, 108–09, 120, 179
Genovese, Eugene D., 161 n.51,
  163 n.58, 172 n.78
gens de couleur libre, 163, 167–68
Geyer, Michael, 92
Gilroy, Paul, 180
Ginsburg, Ruth Bader, Justice,
  272 n.59
Gobineau, Arthur de, 144, 151–52,
  159 n.46
Goethe, Johann Wolfgang von, 48
Gore Jr., Albert, 272 n.59
Gould, Carol C., 218 n.3
Great Awakening, 267
Greene, Jack, 82, 116
Greenfeld, Liah, 175 n.85
Grotius, Hugo, 104
Guéhenno, Jean-Marie, 288 n.17
Guillemin (French Consul at New
  Orleans), 163
Guizot, François, 32, 105–06, 111
Gutman, Herbert G., 156 n.40
Gutmann, Amy, 254 n.17

Habermas, Jürgen, 9 n.3, 59 n.17,
  68 n.19, 76 n.1, 223, 273 n.61,
  282–83
Hacker, Andrew, 205, 230–31 n.33
Hamilton, Alexander, 24, 25, 248,
  248 n.10, 262–63, 271–72
Hardt, Michael, 234
Hartz, Louis, 119
Havel, Vaclav, 242 n.1
Hawthorne, Nathaniel, 205
Hebrew Bible, 108, 116
Hegel, Georg Wilhelm Friedrich,
  54 n.8, 58–59, 179 n.92
Heidegger, Martin, 201
Herder, Johann Gottfried, 70
Herrnstein, Richard, 180
Hirschman, Albert, 27 n.8, 227–28
Hispanic Americans, 191, 201
Hitchens, Christopher, 211

Hobbes, Thomas, 66, 178
Hollinger, David, 228
Hollis, Martin, 220 n.9
Hont, Istvan, 104
Houston, Sam, 97, 100 n.51
Huckleberry Finn, 176
human nature, 27, 85–86, 153, 262, 282, 285–86
humanism, 11, 119, 176–78
  and universality, 11, 177–78
  Christian, 164, 172, 176–77
  non-Christian, 119, 164, 177
Hunter, James, 120, 259–60

identity politics, *see* politics
immigrants, 16, 18, 112–13, 191
Indian Reorganization Act, 107
Indians, *see* Native Americans
individualism, 11, 14, 32, 62, 71, 119, 160, 176, 226, 229, 261, 274, 276, 278, 292
information technology, 20, 231–34, 237, 257, 276, 283–84
Inglehart, Ronald, 219
Internet, *see* information technology
Invisible Man, 203, 205
Iroquois Confederation, 79
Isocrates, 55

Jackson, Andrew, 30, 97–98, 164, 166
Jacobinism, 76–77
Jay, John, 24
Jefferson, Thomas, 24–25, 30, 90, 90 n.34, 135 n.7, 267
Jeffersonian Republicans, 240
Jews, 18, 150–51, 209
Johnson, Lyndon, 187
Judeo-Christian thought, 87
judicial review, 271–72
judicial supremacy, 262
judiciary, 33, 61, 248, 261–62, 271–72
justice, 16, 29–30, 32, 40, 55, 96, 134, 186, 199–200, 213, 223, 225, 229, 244, 247, 251, 257, 261, 283, 291

Kabyles, 142, 145–46, 154
Kahnawake Mohawk Band, 193
Kammen, Michael, 208
Kant, Immanuel, 178, 199–200
Kateb, George, 254 n.17
Keane, John, 230 n.34
Kelly, George Armstrong, 118, 207–08
Key, V.O., 233
Kiernan, V.J., 102 n.55
Kymlicka, Will, 190–92

labor unions, 229, 253
Lacordaire, Henri, 50 n.1
laicisme, 17
Laqueur, Thomas, 238 n.49
La Rochefoucauld-Liancourt, 92
Las Casas, Bartolomé de, 96
Latrobe, John Hazelhurst, 162 n.53
law of contract, 93–96
Lévi-Strauss, Claude, 83–84
liberalism, 4, 13, 23, 69, 76, 179, 213, 223, 226, 242, 270
Liberator The, 158
Liberia, 158
libertarianism, 252
liberty
  absolute, 3
  and authority, 13, 16, 49, 118, 121–24, 130, 134, 140, 293
  and choice, 118, 125, 135–36
  and conformity, 51, 66–67
  and democracy, 123, 141
  and equality, 125
  and history, 136
  and individualism, 86
  and law, 224
  and license, 50
  and modernity, 136
  and necessity, 136
  and public order, 34, 43
  and reason, 117–18
  and religion, 62–63, 118, 121–22, 128, 159
  and self-discipline, 35–36, 47–48, 53, 118, 141
  and solidarity, 206

liberty (*cont.*)
  and universality, 147, 206
  and voluntary associations, 215,
    242
  as will, 88–89, 112
  Athenian, 11–12
  civil, 121
  negative and positive, 252
  political, 121
Liberty Bell, The, 158, 160
Lieber, Francis, 145, 145 n.20
Liebersohn, Harry, 90 n.32
literature, 21, 42–43, 48, 154, 189,
    205
Lochner v. New York, 253
Locke, John, 13, 101, 101 n.54, 104,
    120, 179, 248, 252
Lukas, J. Anthony, 200–03
Luttwack, Edward, 261
Lyotard, Jean-François, 256 n.21

McLoughlin, William G., 106 n.66
Madison, James, 24–27, 29, 34, 132,
    132 n.1, 264
majority rule
  Hannah Arendt on, 28–29
  James Madison on, 26–27
  John Quincy Adams on, 30–31
  See also Tocqueville
Malcomson, Scott L., 188 n.5
Mansfield, Jr., Harvey, 251 n.14,
    253 n.15, 258 n.29, 271, 273–74
Margalit, Avishai, 150 n.26
Marie, 169
market society, 3–4, 8, 10, 58, 60,
    66, 71, 227, 241, 276, 289
Marshall, John, 97, 97 n.45
Marx, Karl, 59–60, 71, 102, 154,
    291 n.28
Masuda, Yoneji, 231
Meek, Ronald L., 153 n.34
Mélonio, Françoise, 86
Melville, Herman, 205, 207
Michelman, Frank, 224
Mill, John Stuart, 20, 32–33, 35
Miller, Arthur, 125
Mills, Charles, 178–79

Milton, John, 84
minorities, 4, 191, 197, 226, 240,
    260–61, 283, 292
Missouri Compromise, 163
modernity, *see* American democracy
moeurs, 24, 35–36, 42, 80, 106, 122,
    175
Momaday, N. Scott, 188–89, 193
Montesquieu, Charles-Louis de
  Secondat, baron de, 56–59, 88,
    127, 148 n.24, 248
Morris, Gouverneur, 132 n.1
Morrison, Toni, 210–11
Morse, Jedediah, 90
multiculturalism, 228
Murray, Charles, 180
Muslims, 17–18, 142–45
Myrdal, Gunnar, 204–05

NAACP Legal Defense Fund, 236
Nandy, Ashis, 103, 103 n.58
National Indian Youth Congress, 187
National Labor Relations Act,
    230 n.33
Nation of Islam, 239
Native Americans, 5, 8–9, 15–16, 69,
    77, 135, 145, 154, 165, 168–69,
    178, 186–87, 205, 211, 254,
    260
  and affirmative action, 292
  and self-government, 106–08,
    190–92
  and victimhood, 190, 192
  assimilation of, 165, 167–68, 187
  comparison with Kabyles, 145–46,
    154
  differences among, 116, 188
  integration of, 187
  land claims of, 190, 192
  languages of, 94, 100
  "primitivism" of, 77, 90–91, 111
  reservation life of, 187–88, 211
  seizure of their lands, 91, 94–98,
    135
  their ancient memories, 93–95,
    100, 103, 113
  their decimation, 99, 293

their notions of property, 94, 96,
101–03
their search for positive identity,
187–89, 191–92
their sense of history, 93–95, 113,
189
their uncertain status, 187–90, 193
Nazism, 150–51
Negri, Antonio, 234, 267–70
Negroes, *see* Afro-Americans
New Deal, 228, 259, 264, 266
New England township, 10, 21, 33, ·
113
as an ideal, 118, 125–26
authority in the, 115, 118–19,
122–24, 126, 129
beginnings in the, 117–18, 124,
128–31
communalism in, 49, 119–20, 127,
200
dissent in the, 126
individualism in, 119–20, 124
liberty in the, 118, 121, 123–24,
126, 129
myth of, 114, 117, 137
Puritanism in, 45, 117
religion in, 119–25, 128
New Orleans, 163, 165–69
newspaper press, 33, 65, 137–38,
257
Nietzsche, Friedrich, 201
Ninth Amendment, 254
Nolla, Eduardo, 84 n.22, 159 n.47
Nussbaum, Martha, 70, 70 n.23

Ober, J., 12 n.5
O'Brien, Conor Cruise, 135 n.7
Offe, Claus, 219
Ottomans, 142

Pagden, Anthony, 102–03
Paine, Thomas, 248
Paradise, 210–11
Pascal, Blaise, 37, 244–45
patriotism, 175–76
Patterson, Orlando, 172 n.79,
195–96, 236, 237 n.45

Paul III's *Sublimus Deus* (1537), 178
people, *the*, 263–74
Pericles, 11–12, 27, 32, 193
personal autonomy, 11, 52–53, 119,
172–73, 176, 191, 200, 282–83
phronēsis, 284
Pinckney, Darryl, 176
Plato, 28, 50–51, 287
pleasure principle, 45
Plessy v. Ferguson, 163 U.S. 537, 168
Poe, Edgar Allan, 208
Poinsett, John Roberts, 161
political associations, 49, 60–61, 64,
106, 215–19, 224, 225, 232
political class, 267, 287
political parties, 65, 215, 218, 228,
233, 255, 260, 265, 266, 280,
283
political philosophy, *see* political
theory
political polling, 232–33, 235
political, *the*, 8, 59–60, 256, 288
political theory, 20–21, 256, 270,
276, 288
politics
and economic life, 4, 214, 216,
218–19, 224, 227, 229
as theater, 35, 282–83
conflict in, 4, 14–15, 213, 215–16,
223, 227–28, 240, 248, 256,
287
degradation of, 8, 22, 69, 234,
255–56
dissent in, 214, 220
ethnicity in, 222, 228
gender, 222
identity, 8, 69, 187–88, 194–99,
201–02, 224–25
inclusion and exclusion in, 12–15,
17, 69, 179, 197, 224, 238, 244,
284, 292
of affection, 20, 128, 134, 137,
154, 174, 160–61
of consensus, 4, 16, 213–16,
221–23, 233, 235, 240–41, 255,
287–90
of victimhood, 187, 190–93

politics (*cont.*)
  parties in, 215
  passion in, 223, 271
  passivity in, 231
  power in, 216
  virtue and, 61, 248, 258, 261,
    283
popular sovereignty, 23, 57, 76, 141,
  249, 273–74, 284
populism, 34, 69, 259, 261, 270, 273
Portugal, 17
post-industrial society, 219
power
  and authority, 9, 244, 255–56
  constituent, 267–69, 271
  constituted, 244, 265, 268–69
  constitutive, 265, 269, 273
  disguised forms of, 284
pressure groups, 68–69, 216, 232,
  240–41, 242 n.50, 285
property, conflicting concepts of,
  101–08
public opinion, 6, 23, 27, 49, 65–67,
  235, 286
public spirit, 65
Puerto Rican Americans, 191
Pufendorf, Samuel, 104
Puritanism, 45, 62, 116–17, 140,
  160, 172, 174, 179
Putnam, Robert, 218–20, 240

quality
  and equality, 36–43
  and excellence, 40
  aristocratic, 38
  capacities and, 38–39
  caste and, 36–37
  idealized, 37, 42
  in democracies, 41, 47, 291
Québec, 191–93
Quinze jours dans le désert, 90

race
  and civilization, 178–79
  and color, 23, 80, 165–68, 185,
    193–96
  and culture, 193

and inequality, 218
and liberty, 165
"biology" of, 193
riots, 210
racial assimilation, 198, 200
racial contract, 178
racial discrimination, 135, 237–38,
  249
racial disenfranchisement, 238–39
racial divisions, 72, 148, 169–70,
  188, 196, 203–06, 236–37,
  239
racial inferiority, 151–52, 195, 218
racial mixing, 165–67, 169, 192
racial preferences, 236
racial solidarity, 194, 196, 198, 239
racism, 72, 160, 179–80, 185–86,
  193–95, 198, 202–03, 209–11,
  223, 238
  and liberalism, 179
Rawls, John, 15–16, 191, 221–23,
  223 n.13, 225, 257, 290
Raynal, Guillaume-Thomas, abbé,
  104
Reconstruction, 146, 168, 176, 215,
  264
Red-Jacket, 93, 93 n.43
religious Right, 258–60
Relocation Program, 187
Republic The, 49–50
Republican Party, 267, 277
republicanism, 18, 22, 62, 134,
  140–41, 175
  democracy and, 24–29
Reservation Blues, 189, 211
Revolution of 1830, 76–77
Revolution of 1848, 35
Richter, Melvin, 145 n.20
Ridge, John, 167 n.65
rights
  absolute, 252–53, 268, 273
  and history, 252–54
  and litigation, 254
  civil, 7, 31–39, 130, 191, 225,
    235, 245, 252, 267
  expansion of, 255–58
  group, 191–92

human, 84, 213, 215, 222,
251–53, 283
natural, 39
political, 7, 38–39, 61–62, 123,
130, 161, 191, 218, 245,
251–52, 283
Roberts v. Jaycees, 254
Roelofs, Mark, 119
Rogin, Michael, 135, 135 n.7
Rome, barbarian invasions of, 98–99,
111
Rorty, Richard, 54 n.8, 159–60 n.48,
201, 228–30, 230 n.34, 261,
289–90
Roth, Philip, 209–10
Rousseau, Jean-Jacques, 13, 14, 34,
38, 55–57, 104–05, 107,
109–12, 120, 127, 142, 245–46,
268, 273
Royer-Collard, Pierre-Paul, 76
Russia, 17

Sahagun, Bernadino de, 96
Sandel, Michael, 258, 258 n.30, 260
Schleifer, James T., 53 n.5
Schmitt, Carl, 245, 246 n.6,
250 n.11, 269
Schneck, Stephen F., 126 n.19
Schudson, Michael, 126 n.20
Schumpeter, Joseph, 286
science and technology, 42–43, 265,
276
Sen, Amartya, 239, 239 n.51,
291–92, 291 n.28, 292 n.29
separation of powers, 22, 136, 242,
247
Shain, Barry, 119
Shklar, Judith, 175 n.85, 223,
223 n.14, 227–28
Sieyès, Emmanuel-Joseph, 38–39,
38 n.29, 264, 268
Singer, Brian C. J., 118 n.6
slavery, 16–18, 134, 260
abolition of, 147, 164, 171–72,
179, 238
abolitionists and, 157–59, 176,
222

and anti-slavery movement, 157,
162, 164, 171–72
and color, 146
and insurrection, 135, 149, 161–62
and racism, 147, 149, 160,
168–69, 193
and revolution, 146, 151, 161,
162–63
Christianity and, 172–73
culture of, 156
economics of, 149, 156, 169–70
emancipation and, 157
Frederick Douglass on, 151
humiliation and shame of, 150–51,
198
in the British West Indies, 17
in the French colonies, 17
Nullification and, 137, 162–63
resettlement campaign and, 158
secession and, 137
slaveholders and, 122, 149–51,
156, 160, 162, 177
Tocqueville and, 85, 122, 146–65,
170–73, 293
Smith, Adam, 108, 147, 147 n.23,
239 n.51
Smith, Bruce J., 128 n.24
Smith, John Jay, 152
social capital, 218
social class, 10, 36, 59, 115, 122,
154, 171, 197–98, 215, 218,
226–27, 231, 240, 243, 263,
277, 280, 283–84, 290
social democracy, 230
social mobility, 226
social trust, 220–21
socialism, 52
Société française pour l'abolition de
l'esclavage, 171
Sources of the Self, 194
South Asia, 103
Spain, 163
Spanish America, 17, 80
Sparta, 12, 32, 54
stadial theory of social development,
104, 106–10, 153
Starobinski, Jean, 89 n.29, 109

state, 224, 241
  absolutist, 244
  administrative, 242–43, 247, 270
  and authority, 60, 133, 242–43
  and civil society, 225–27, 242–43,
    251, 270
  and coercion, 129, 227, 290
  and violence, 260
  authoritarian, 247
  bureaucratic, 33, 247, 276, 280
  centralized, 128–30, 133, 137,
    143, 242, 279–80
  democratic, 225, 250, 288–89
  expanding role of, 251, 277
  fear of the, 247–50, 259, 278
  good forms of the, 225, 249, 289
  justice and the, 251
  Marxist theory of the, 59
  modern activist, 249
  post-modern, 269–70
  powers of, 242
  the infantilizing, 243
  welfare, 226, 248, 250, 259, 261,
    269–70
Steele, Shelby, 194 n.15
Stevens, John Paul, Justice, 272 n.59
Stevens, Wallace, 209–10
Stokes, Curtis, 146 n.21
Story, Joseph, 98, 98 n.48
Supreme Court of Canada, 101 n.54
Swiss cantons, 145

Tammany Hall, 280
Taylor, Charles, 69, 194–95
The Lynchers, 210
"The Sick Man," 209–10
third parties, 228
Thoreau, Henry David, 165
Thuycidides, 11, 32
Tocqueville, Alexis de
  and Algeria, 142–46, 154
  and American belief in chance,
    5–6
  and American ethos of success,
    10
  and authority, 43, 51, 75, 140–41,
    243–46
  and beginnings, 23–24, 75, 77, 80,
    82–83, 85, 88, 112, 116–18,
    124, 128–32, 134, 136, 146–48,
    174
  and centralization, 128–30, 133,
    137, 143, 279–80, 293
  and cities, 111–12, 136
  and commerce, 6–7, 58–61, 67,
    71
  and conformity, 27, 47, 66–67,
    126
  and democratic despotism, 8, 35,
    45, 50–51, 66, 139, 160,
    242–43, 279–80
  and difference, 43, 46, 51, 54, 69,
    71–72, 80, 285–86
  and dissent, 66–67, 126
  and diversity, 47–50
  and elections, 10, 30–31, 34, 36,
    290
  and Enlightenment, 31, 86–87, 115
  and error, 245–46, 273
  and excellence, 40, 42, 46–47, 69,
    204, 293
  and history, 5, 18–19, 24, 51,
    85–89, 102–03, 111–13, 115,
    125, 130, 133, 136, 138, 141,
    148, 153–54, 160, 206
  and honor, 153
  and human nature, 27, 83, 85–86,
    153, 282
  and human perfectibility, 5, 115,
    154
  and individualism, 120, 160, 176,
    278, 292
  and Islam, 142–44
  and judiciary, 61
  and localism, 56–57, 115, 123–24,
    130
  and majority rule, 27–30, 51,
    67–68, 134, 138, 149, 245–46,
    263, 273, 286
  and materialism, 7, 45, 47, 54, 62,
    85, 127, 219, 234, 277–78
  and mediocrity, 46–47, 56
  and miscegenation, 165–68,
    169–70

and *moeurs*, 24, 35–36, 42, 80, 106, 122, 175
and Native Americans, 77–100, 104–06, 146, 165, 169
and New England township, 21, 54, 56–57, 114–32, 137, 140–41, 231
and patriotism, 130, 174–76
and political parties, 265
and press, 33, 65, 137–38
and property, 104–05
and public opinion, 65–68
and quality, 36, 40–41, 43, 46
and race, 85–87, 130, 147–48, 152–55, 161, 168–69, 203, 205
and religion, 62–63, 116, 125, 127–28, 176–79
and rights, 61–62
and self-interest, 63, 258
and slavery, 85, 122, 146–65, 170–73, 293
and stadial theory of civilization, 153
and state control of the economy, 278
and success, 5–6
and the Enlightenment, 77
and the Federalists, 20, 24, 29–31, 133
and the state, 60, 129, 141, 243–44, 249–50
and U.S. Constitution, 33–35
and virtue, 6, 8, 86, 127–28, 256
and voluntary associations, 8–9, 21–22, 63–64, 71, 160, 203, 216, 221, 284–85
and wealth, 10, 54, 86, 136, 204, 219, 276–77, 279
clash of cultures in his theory of civilization, 21, 77–86, 89–93, 96, 98–100, 104, 106–08, 111–13, 120, 144–45, 181
his incomplete analysis of capitalism, 276–77
his notion of *consensus universalis*, 140, 174–75

on American conservatism, 139, 287, 290
on caste and class in America, 46–47
on knowledge and intelligence, 115, 138, 161, 175, 204
on political corruption, 62
on revolution in democratic times, 287
on science and art of politics, 284
on utility, 258
optimism of, 5, 58, 115–16, 131
paradox in, 88
pessimism of, 5, 58, 43, 45, 67, 154, 174, 250
political theory of, 20, 24, 58, 127–28, 133, 207, 273
republicanism, virtues of, as seen by, 29, 62, 134, 140, 175–76, 243
theory and history of civilization in, 5, 8, 24, 76–86, 89–93, 96, 98–100, 104, 106–08, 111–13, 115–16, 144–45, 153–55, 205
Todorov, Tzvetan, 89
Touraine, Alain, 118 n.6
Toussaint L'Ouverture, 162
Tully, James, 290 n.24
Turner, Nat, 162
Twain, Mark, 176

Unitarians, 63
U.S. Congress, 30, 33, 90, 95, 134, 266
U.S. Constitution, 13, 20, 23, 28–29, 33–35, 97, 132–34, 140, 174, 187, 200, 235, 240, 252–53, 255, 262–64, 267, 271–74
U.S. Presidency, 247, 273
U.S. Supreme Court, 18, 97, 168, 236, 253, 266, 271–72
universality, 8, 10–12, 14, 21, 48, 69, 83, 87, 159, 172, 174, 177–78, 200, 206, 254, 283
unsocial sociability, 110
utilitarianism, 42, 258
utopianism, 4, 10–11, 225, 283

Van Buren, Martin, 161
Vaughan, Alden T., 79 n.6
victimhood, 187, 190–93
Vietnam War, 209–10
Vitoria, Francisco, 104 n.59
Volney, Constantin François de
    Chasseboeuf, comte de, 91
voluntary associations, 8–9, 21–22,
    64, 119, 139, 213–14, 217, 221,
    224, 231, 235, 239–43, 250,
    260
  and localism, 140, 214, 220, 225,
    227, 285
  and special interest groups, 68,
    216, 232, 240–41, 285
  declining power of, 218–19, 285
  Putnam's faith in, 218–19, 240
  Walzer and, 225–27
  Tocqueville's belief in, 8–9, 21–22,
    63–64, 216–18
Voyage to Lake Oneida, 89

Walzer, Michael, 225–27, 226 n.23
Washington, George, 90
Wattell, M. de, 105
Weber, Max, 125 n.18, 140, 279–
    80
West Indies, 99, 162, 279–80, 282
Whitman, Walt, 229
Wideman, John Edgar, 210
Williams, Bernard, 150 n.26
Williams, Roger, 118
Williams, William Appleman, 30
Wilson, William Julius, 237
Winthrop, John, 121
Worcester v. Georgia, 97
work principle, 45
working-class protest, 153, 260–61
World War I, 279
World War II, 218
Wounded Knee, South Dakota, 187

Young, Iris Marion, 198–99